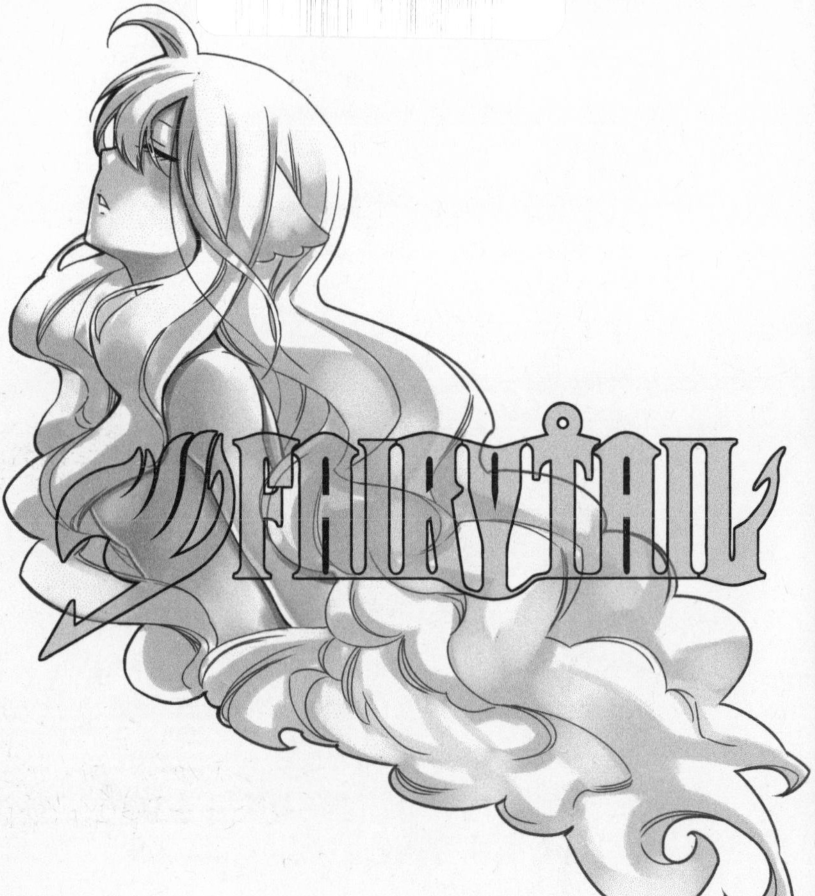
FAIRY TAIL

62

HIRO MASHIMA

FAIRY TAIL 62
CONTENTS

FAIRY TAIL
フェアリーテイル

Chapter 528: Dragon of Magic

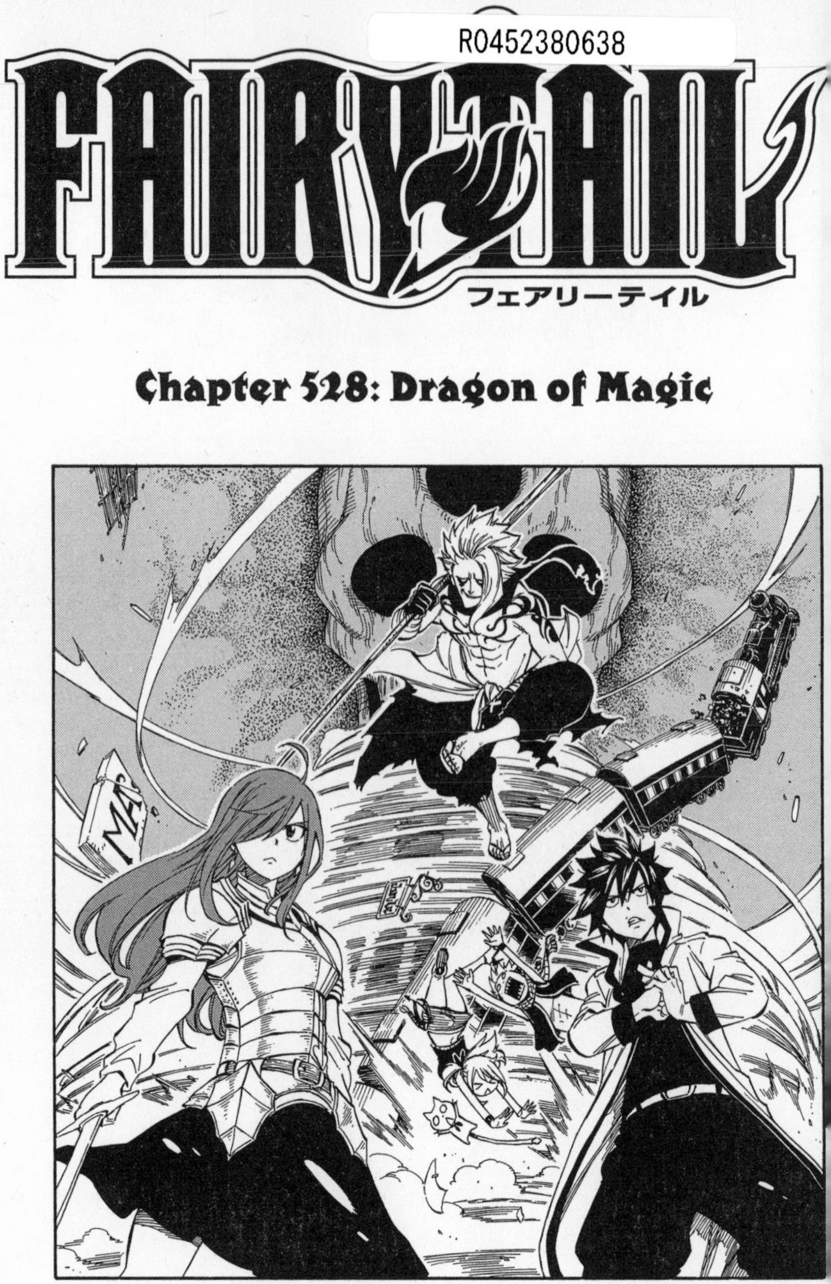

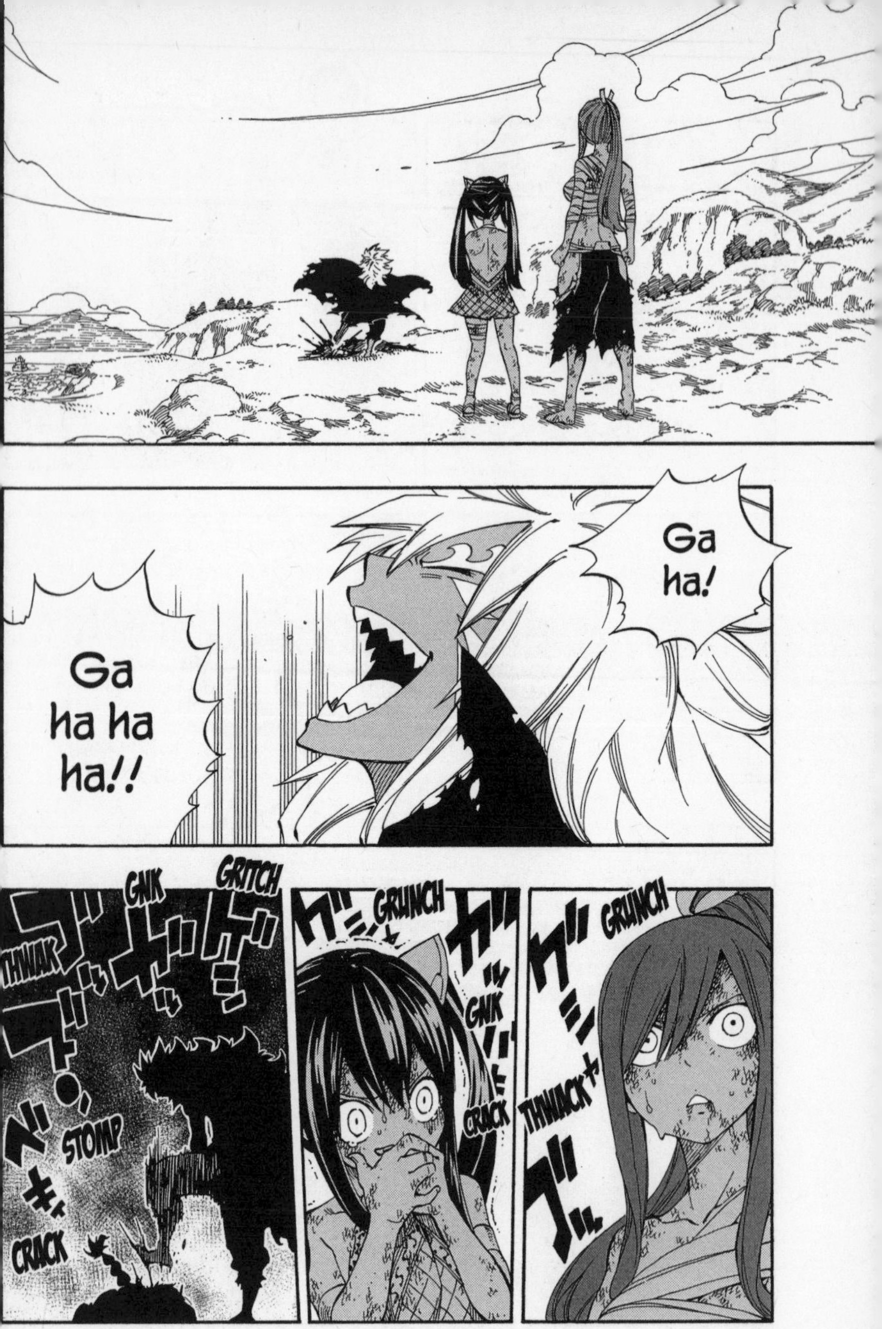

Ga ha!
Ga ha ha ha!!
GRUNCH
THWACK
GRUNCH
GNK
CRACK
GRITCH
GNK
THWAK
STOMP
CRACK

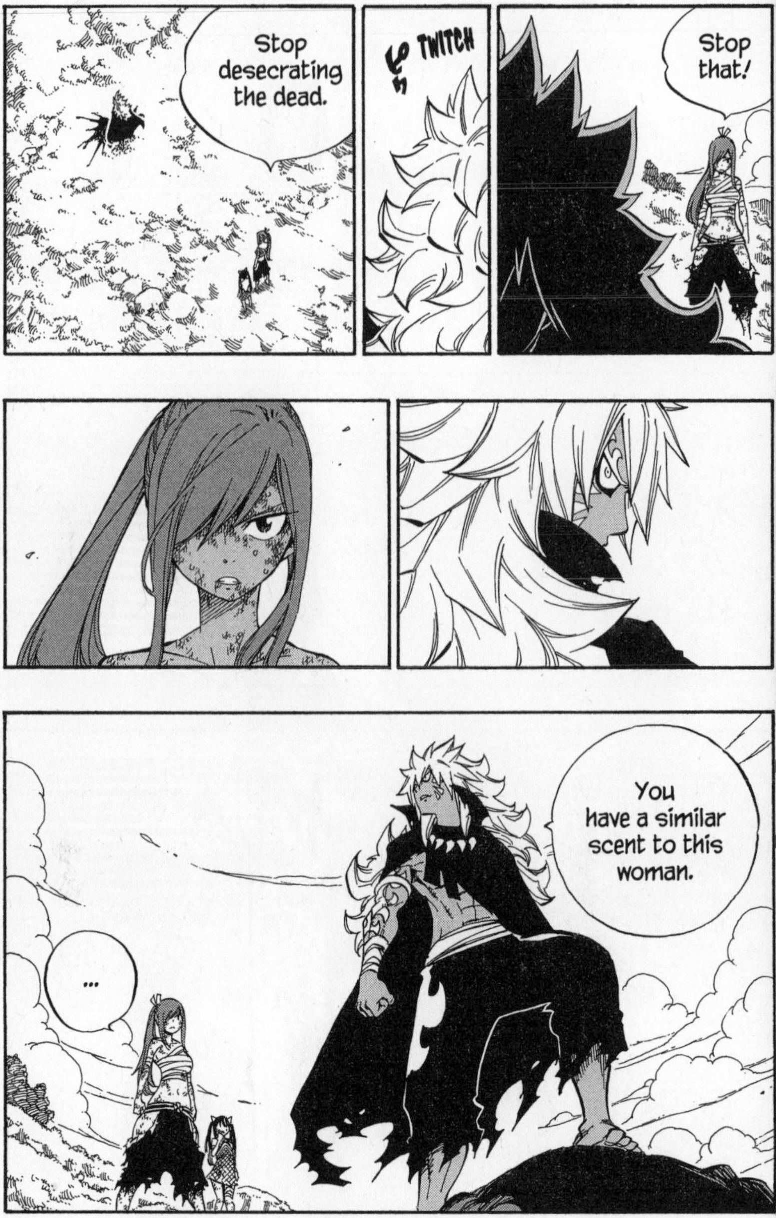
Stop that!
TWITCH
Stop desecrating the dead.
You have a similar scent to this woman.
...

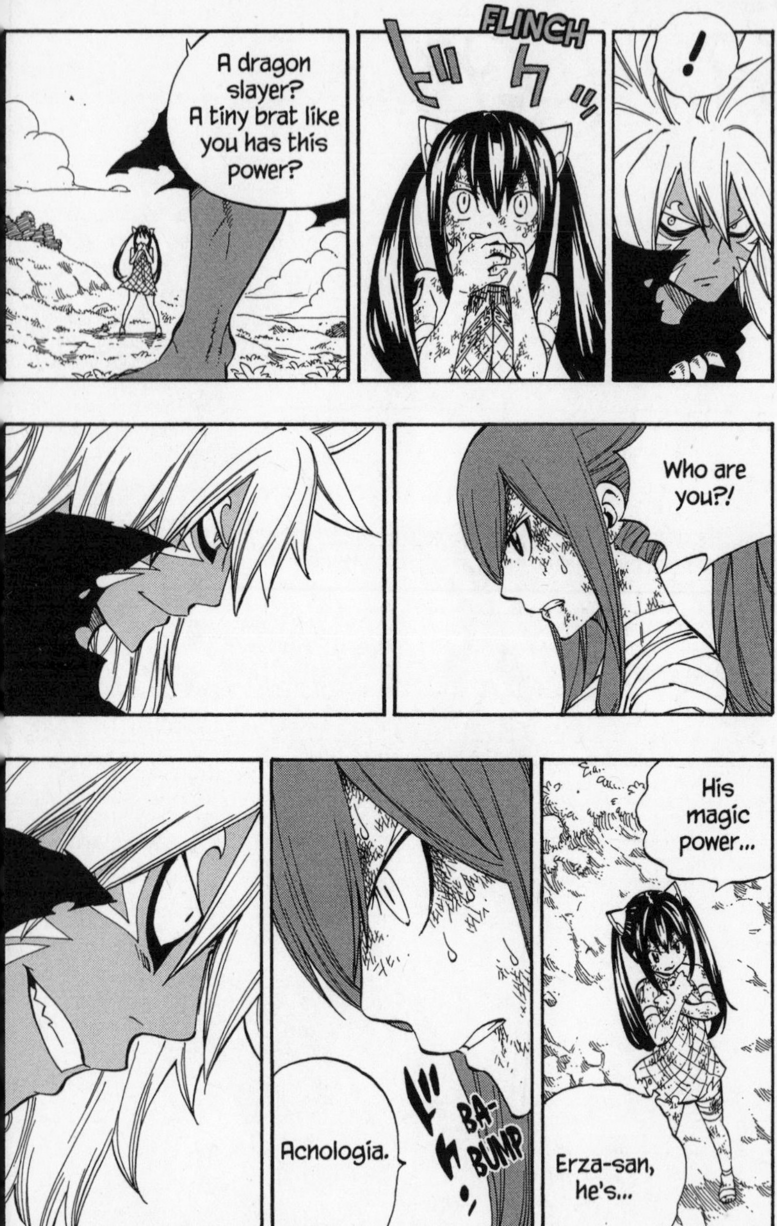
!
FLINCH
A dragon slayer? A tiny brat like you has this power?
Who are you?!
His magic power...
Erza-san, he's...
BA-BUMP
Acnologia.

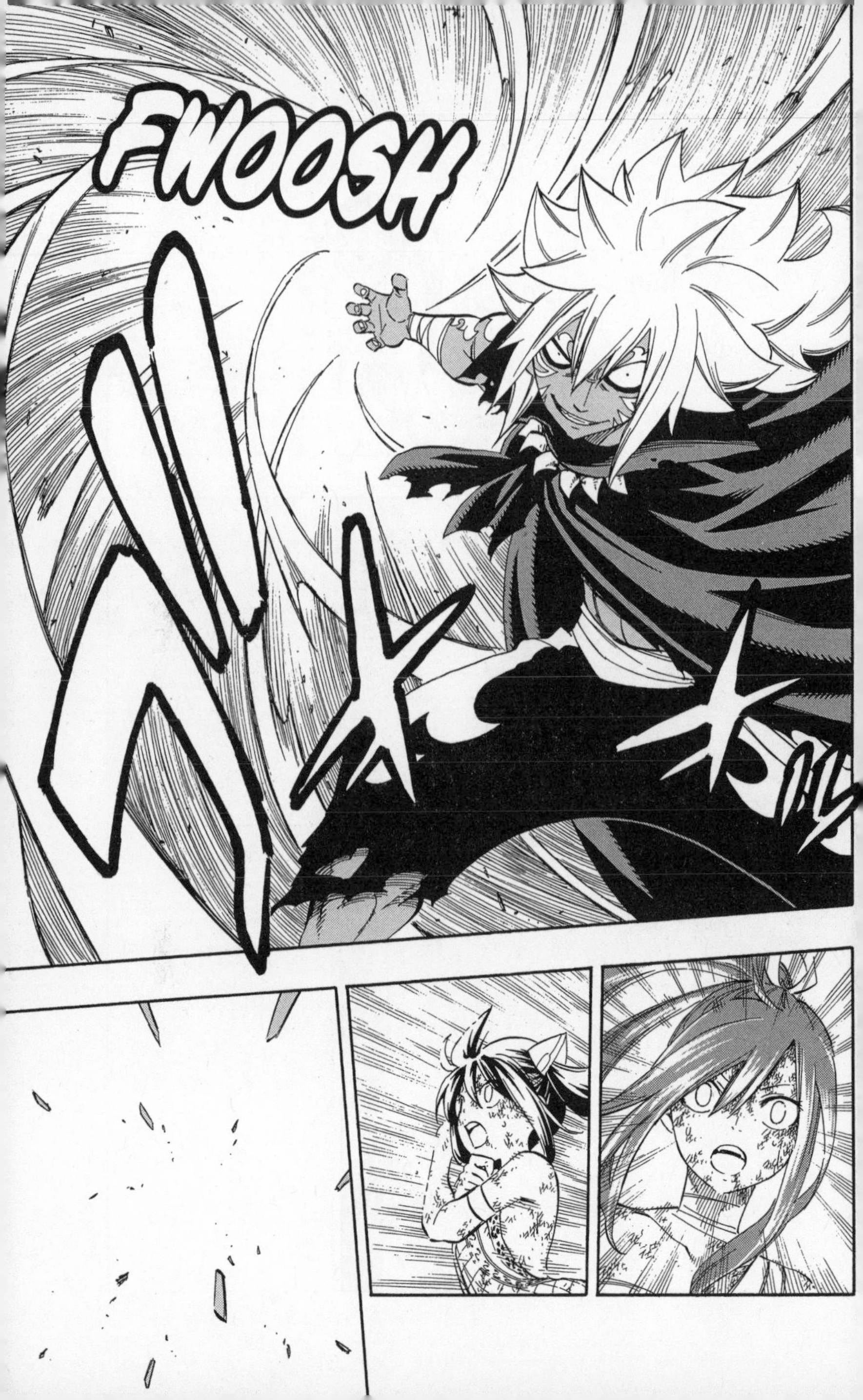
FWOOSH

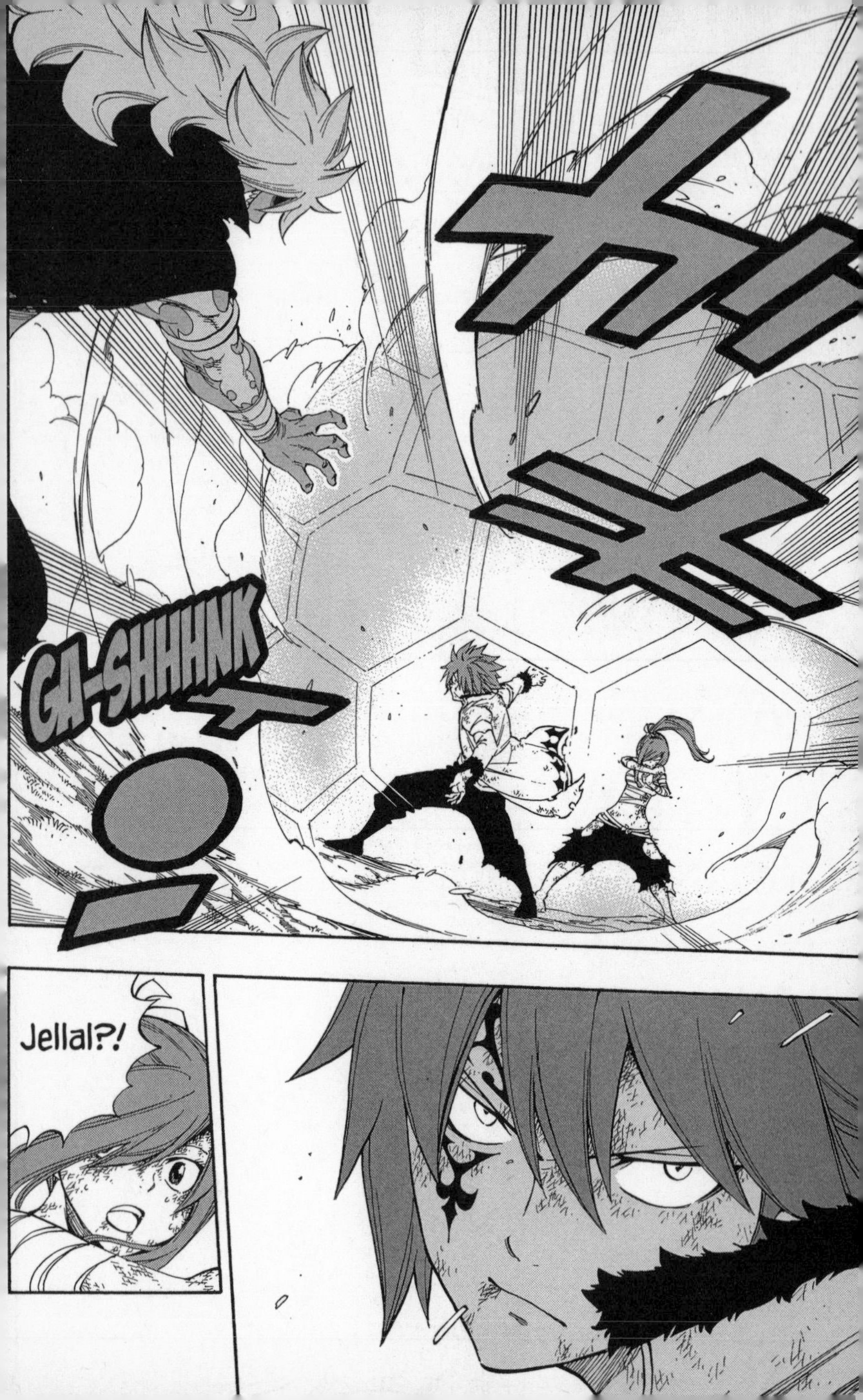
GA-SHHHNK
Jellal?!

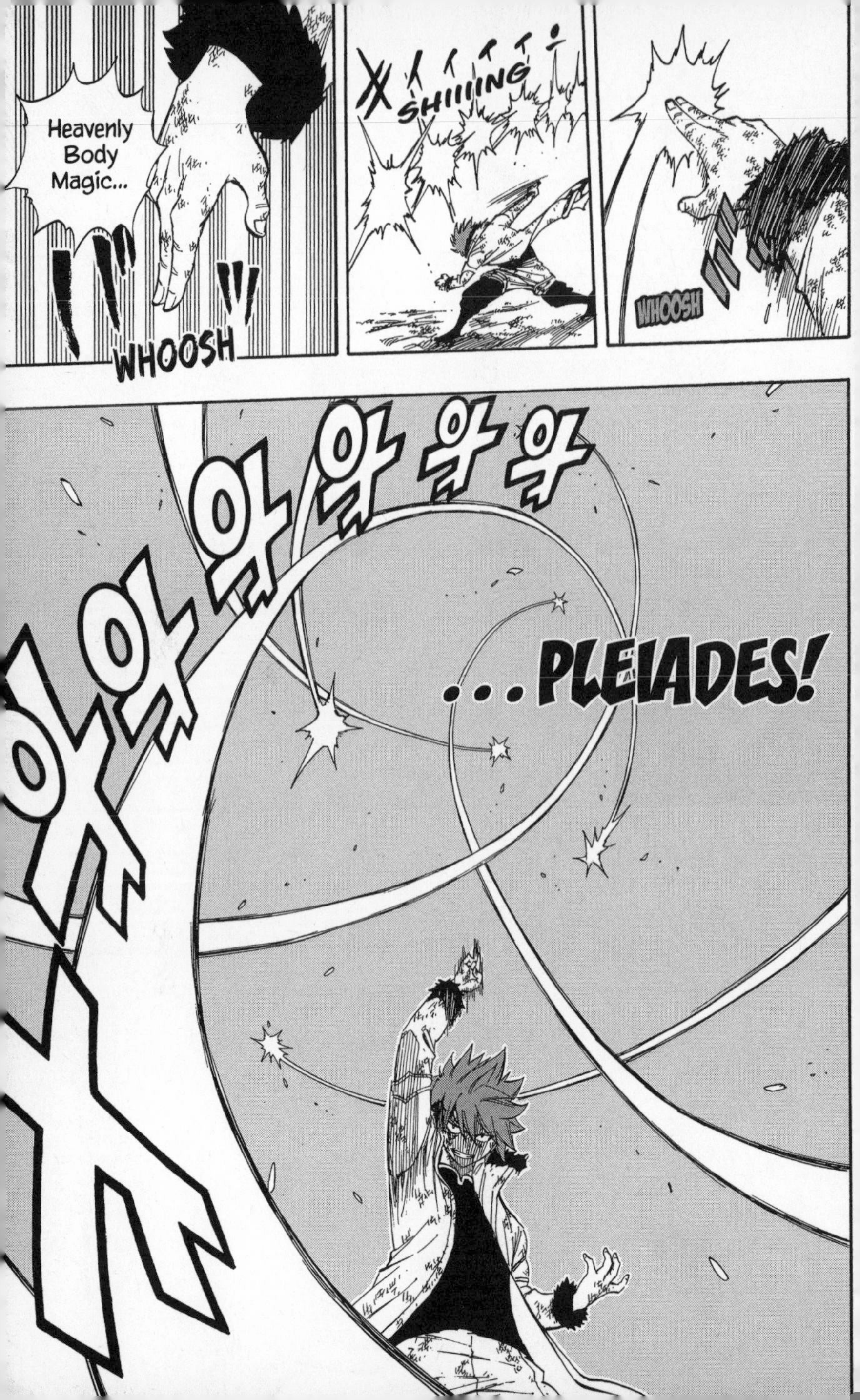
WHOOSH
SHIIIING
Heavenly Body Magic...
WHOOSH
...PLEIADES!

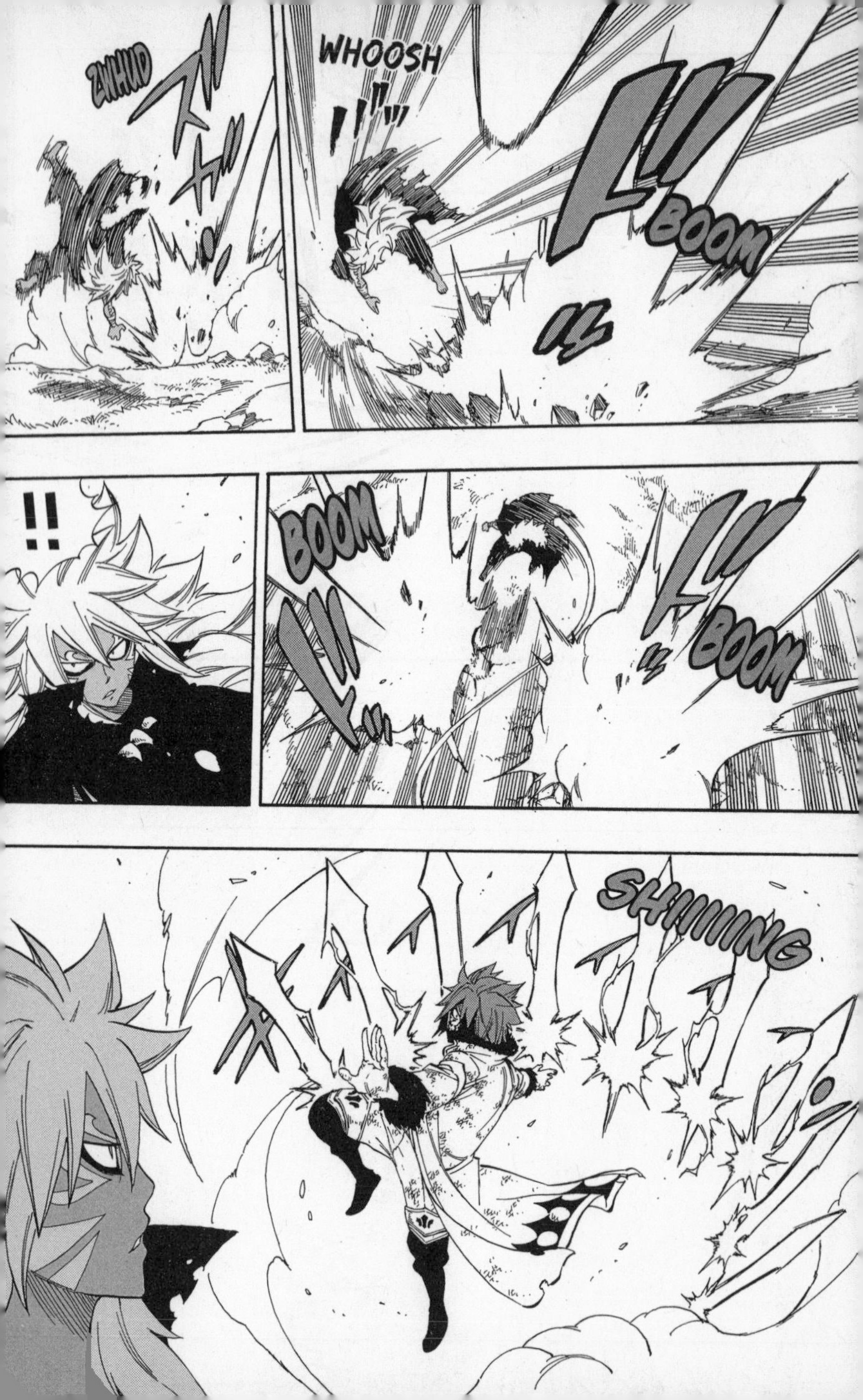
WHOOSH
BOOM
ZWHUD
BOOM
BOOM
!!
SHIIIIING

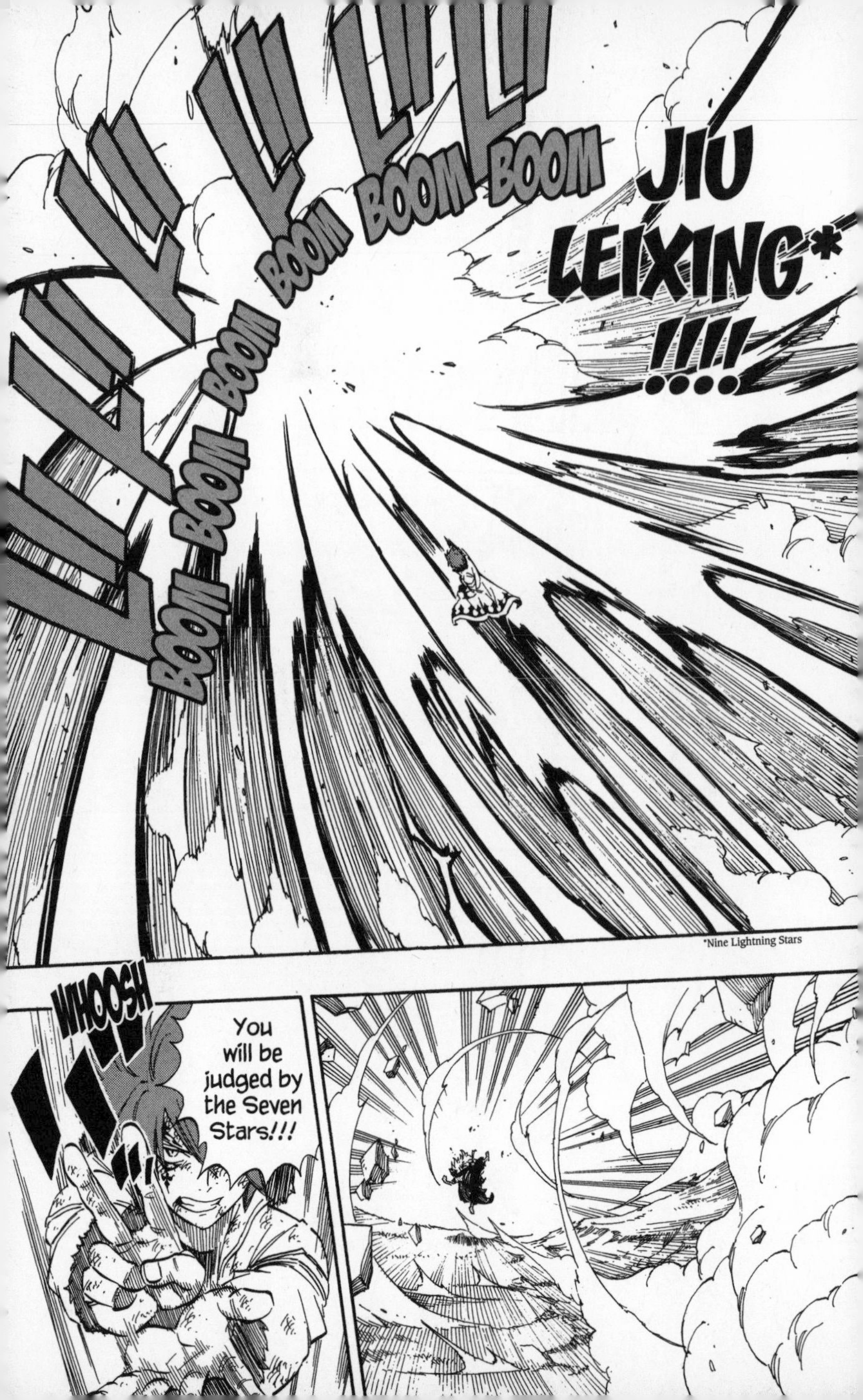
JIU LEIXING*!!!!
BOOM BOOM BOOM BOOM BOOM BOOM
WHOOSH
You will be judged by the Seven Stars!!!

*Nine Lightning Stars

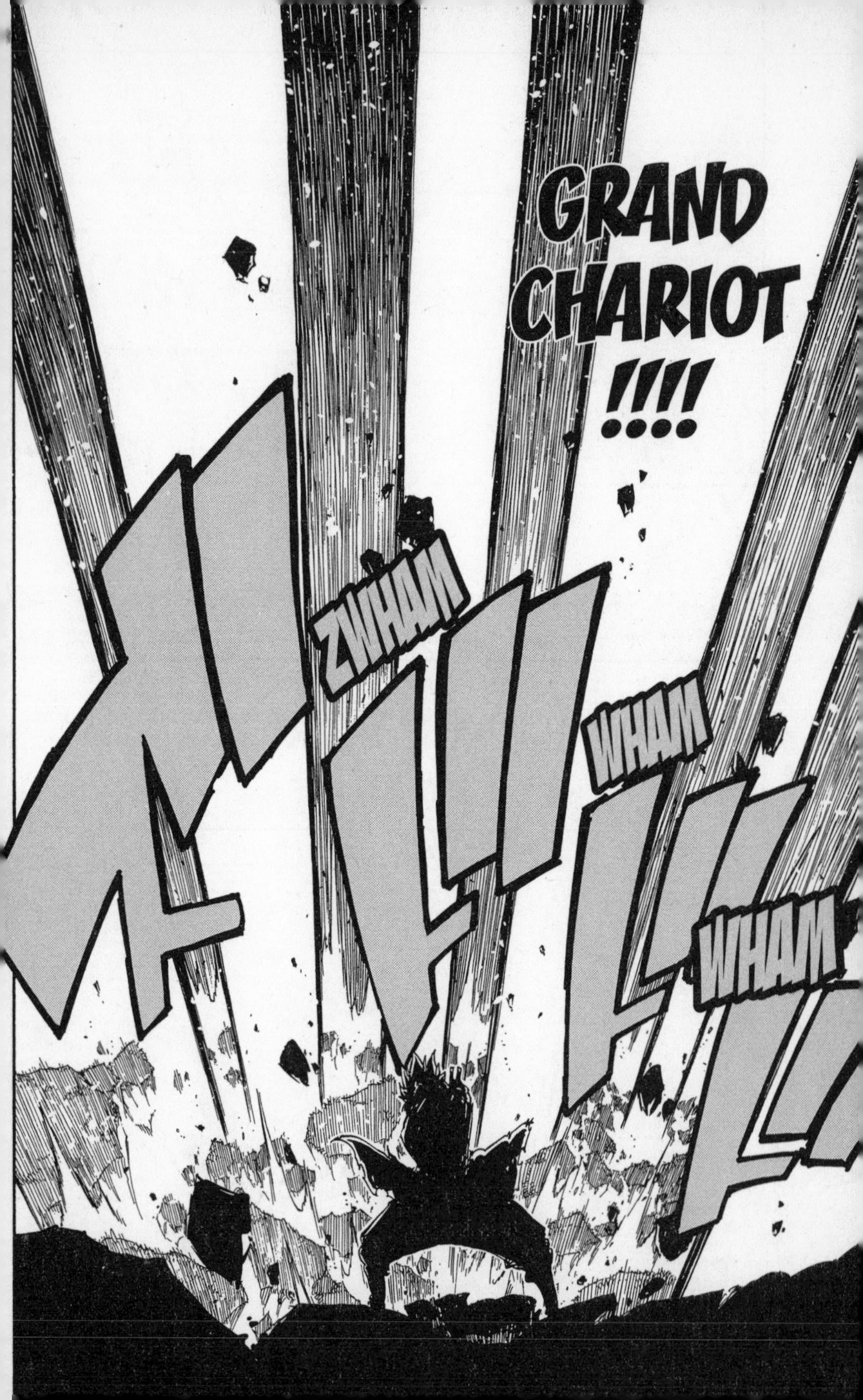

GRAND CHARIOT!!!!
ZWHAM
WHAM
WHAM

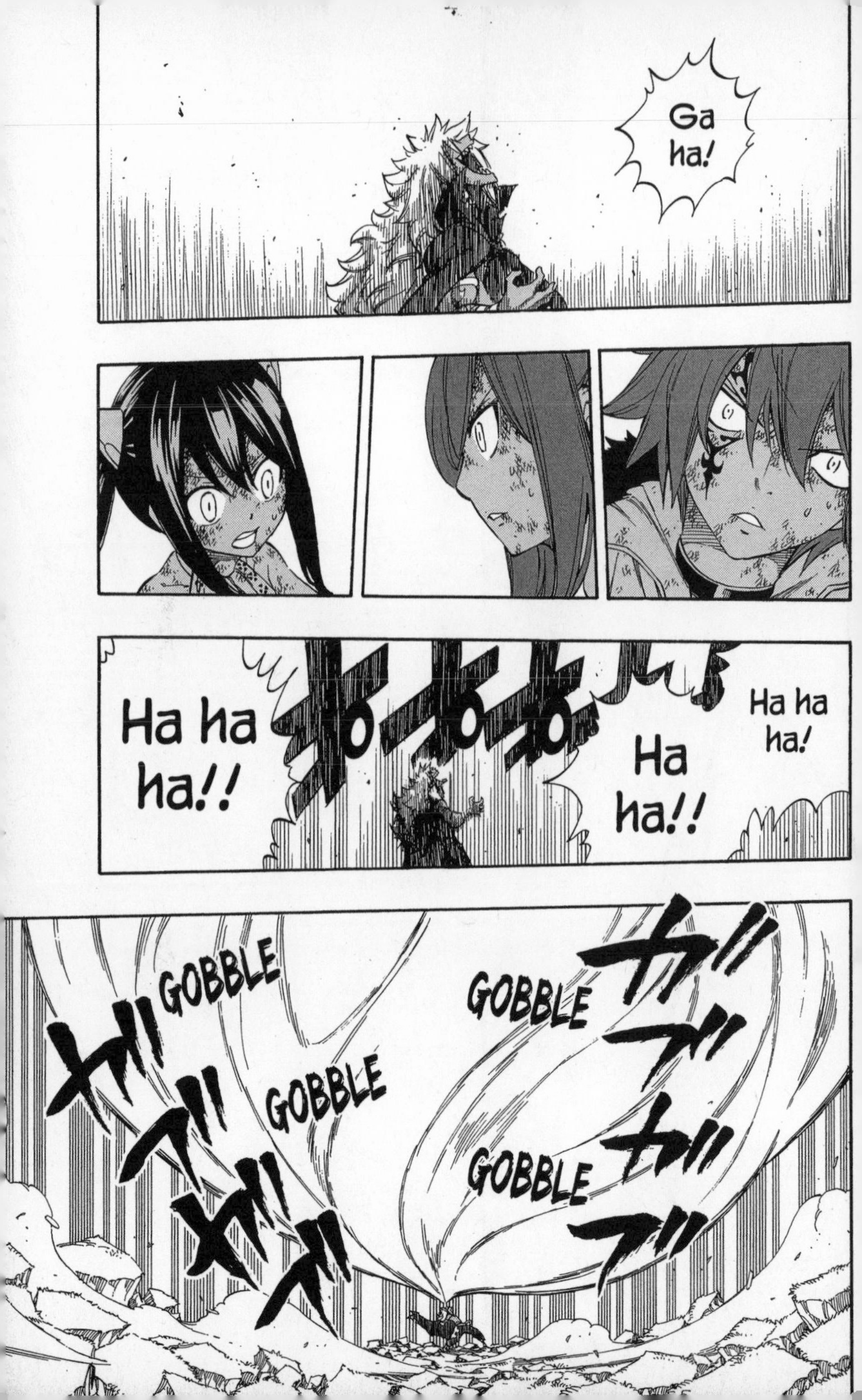
Ga ha!
Ha ha ha!
Ha ha!!
Ha ha ha!!
GOBBLE
GOBBLE
GOBBLE
GOBBLE

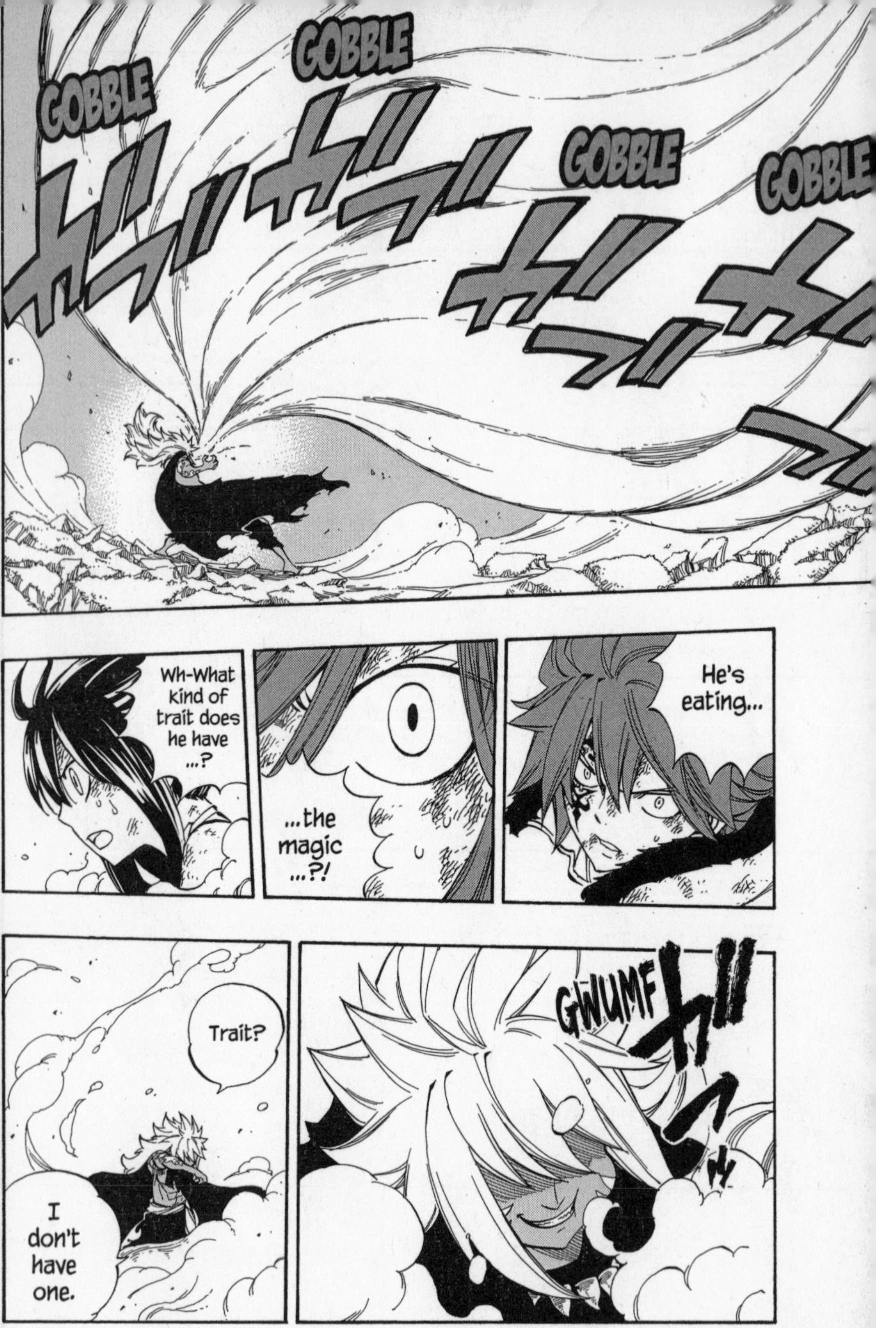
GOBBLE
GOBBLE
GOBBLE
GOBBLE
He's eating...
...the magic ...?!
Wh-What kind of trait does he have ...?
GWUMF
Trait?
I don't have one.

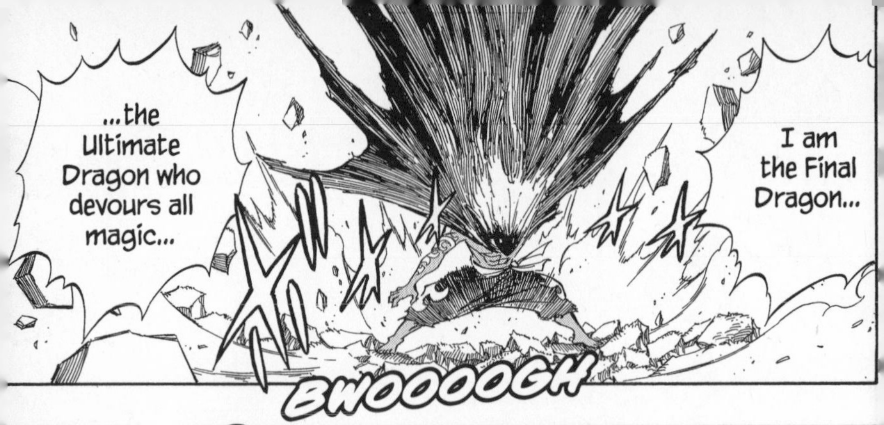
I am the Final Dragon...
...the Ultimate Dragon who devours all magic...
BWOOOOGH

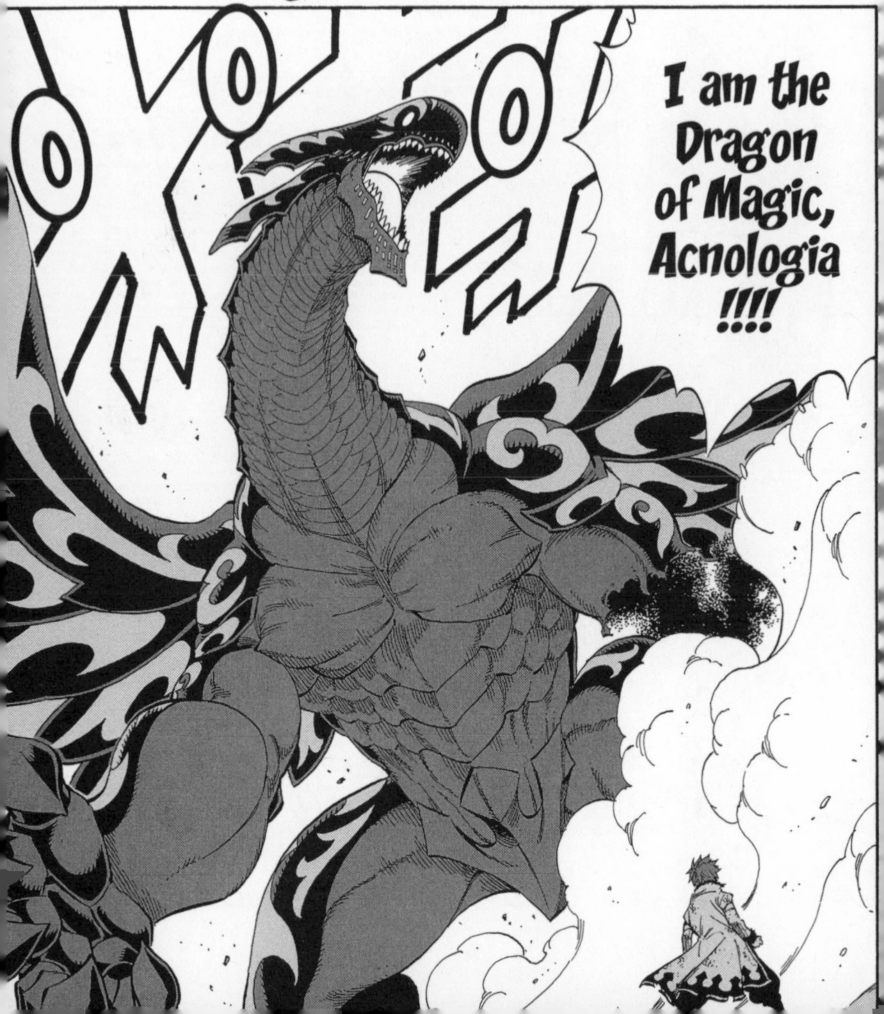
I am the Dragon of Magic, Acnologia !!!!

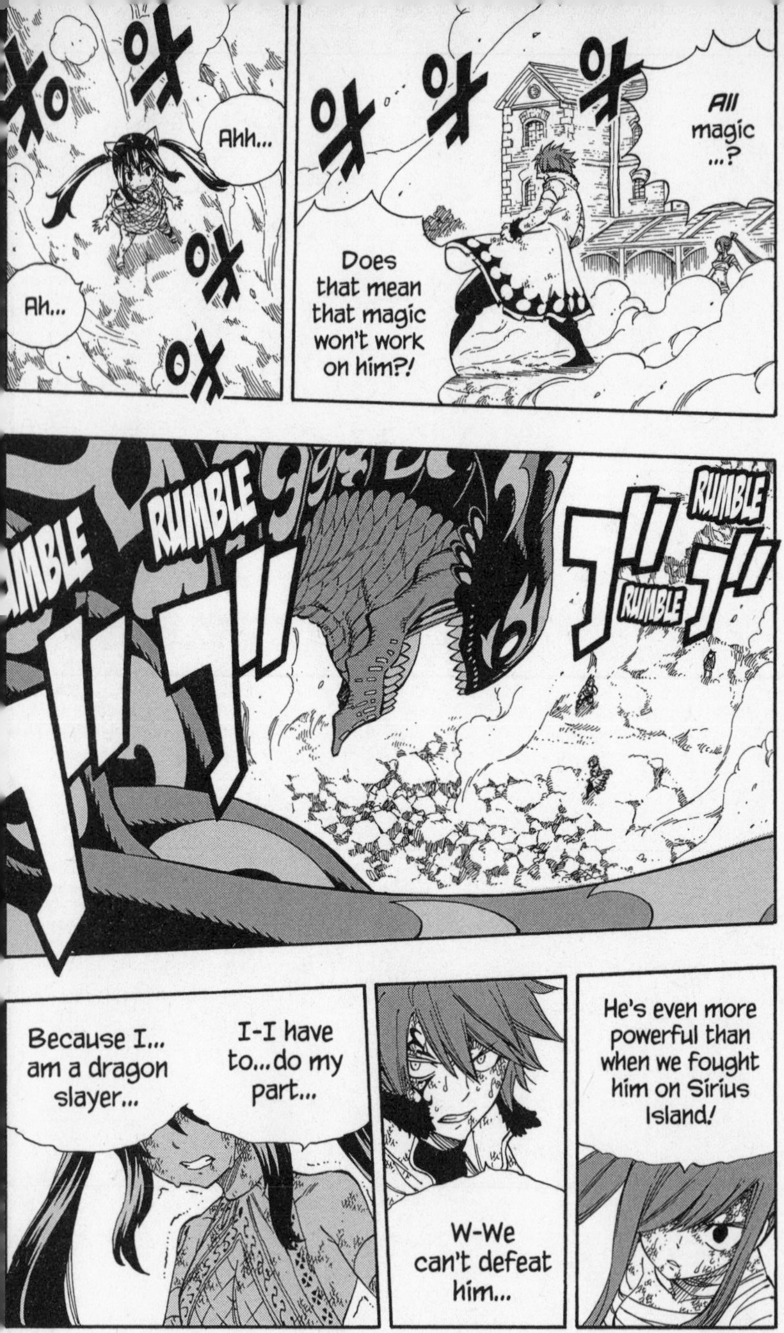
All magic ...?
Does that mean that magic won't work on him?!
Ahh...
Ah...
RUMBLE
RUMBLE
RUMBLE
RUMBLE
He's even more powerful than when we fought him on Sirius Island!
W-We can't defeat him...
I-I have to...do my part...
Because I... am a dragon slayer...

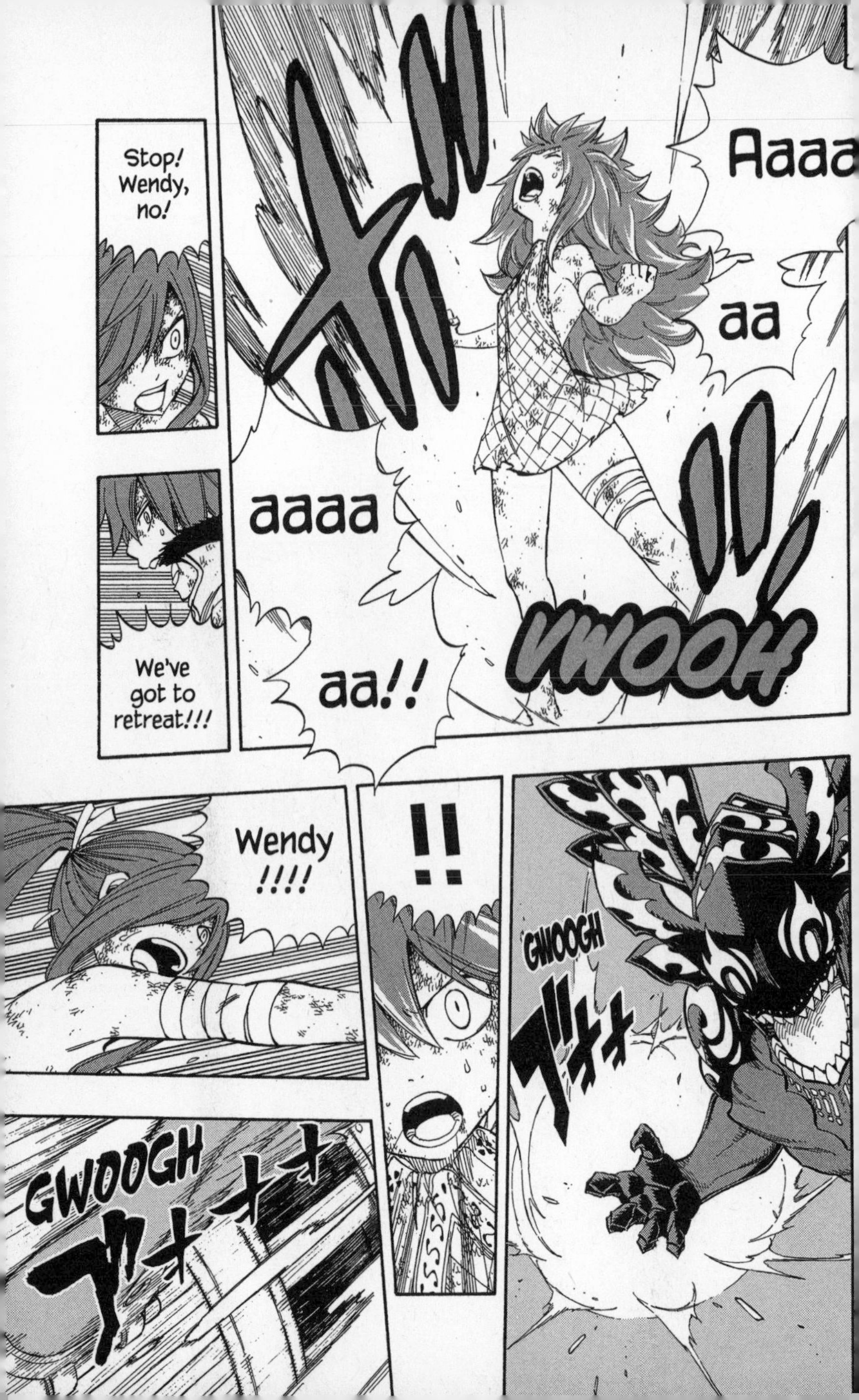
Aaaa
aa
aaaa
aa!!
VWOOH
Stop! Wendy, no!
We've got to retreat!!!
GWOOGH
!!
Wendy !!!!
GWOOGH

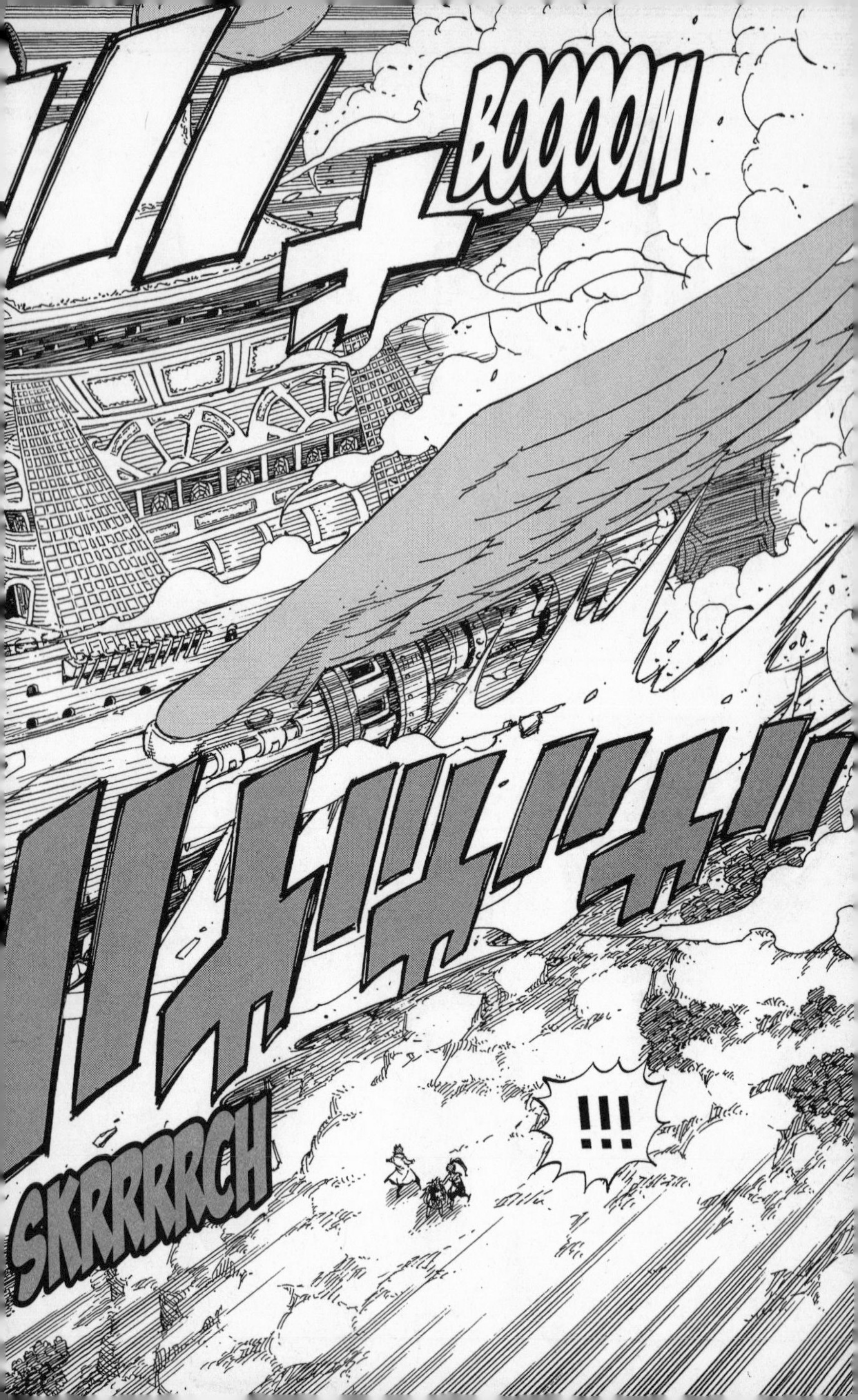
BOOOOM
SKRRRRCH
!!!

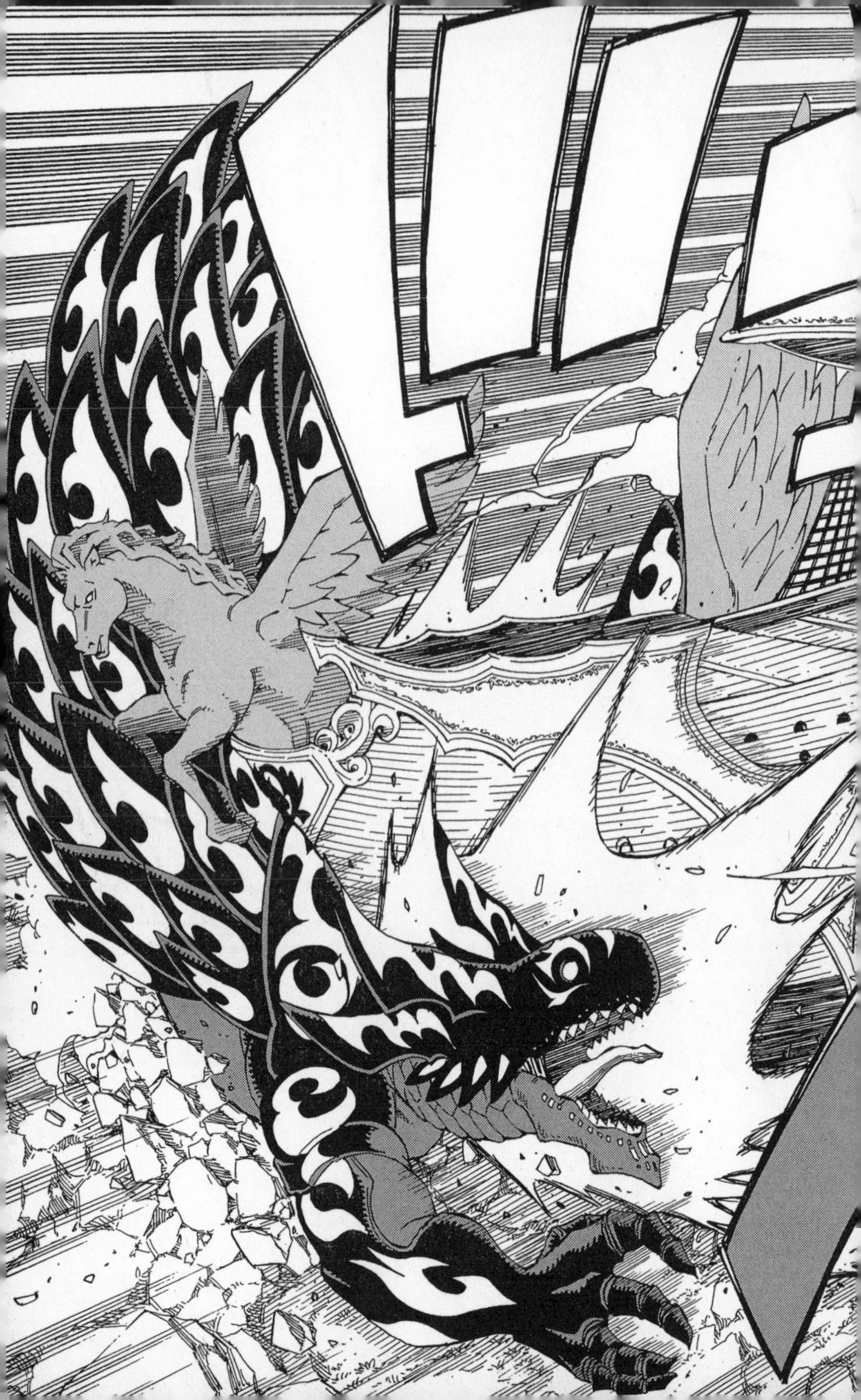

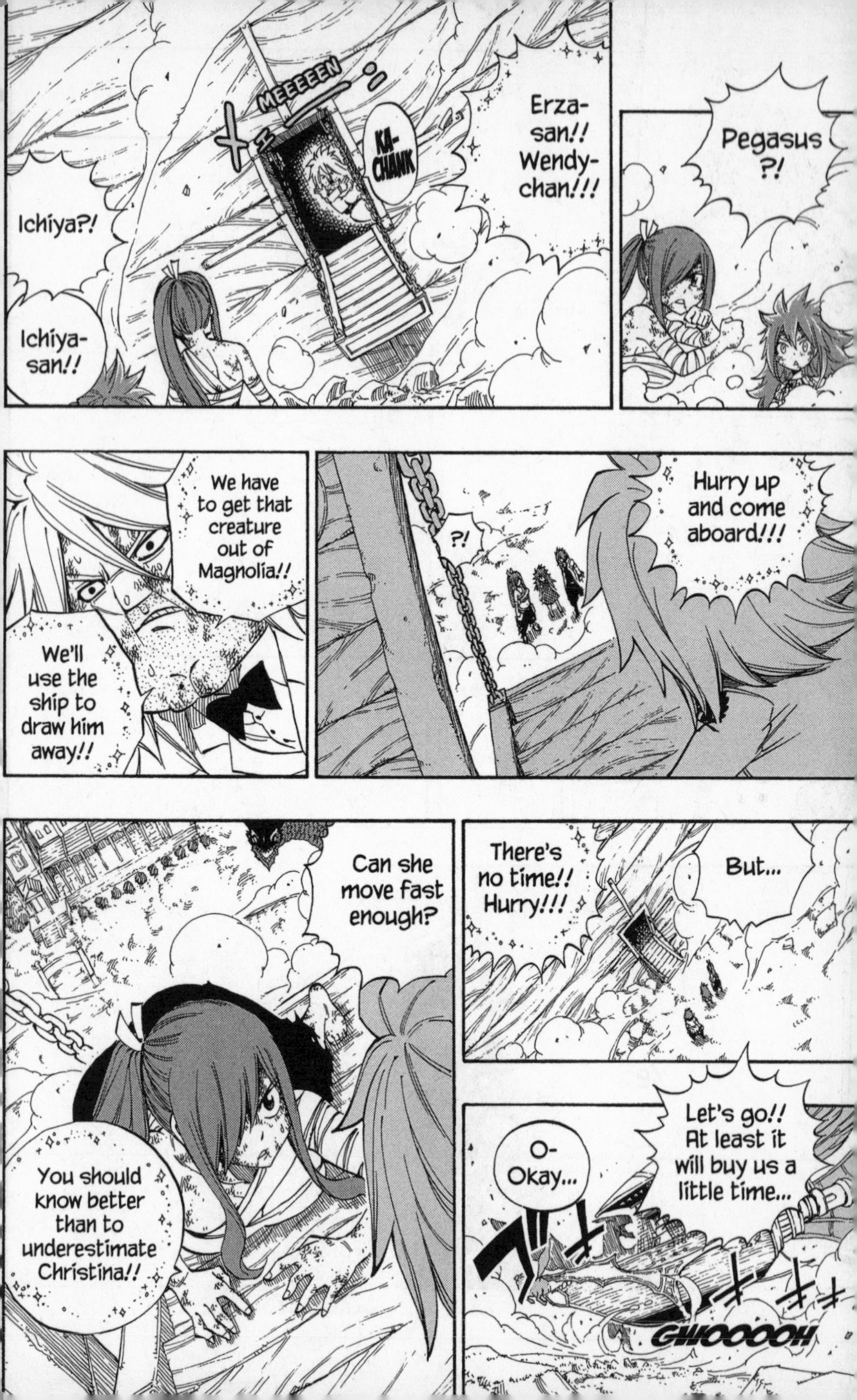
Pegasus ?!
Erza-san!! Wendy-chan!!!
KA-CHANK
MEEEEEN
Ichiya?!
Ichiya-san!!
Hurry up and come aboard!!!
?!
We have to get that creature out of Magnolia!!
We'll use the ship to draw him away!!
But...
There's no time!! Hurry!!!
Let's go!! At least it will buy us a little time...
O-Okay...
GWOOOOH
Can she move fast enough?
You should know better than to underestimate Christina!!

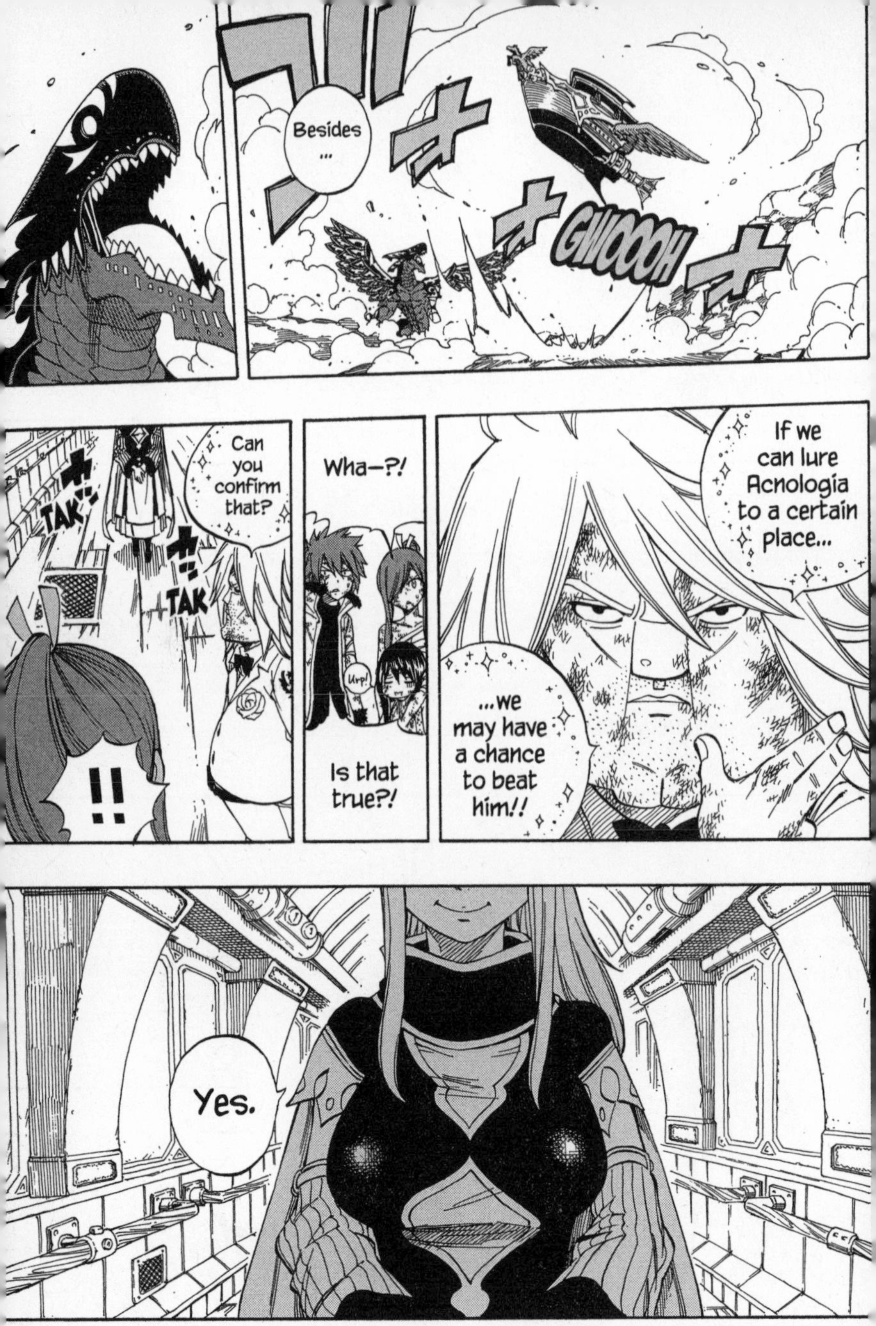
Besides...
GWOOOH
If we can lure Acnologia to a certain place...
...we may have a chance to beat him!!
Wha–?!
Urp!
Is that true?!
Can you confirm that?
TAK
TAK
!!
Yes.

FAIRY TAIL
フェアリーテイル

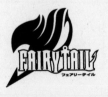

FAIRY TAIL

フェアリーテイル

Chapter 529: Teacher

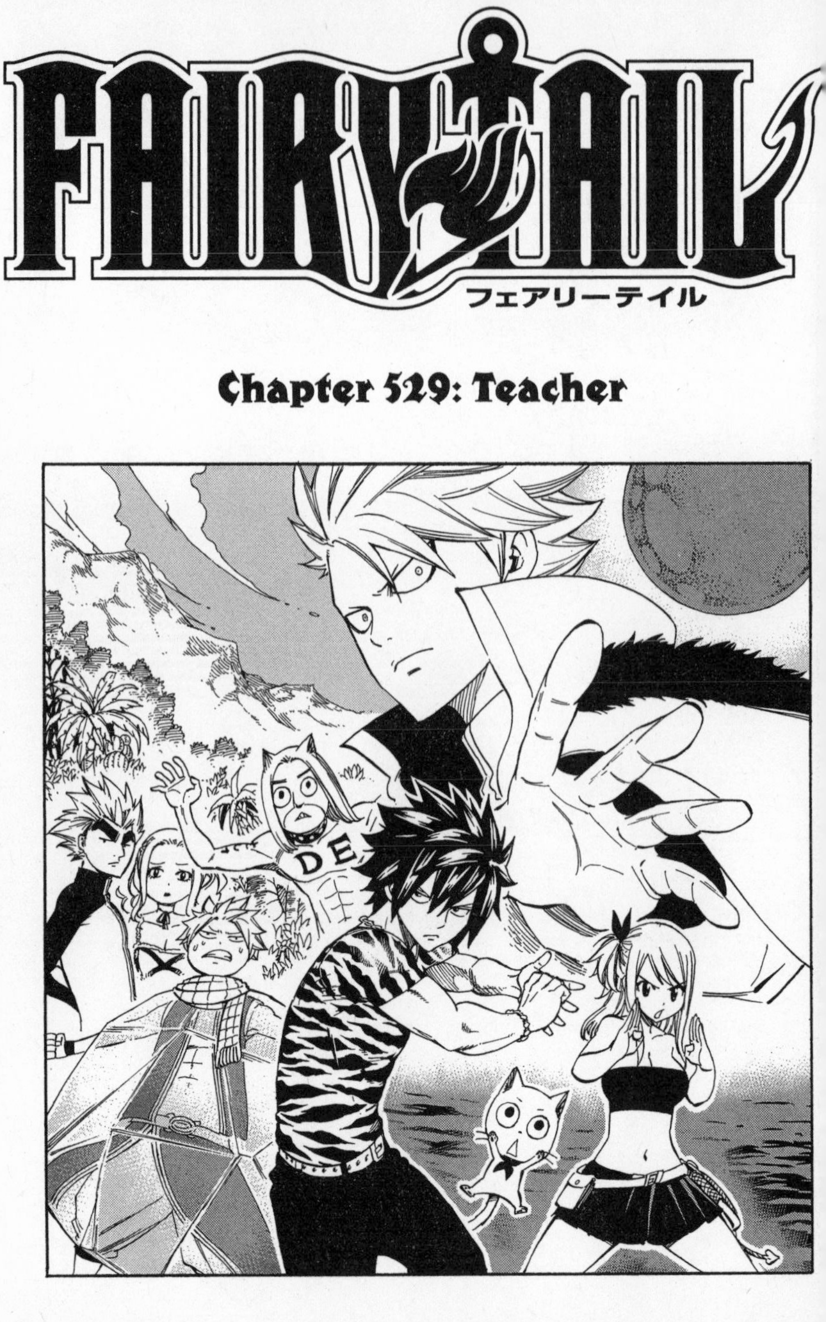
DE

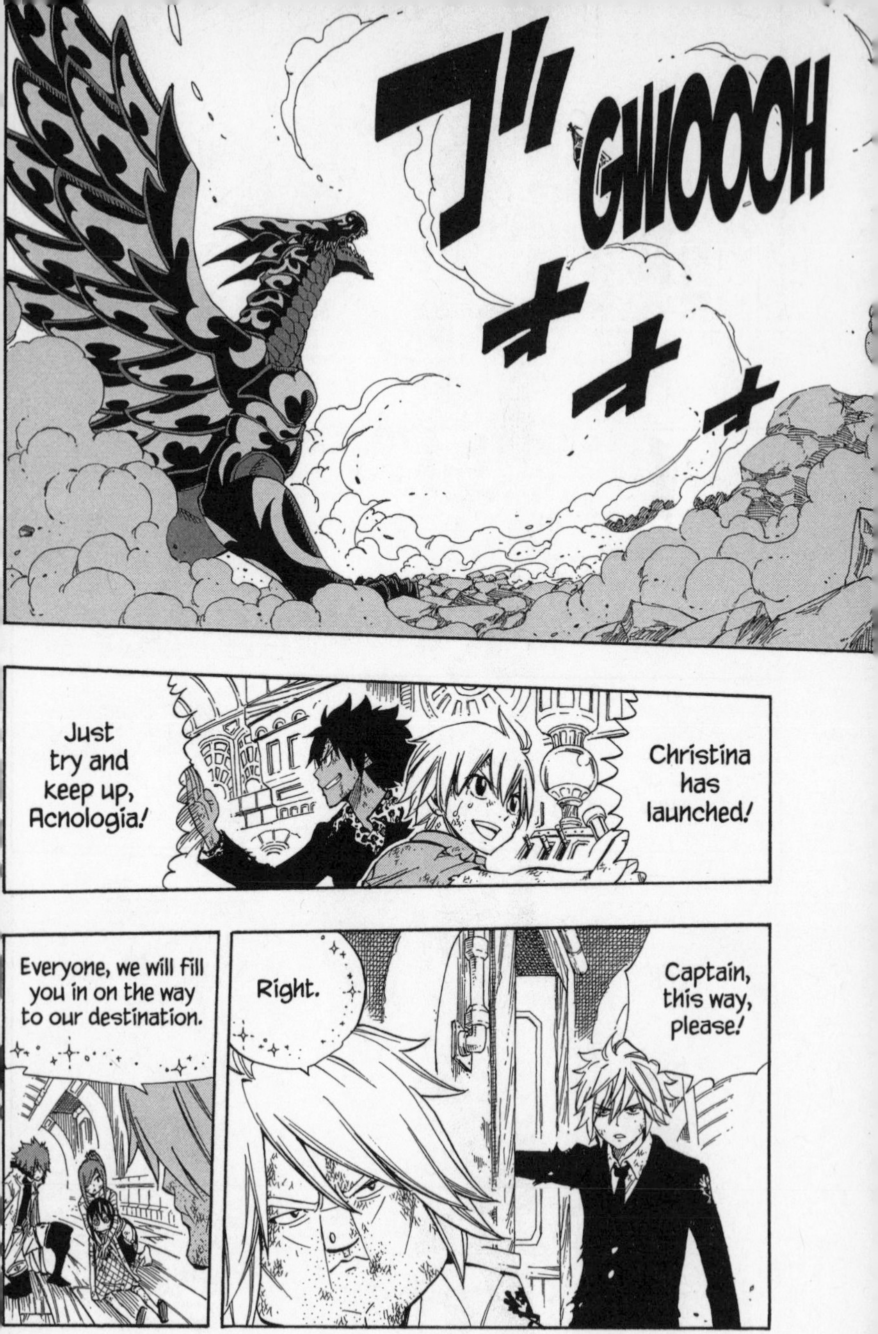
ゴォォォ
GWOOOH
Christina has launched!
Just try and keep up, Acnologia!
Captain, this way, please!
Right.
Everyone, we will fill you in on the way to our destination.

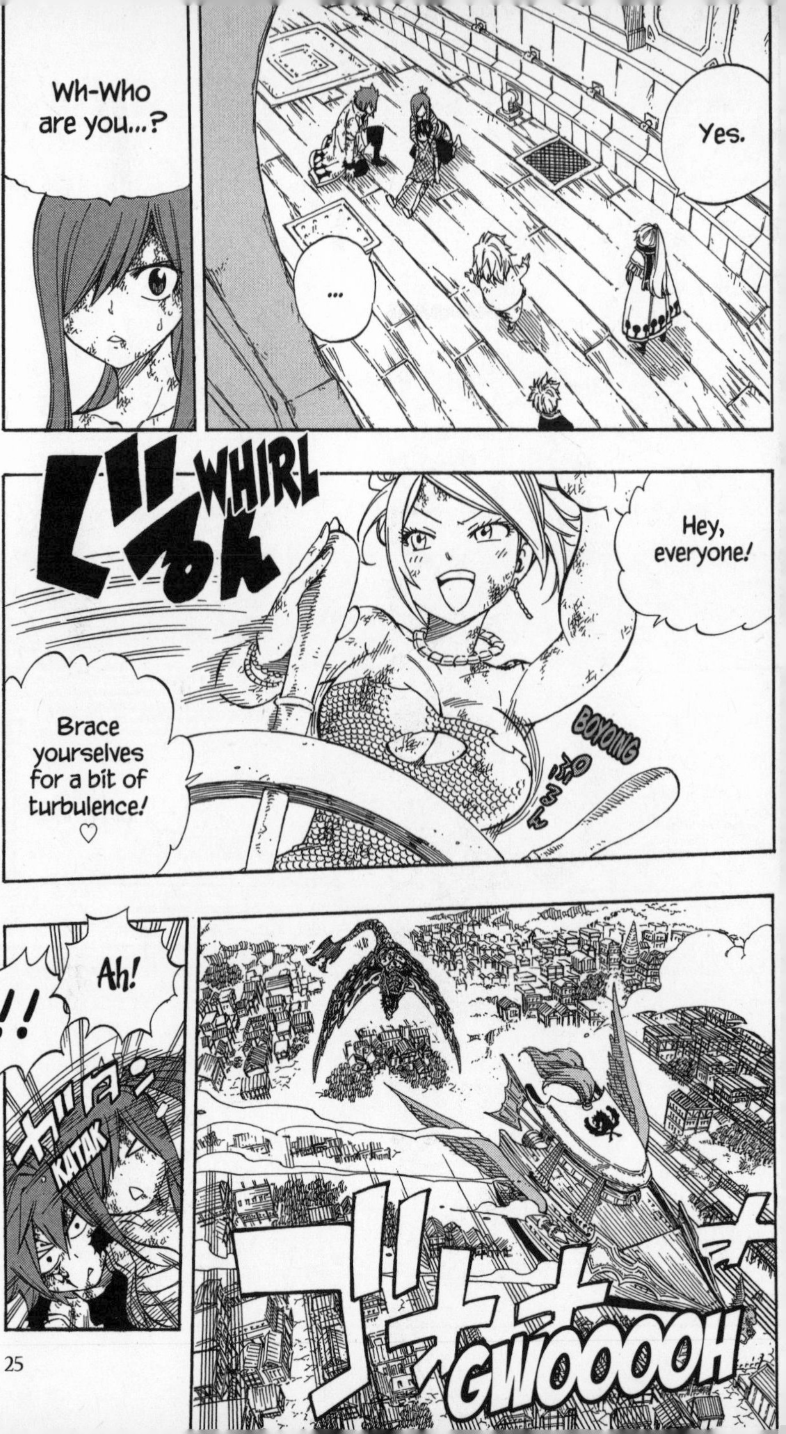
Yes.
...
Wh-Who are you...?
WHIRL
Hey, everyone!
Brace yourselves for a bit of turbulence! ♡
BOYOING
GWOOOOH
Ah!
!!
KATAK

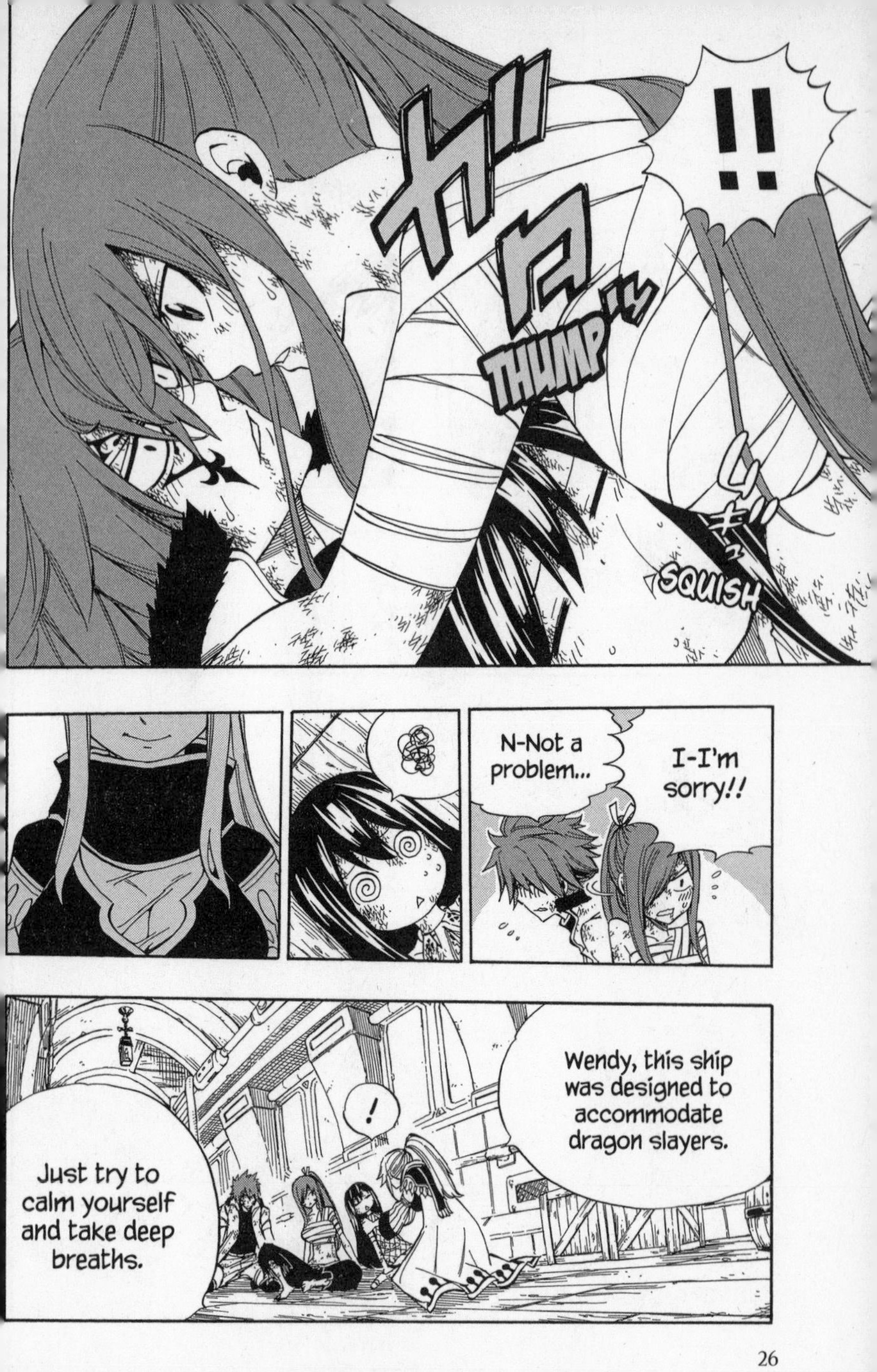
!!
THUMP
SQUISH
I-I'm sorry!!
N-Not a problem...
Wendy, this ship was designed to accommodate dragon slayers.
!
Just try to calm yourself and take deep breaths.

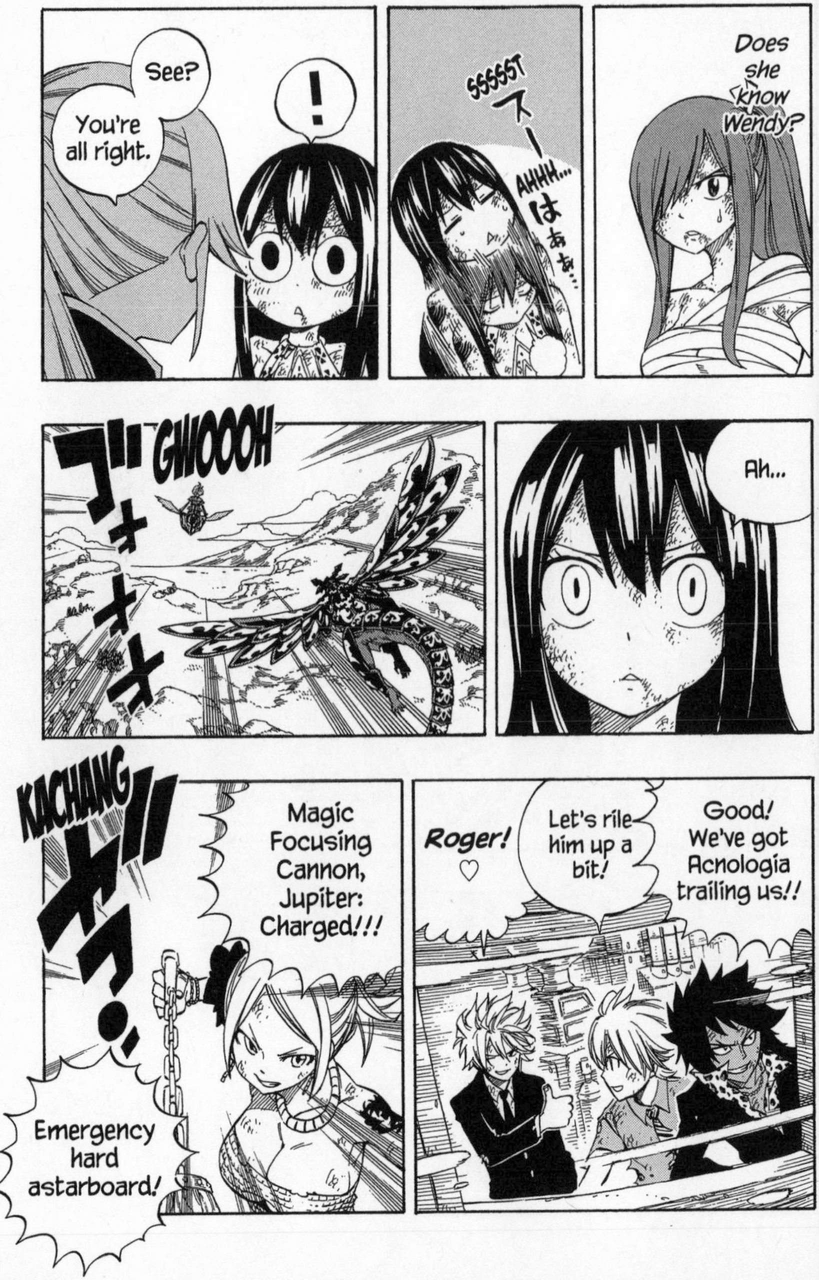
Does she know Wendy?
SSSSST
スー
AHHH...
はぁぁ…
!
See?
You're all right.
Ah...
GWOOOH
ゴォォォォ
Good! We've got Acnologia trailing us!!
Let's rile him up a bit!
Roger! ♡
Magic Focusing Cannon, Jupiter: Charged!!!
KACHANG
ガコッ
Emergency hard astarboard!

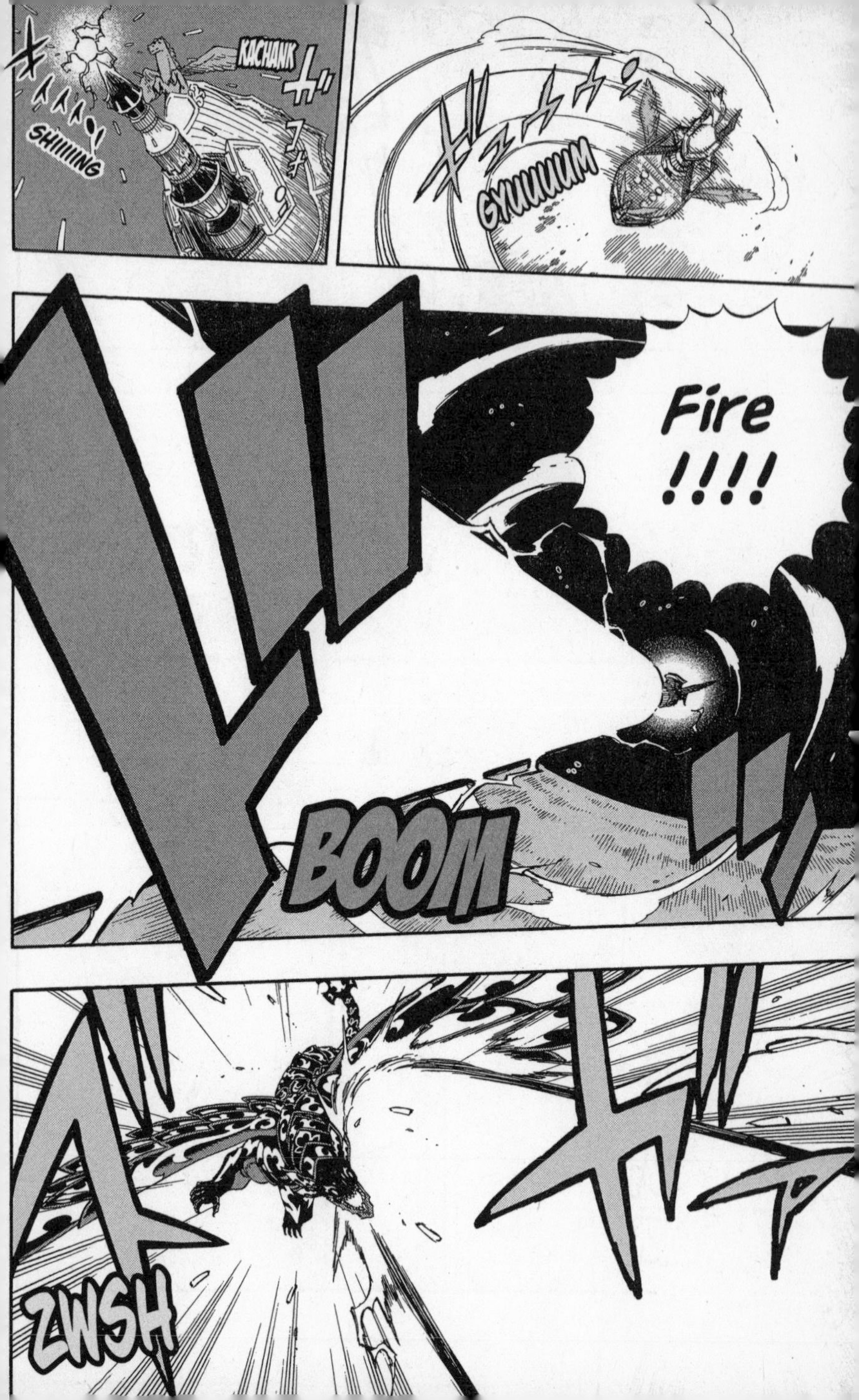
GYUUUUM
KACHANK
SHIIIIING
Fire !!!!
BOOM
ZWSH

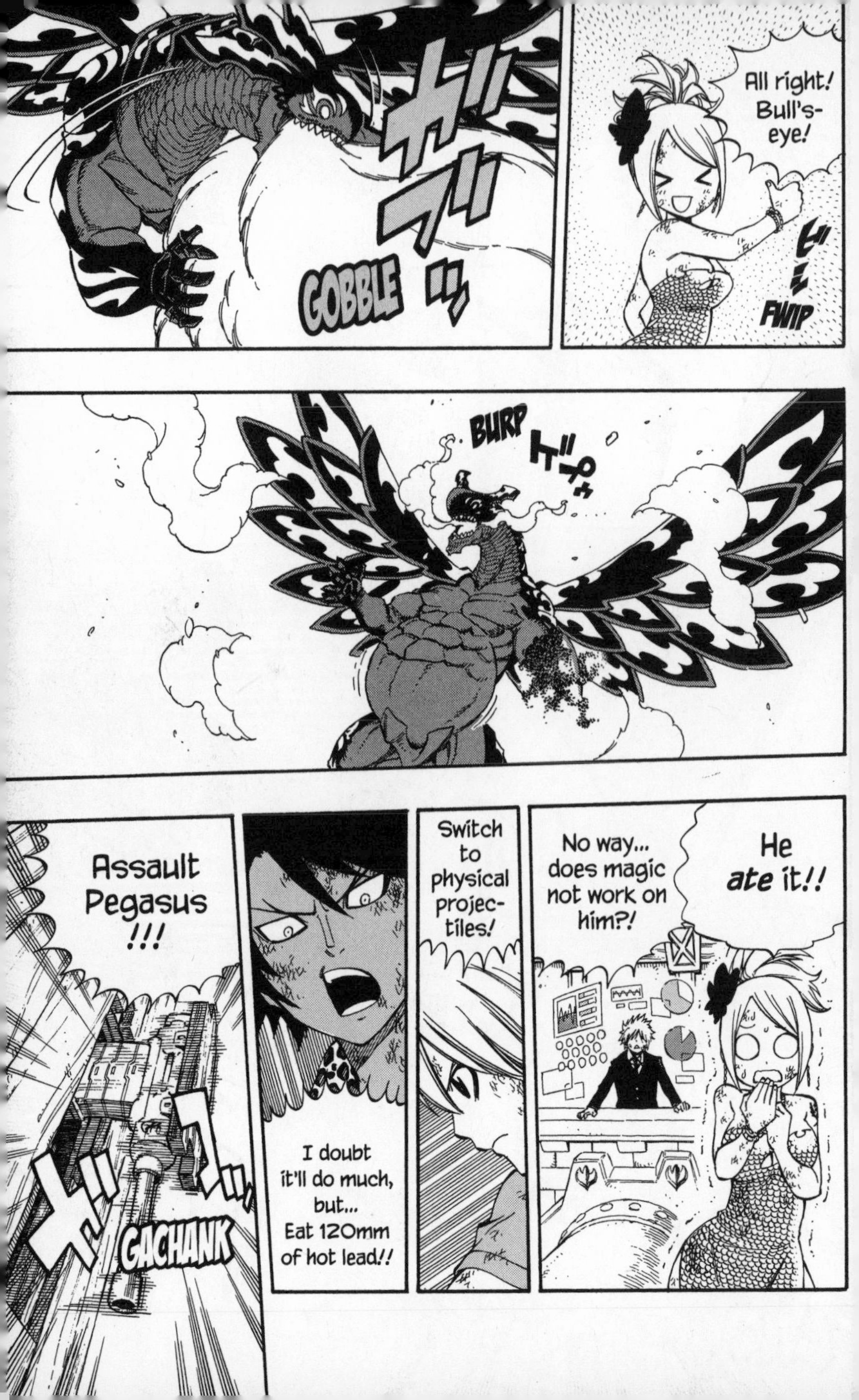
All right! Bull's-eye!
FWIP
GOBBLE
BURP
He *ate* it!!
No way... does magic not work on him?!
Switch to physical projec-tiles!
I doubt it'll do much, but... Eat 120mm of hot lead!!
Assault Pegasus !!!
GACHANK

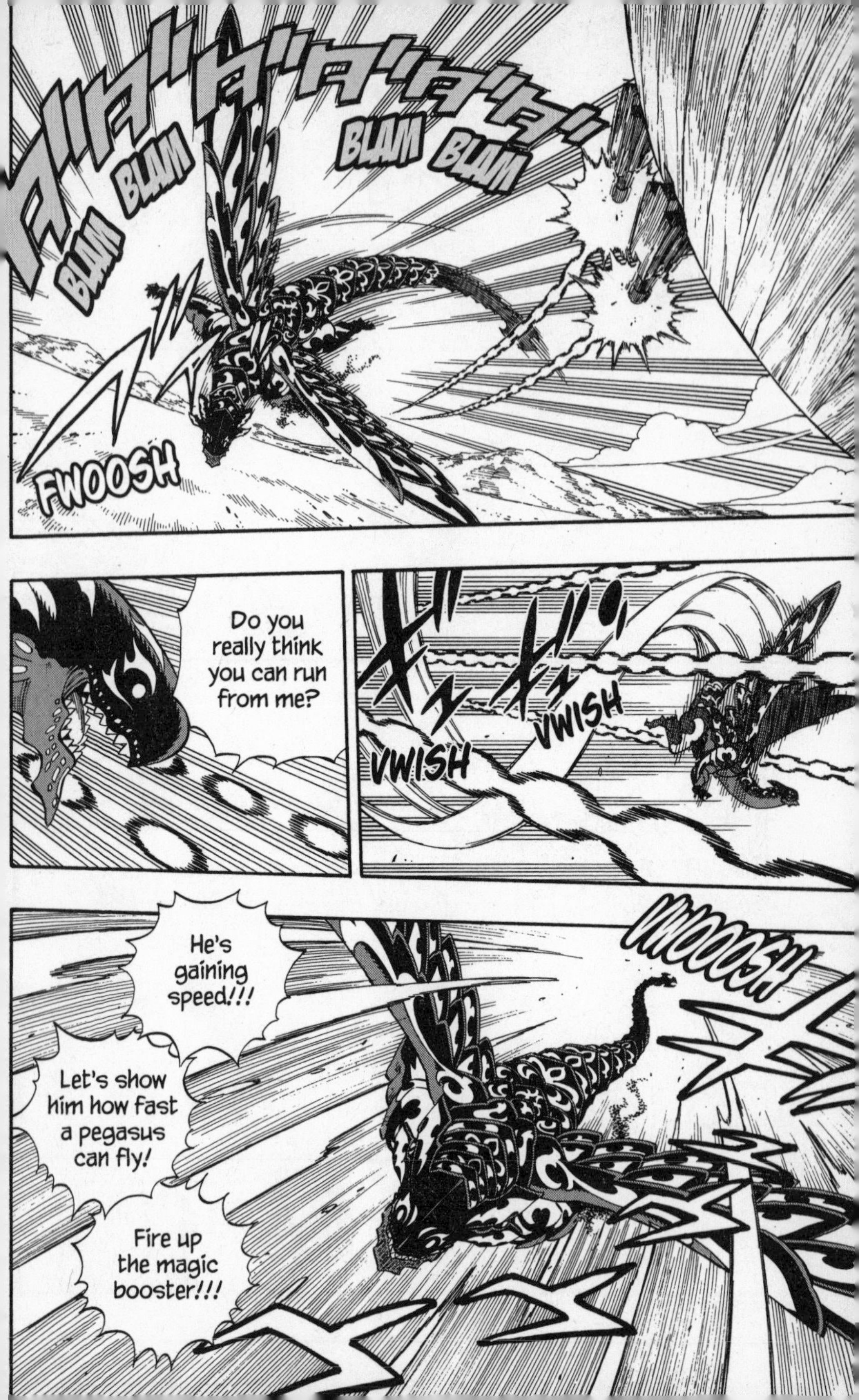
BLAM BLAM
BLAM BLAM
FWOOSH
VWISH
VWISH
Do you really think you can run from me?
WOOOSH
He's gaining speed!!!
Let's show him how fast a pegasus can fly!
Fire up the magic booster!!!

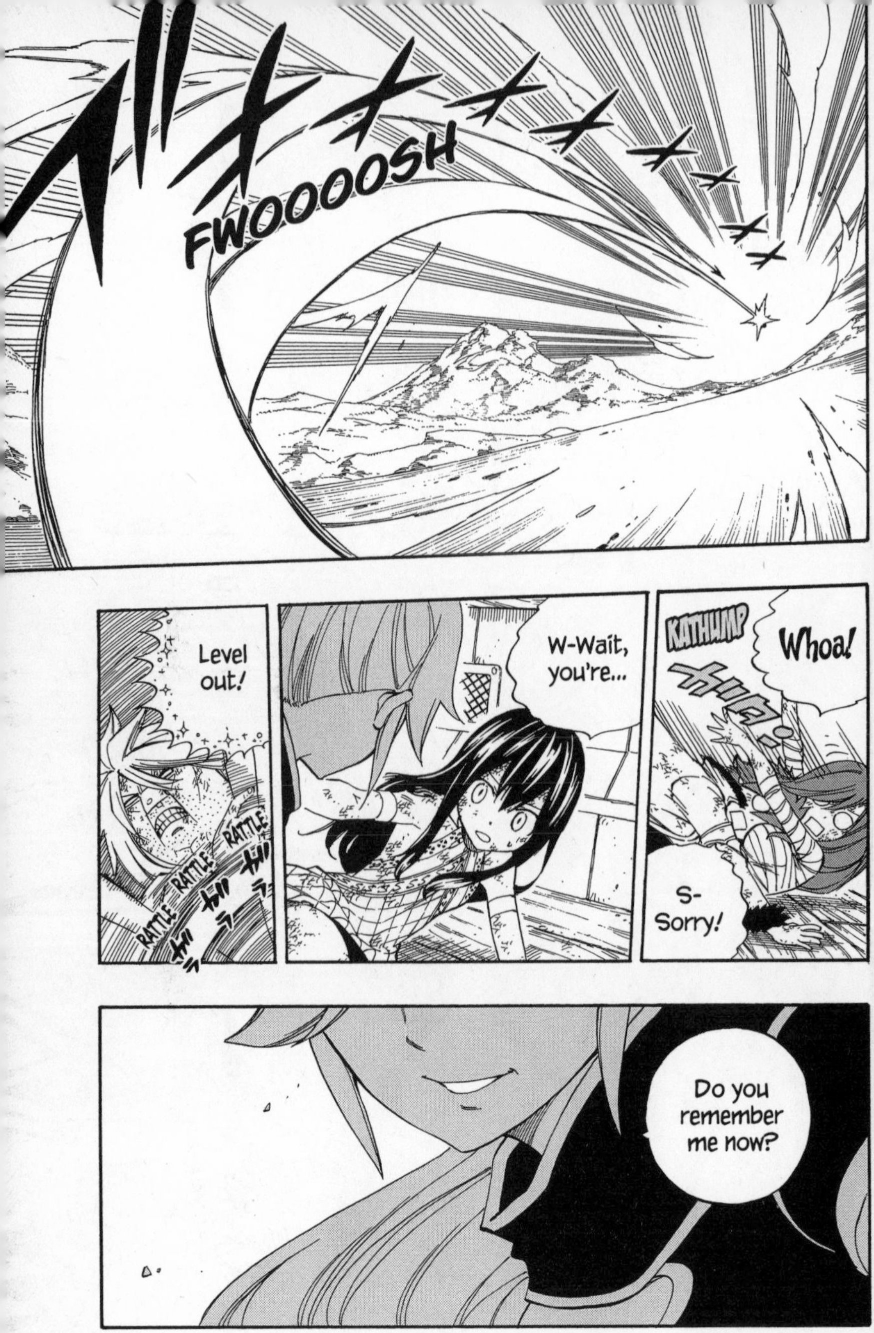
FWOOOOSH
Whoa!
KATHUMP
S-Sorry!
W-Wait, you're...
Level out!
RATTLE RATTLE RATTLE
Do you remember me now?

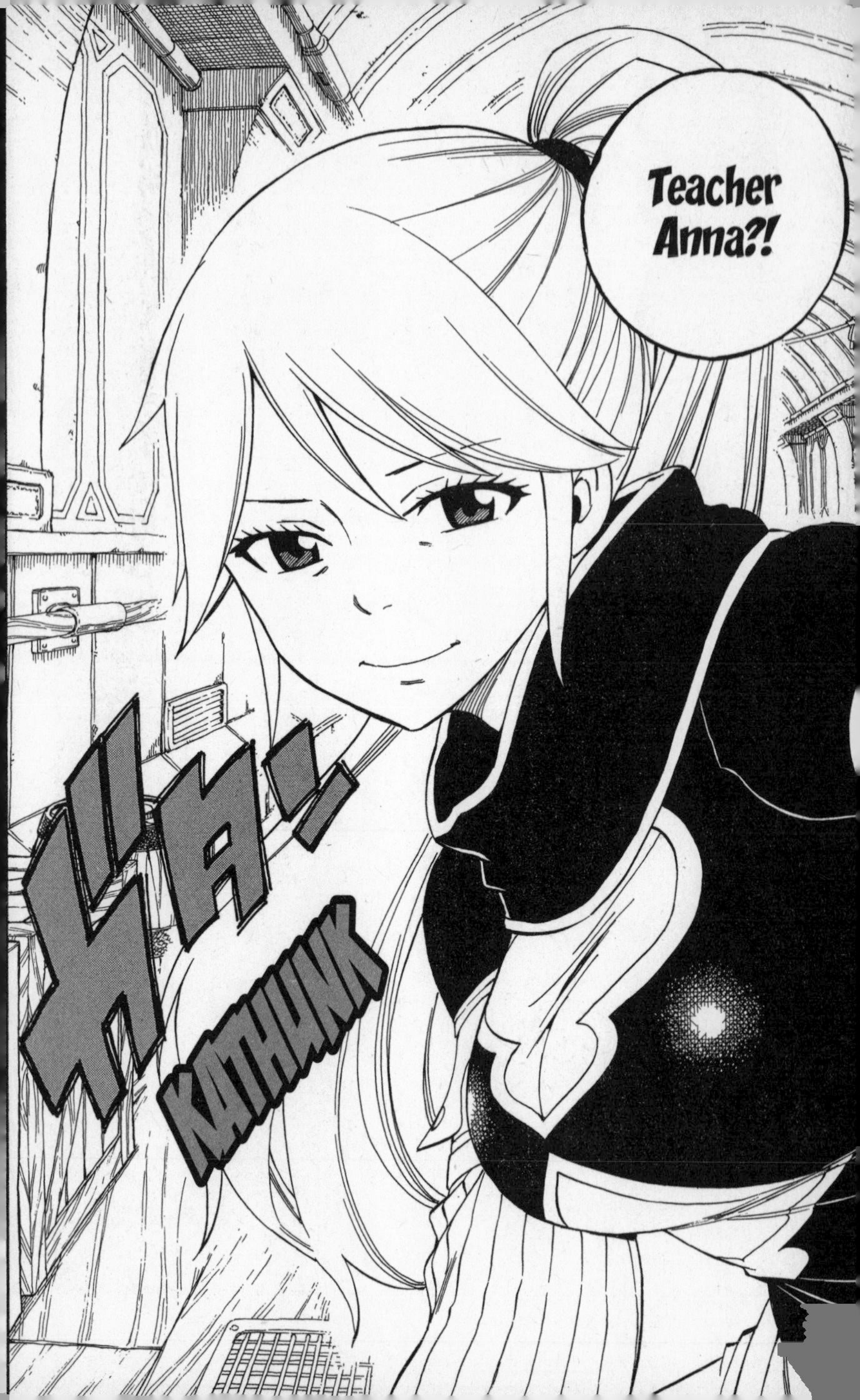
Teacher Anna?!
KATHUNK

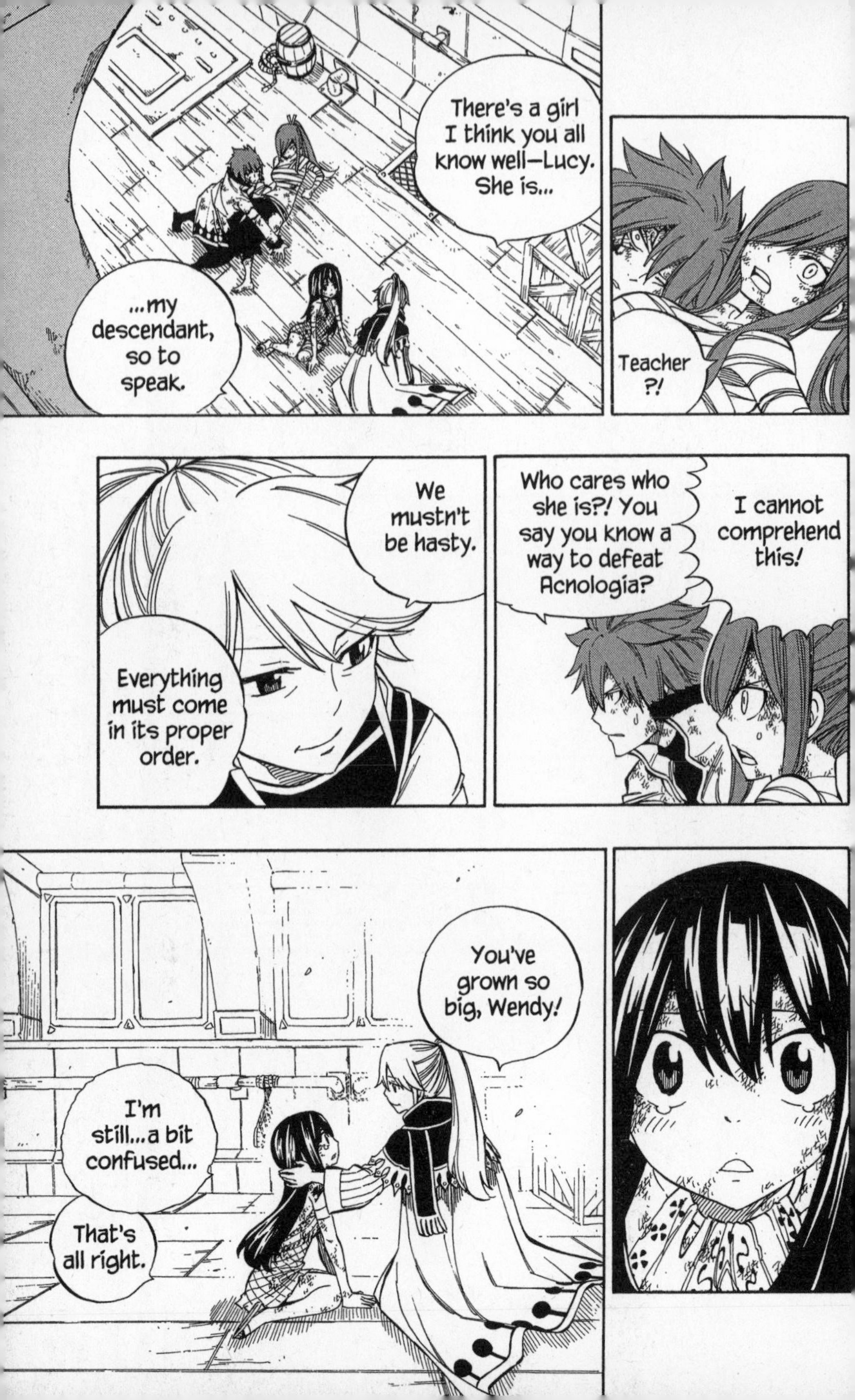
Teacher?!
There's a girl I think you all know well—Lucy. She is...
...my descendant, so to speak.
I cannot comprehend this!
Who cares who she is?! You say you know a way to defeat Acnologia?
We mustn't be hasty.
Everything must come in its proper order.
You've grown so big, Wendy!
I'm still...a bit confused...
That's all right.

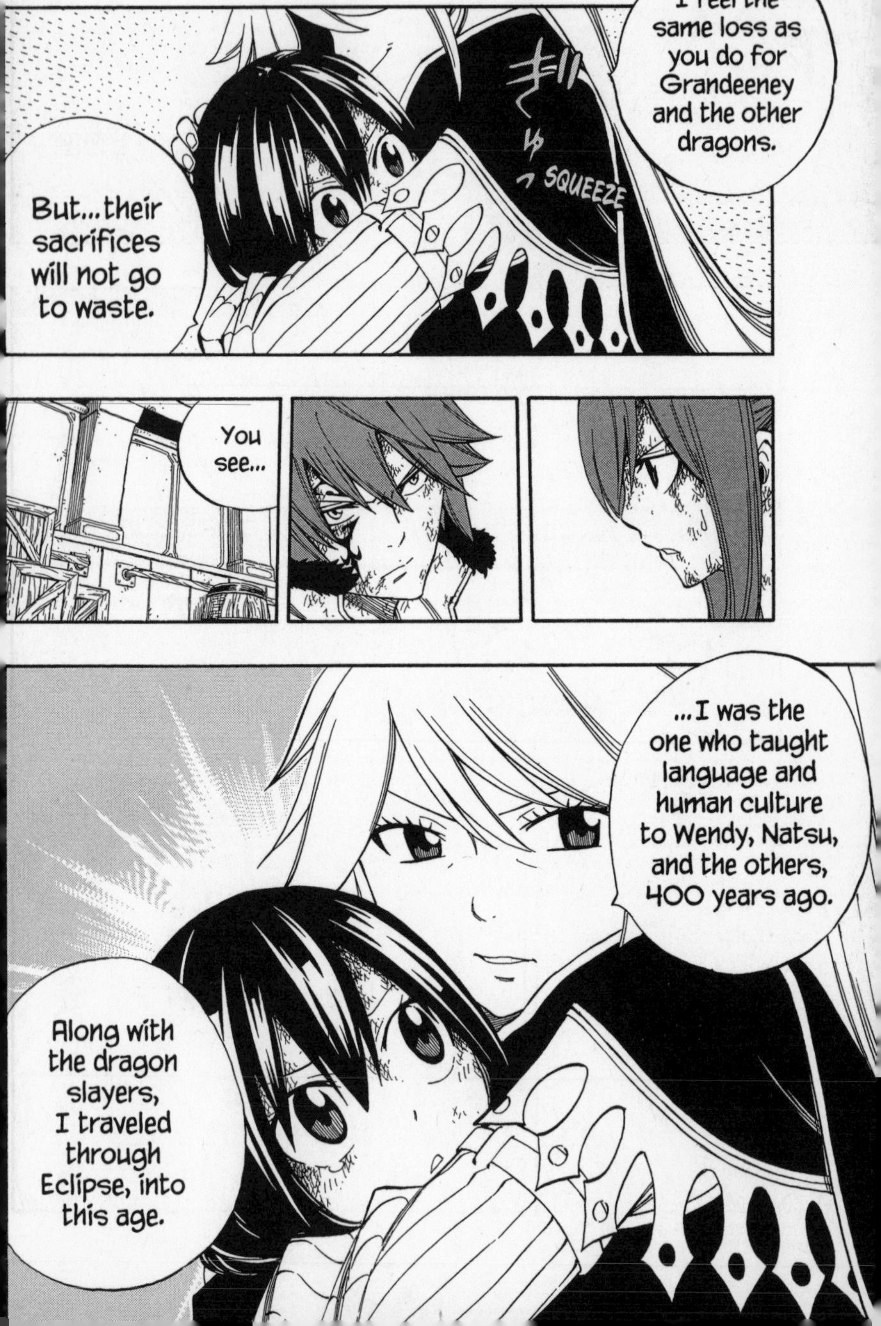
I feel the same loss as you do for Grandeeney and the other dragons.
SQUEEZE
But...their sacrifices will not go to waste.
You see...
...I was the one who taught language and human culture to Wendy, Natsu, and the others, 400 years ago.
Along with the dragon slayers, I traveled through Eclipse, into this age.

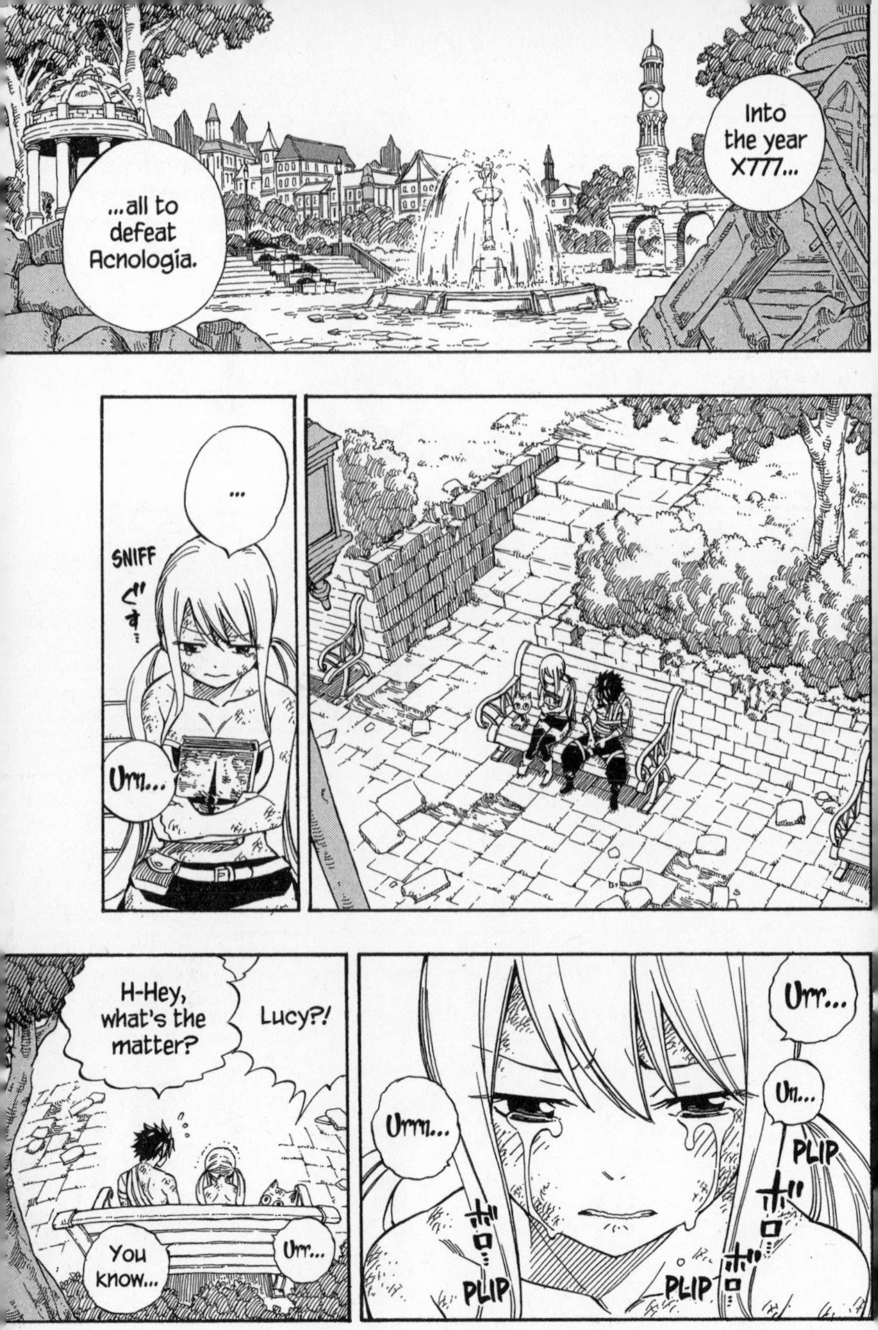
Into the year X777...
...all to defeat Acnologia.
...
SNIFF
ぐす…
Urrn...
Urr...
Un...
PLIP
ボロ…
PLIP
ボロ…
Urrn...
ボロ…
PLIP
Lucy?!
H-Hey, what's the matter?
Urr...
You know...

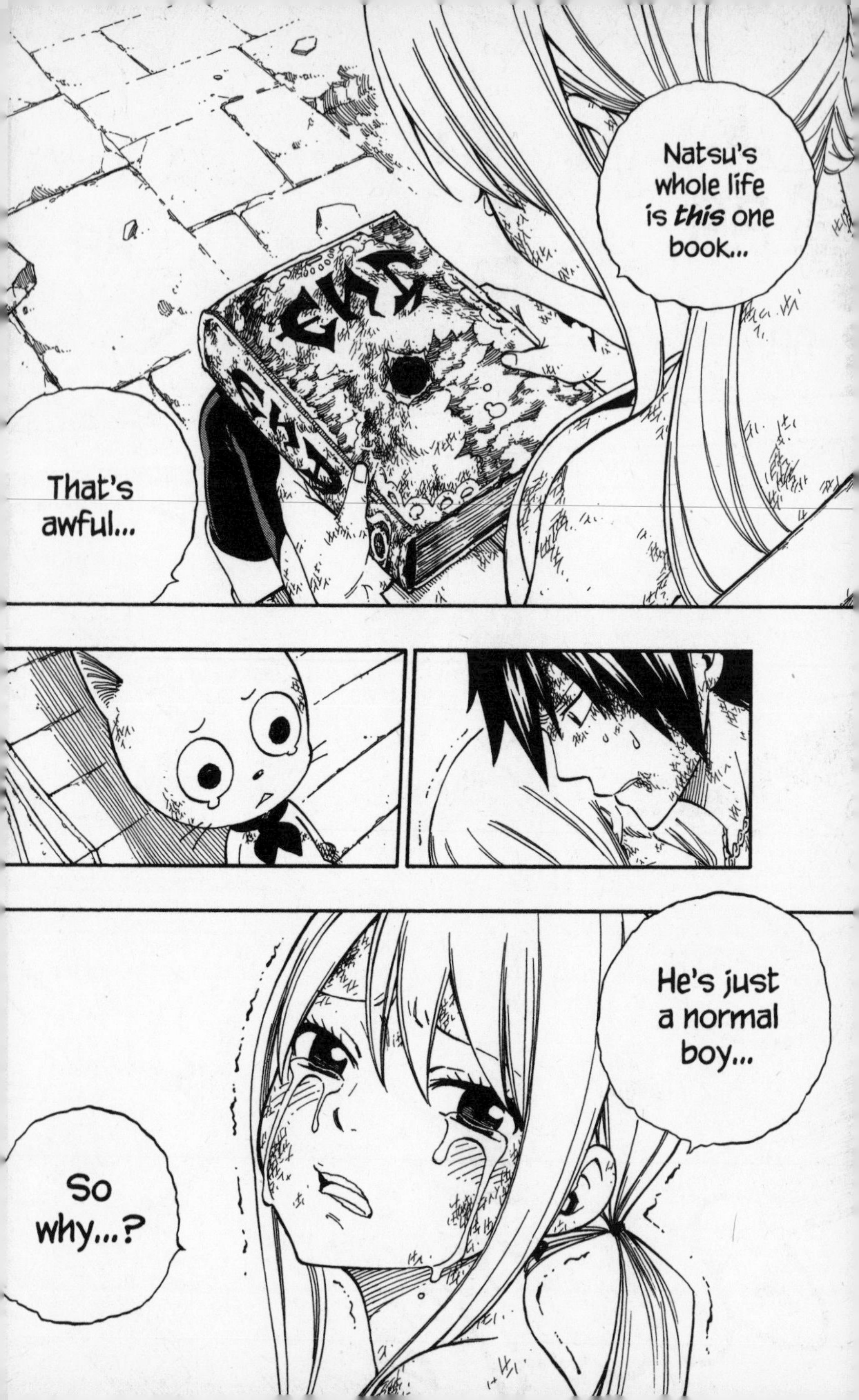
Natsu's whole life is *this* one book...
That's awful...
He's just a normal boy...
So why...?

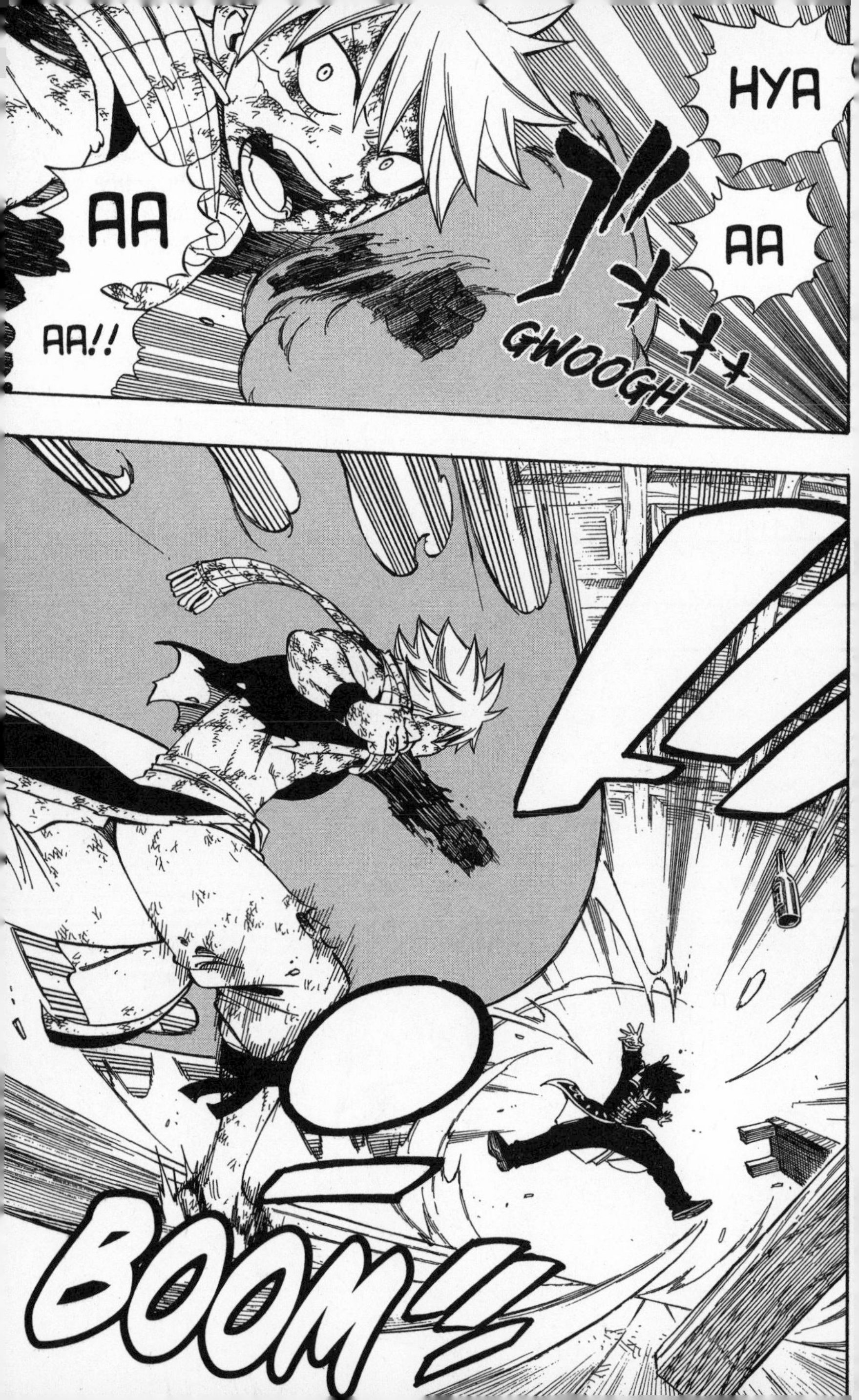
HYA
AA
GWOOGH
AA
AA!!
BOOM!!

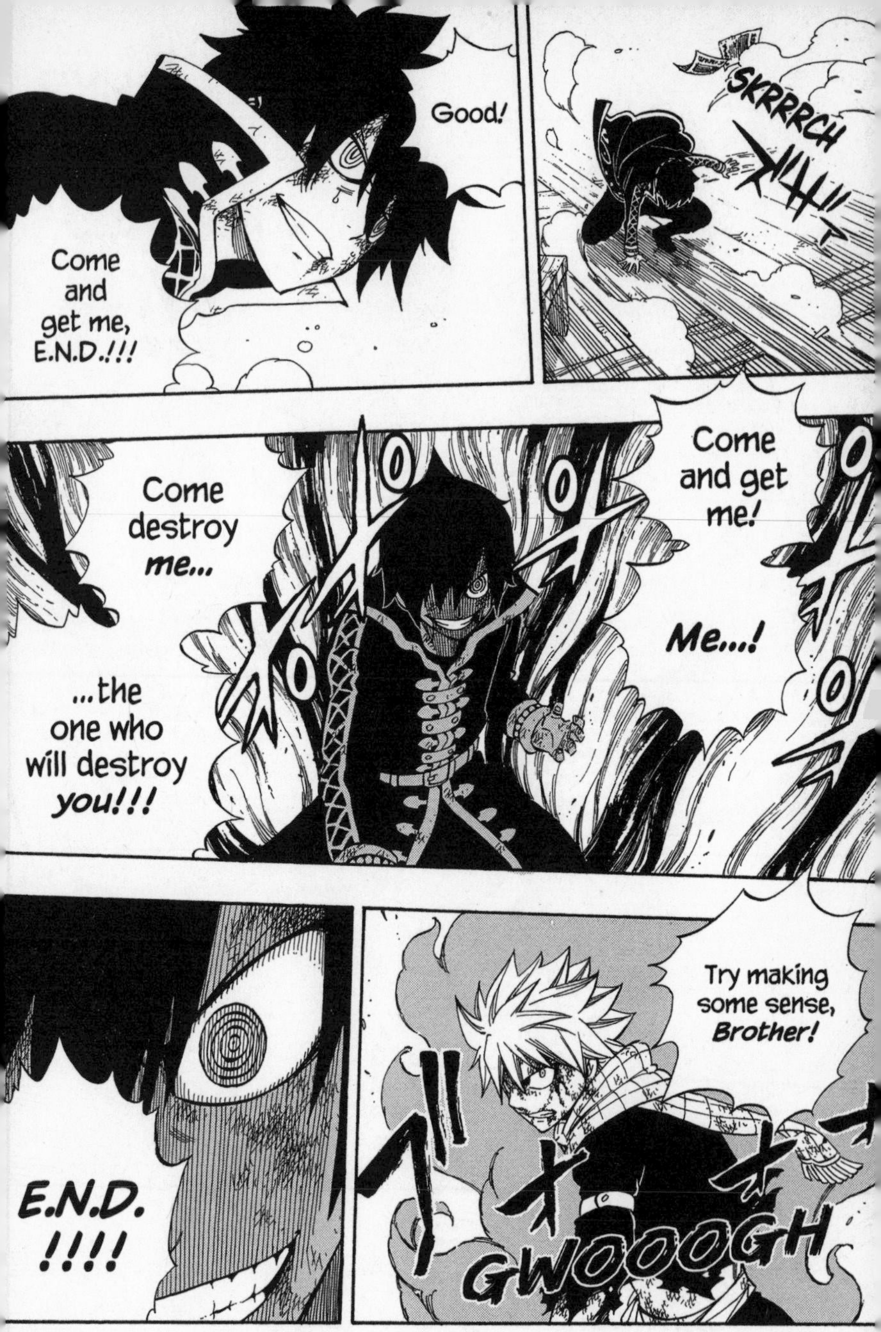
SKRRRCH
Good!
Come and get me, E.N.D.!!!
Come and get me!
Me...!
Come destroy me...
...the one who will destroy you!!!
Try making some sense, Brother!
GWOOOGH
E.N.D. !!!!

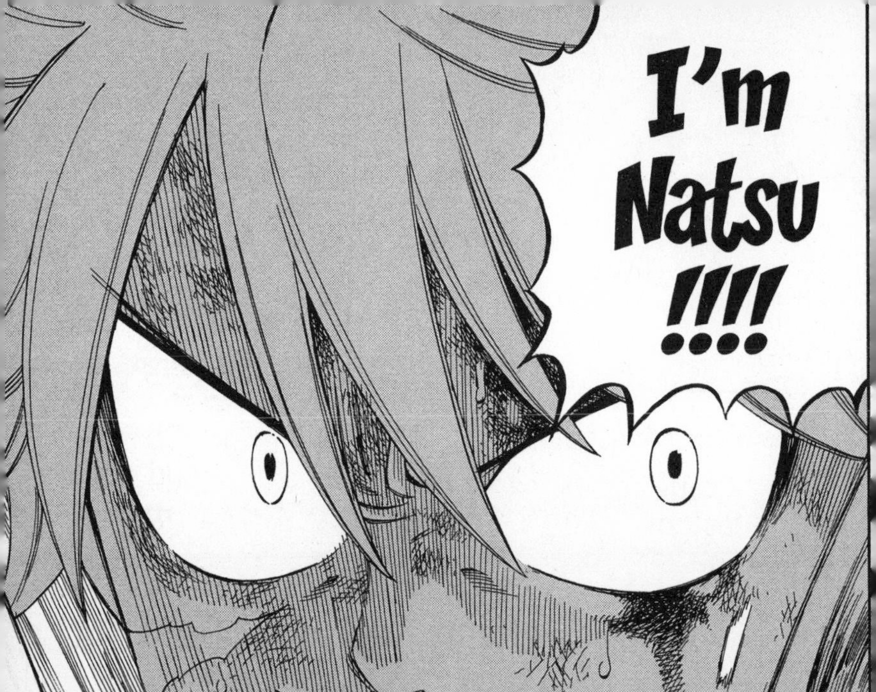
I'm Natsu!!!!
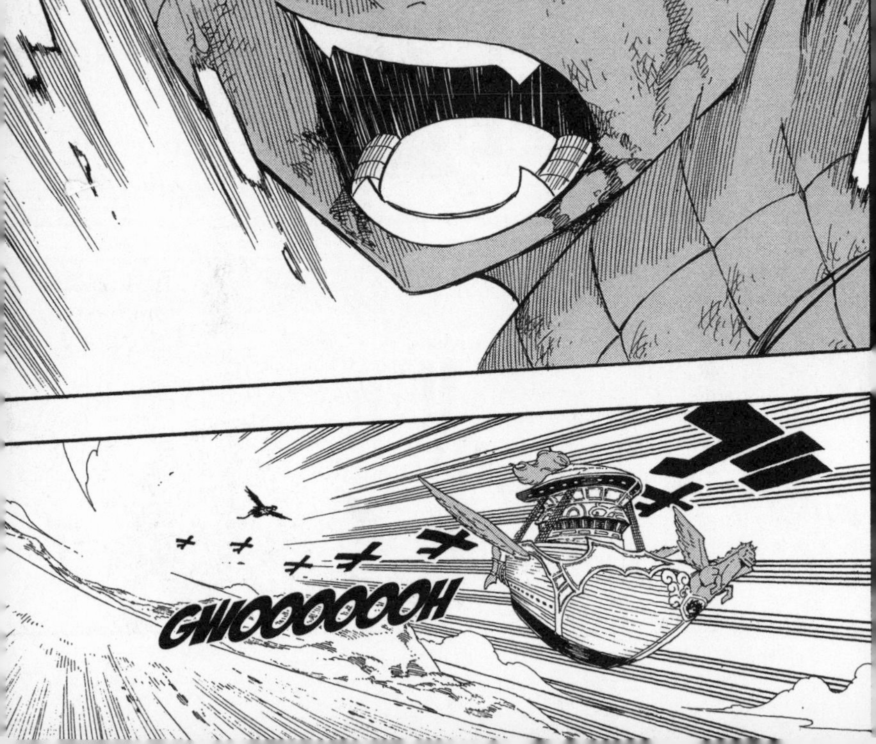
GWOOOOOOH

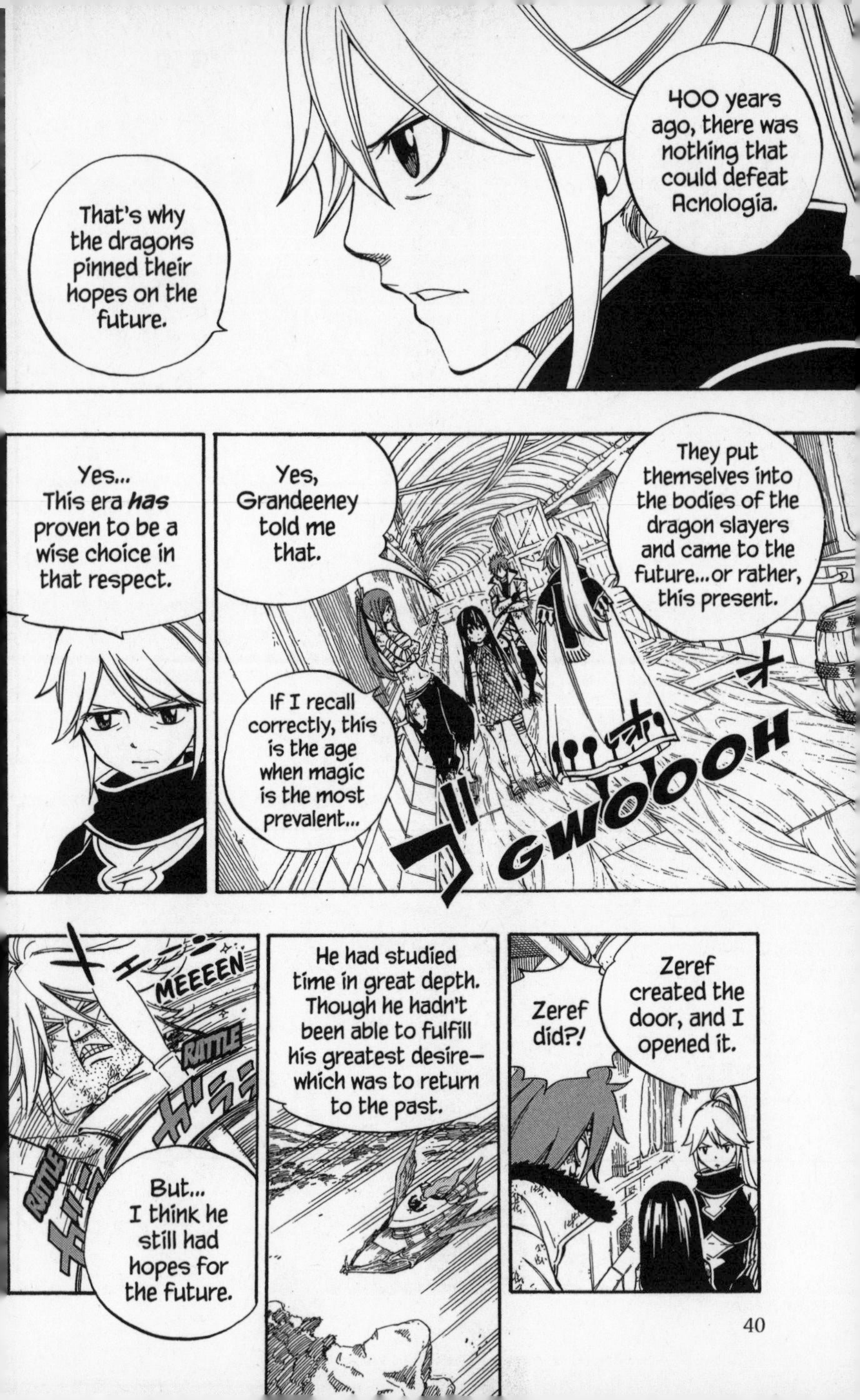
400 years ago, there was nothing that could defeat Acnologia.
That's why the dragons pinned their hopes on the future.
They put themselves into the bodies of the dragon slayers and came to the future...or rather, this present.
Yes, Grandeeney told me that.
If I recall correctly, this is the age when magic is the most prevalent...
GWOOOOH
Yes... This era *has* proven to be a wise choice in that respect.
Zeref created the door, and I opened it.
Zeref did?!
He had studied time in great depth. Though he hadn't been able to fulfill his greatest desire—which was to return to the past.
MEEEEN
RATTLE
RATTLE
But... I think he still had hopes for the future.

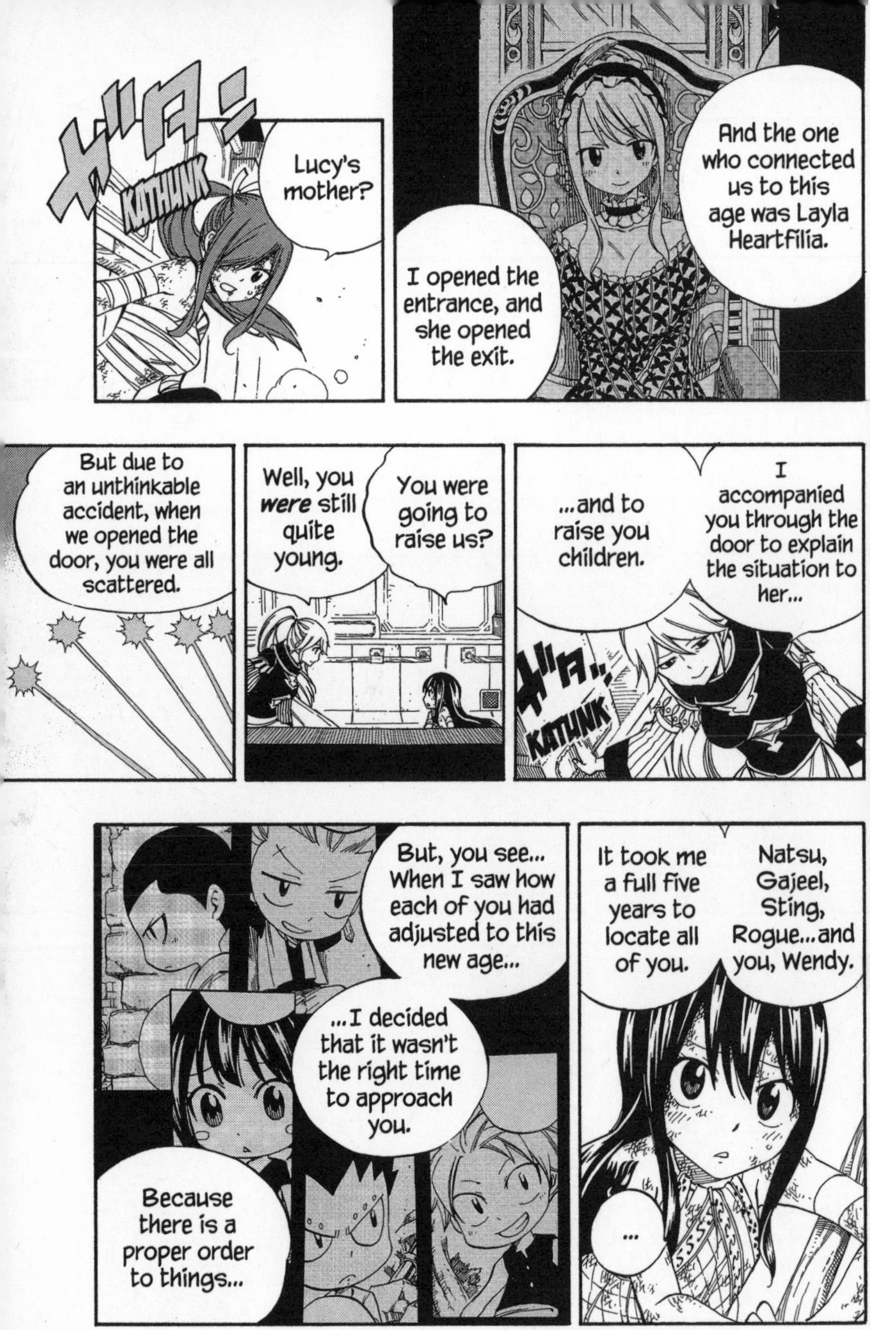
And the one who connected us to this age was Layla Heartfilia.
I opened the entrance, and she opened the exit.
KATHUNK
Lucy's mother?
I accompanied you through the door to explain the situation to her...
...and to raise you children.
KATHUNK
You were going to raise us?
Well, you *were* still quite young.
But due to an unthinkable accident, when we opened the door, you were all scattered.
Natsu, Gajeel, Sting, Rogue...and you, Wendy.
It took me a full five years to locate all of you.
...
But, you see... When I saw how each of you had adjusted to this new age...
...I decided that it wasn't the right time to approach you.
Because there is a proper order to things...

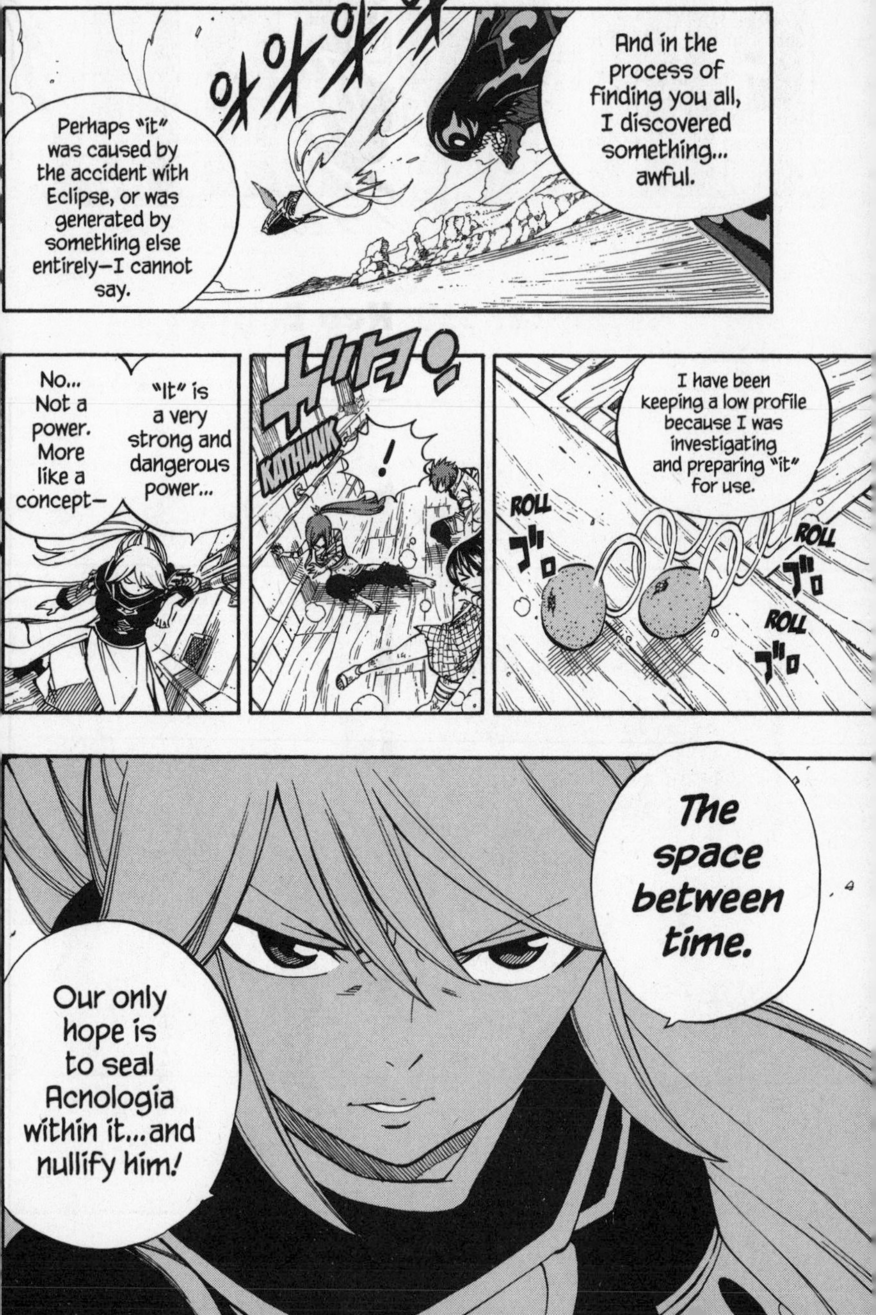
And in the process of finding you all, I discovered something... awful.
Perhaps "it" was caused by the accident with Eclipse, or was generated by something else entirely—I cannot say.
I have been keeping a low profile because I was investigating and preparing "it" for use.
ROLL
ROLL
ROLL
KATHUNK
!
"It" is a very strong and dangerous power...
No... Not a power. More like a concept—
The space between time.
Our only hope is to seal Acnologia within it...and nullify him!

FAIRY TAIL

フェアリーテイル

Chapter 530: Neo Eclipse

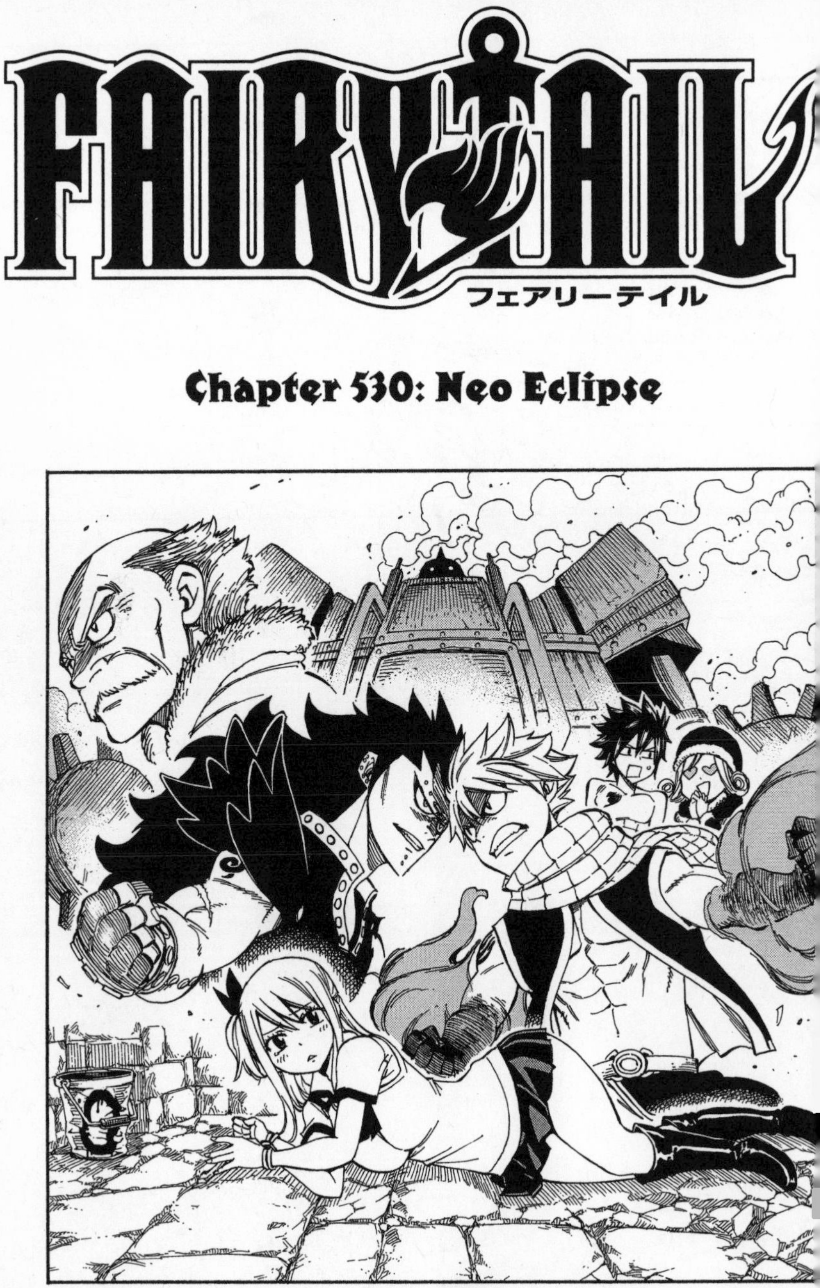

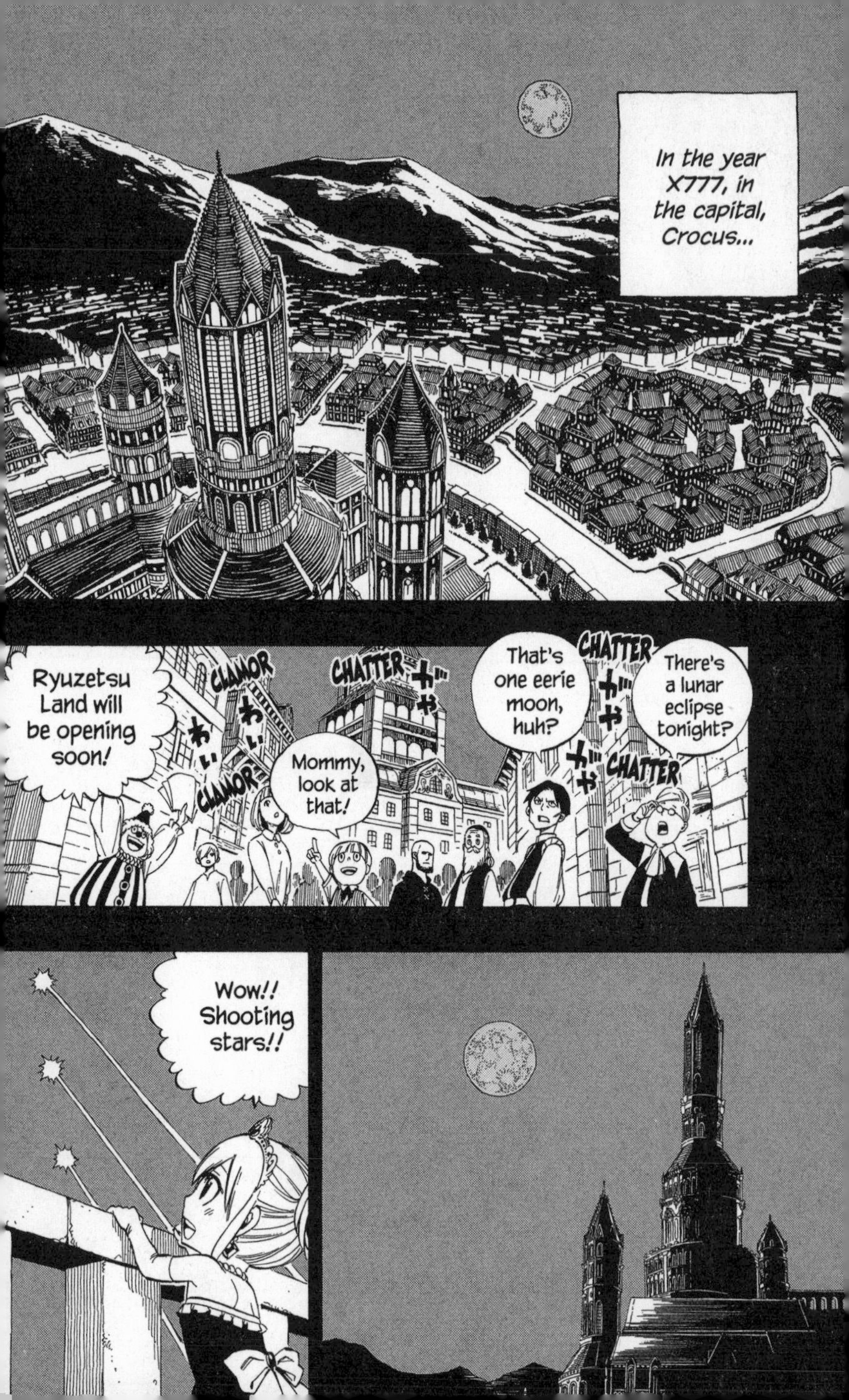
In the year X777, in the capital, Crocus...
CHATTER
There's a lunar eclipse tonight?
CHATTER
That's one eerie moon, huh?
CHATTER
Mommy, look at that!
CLAMOR
CLAMOR
Ryuzetsu Land will be opening soon!
Wow!! Shooting stars!!

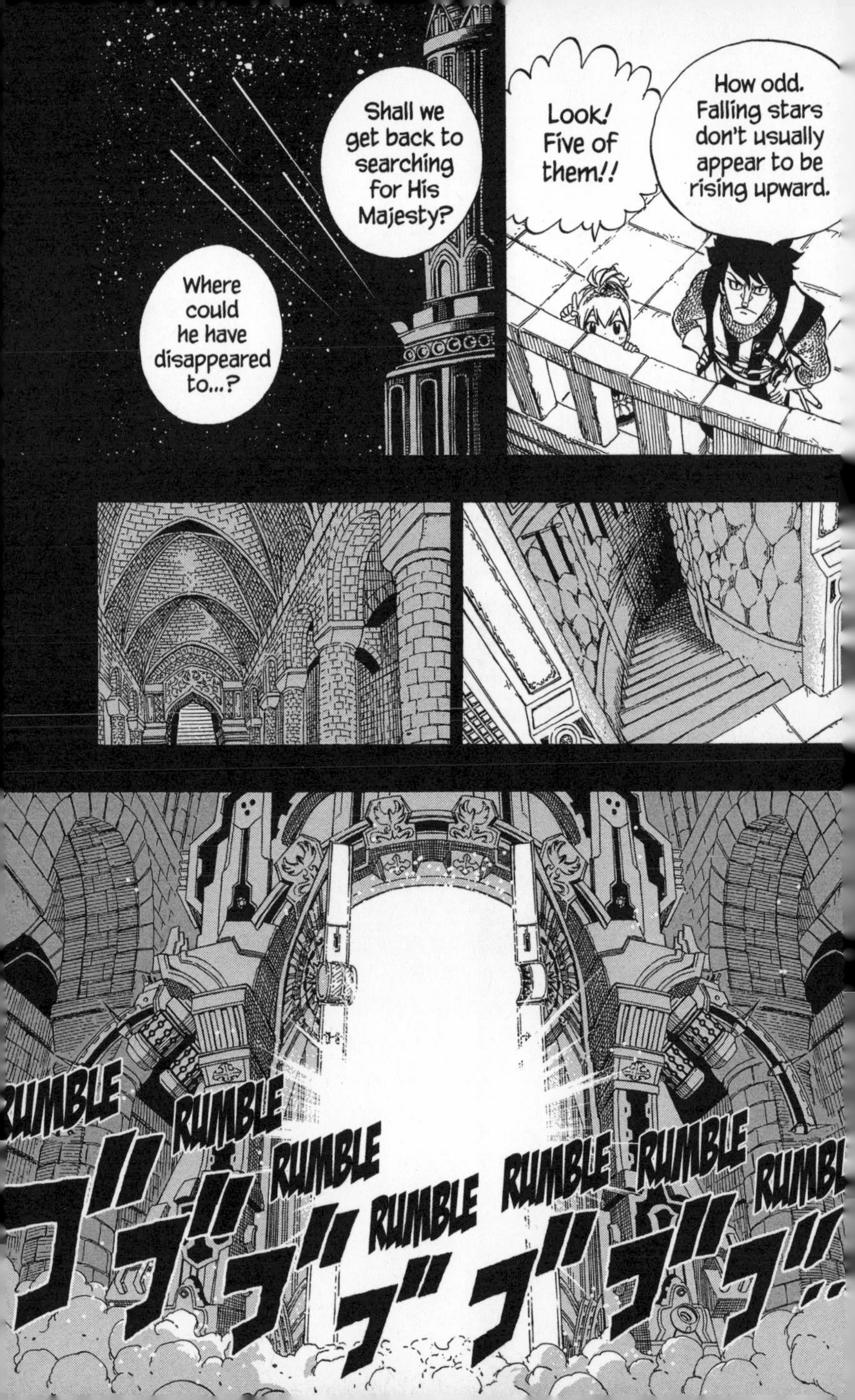
How odd. Falling stars don't usually appear to be rising upward.
Look! Five of them!!
Shall we get back to searching for His Majesty?
Where could he have disappeared to...?
RUMBLE RUMBLE RUMBLE RUMBLE RUMBLE RUMBLE RUMBLE

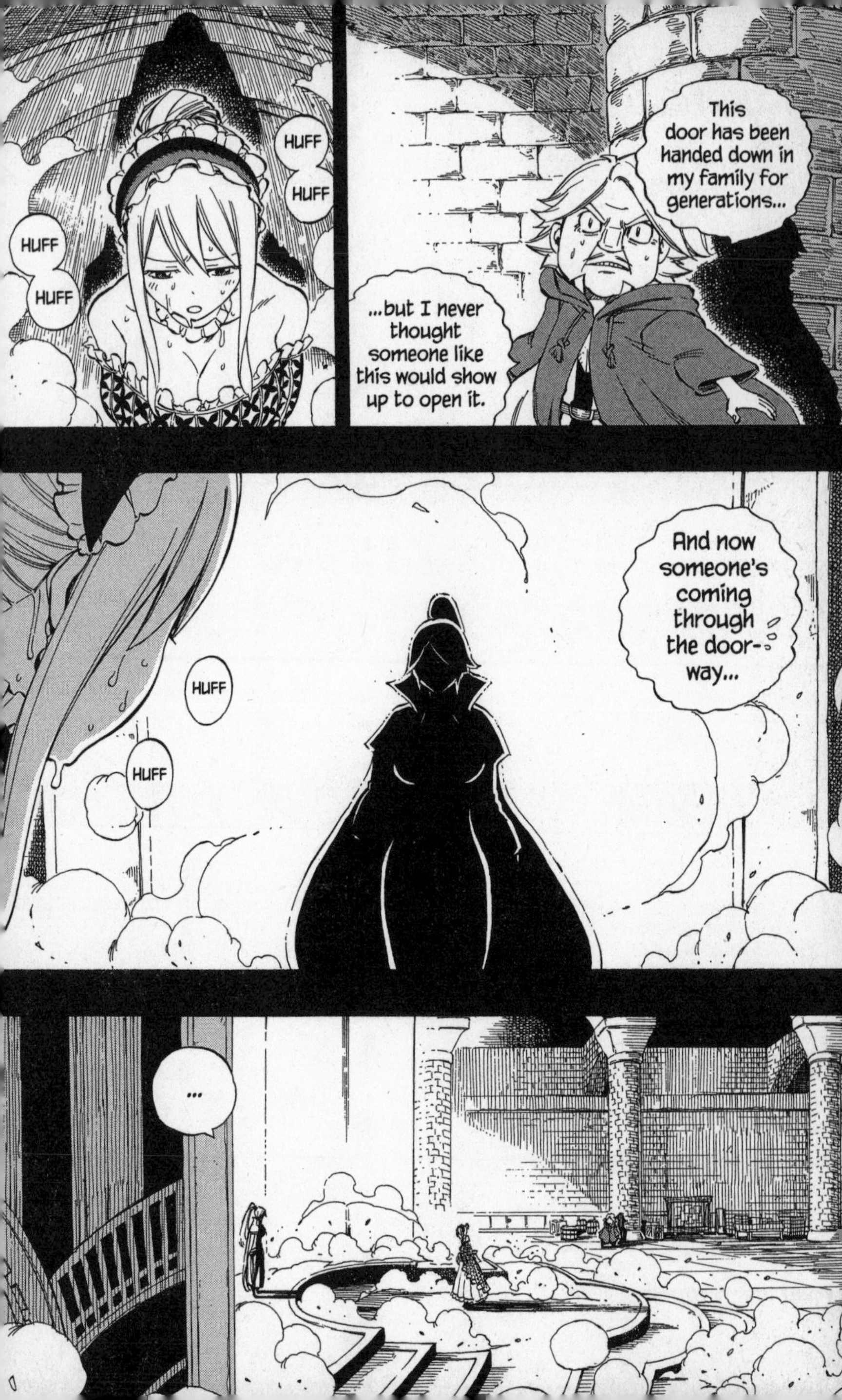
This door has been handed down in my family for generations...
...but I never thought someone like this would show up to open it.
HUFF
HUFF
HUFF
HUFF
And now someone's coming through the door-way...
HUFF
HUFF
...

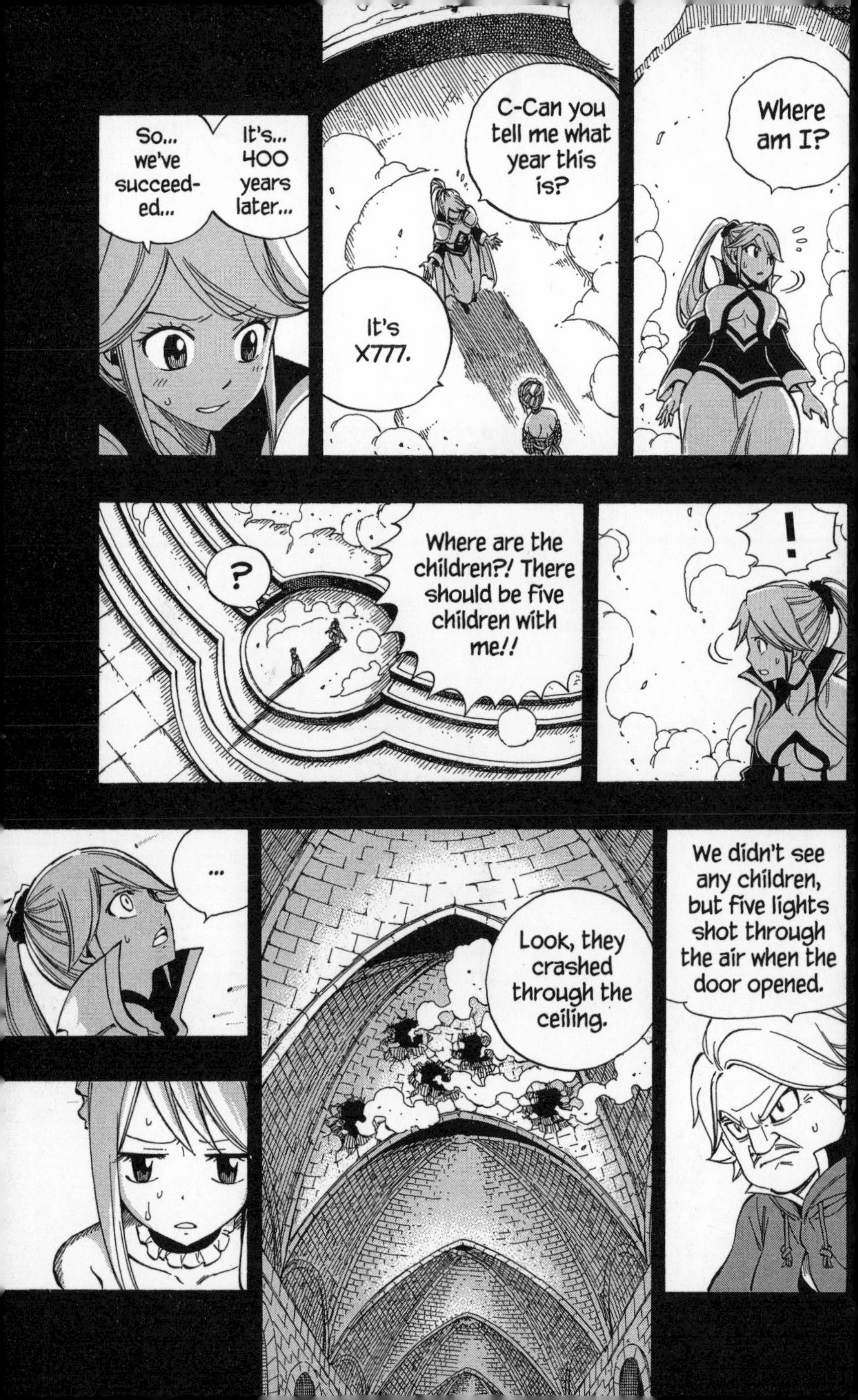
Where am I?
C-Can you tell me what year this is?
It's X777.
It's... 400 years later...
So... we've succeed-ed...
!
Where are the children?! There should be five children with me!!
?
We didn't see any children, but five lights shot through the air when the door opened.
Look, they crashed through the ceiling.
...

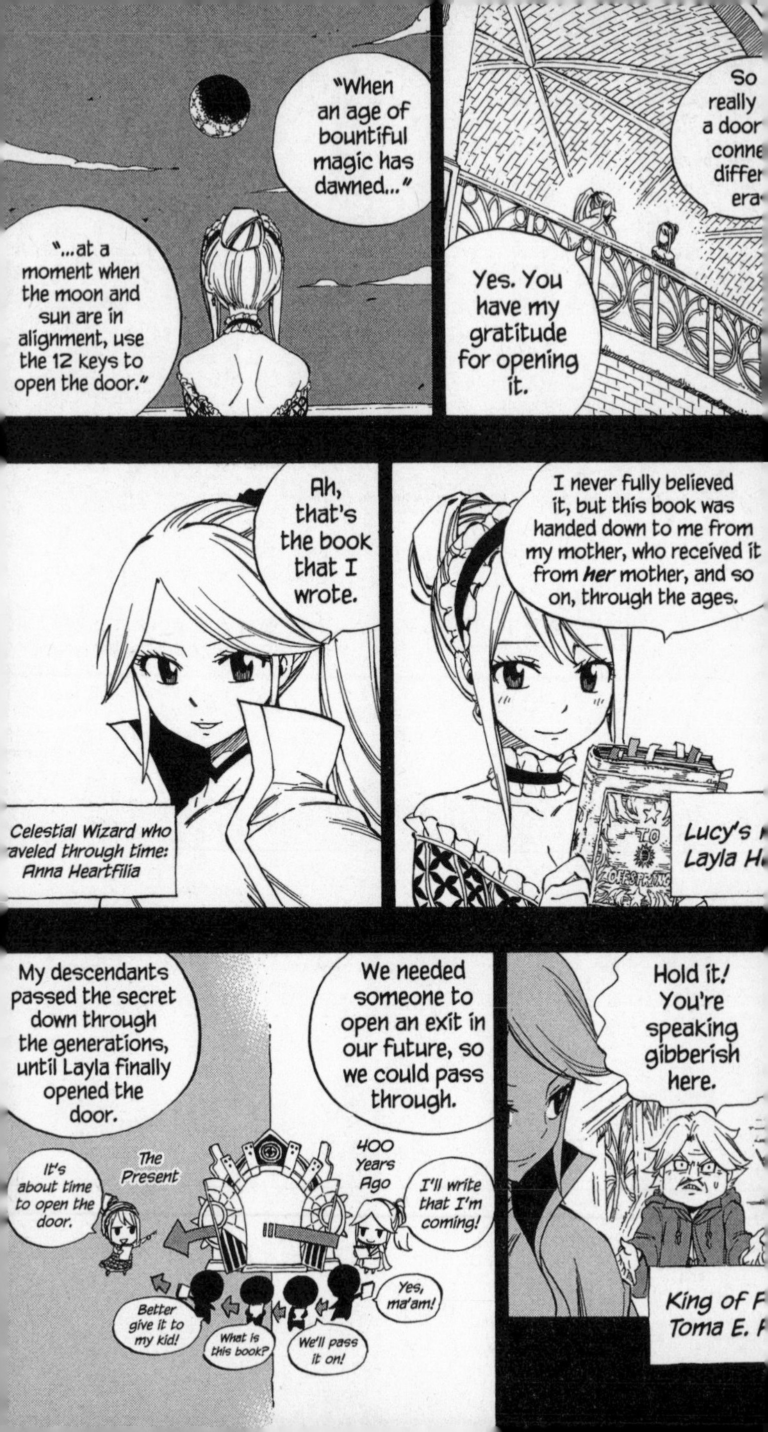
So really a door conne differ era
Yes. You have my gratitude for opening it.
"When an age of bountiful magic has dawned..."
"...at a moment when the moon and sun are in alignment, use the 12 keys to open the door."
I never fully believed it, but this book was handed down to me from my mother, who received it from *her* mother, and so on, through the ages.
TO OFFSPRING
Lucy's Layla H
Ah, that's the book that I wrote.
Celestial Wizard who aveled through time: Anna Heartfilia
Hold it! You're speaking gibberish here.
King of F Toma E.
We needed someone to open an exit in our future, so we could pass through.
My descendants passed the secret down through the generations, until Layla finally opened the door.
400 Years Ago
I'll write that I'm coming!
Yes, ma'am!
We'll pass it on!
What is this book?
Better give it to my kid!
The Present
It's about time to open the door.

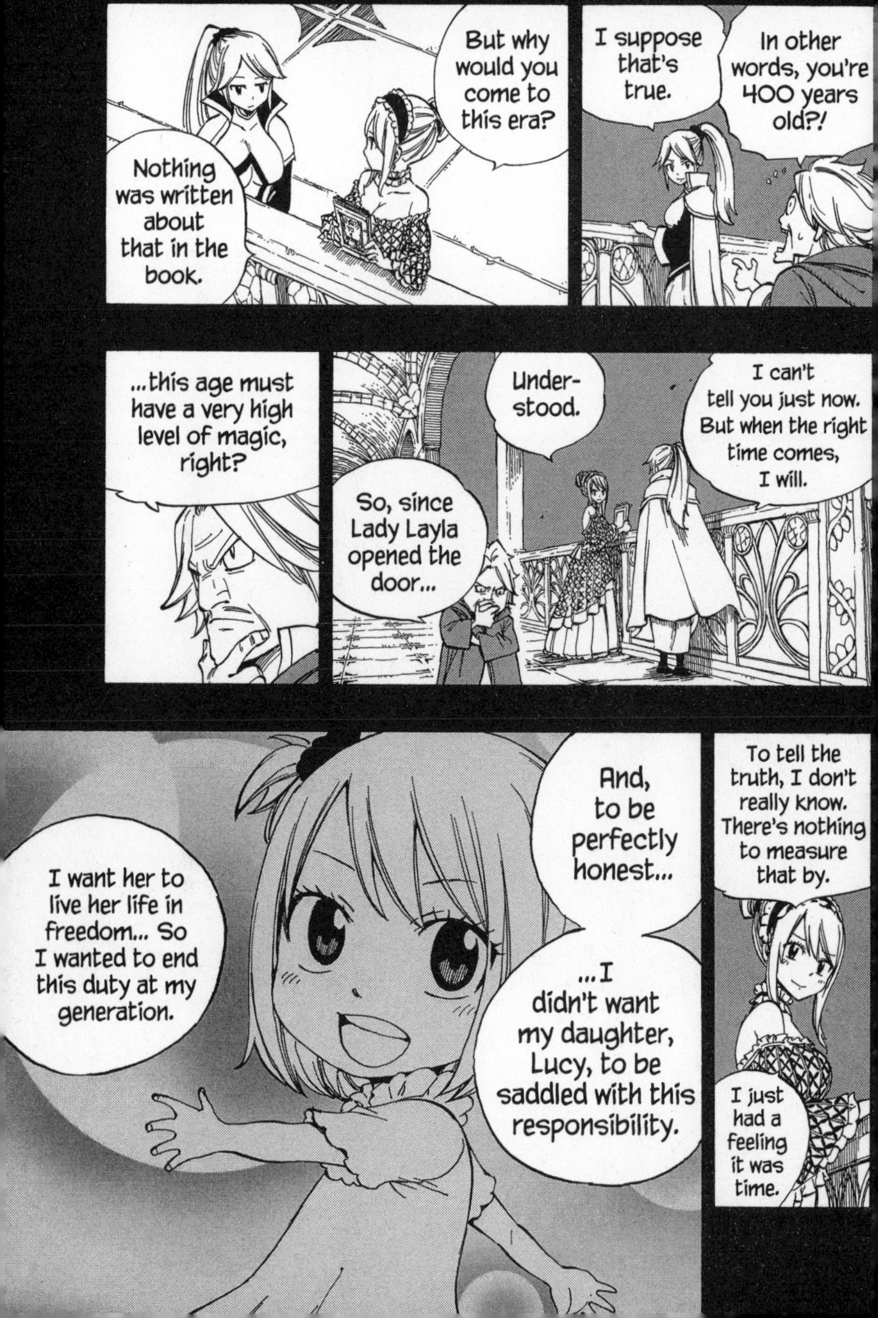
In other words, you're 400 years old?!
I suppose that's true.
But why would you come to this era?
Nothing was written about that in the book.
I can't tell you just now. But when the right time comes, I will.
Under-stood.
So, since Lady Layla opened the door...
...this age must have a very high level of magic, right?
To tell the truth, I don't really know. There's nothing to measure that by.
I just had a feeling it was time.
And, to be perfectly honest...
...I didn't want my daughter, Lucy, to be saddled with this responsibility.
I want her to live her life in freedom... So I wanted to end this duty at my generation.

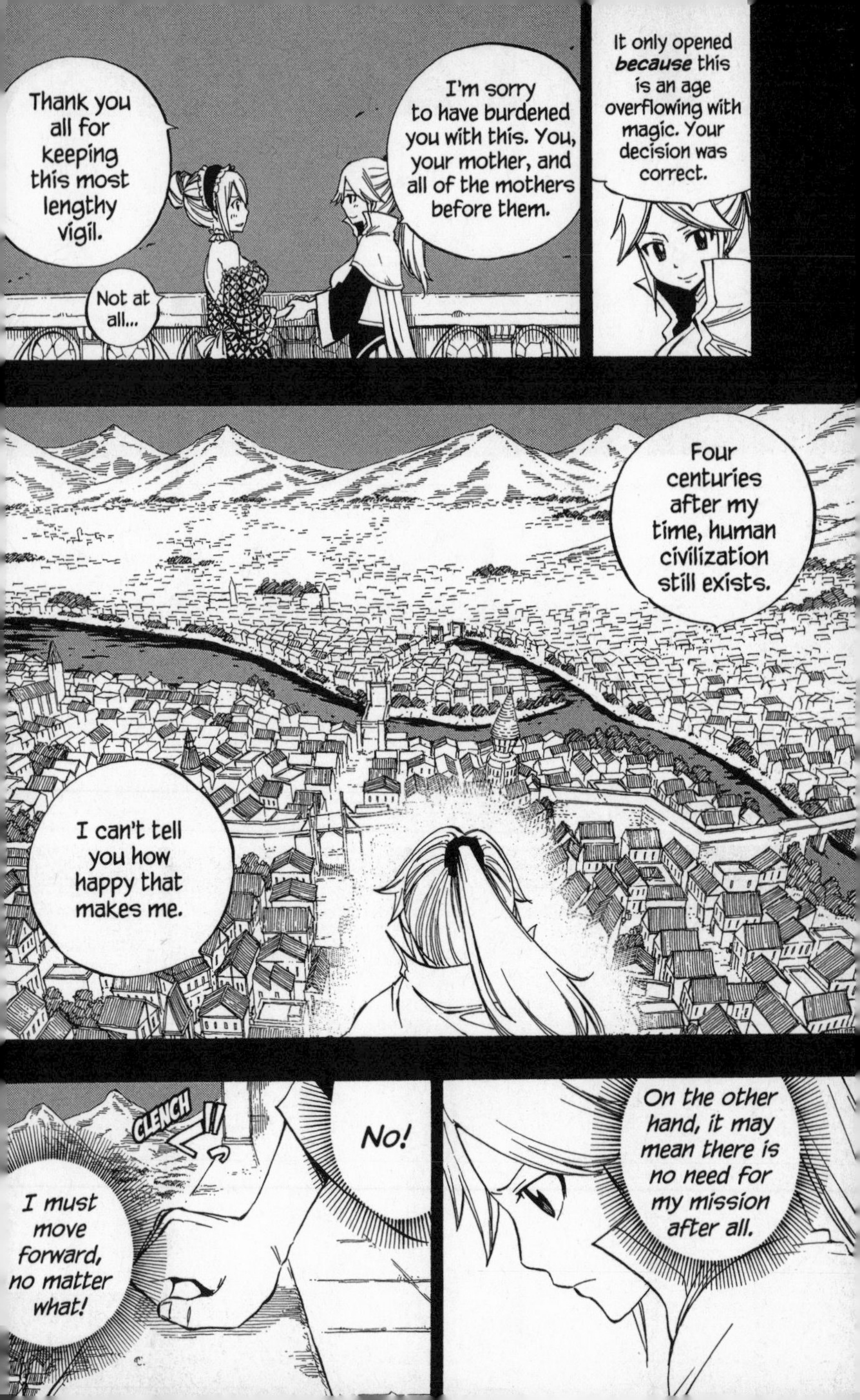

It only opened *because* this is an age overflowing with magic. Your decision was correct.
I'm sorry to have burdened you with this. You, your mother, and all of the mothers before them.
Thank you all for keeping this most lengthy vigil.
Not at all...
Four centuries after my time, human civilization still exists.
I can't tell you how happy that makes me.
On the other hand, it may mean there is no need for my mission after all.
No!
CLENCH
I must move forward, no matter what!

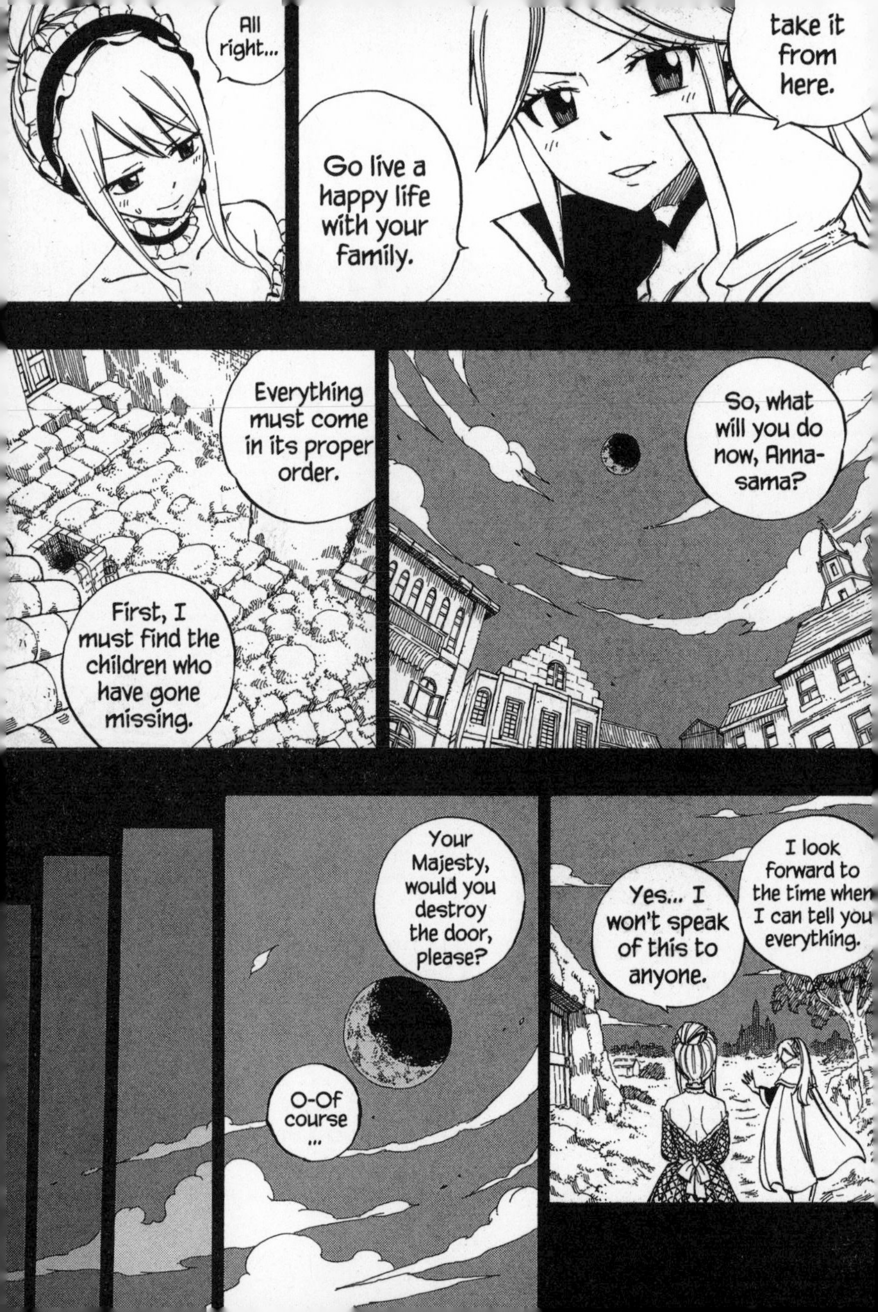
take it from here.
Go live a happy life with your family.
All right...
So, what will you do now, Anna-sama?
Everything must come in its proper order.
First, I must find the children who have gone missing.
I look forward to the time when I can tell you everything.
Yes... I won't speak of this to anyone.
Your Majesty, would you destroy the door, please?
O-Of course ...

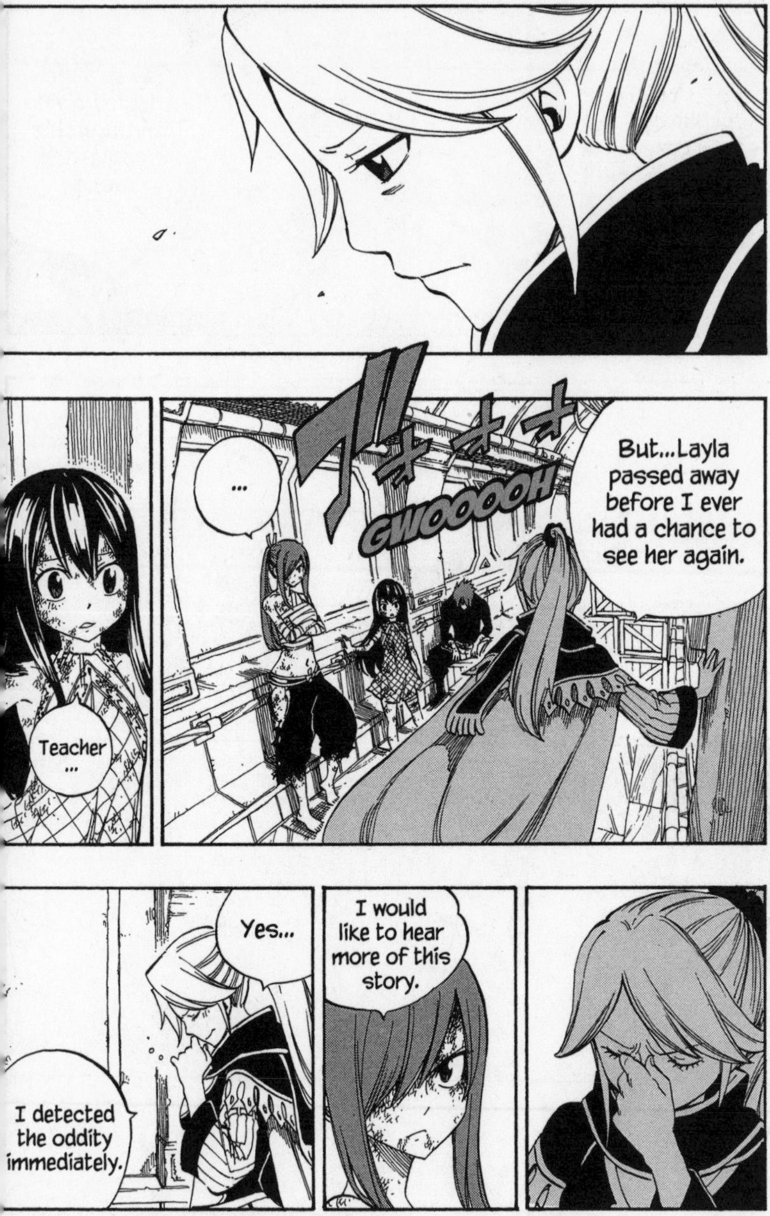
But...Layla passed away before I ever had a chance to see her again.
GWOOOOOH
...
Teacher ...
I would like to hear more of this story.
Yes...
I detected the oddity immediately.

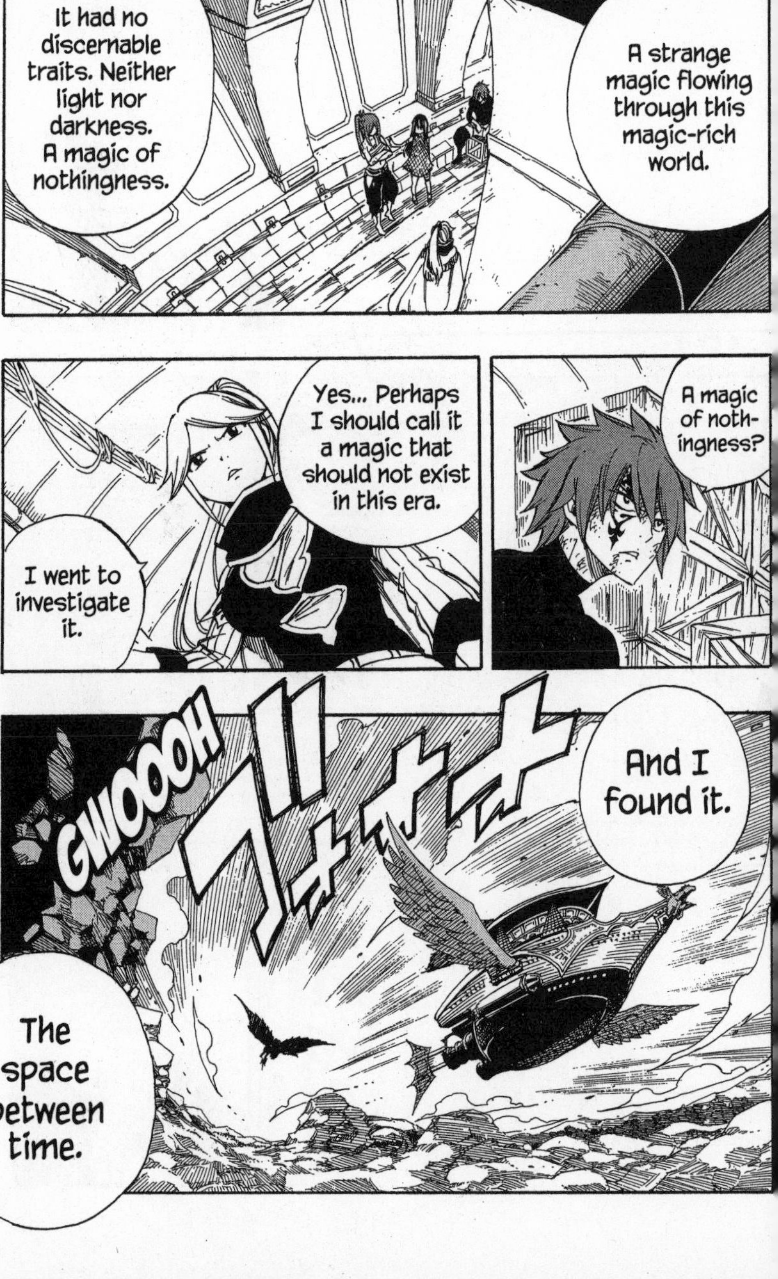
A strange magic flowing through this magic-rich world.
It had no discernable traits. Neither light nor darkness. A magic of nothingness.
A magic of noth-ingness?
Yes... Perhaps I should call it a magic that should not exist in this era.
I went to investigate it.
And I found it.
GWOOOH
The space between time.

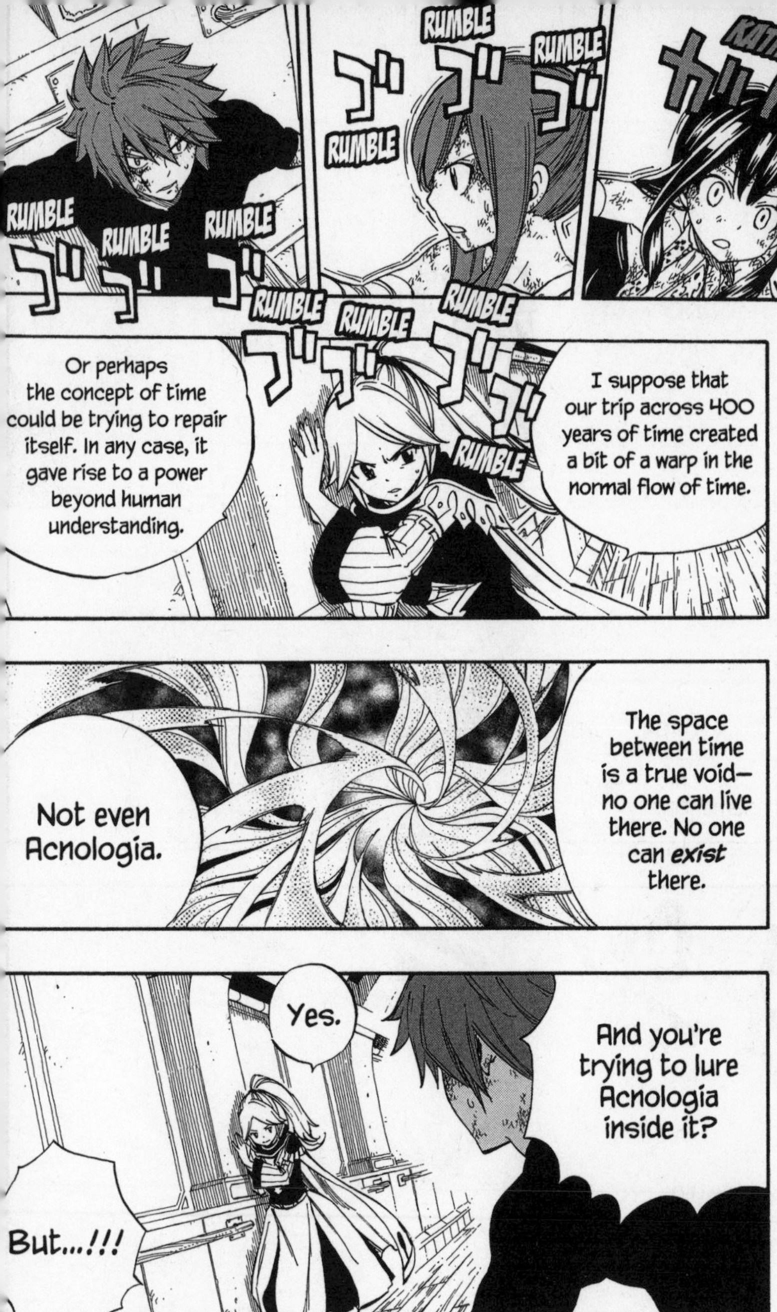
KATHUMP
RUMBLE
RUMBLE
RUMBLE
RUMBLE
RUMBLE
RUMBLE
RUMBLE
RUMBLE
RUMBLE
RUMBLE
I suppose that our trip across 400 years of time created a bit of a warp in the normal flow of time.
Or perhaps the concept of time could be trying to repair itself. In any case, it gave rise to a power beyond human understanding.
The space between time is a true void—no one can live there. No one can *exist* there.
Not even Acnologia.
And you're trying to lure Acnologia inside it?
Yes.
But...!!!

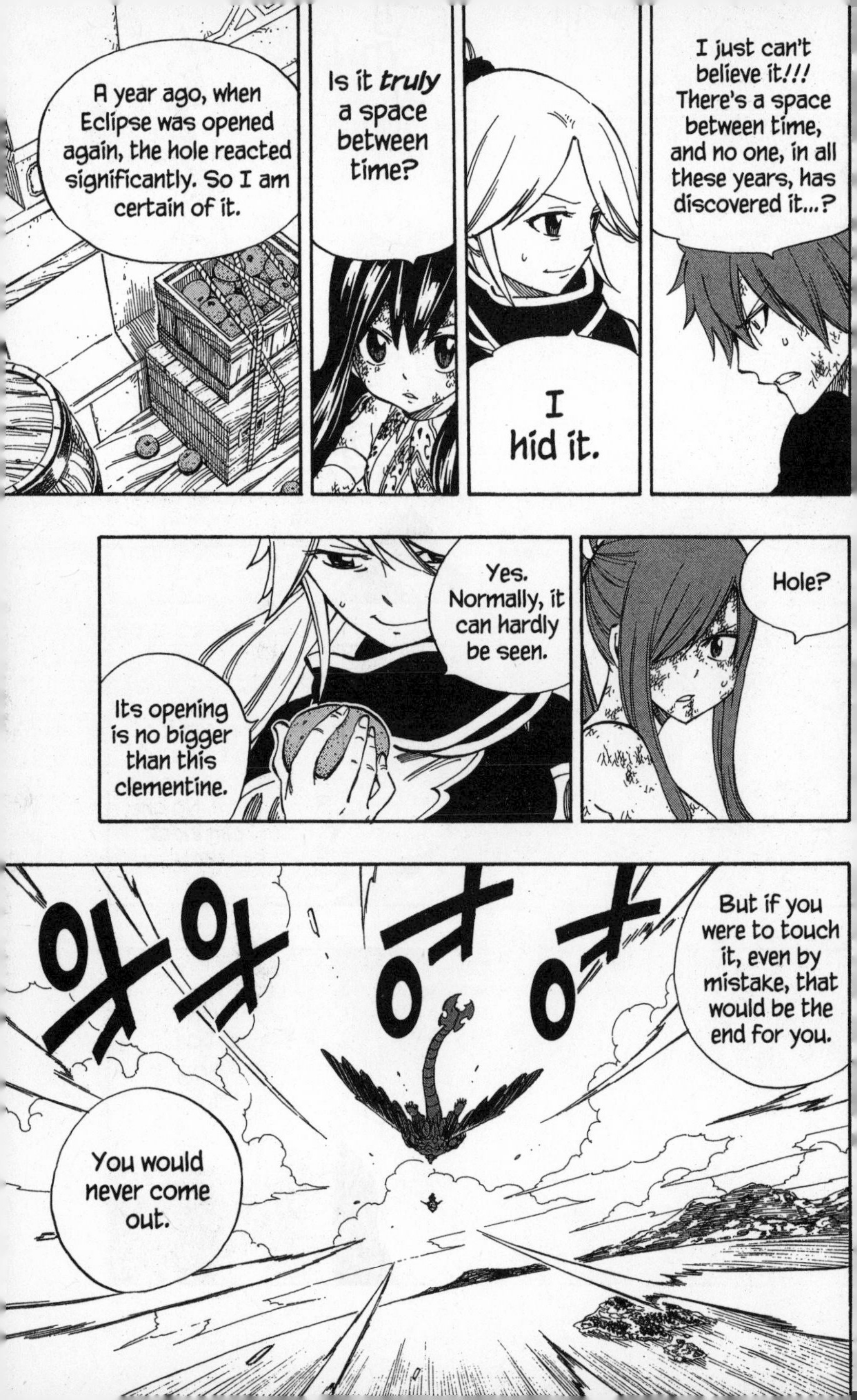
I just can't believe it!!! There's a space between time, and no one, in all these years, has discovered it...?
I hid it.
Is it *truly* a space between time?
A year ago, when Eclipse was opened again, the hole reacted significantly. So I am certain of it.
Hole?
Yes. Normally, it can hardly be seen.
Its opening is no bigger than this clementine.
But if you were to touch it, even by mistake, that would be the end for you.
You would never come out.

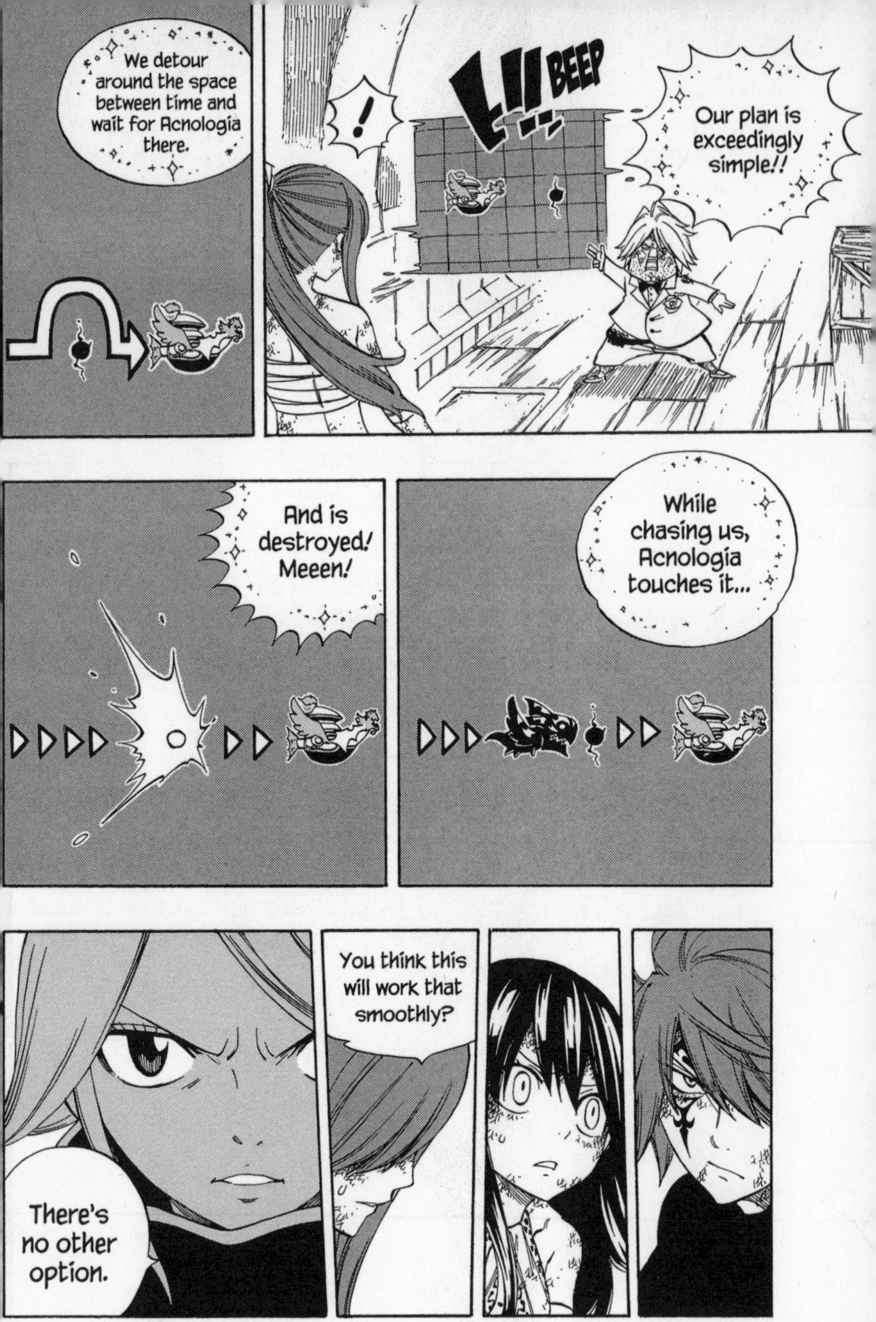

Our plan is exceedingly simple!!
BEEP
!
We detour around the space between time and wait for Acnologia there.
While chasing us, Acnologia touches it...
And is destroyed! Meeen!
You think this will work that smoothly?
There's no other option.

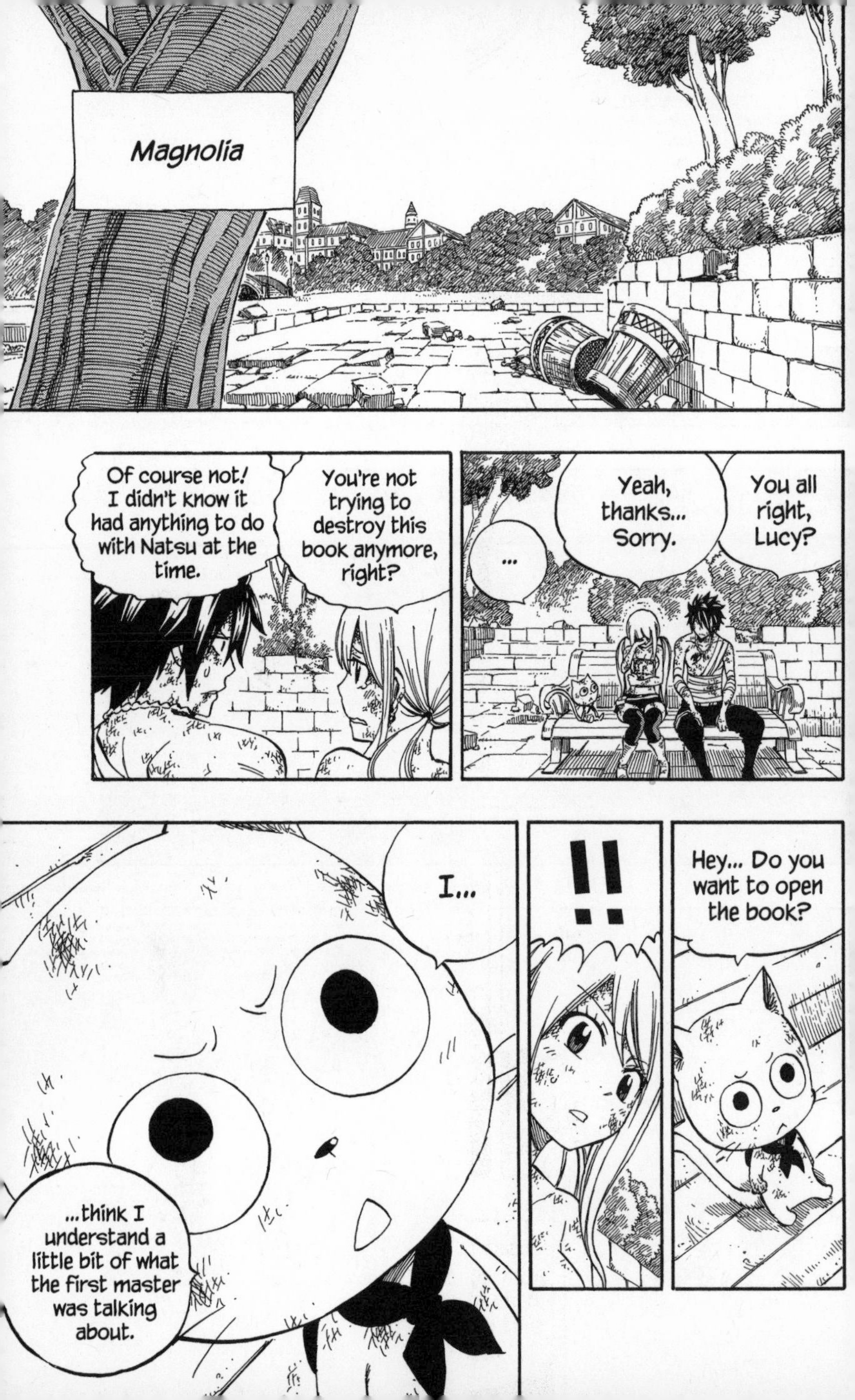
Magnolia
You all right, Lucy?
Yeah, thanks... Sorry.
...
You're not trying to destroy this book anymore, right?
Of course not! I didn't know it had anything to do with Natsu at the time.
Hey... Do you want to open the book?
!!
I...
...think I understand a little bit of what the first master was talking about.

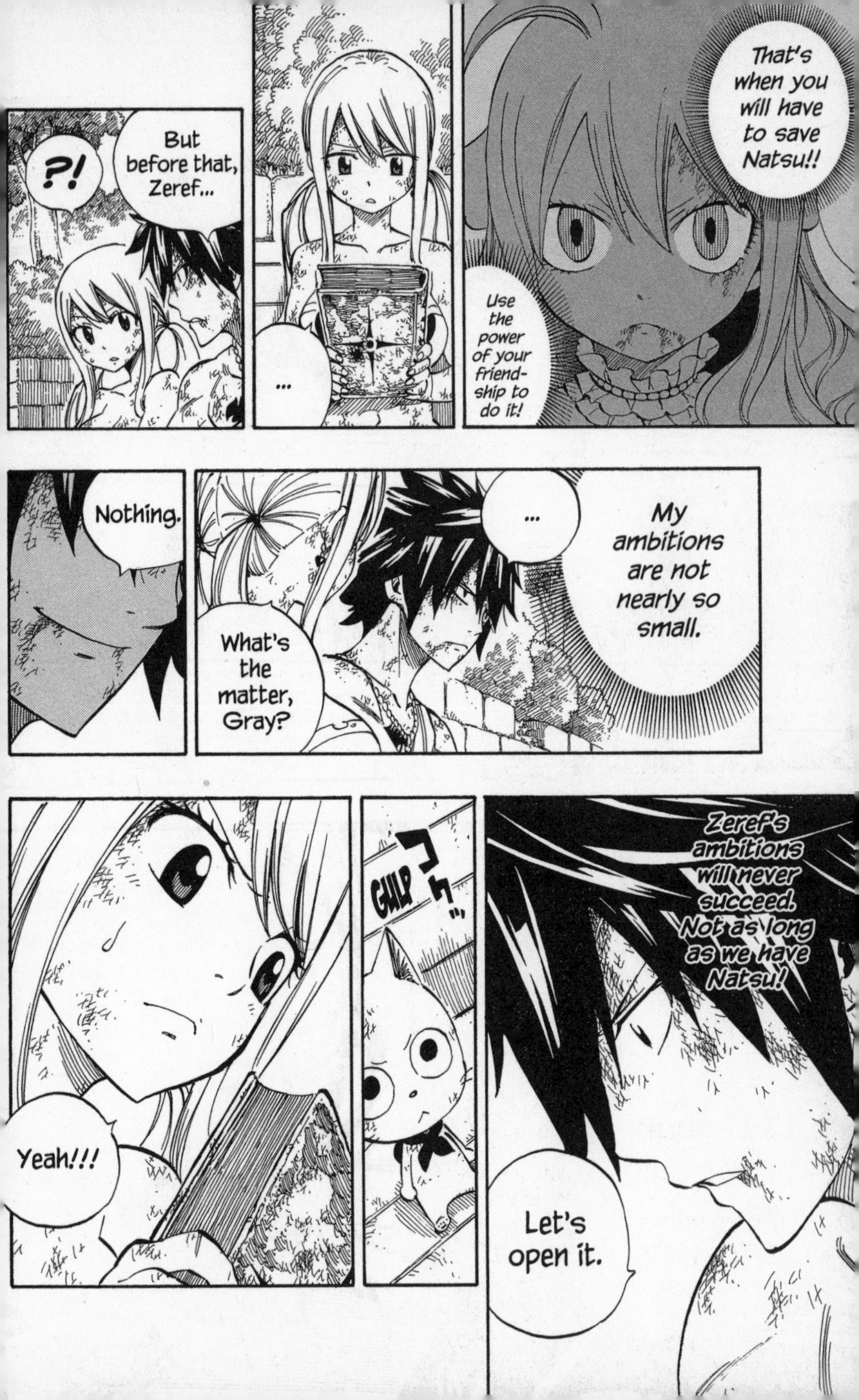
That's when you will have to save Natsu!!
Use the power of your friendship to do it!
...
But before that, Zeref...
?!
...
My ambitions are not nearly so small.
What's the matter, Gray?
Nothing.
Zeref's ambitions will never succeed. Not as long as we have Natsu!
Let's open it.
GULP
Yeah!!!

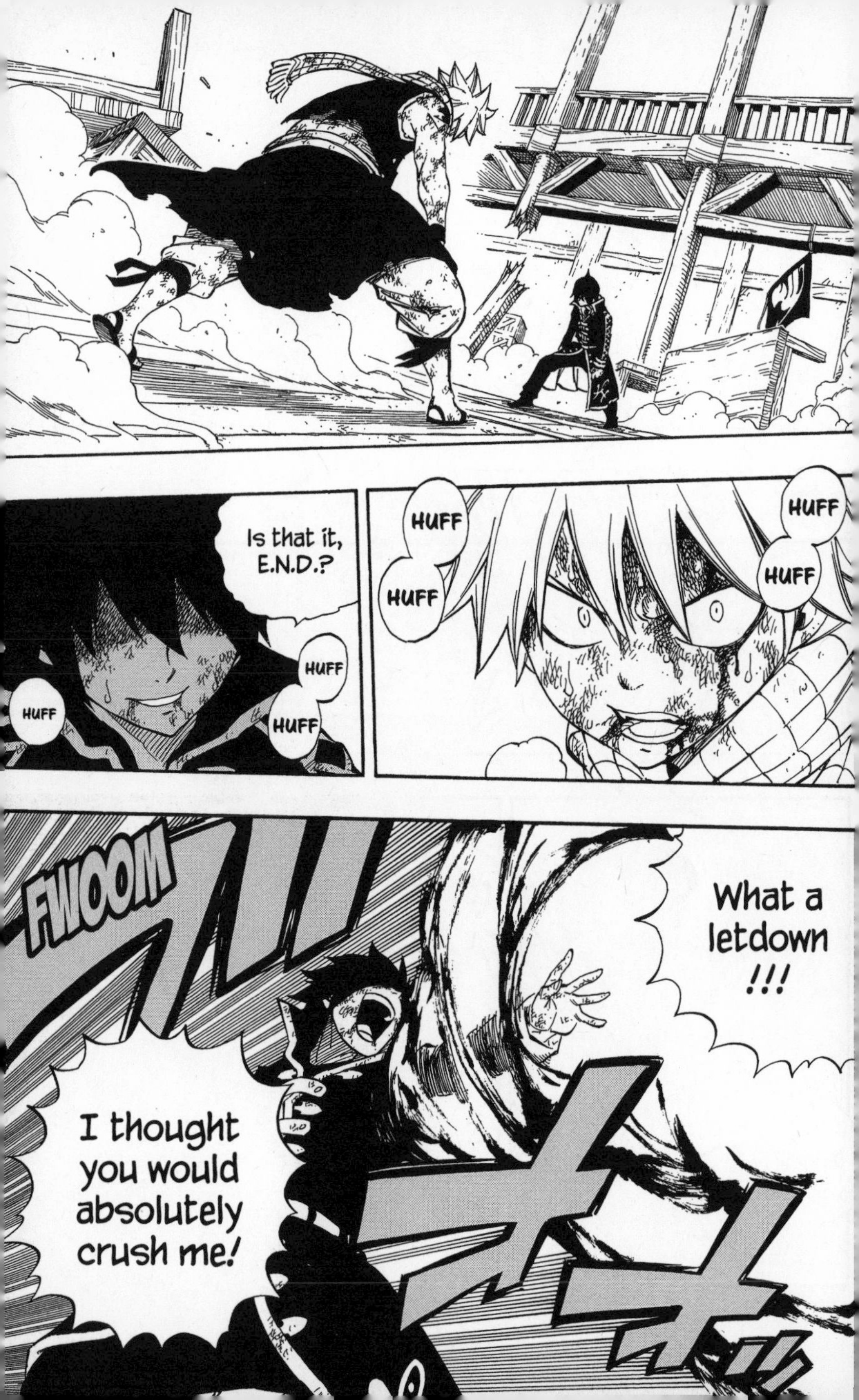
HUFF
HUFF
HUFF
HUFF
Is that it, E.N.D.?
HUFF
HUFF
HUFF
What a letdown!!!
FWOOM
I thought you would absolutely crush me!

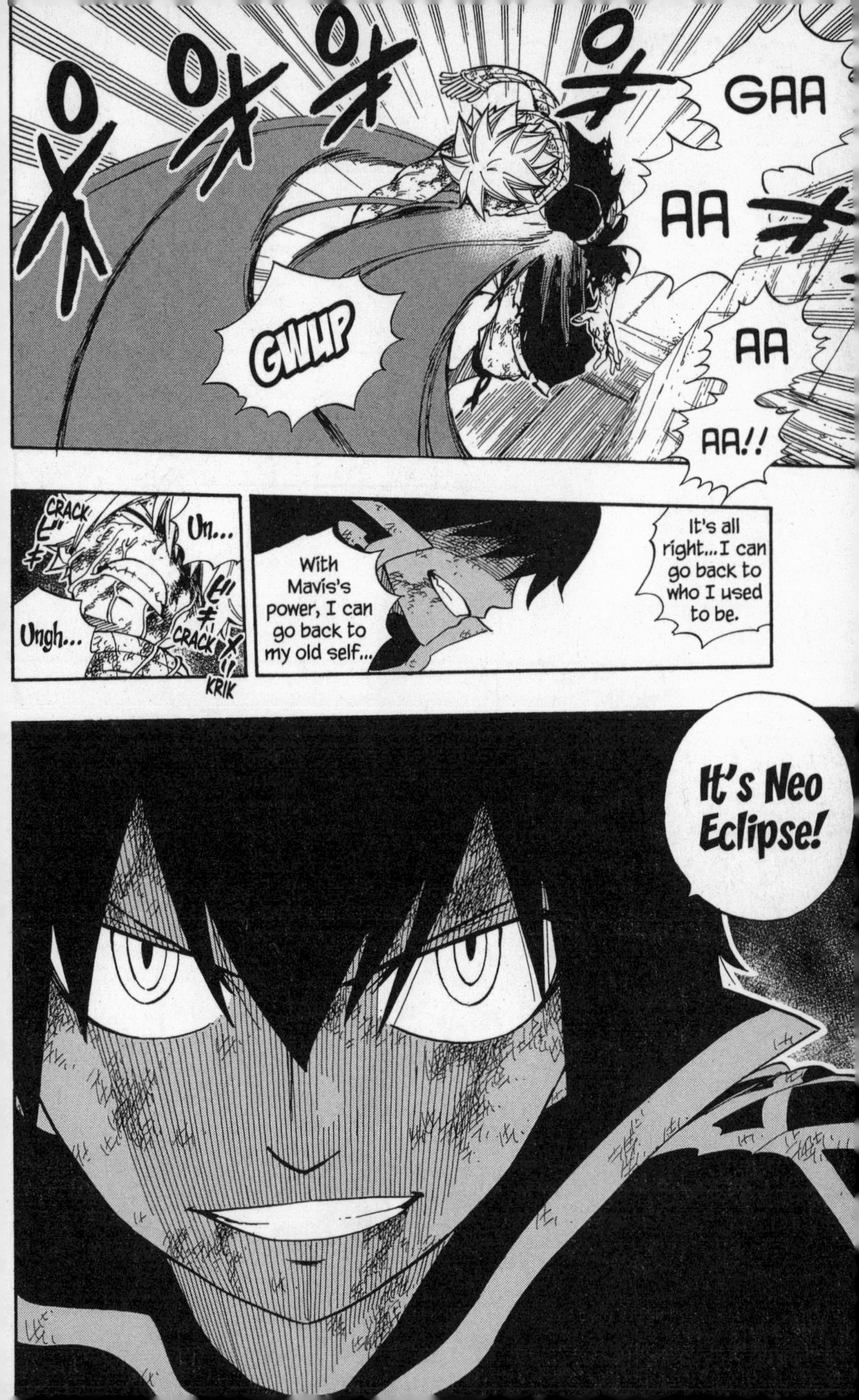
GAA AA AA AA!!
GWUP
It's all right...I can go back to who I used to be.
With Mavis's power, I can go back to my old self...
Un...
CRACK
CRACK
KRIK
Ungh...
It's Neo Eclipse!

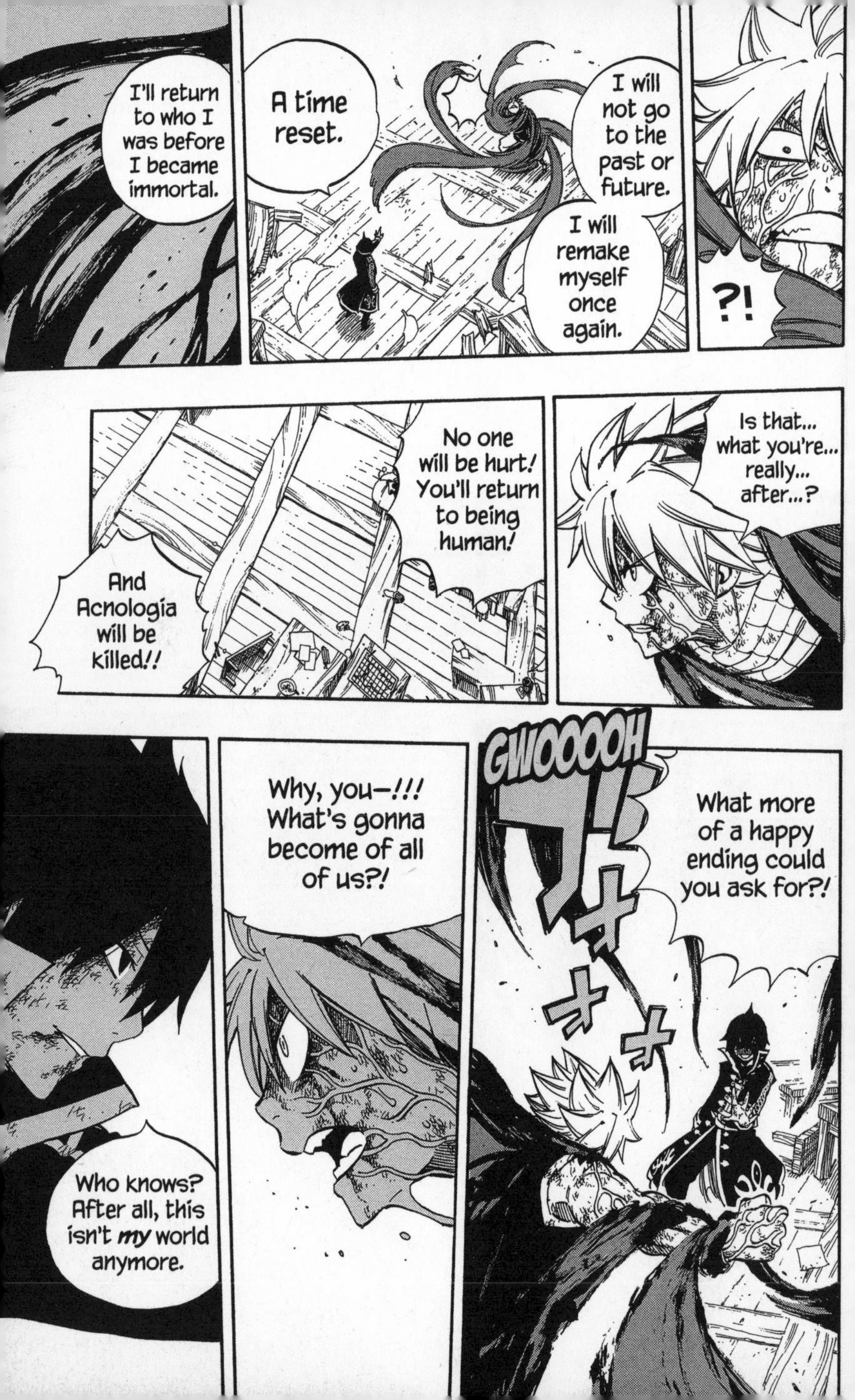

?!
I will not go to the past or future.
I will remake myself once again.
A time reset.
I'll return to who I was before I became immortal.
Is that... what you're... really... after...?
No one will be hurt! You'll return to being human!
And Acnologia will be killed!!
GWOOOOH
What more of a happy ending could you ask for?!
Why, you–!!! What's gonna become of all of us?!
Who knows? After all, this isn't *my* world anymore.

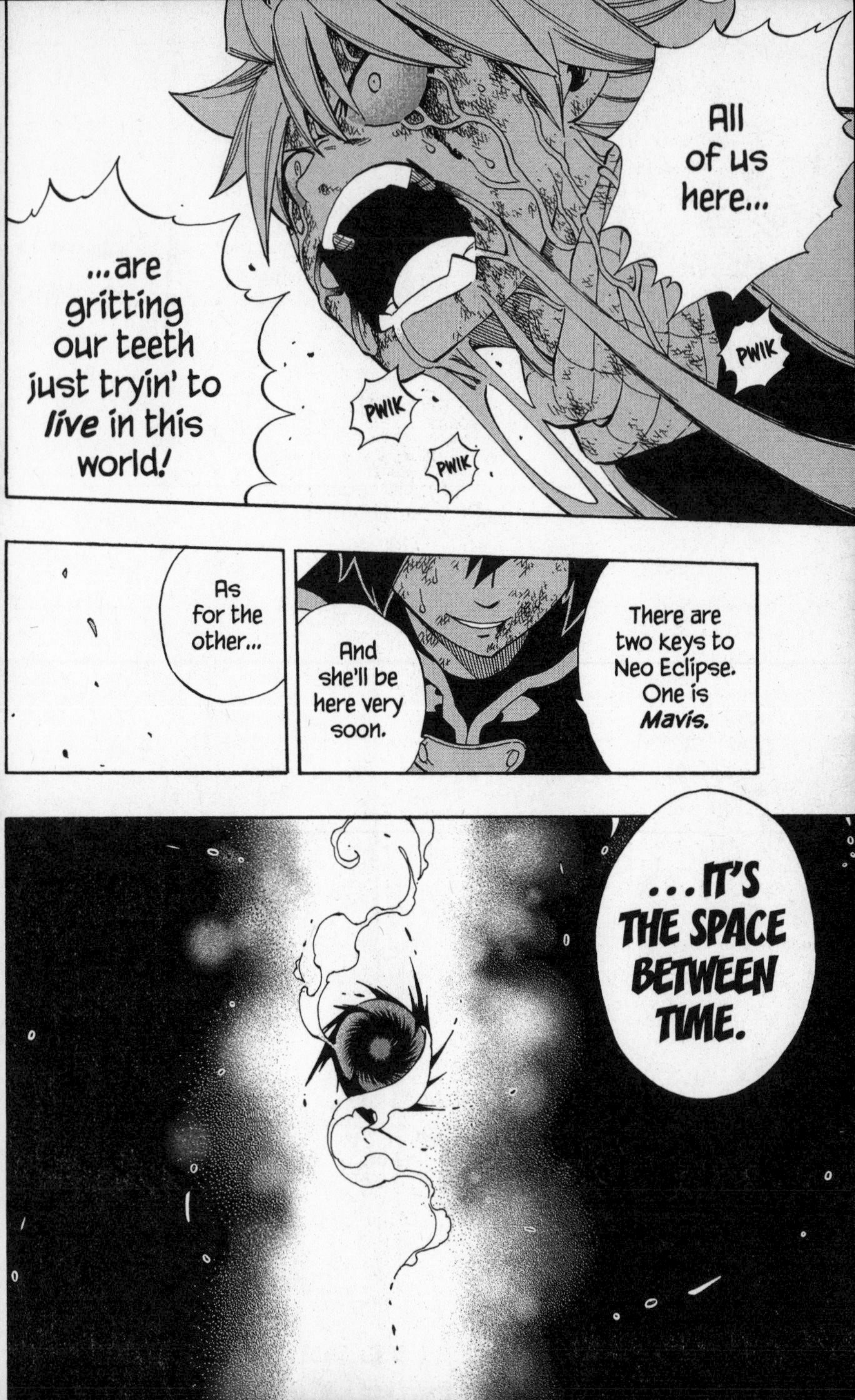
All of us here...
PWIK
...are gritting our teeth just tryin' to *live* in this world!
PWIK
PWIK
There are two keys to Neo Eclipse. One is *Mavis.*
And she'll be here very soon.
As for the other...
...IT'S THE SPACE BETWEEN TIME.

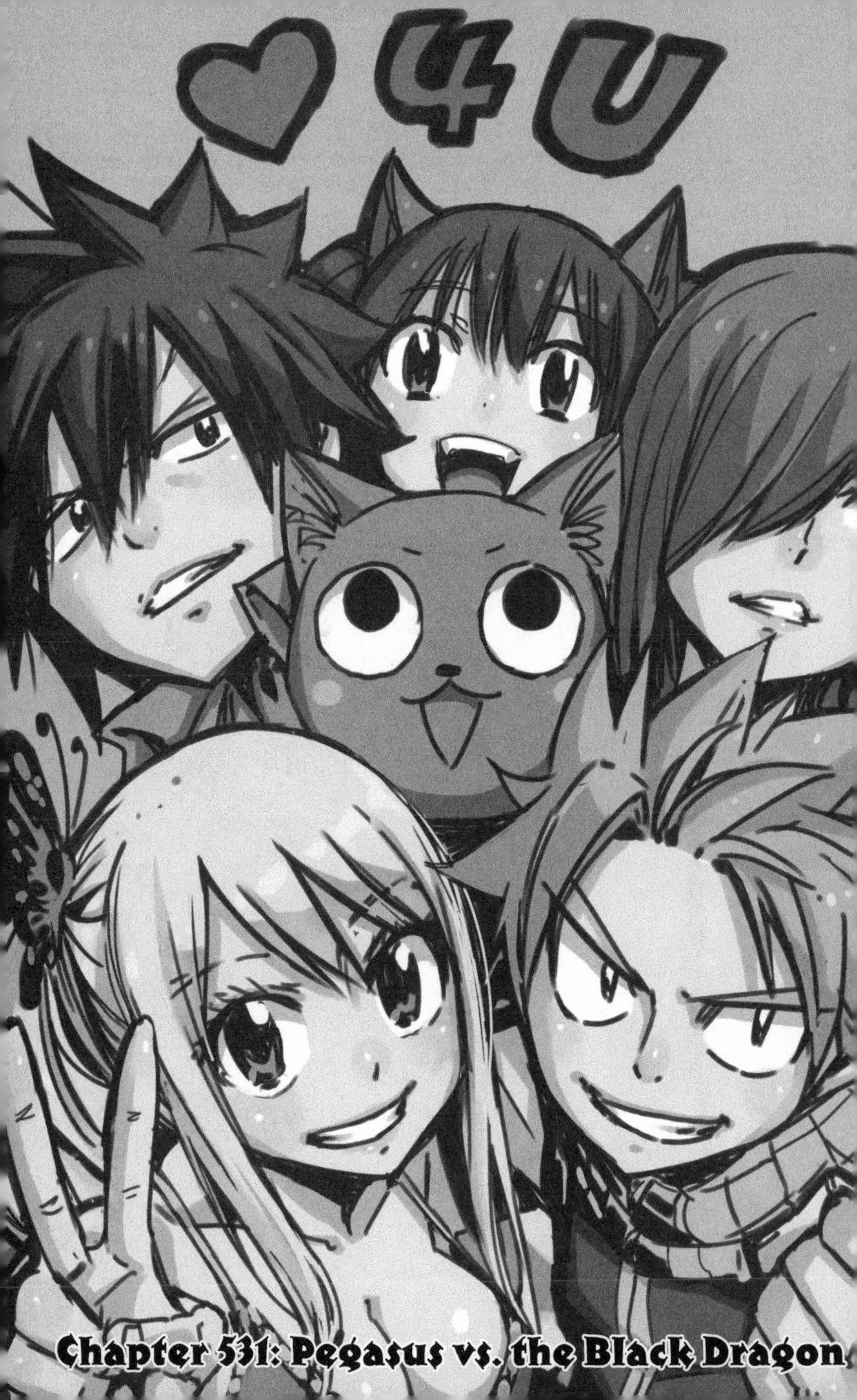
♥ 4 U

Chapter 531: Pegasus vs. the Black Dragon

Those chosen to be published will get a signed mini poster! ♪

FAIRY TAIL GUILD de ART

▼ Thanks for the message of support! I took it to heart!

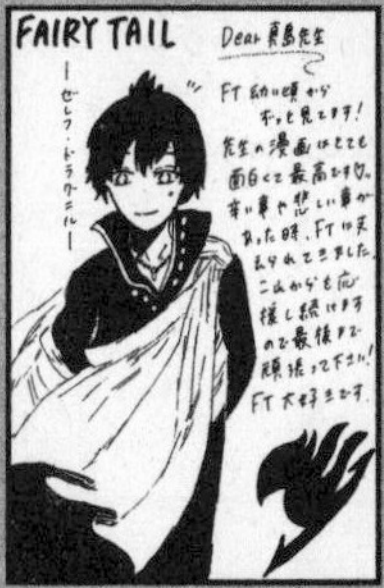
FAIRY TAIL
Dear 真島先生

Saitama Prefecture, Megumi Kumada

Nara Prefecture, Ami Konishi

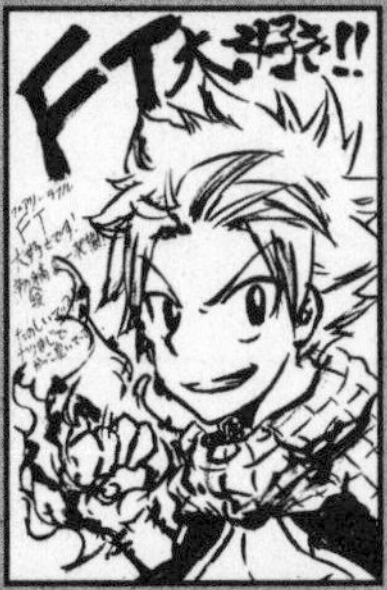
FT大好き!!

▲ This really captures his fired-up feel!!

▼ I hope someday they can meet again and work it all out.

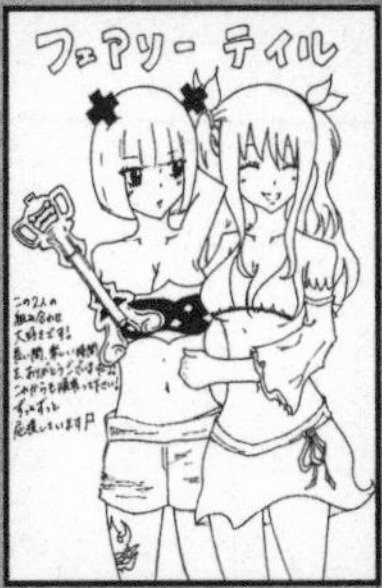
フェアリーテイル

Saitama Prefecture, Natsuki Ino

Chiba Prefecture, Momo

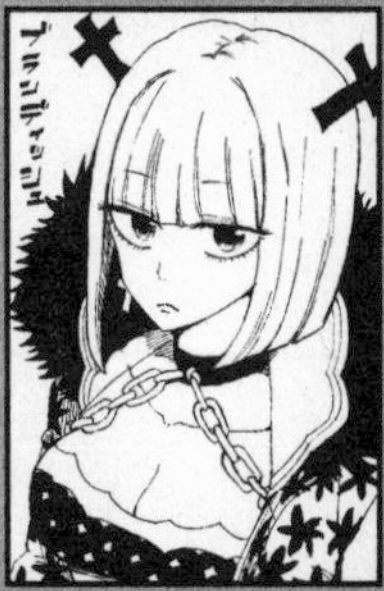

▲ She's far, far more popular than I expected! I like her, too!

▼ Oh! Cute! I like the marks of the constellations behind her, too!

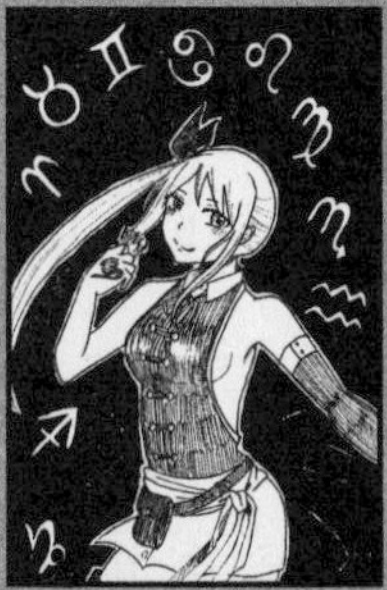

Fukuoka Prefecture, Kikitto Kinoko Ichinin-mae

Aichi Prefecture, Kouichirou Watanabe

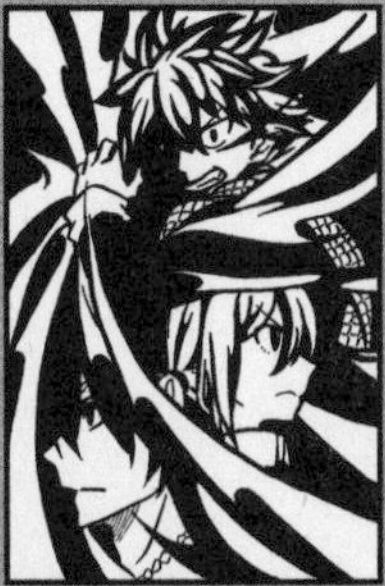

▲ Everybody appearing on that black background looks so cool!

Hokkaido, Doctor U

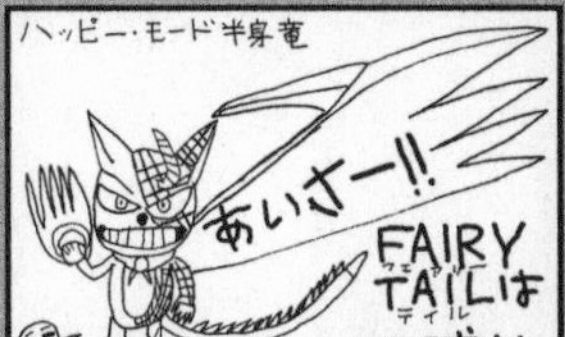
ハッピー・モード半身竜
あいさー!!
FAIRY TAILは不滅!!

▲ Happy!! What's happened to you?! You're looking really strong!

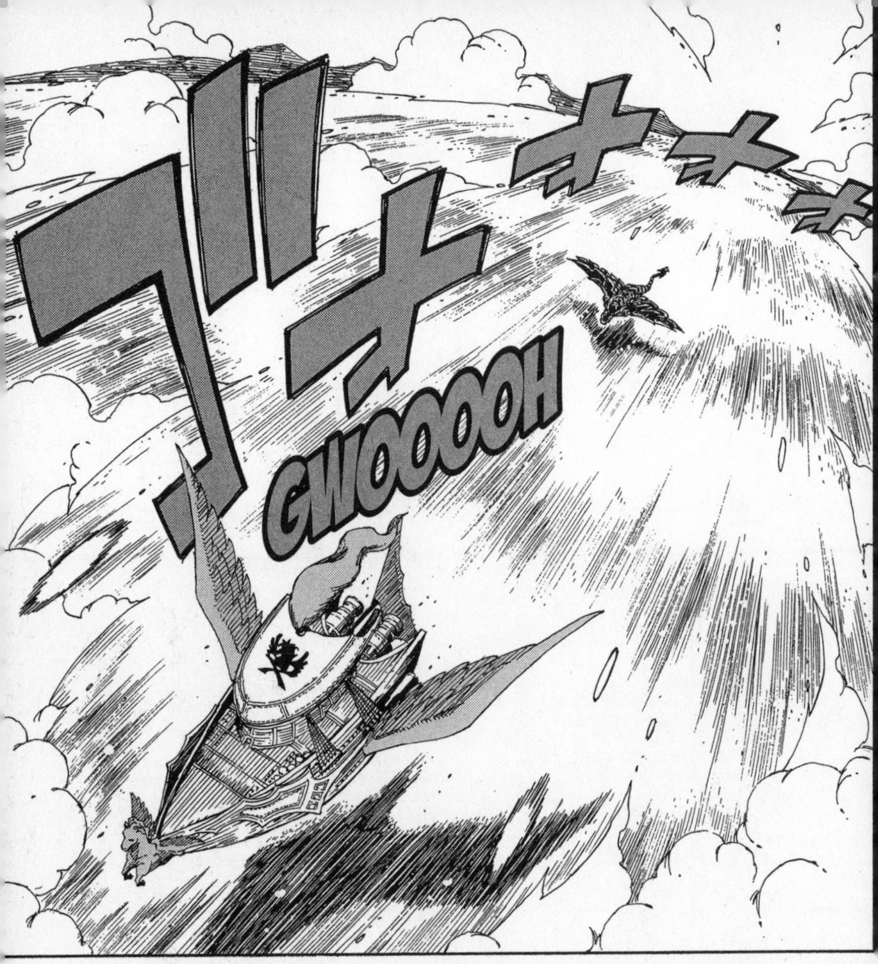
GWOOOOH

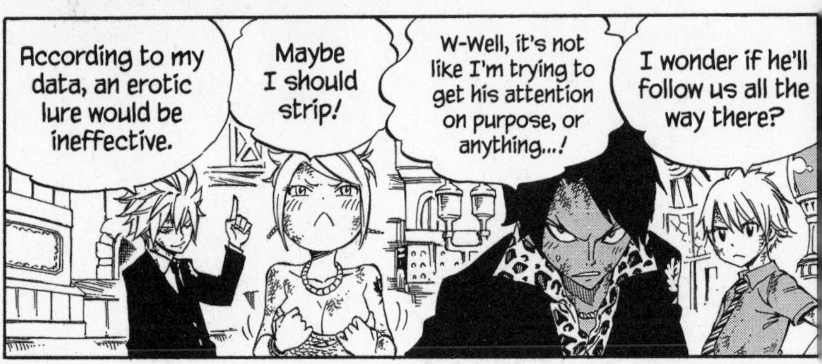
I wonder if he'll follow us all the way there?
W-Well, it's not like I'm trying to get his attention on purpose, or anything...!
Maybe I should strip!
According to my data, an erotic lure would be ineffective.

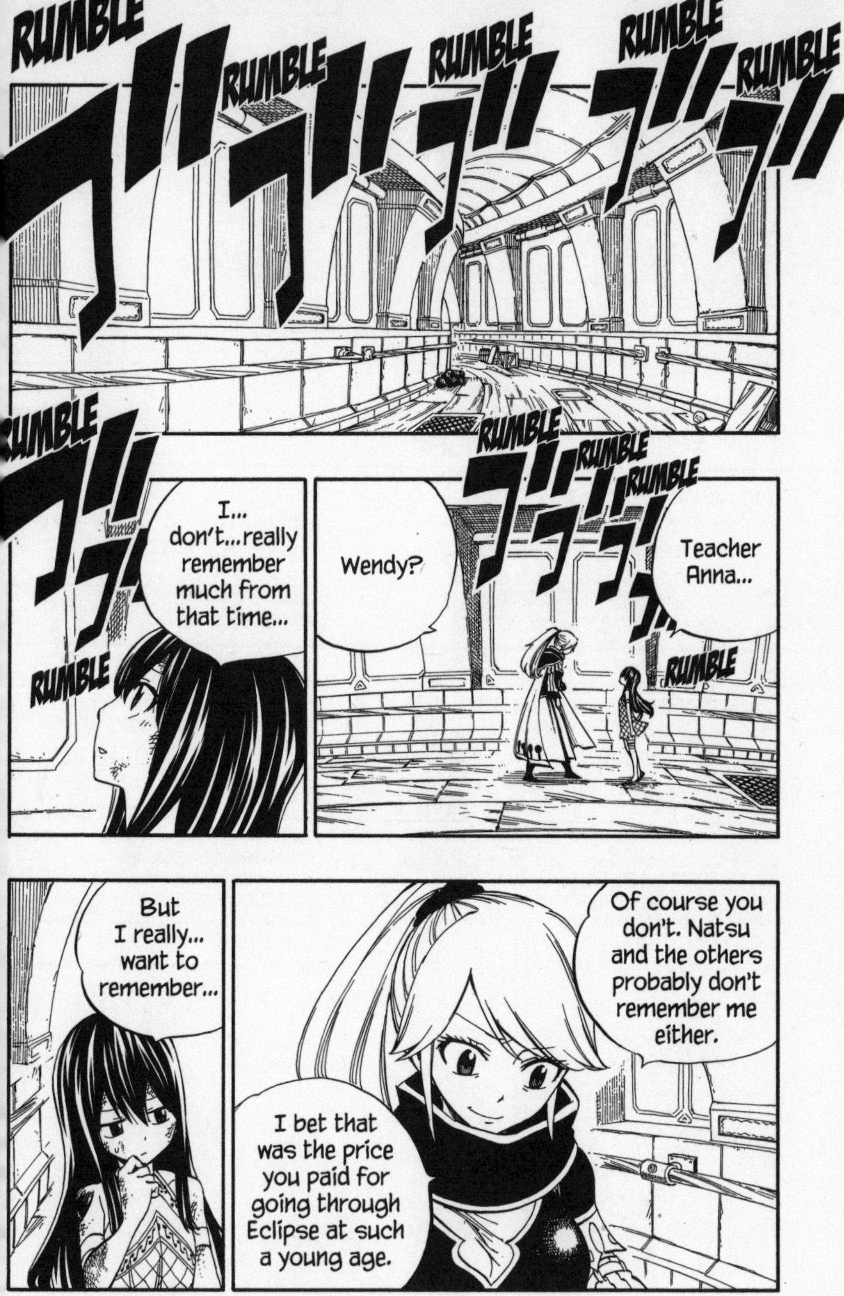
RUMBLE
RUMBLE
RUMBLE
RUMBLE
RUMBLE
RUMBLE
RUMBLE
RUMBLE
Teacher Anna...
RUMBLE
Wendy?
RUMBLE
I... don't...really remember much from that time...
RUMBLE
Of course you don't. Natsu and the others probably don't remember me either.
I bet that was the price you paid for going through Eclipse at such a young age.
But I really... want to remember...

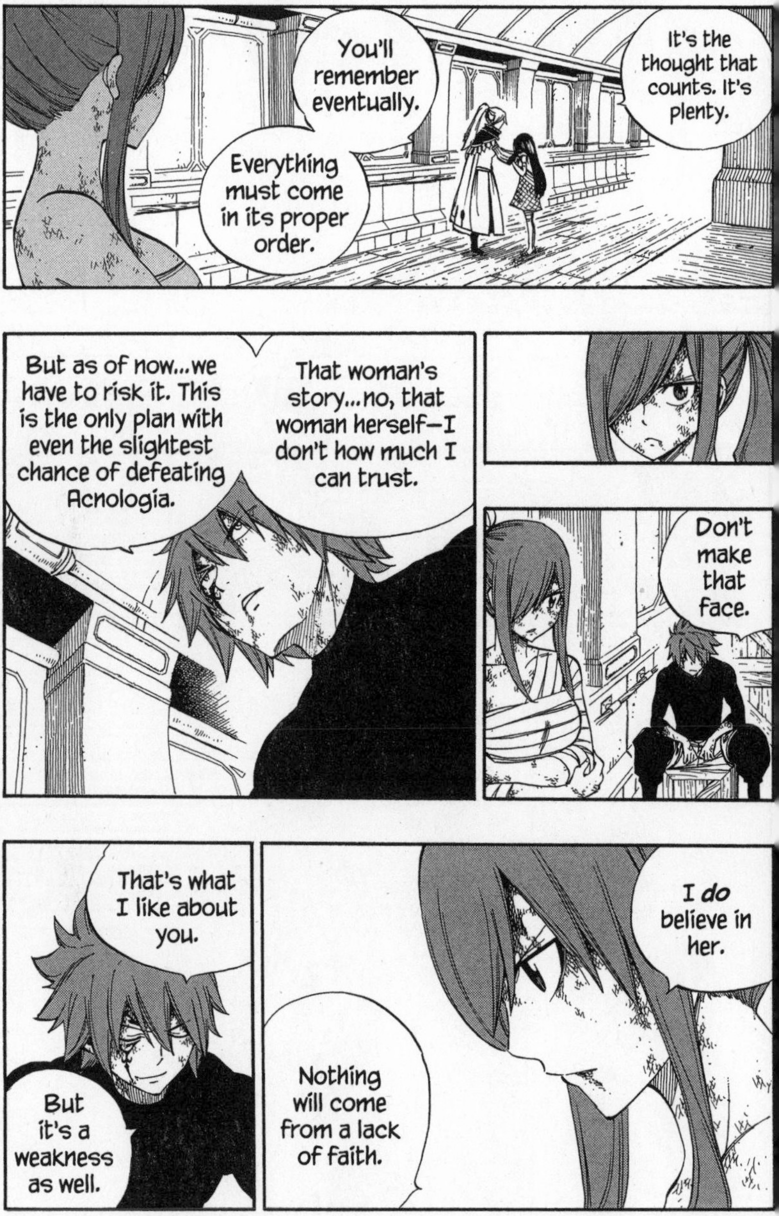
It's the thought that counts. It's plenty.
You'll remember eventually.
Everything must come in its proper order.
Don't make that face.
That woman's story...no, that woman herself—I don't how much I can trust.
But as of now...we have to risk it. This is the only plan with even the slightest chance of defeating Acnologia.
I *do* believe in her.
Nothing will come from a lack of faith.
That's what I like about you.
But it's a weakness as well.

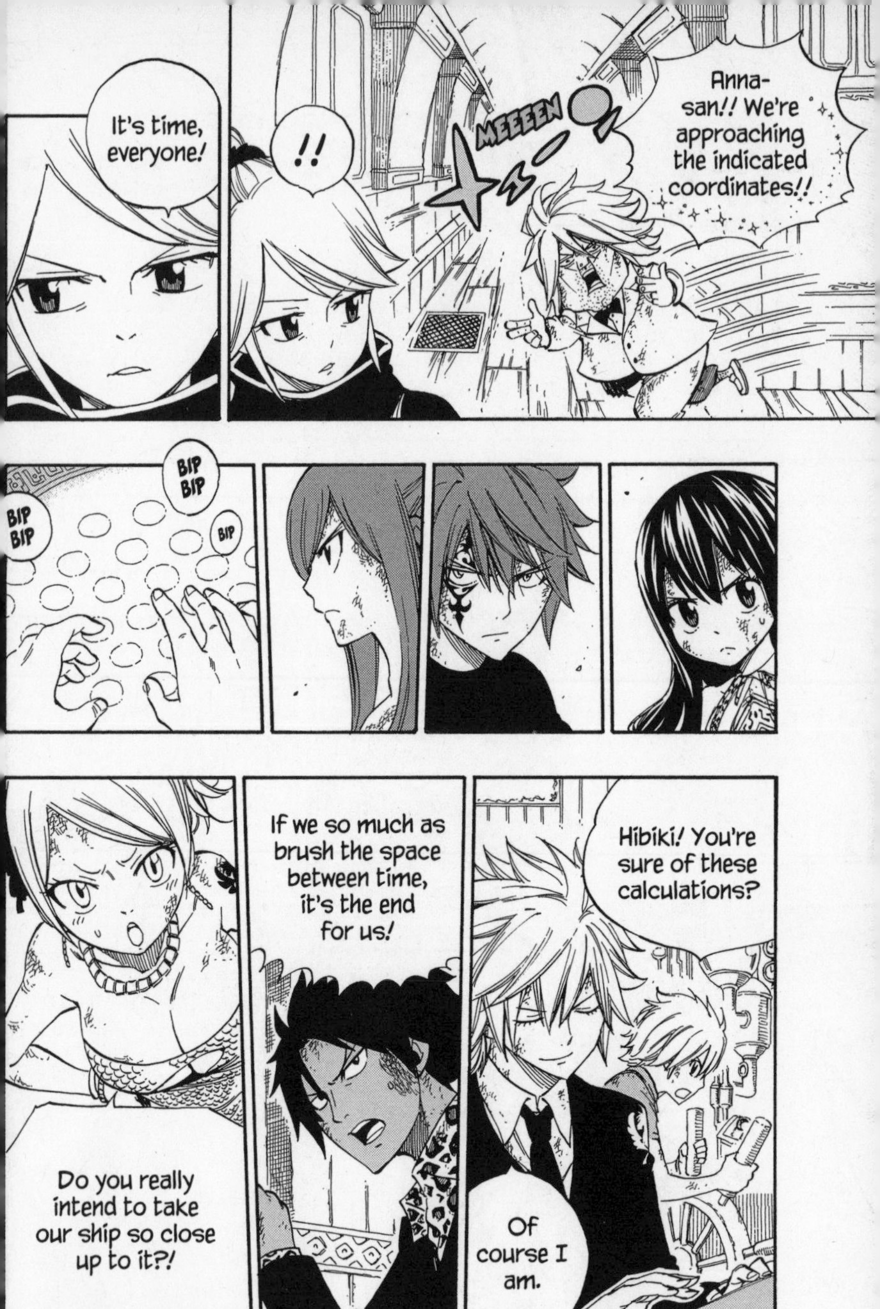
Anna-san!! We're approaching the indicated coordinates!!
MEEEEN
!!
It's time, everyone!
BIP BIP
BIP
BIP BIP
Hibiki! You're sure of these calculations?
Of course I am.
If we so much as brush the space between time, it's the end for us!
Do you really intend to take our ship so close up to it?!

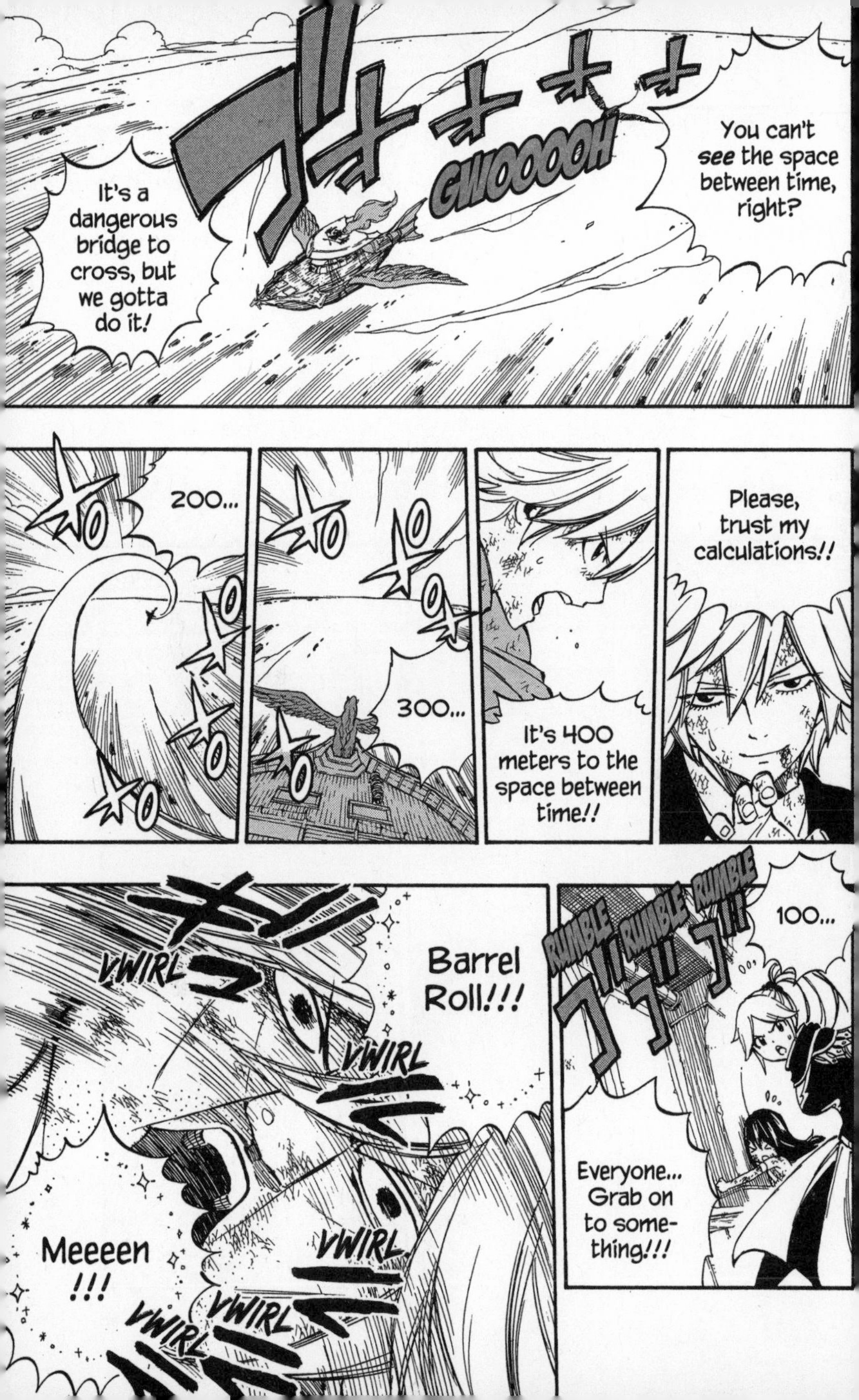

You can't *see* the space between time, right?
GWOOOOOH
It's a dangerous bridge to cross, but we gotta do it!
Please, trust my calculations!!
It's 400 meters to the space between time!!
300...
200...
100...
RUMBLE RUMBLE RUMBLE
Everyone... Grab on to some-thing!!!
Barrel Roll!!!
VWIRL
VWIRL
VWIRL
VWIRL
VWIRL
Meeeen !!!

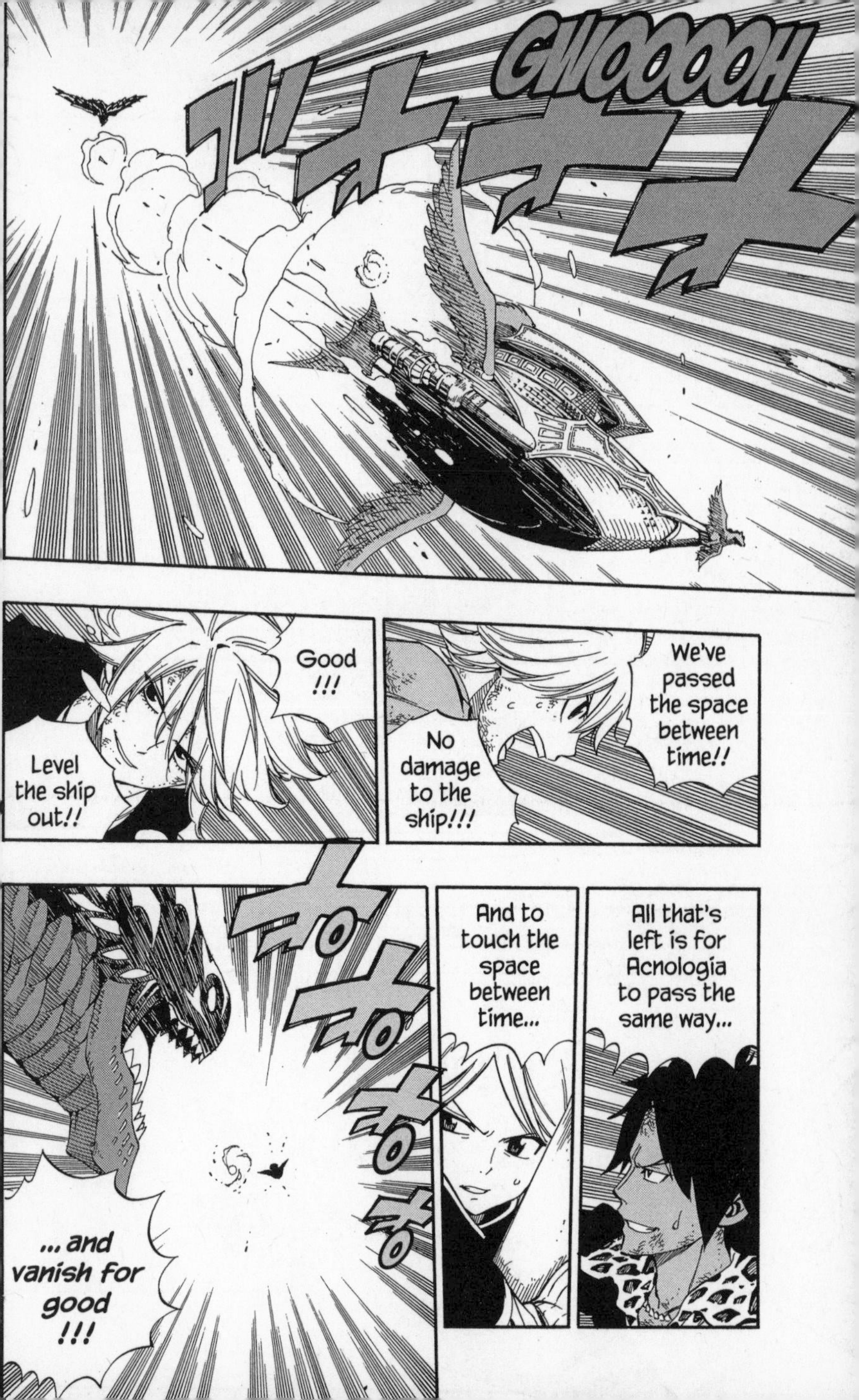
GWOOOOOH
We've passed the space between time!!
No damage to the ship!!!
Good!!!
Level the ship out!!
All that's left is for Acnologia to pass the same way...
And to touch the space between time...
...and vanish for good!!!

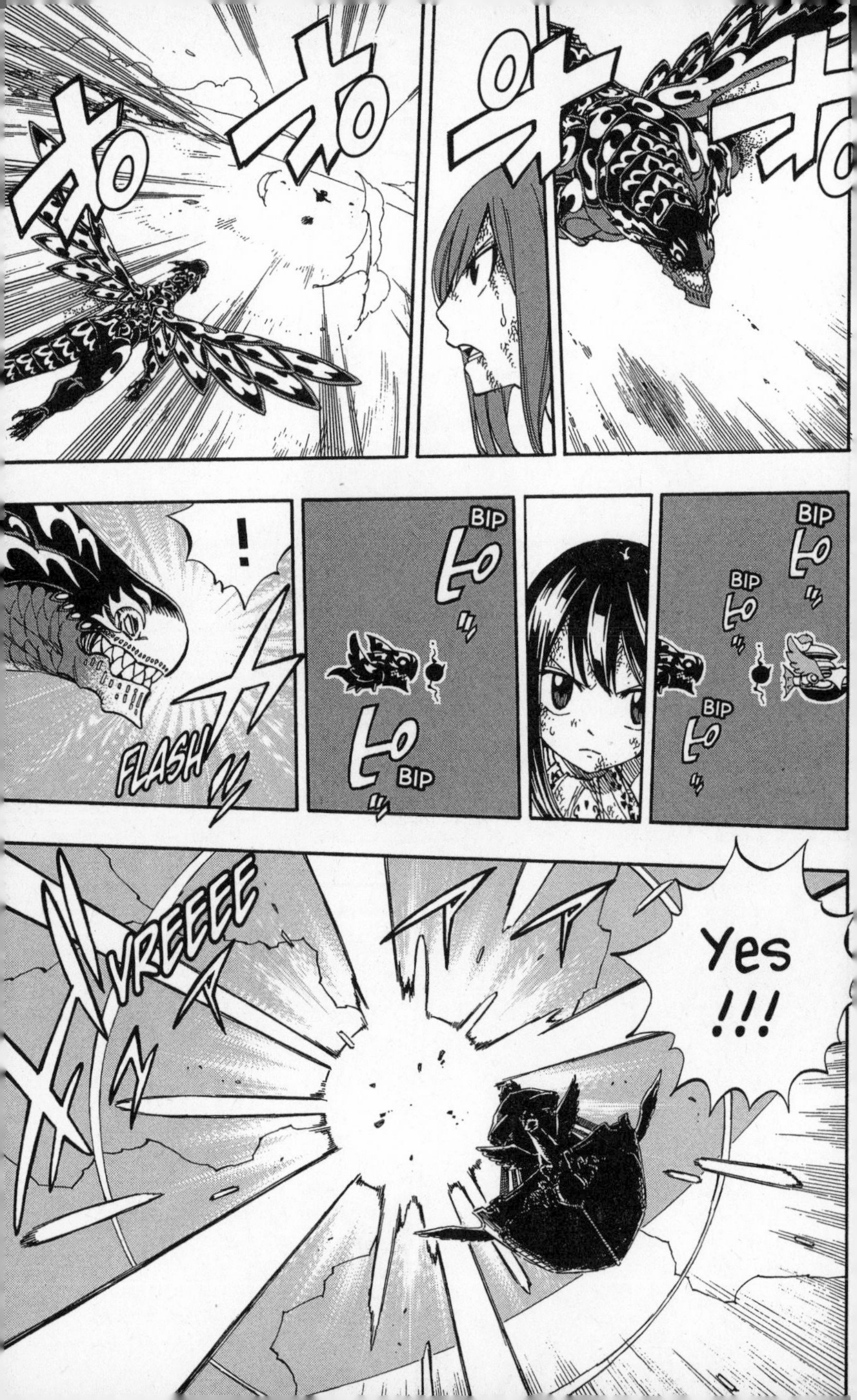
BIP
BIP
BIP
BIP
BIP
!
FLASH
Yes!!!
VREEEE

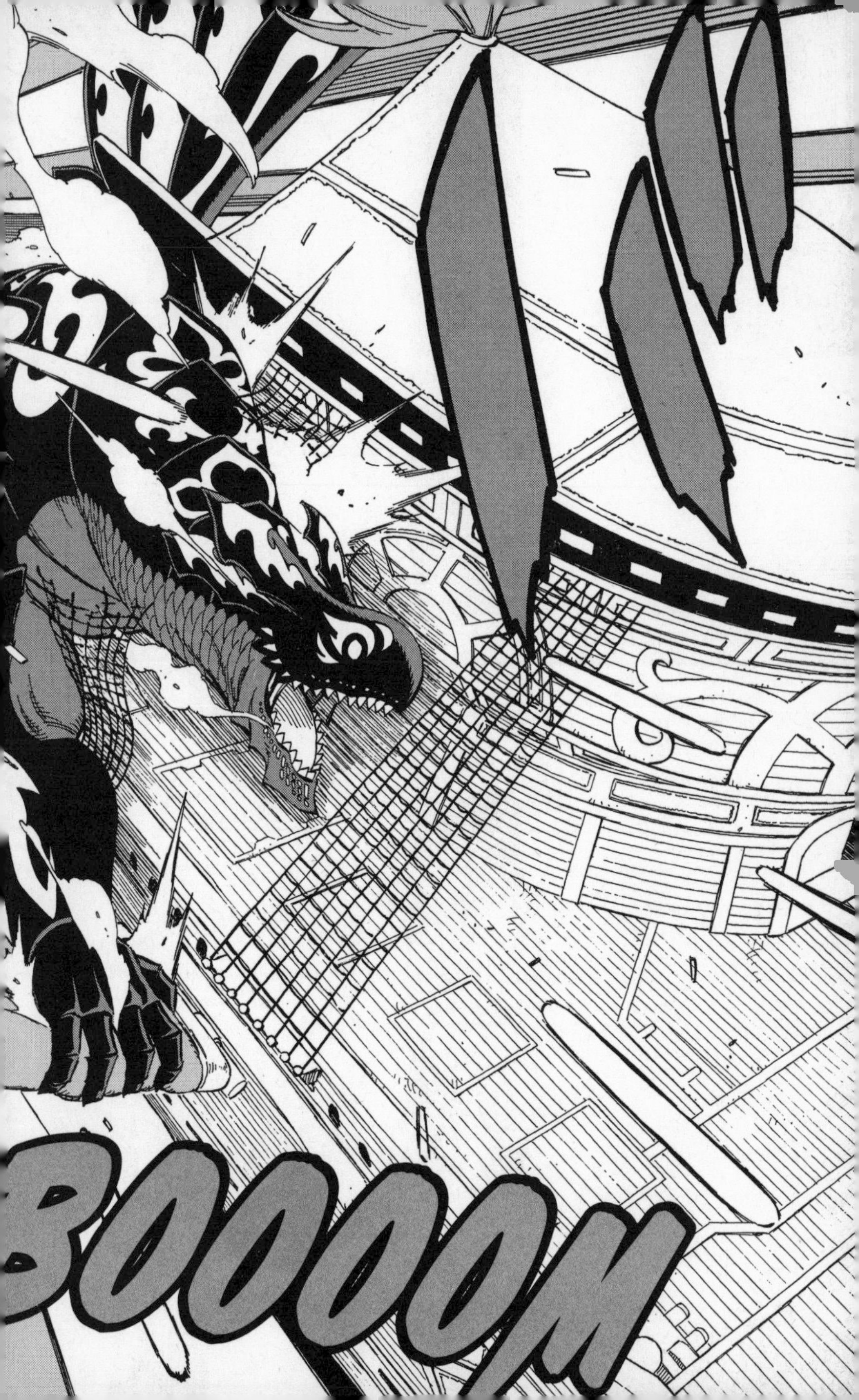
BOOOOM

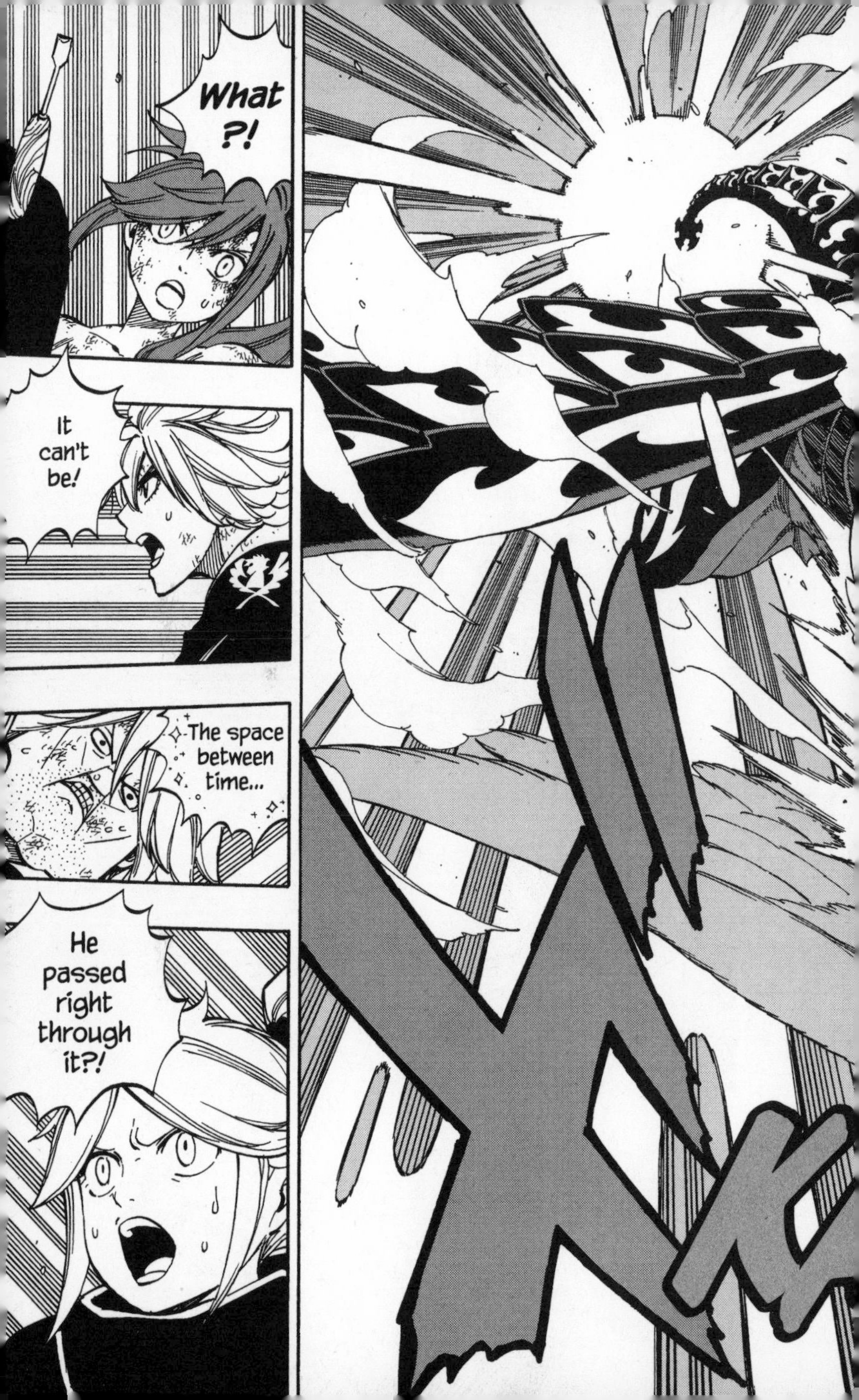
What?!
It can't be!
The space between time...
He passed right through it?!

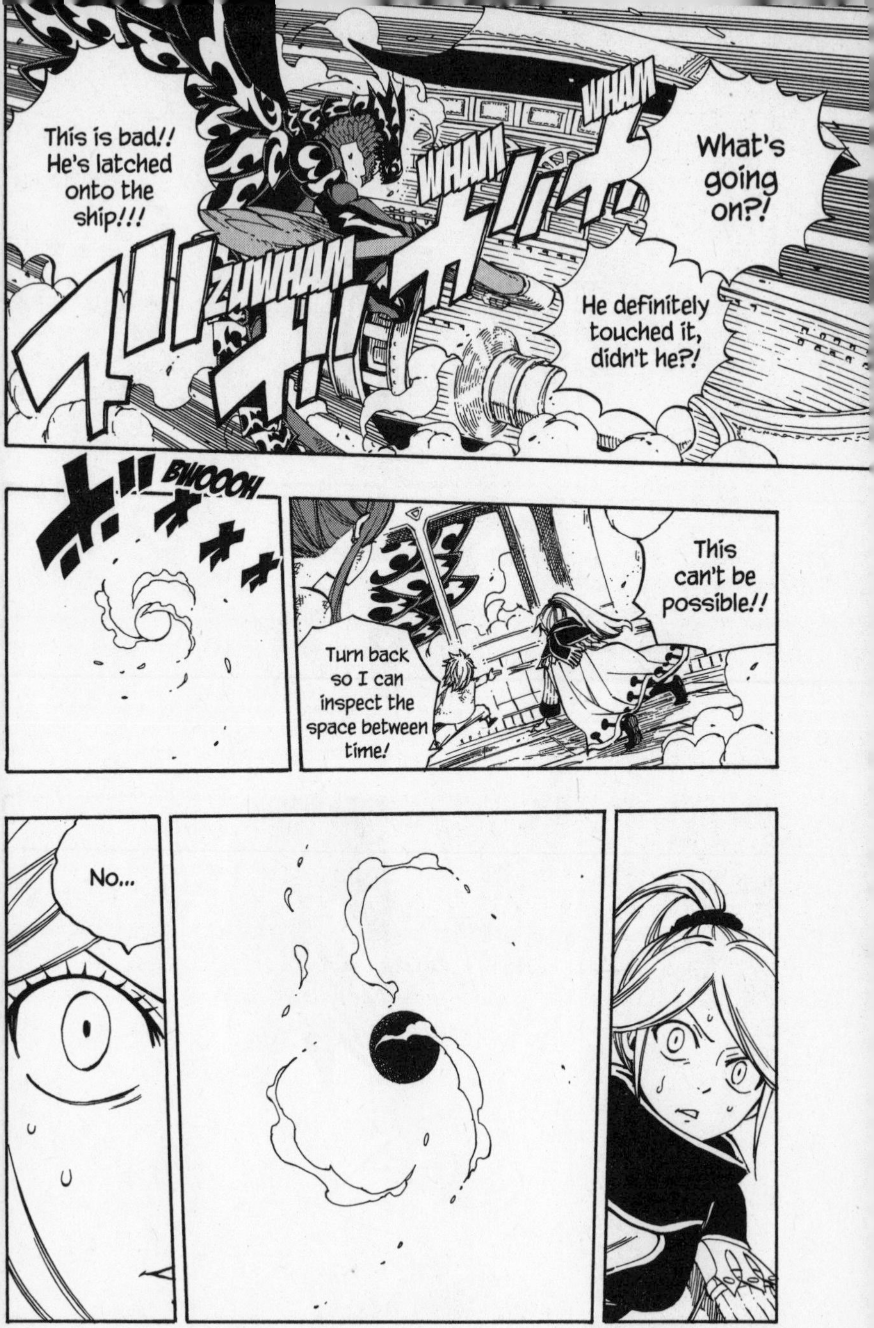
What's going on?!
WHAM
WHAM
He definitely touched it, didn't he?!
This is bad!! He's latched onto the ship!!!
ZUWHAM
This can't be possible!!
Turn back so I can inspect the space between time!
BWOOOH
No...

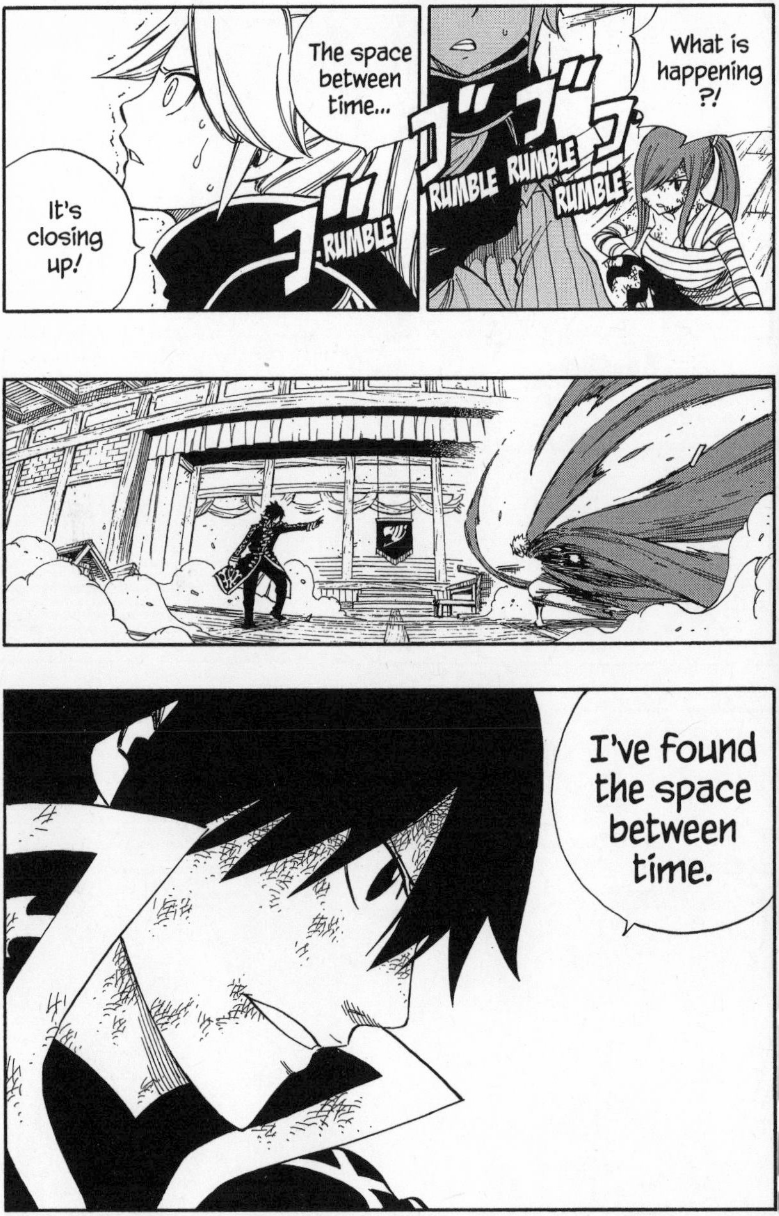
What is happening ?!
RUMBLE RUMBLE RUMBLE
The space between time...
It's closing up!
RUMBLE
I've found the space between time.

Urrgh...

It's brimming with so much Time Magic, it beggars the imagination.

And that Time Magic belongs *to me!!*

So I sealed it away!

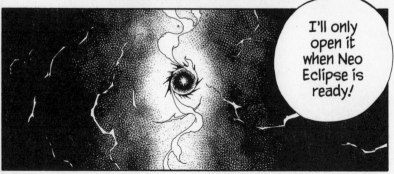

I'll only open it when Neo Eclipse is ready!

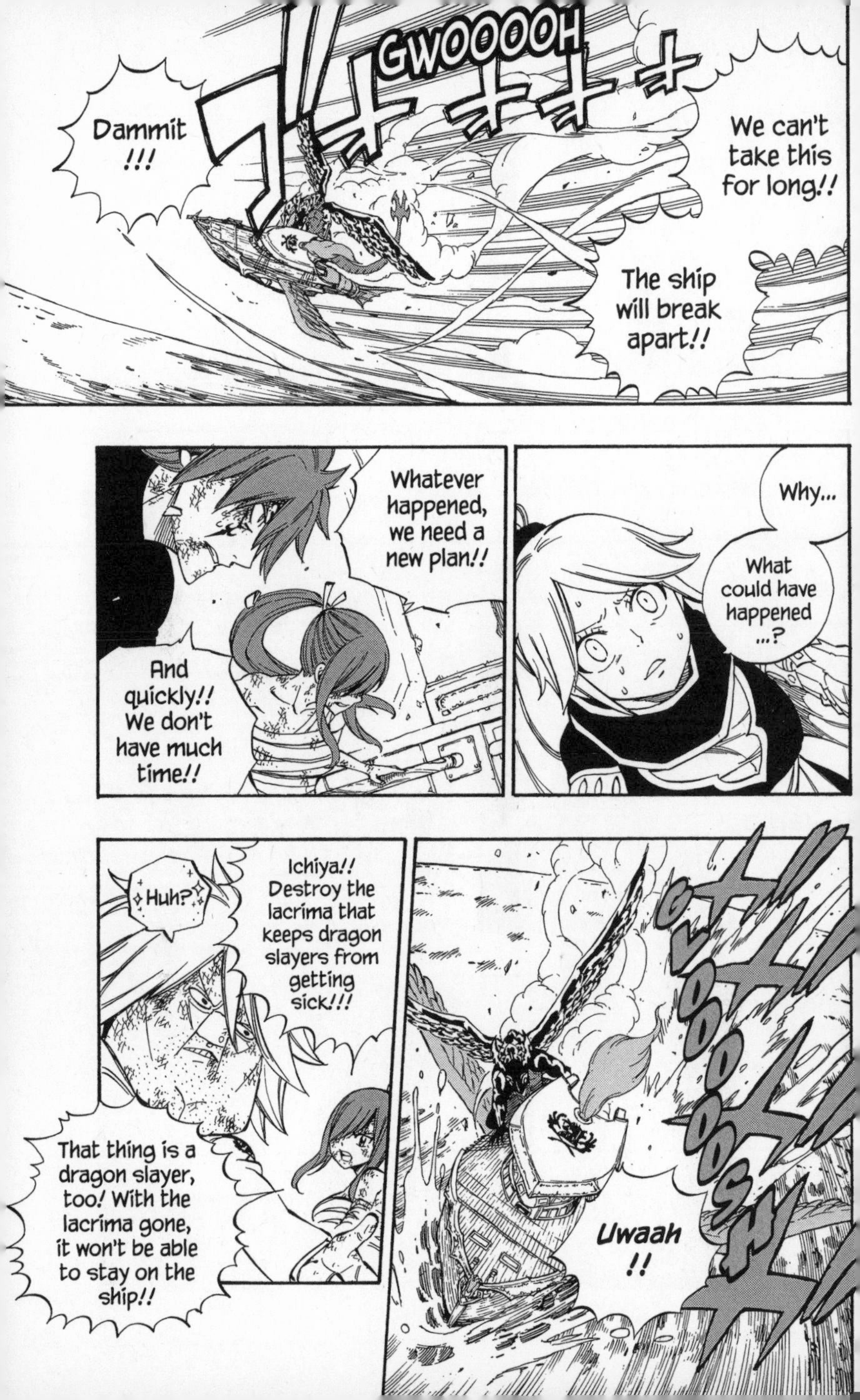
GWOOOOH
We can't take this for long!!
The ship will break apart!!
Dammit!!!
Why...
What could have happened...?
Whatever happened, we need a new plan!!
And quickly!! We don't have much time!!
GWOOOOOSH
Uwaah!!
Huh?
Ichiya!! Destroy the lacrima that keeps dragon slayers from getting sick!!!
That thing is a dragon slayer, too! With the lacrima gone, it won't be able to stay on the ship!!

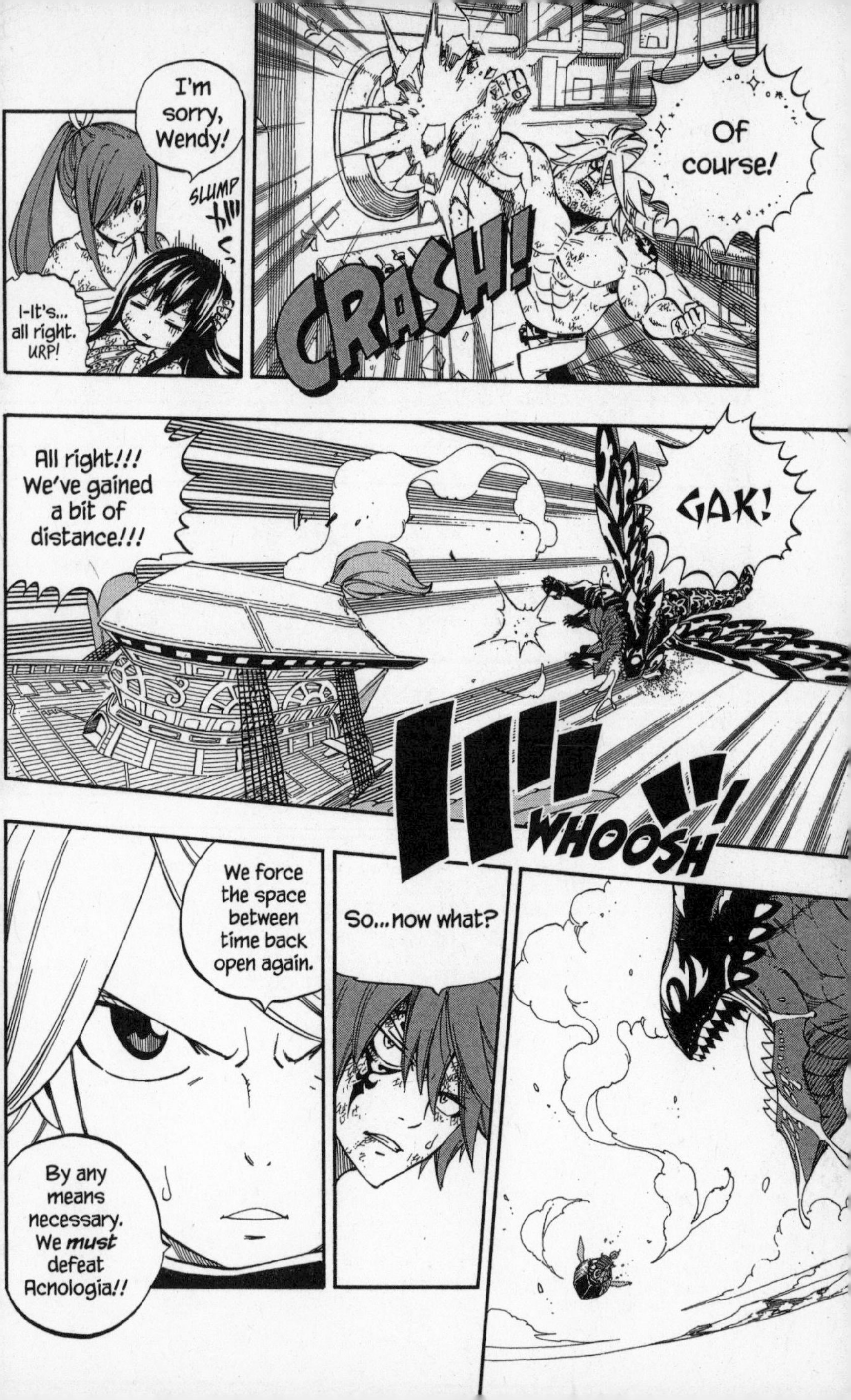
Of course!
CRASH!
I'm sorry, Wendy!
SLUMP
I-It's... all right. URP!
GAK!
All right!!! We've gained a bit of distance!!!
WHOOSH
So...now what?
We force the space between time back open again.
By any means necessary. We *must* defeat Acnologia!!

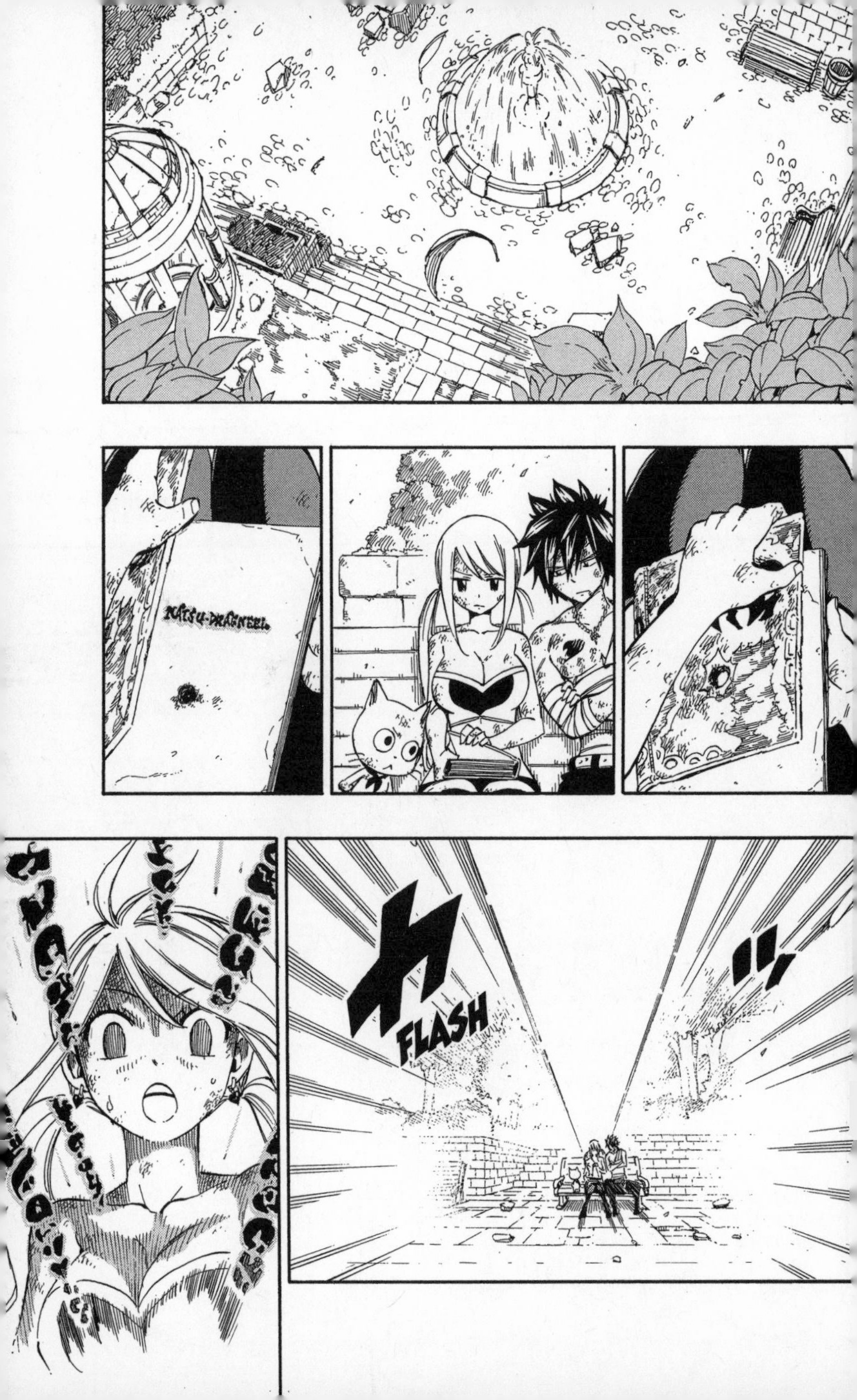

NATSU-DRAGNEEL
FLASH

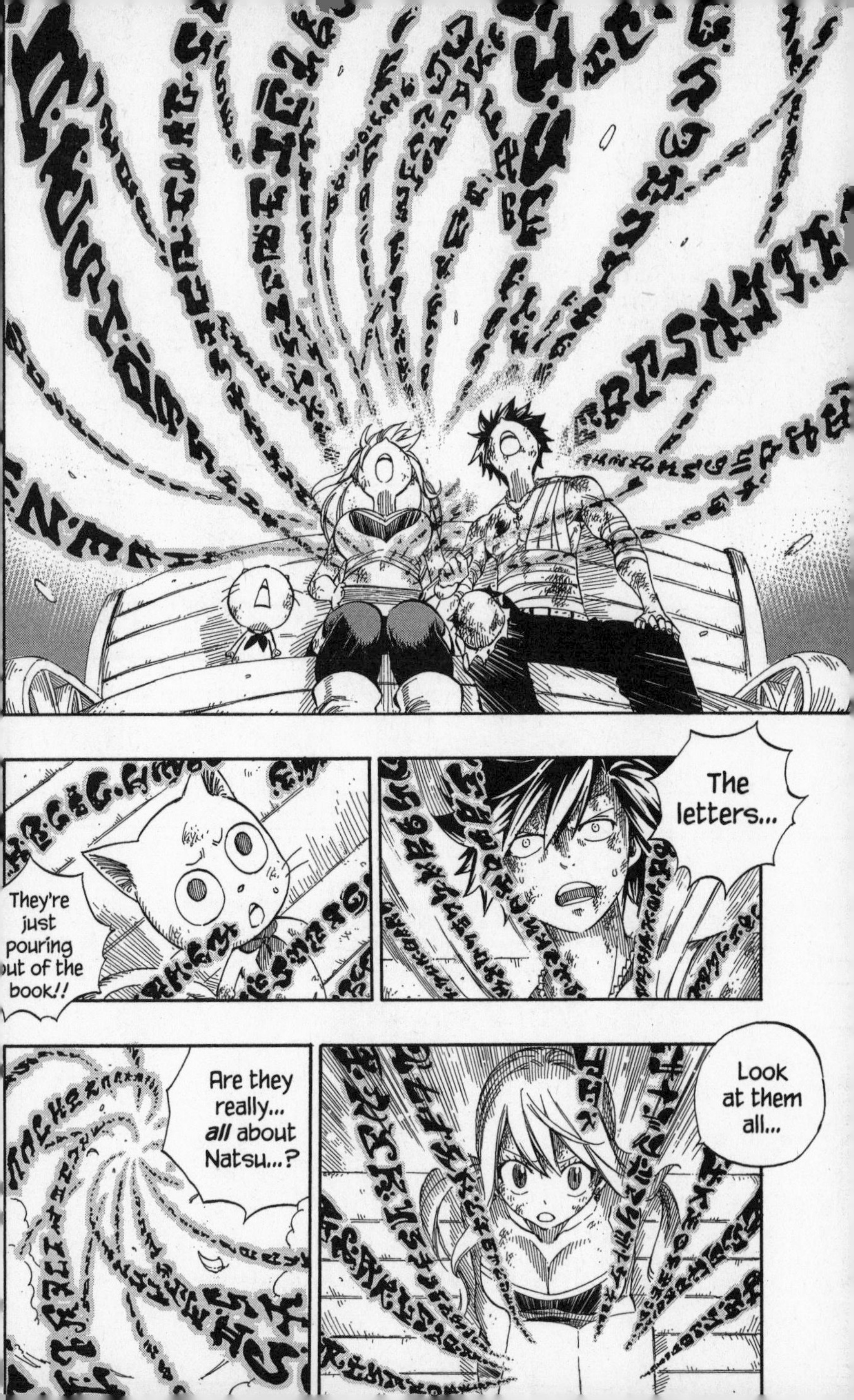
The letters...
They're just pouring out of the book!!
Look at them all...
Are they really... *all* about Natsu...?

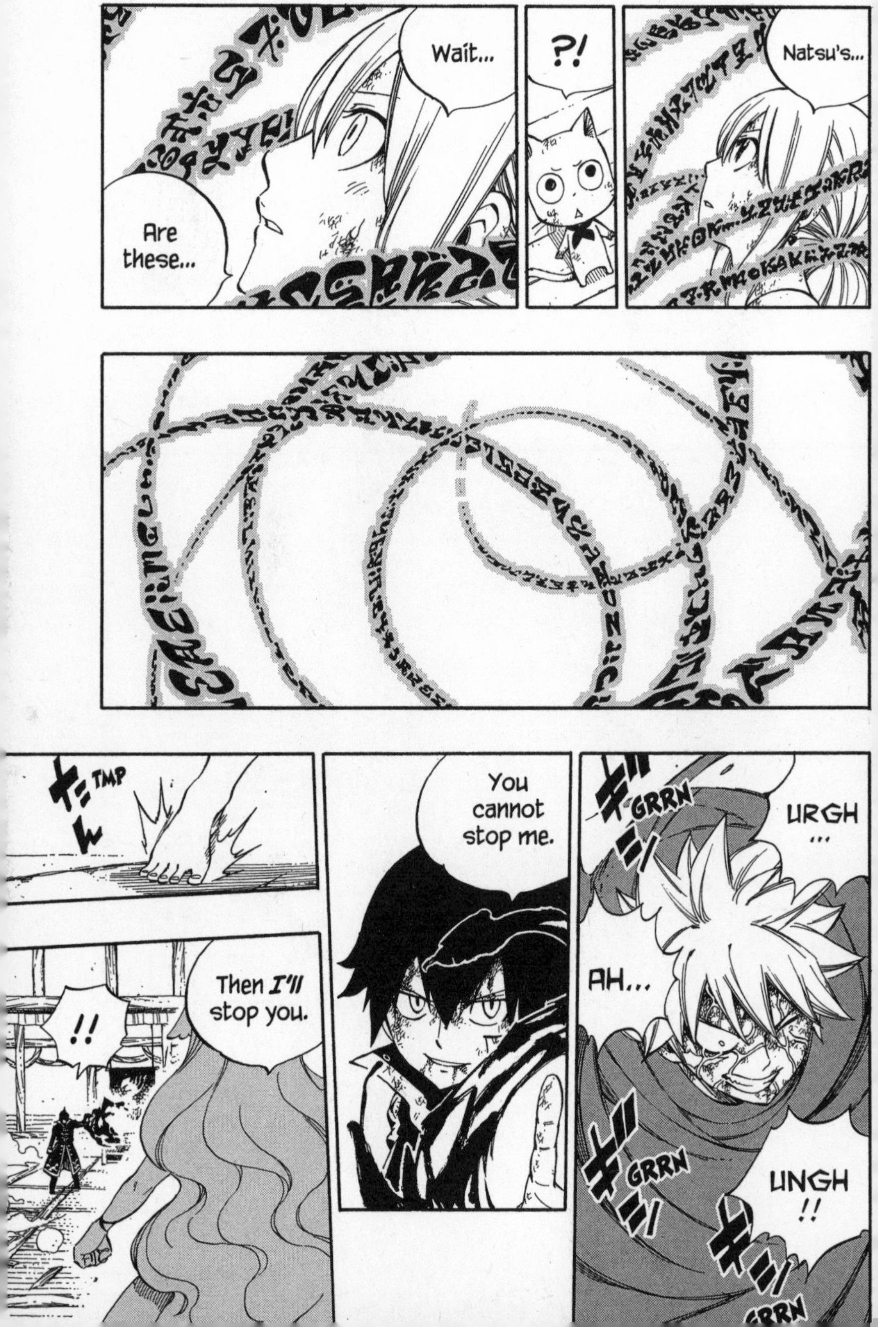

Natsu's...
?!
Wait...
Are these...
URGH ...
GRRN
AH...
UNGH !!
GRRN
GRRN
You cannot stop me.
TMP
Then *I'll* stop you.
!!

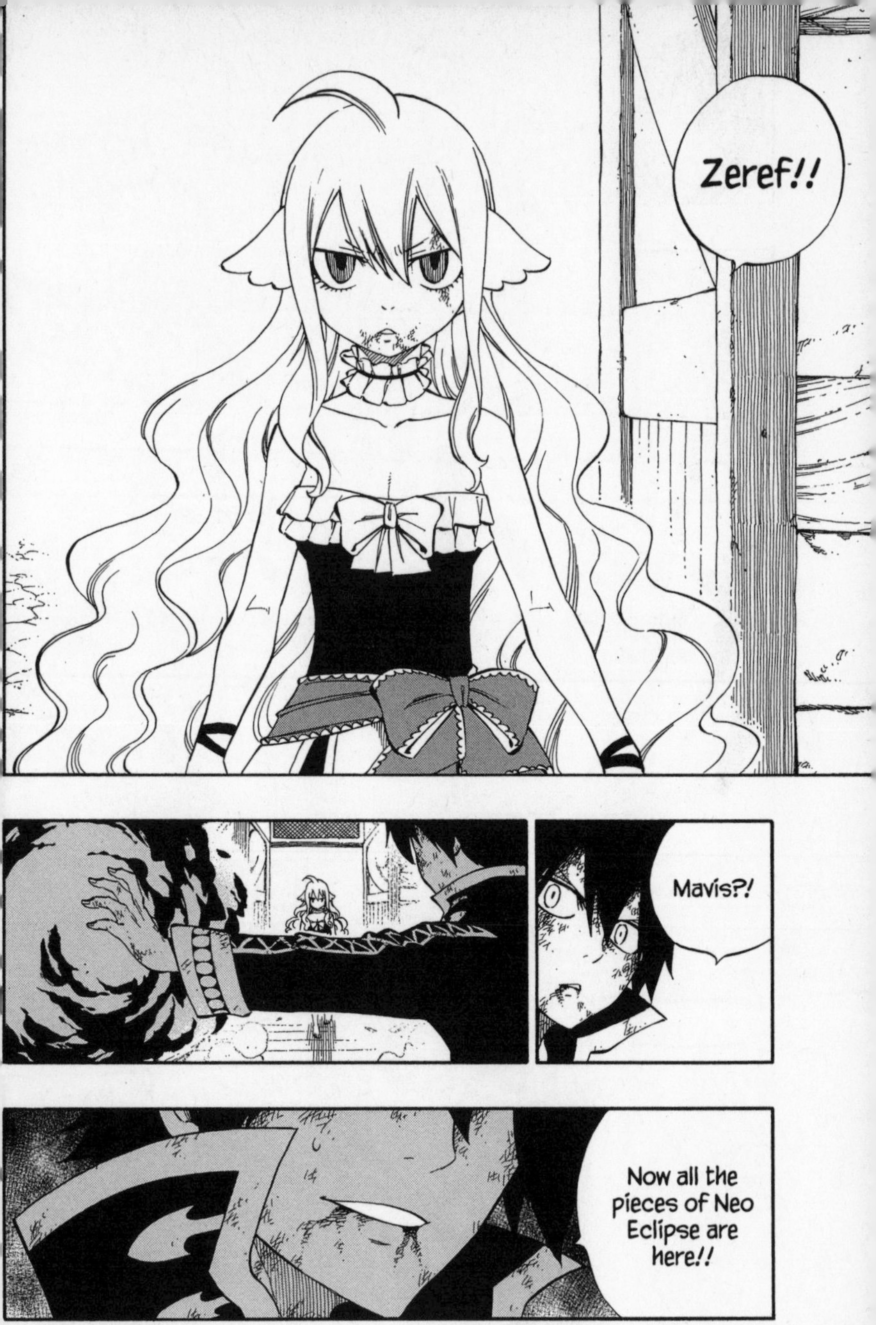
Zeref!!
Mavis?!
Now all the pieces of Neo Eclipse are here!!

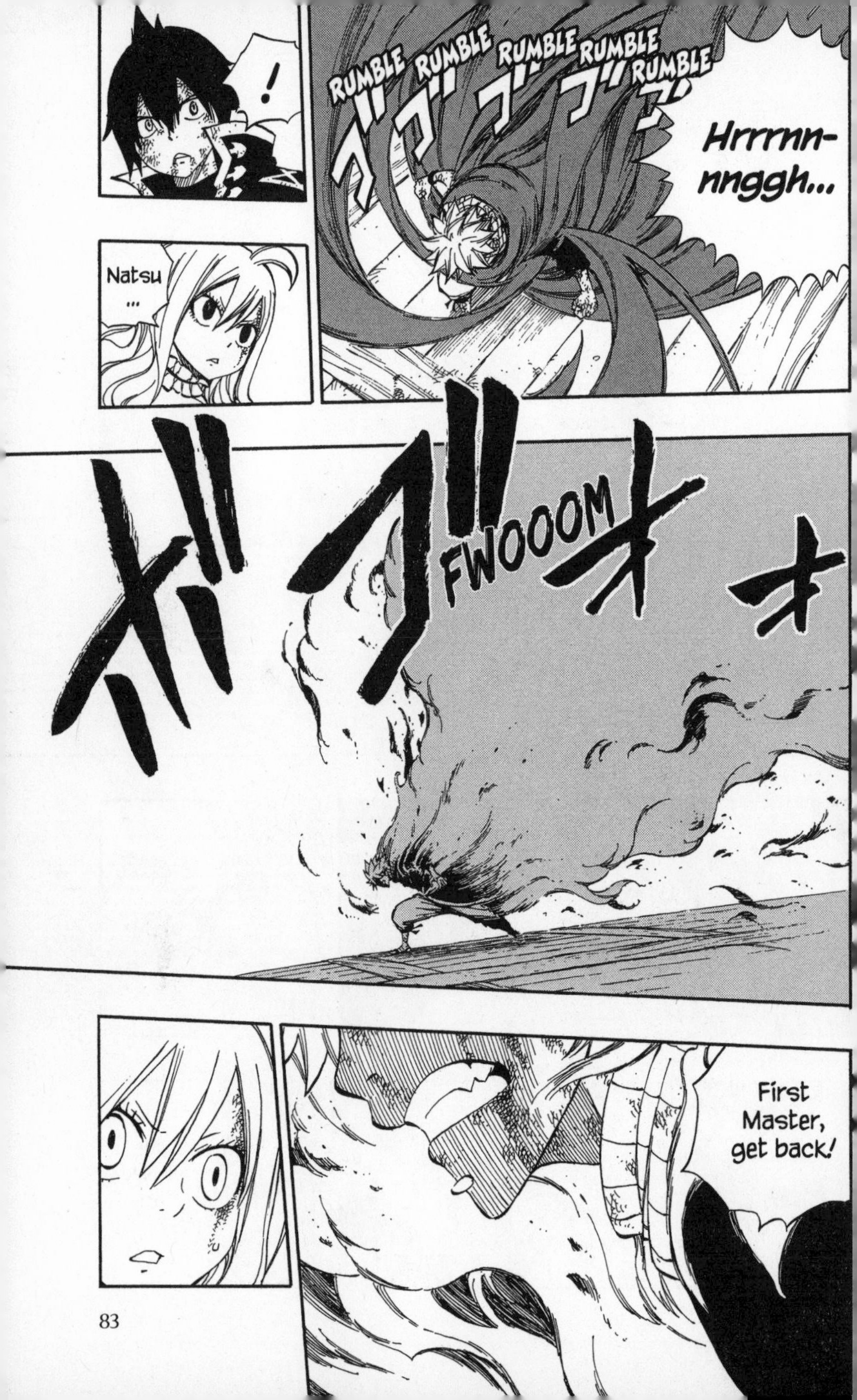
RUMBLE RUMBLE RUMBLE RUMBLE RUMBLE
Hrrrnn-nnggh...
!
Natsu ...
FWOOOM
First Master, get back!

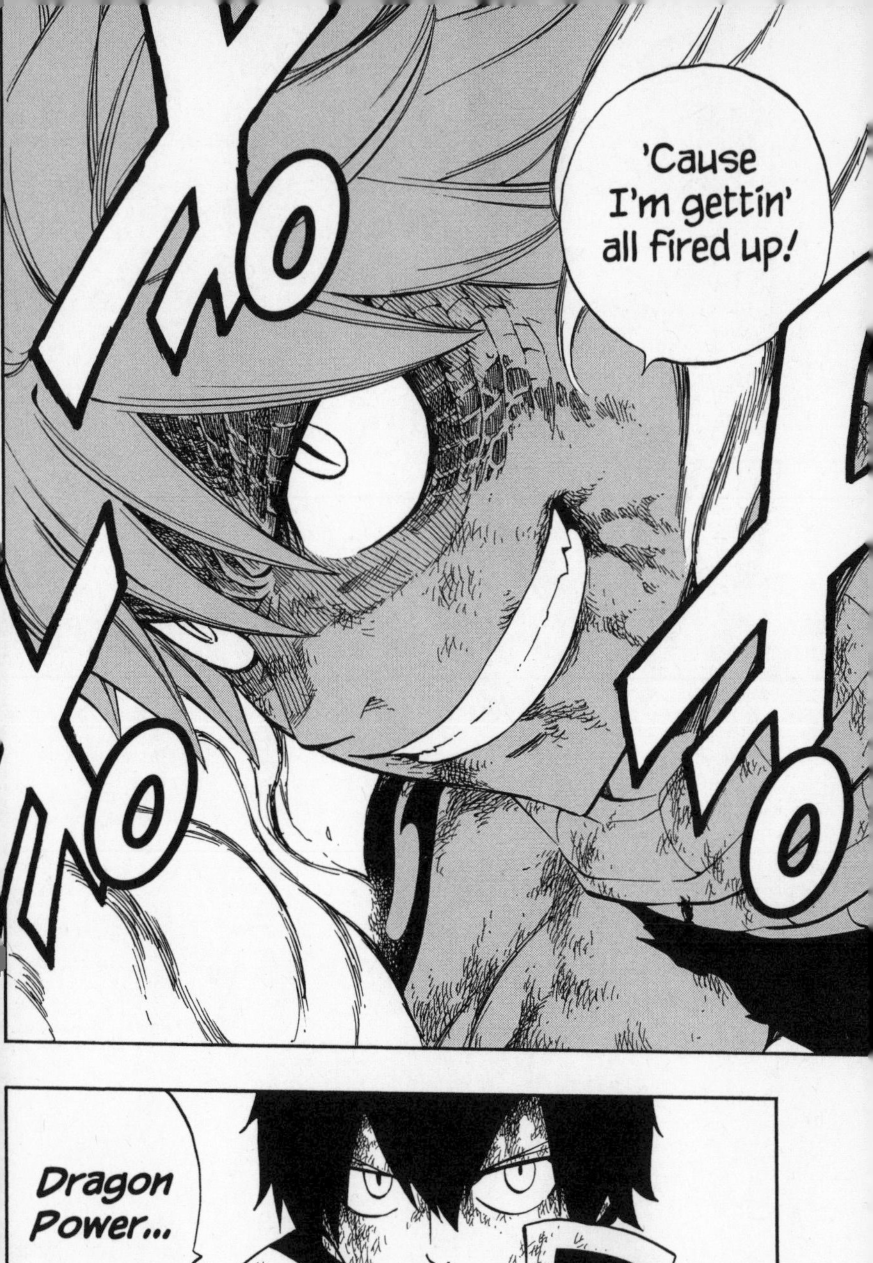
'Cause I'm gettin' all fired up!
Dragon Power...

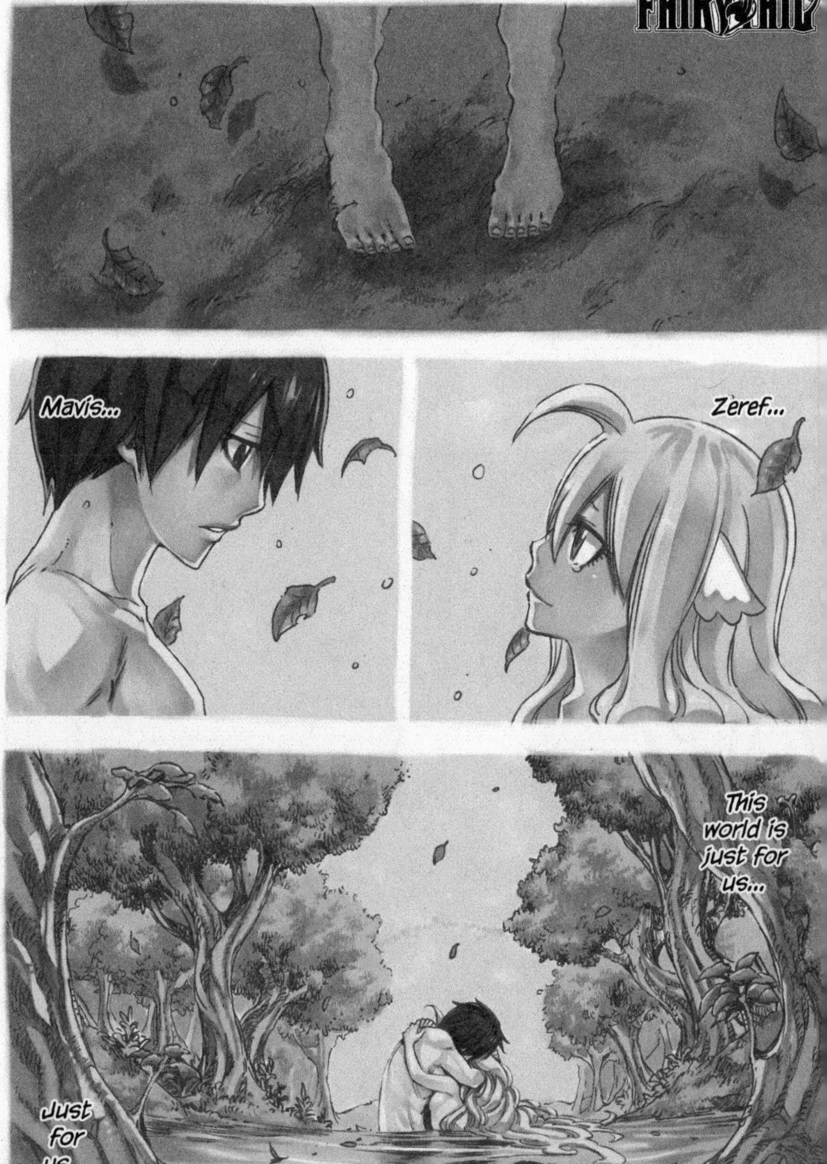
Zeref...
Mavis...
This world is just for us...
Just for us...

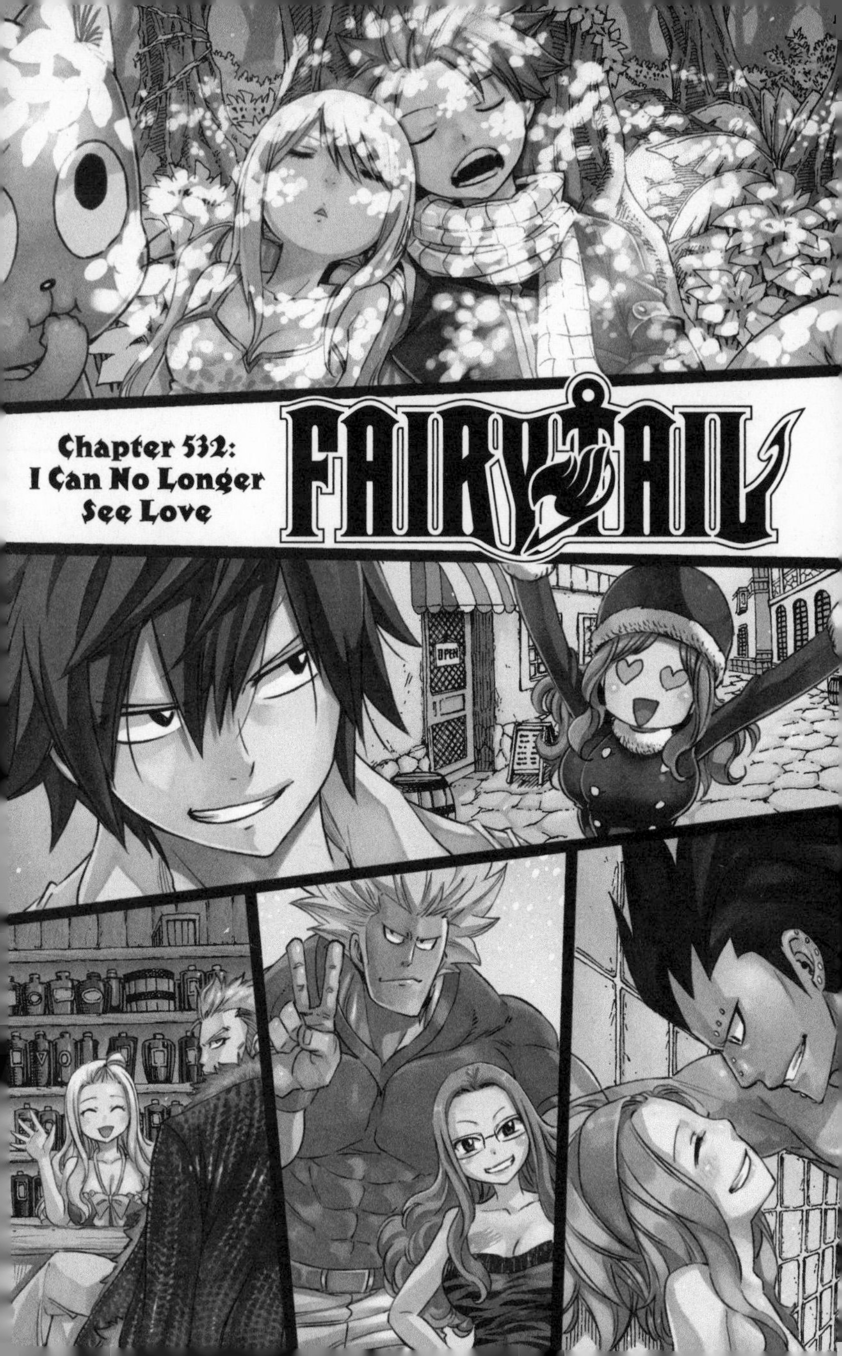
Chapter 532:
I Can No Longer
See Love
OPEN

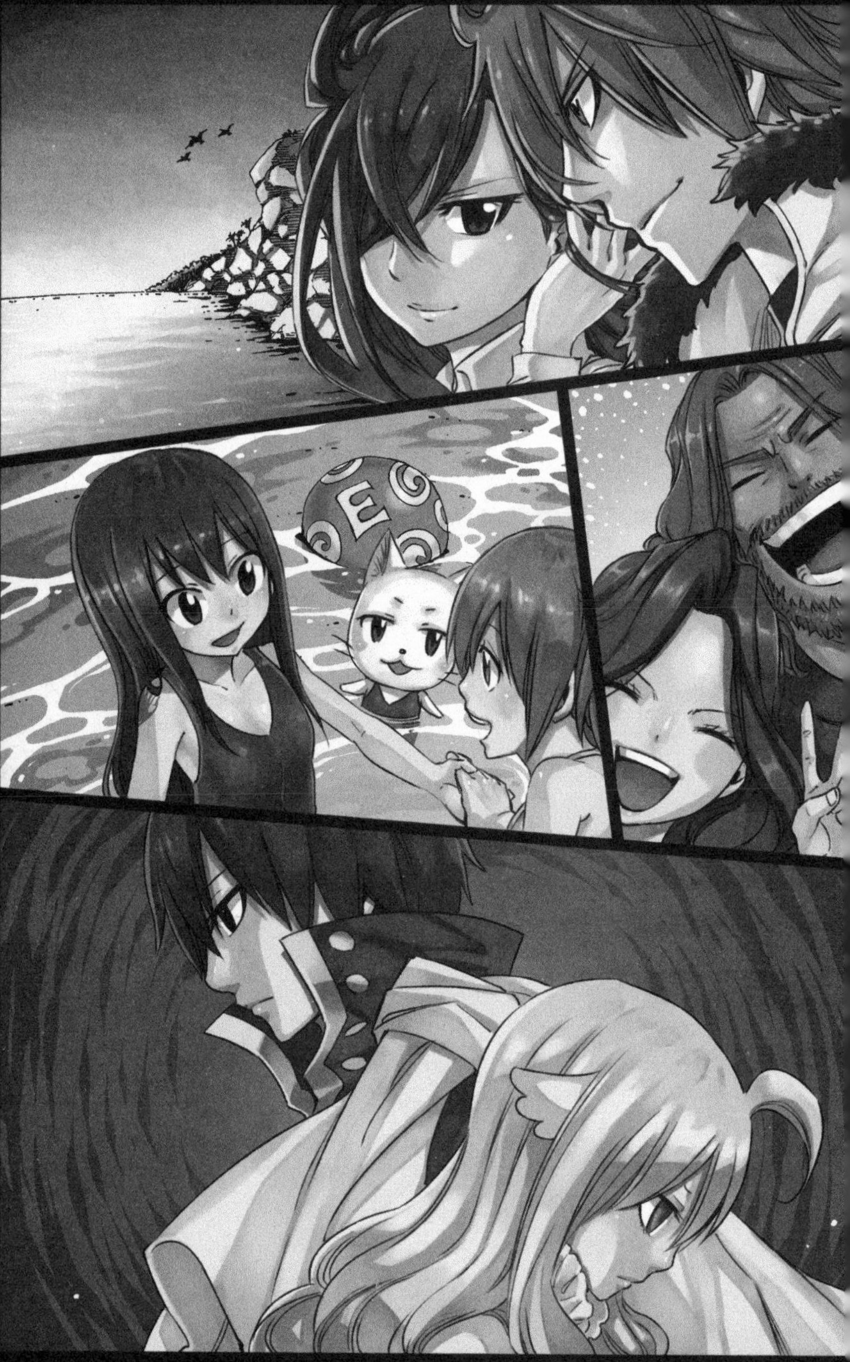

Those chosen to be published will get a signed mini poster! ♪

FAIRY TAIL GUILD de ART

▼ That's well done! And thanks for the message, too!

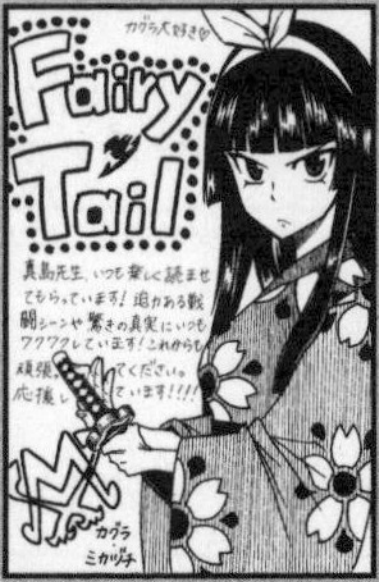
Fairy Tail
カグラ ミカヅチ

Hokkaido, Hikari Honda

Aichi Prefecture, Nijirou

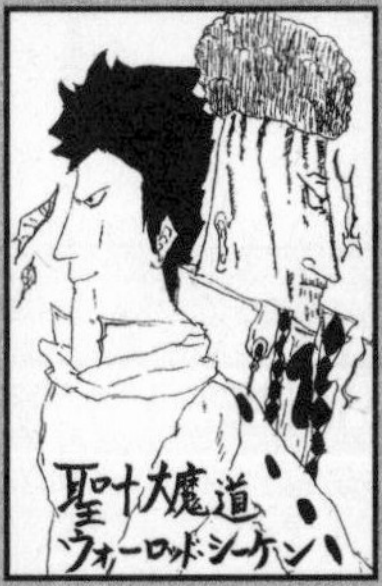
聖十大魔道
ウォーロッド・シーケン

▲ An illustration of Warrod! That's pretty uncommon!

▼ Whoa! Cute! And I love the costume!

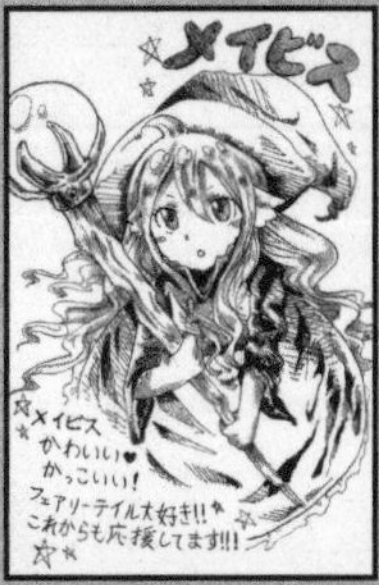
メイビス
メイビス かわいい♥ かっこいい! フェアリーテイル大好き!! これからも応援してます!!!

Aichi Prefecture, Raumu

Aichi Prefecture, Rion Tomioka

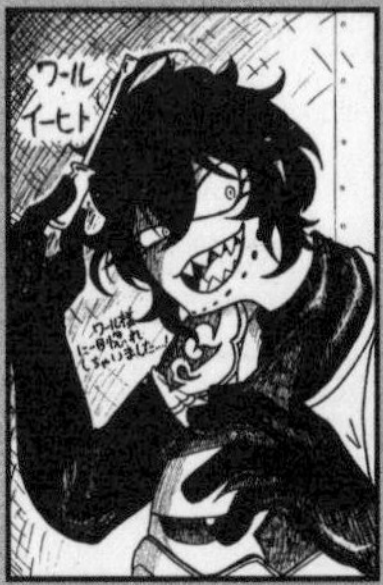
ワール イーヒト

▲ Thanks! This is a rare character to get a drawing of!

REJECTION CORNER

Hiroshima Prefecture, Ebi

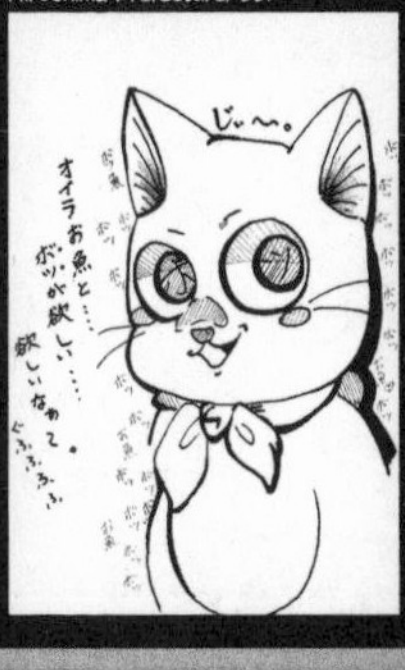
じぃ〜。

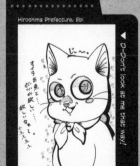

▼ D-Don't look at me that way!

Osaka, Maashii

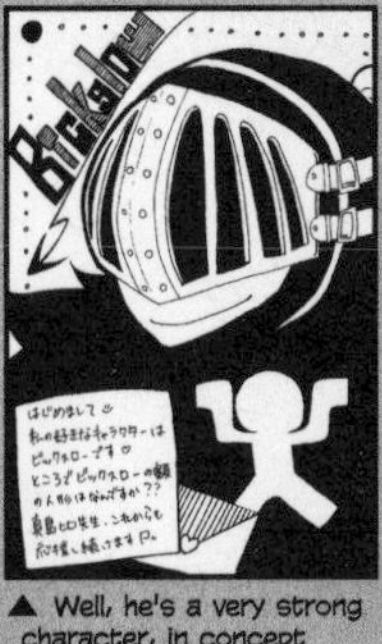
Bickslow

▲ Well, he's a very strong character, in concept anyway.

Nara Prefecture, Rui Uranaka

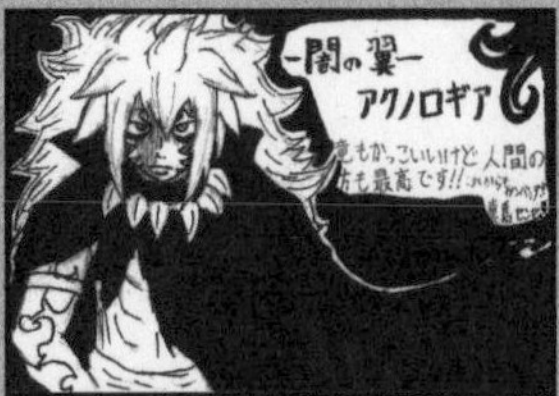
ー闇の翼ー
アクノロギア

▲ In his human form. I think he's pretty darn cool, too!

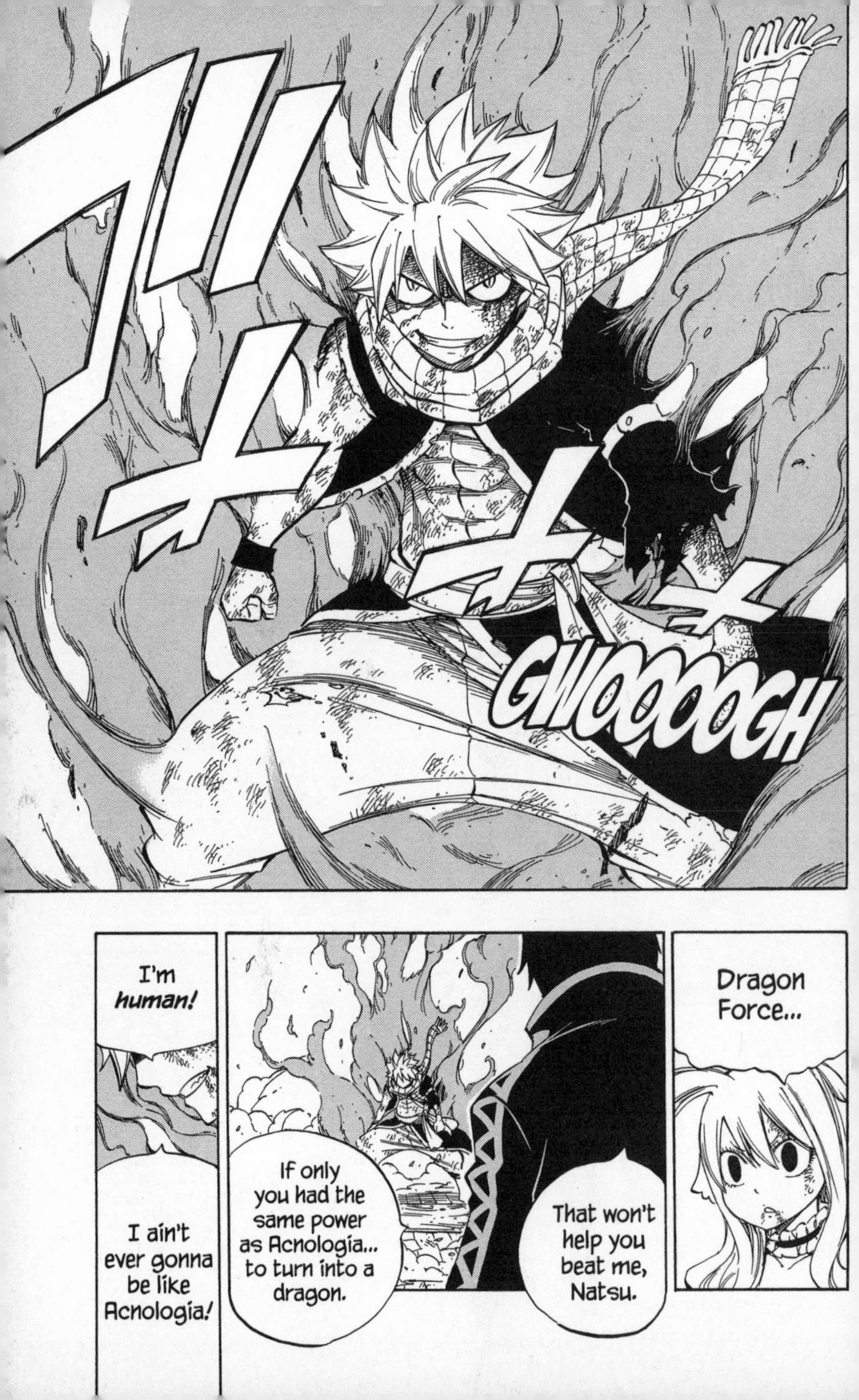
GWOOOOGH
Dragon Force...
That won't help you beat me, Natsu.
If only you had the same power as Acnologia... to turn into a dragon.
I'm *human!*
I ain't ever gonna be like Acnologia!

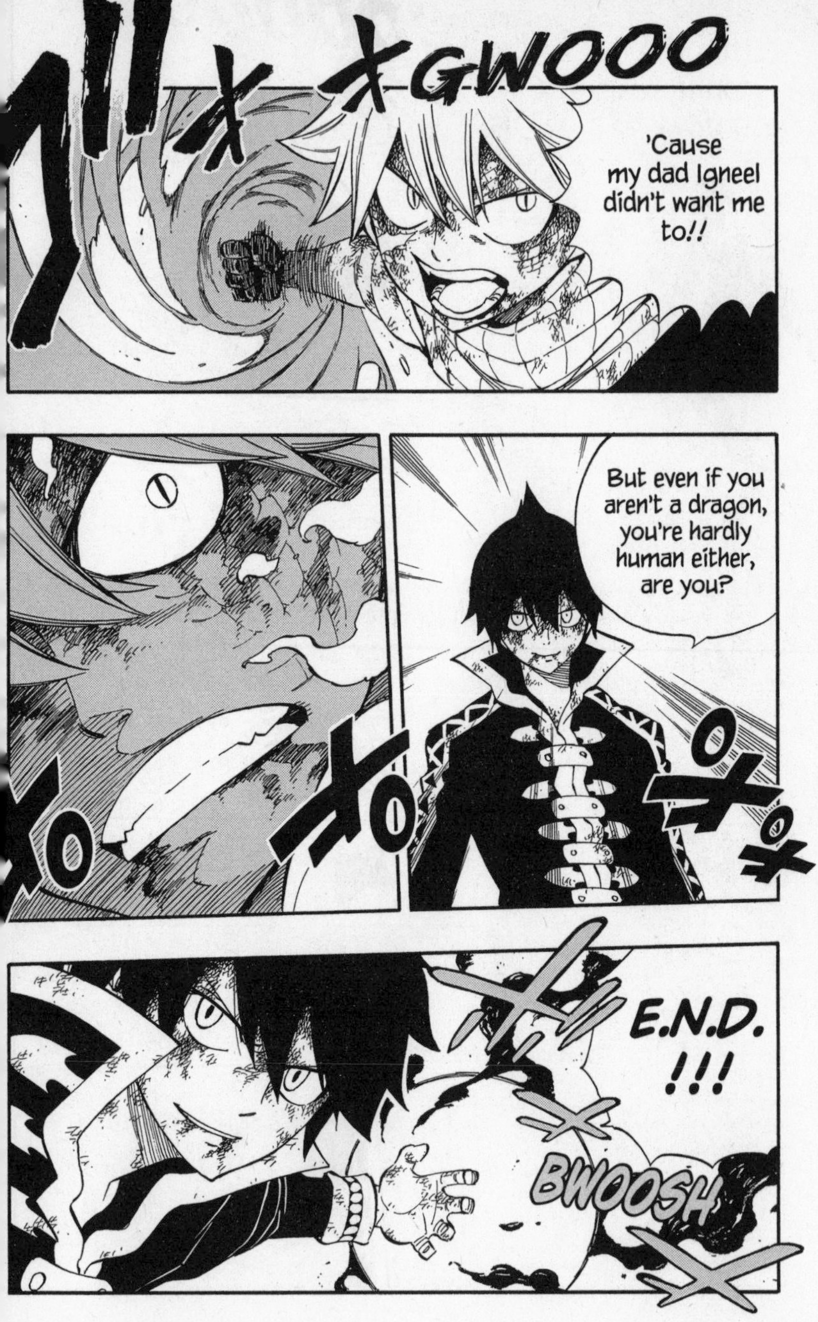
GWOOO
'Cause my dad Igneel didn't want me to!!
But even if you aren't a dragon, you're hardly human either, are you?
E.N.D. !!!
BWOOSH

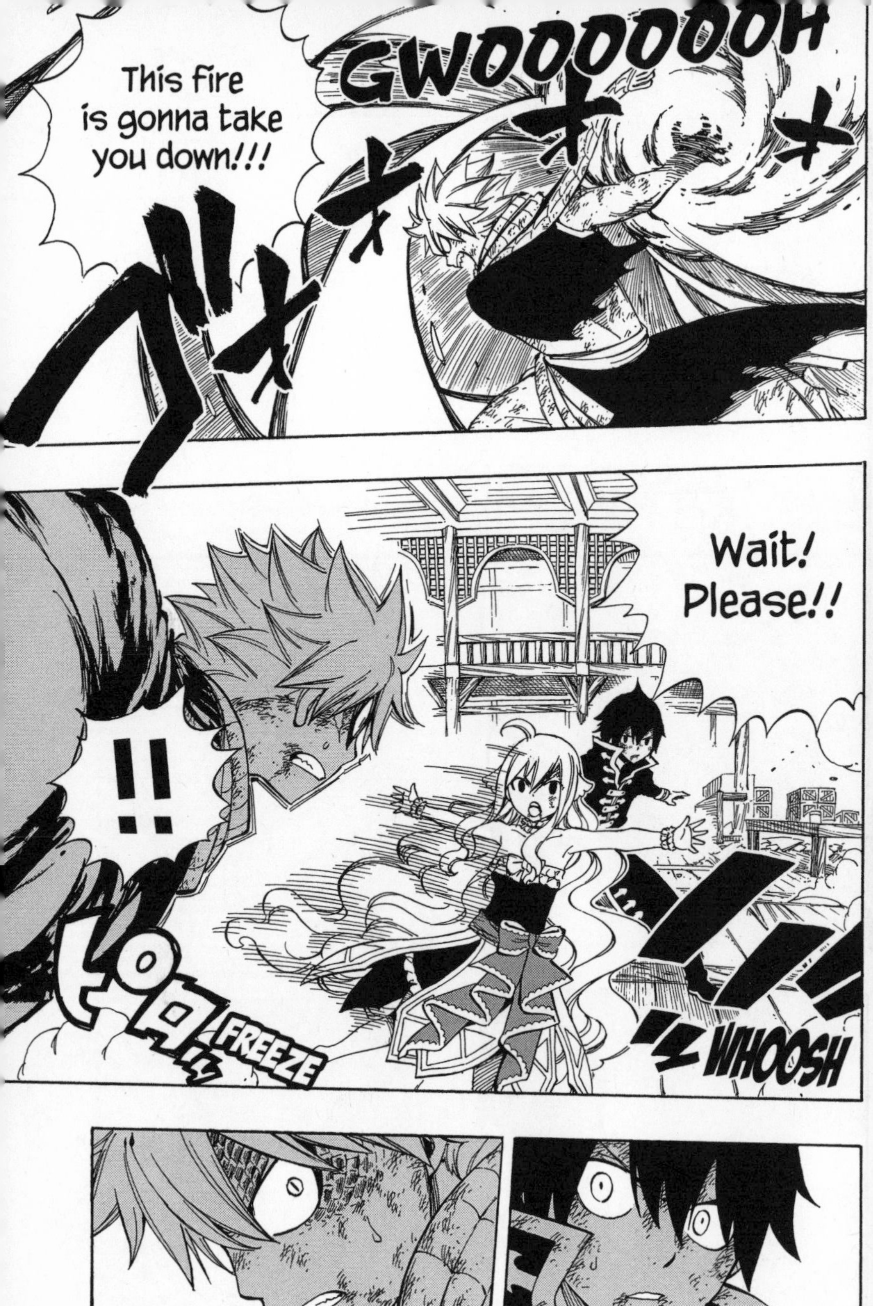
GWOOOOOOH
This fire is gonna take you down!!!
Wait! Please!!
!!
WHOOSH
FREEZE

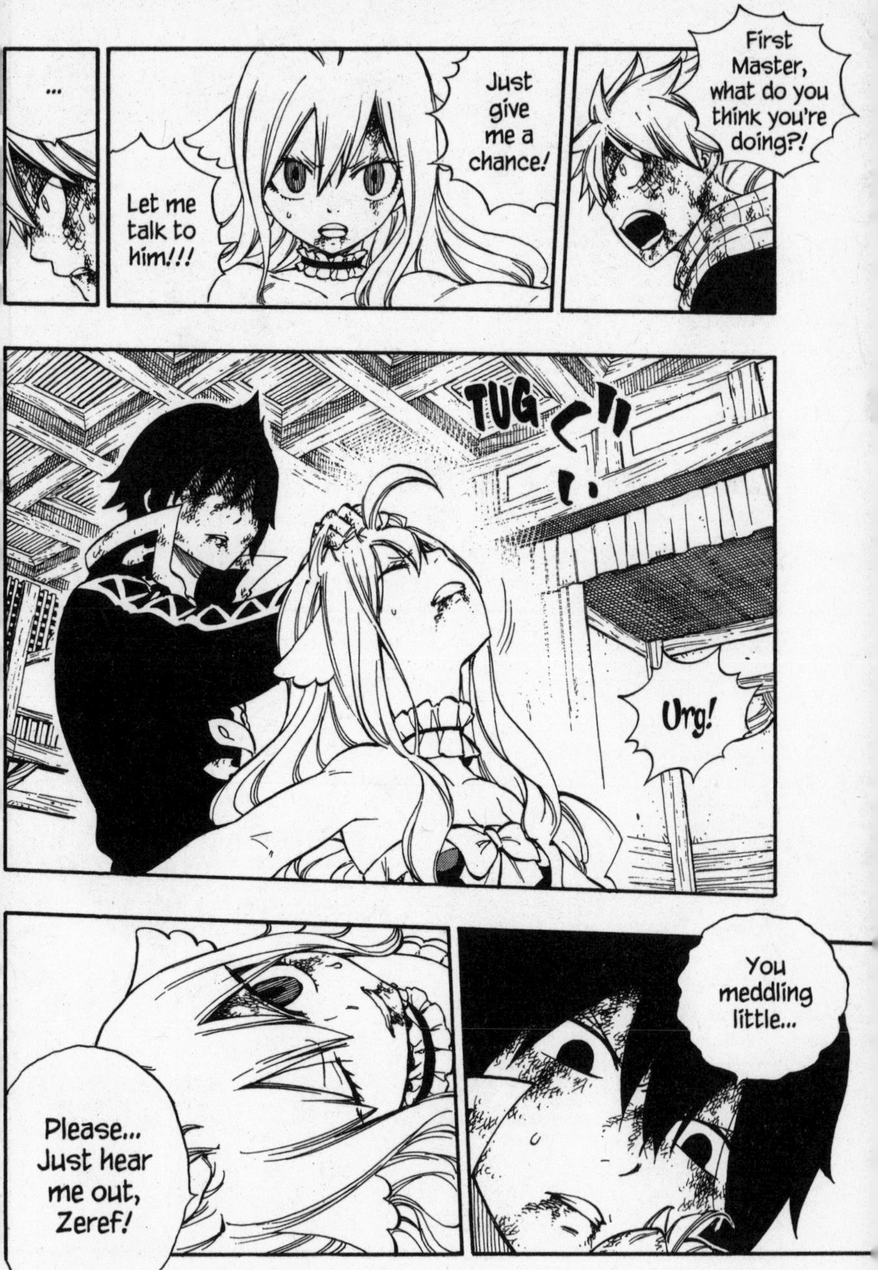
First Master, what do you think you're doing?!
Just give me a chance!
Let me talk to him!!!
...
TUG
Urg!
You meddling little...
Please... Just hear me out, Zeref!

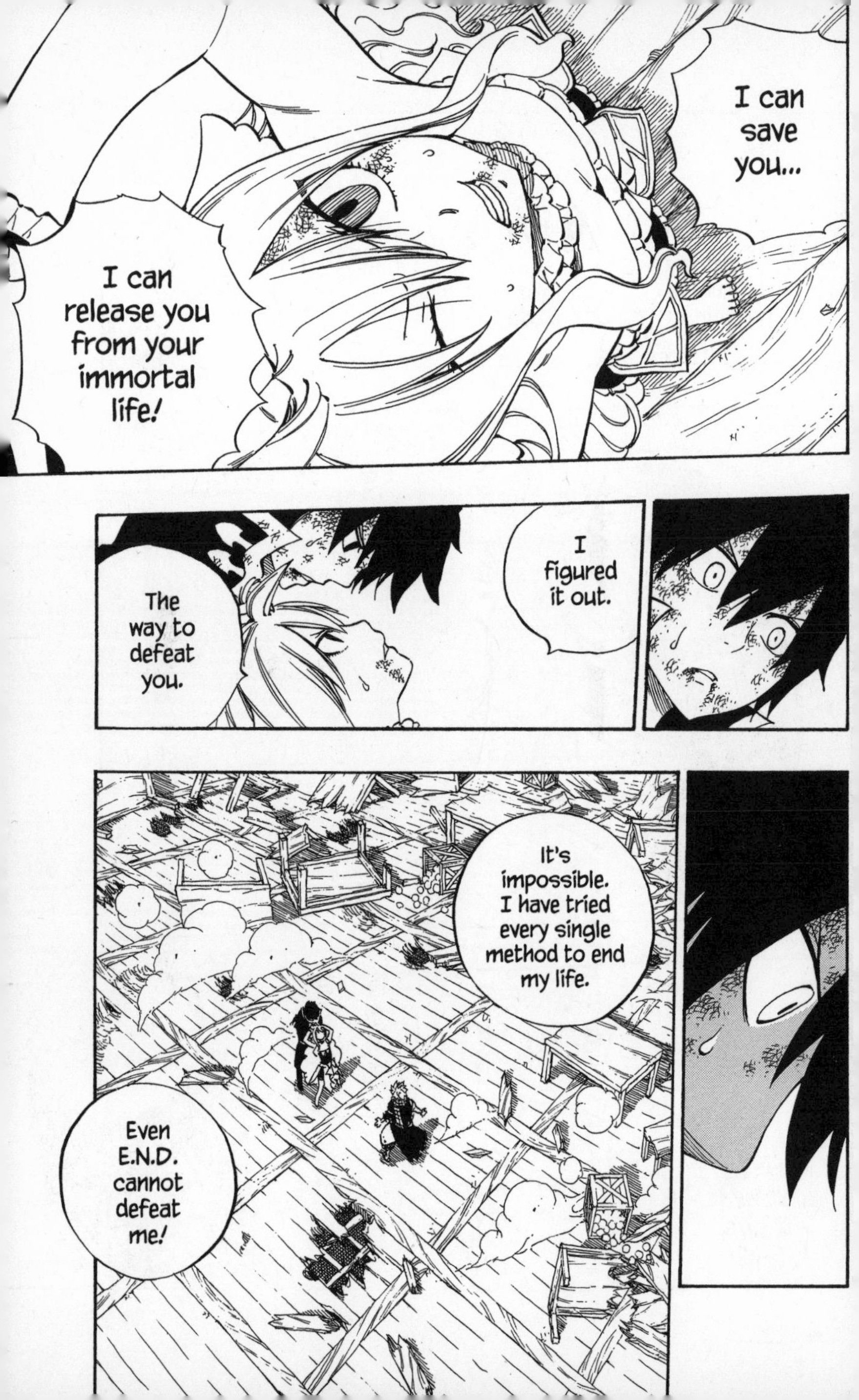
I can save you...
I can release you from your immortal life!
I figured it out.
The way to defeat you.
It's impossible. I have tried every single method to end my life.
Even E.N.D. cannot defeat me!

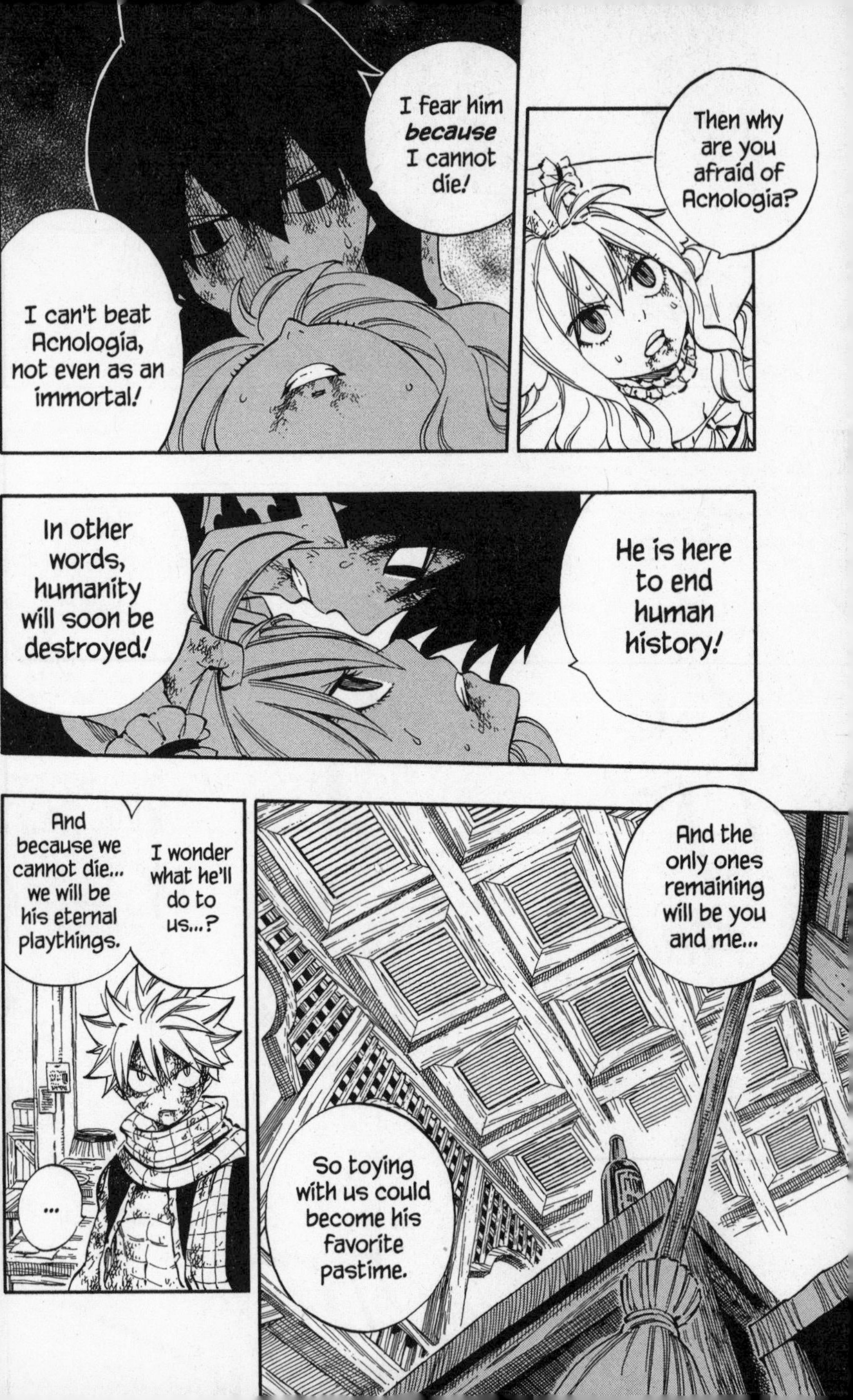
Then why are you afraid of Acnologia?
I fear him ***because*** I cannot die!
I can't beat Acnologia, not even as an immortal!
He is here to end human history!
In other words, humanity will soon be destroyed!
And the only ones remaining will be you and me...
So toying with us could become his favorite pastime.
And because we cannot die... we will be his eternal playthings.
I wonder what he'll do to us...?
...

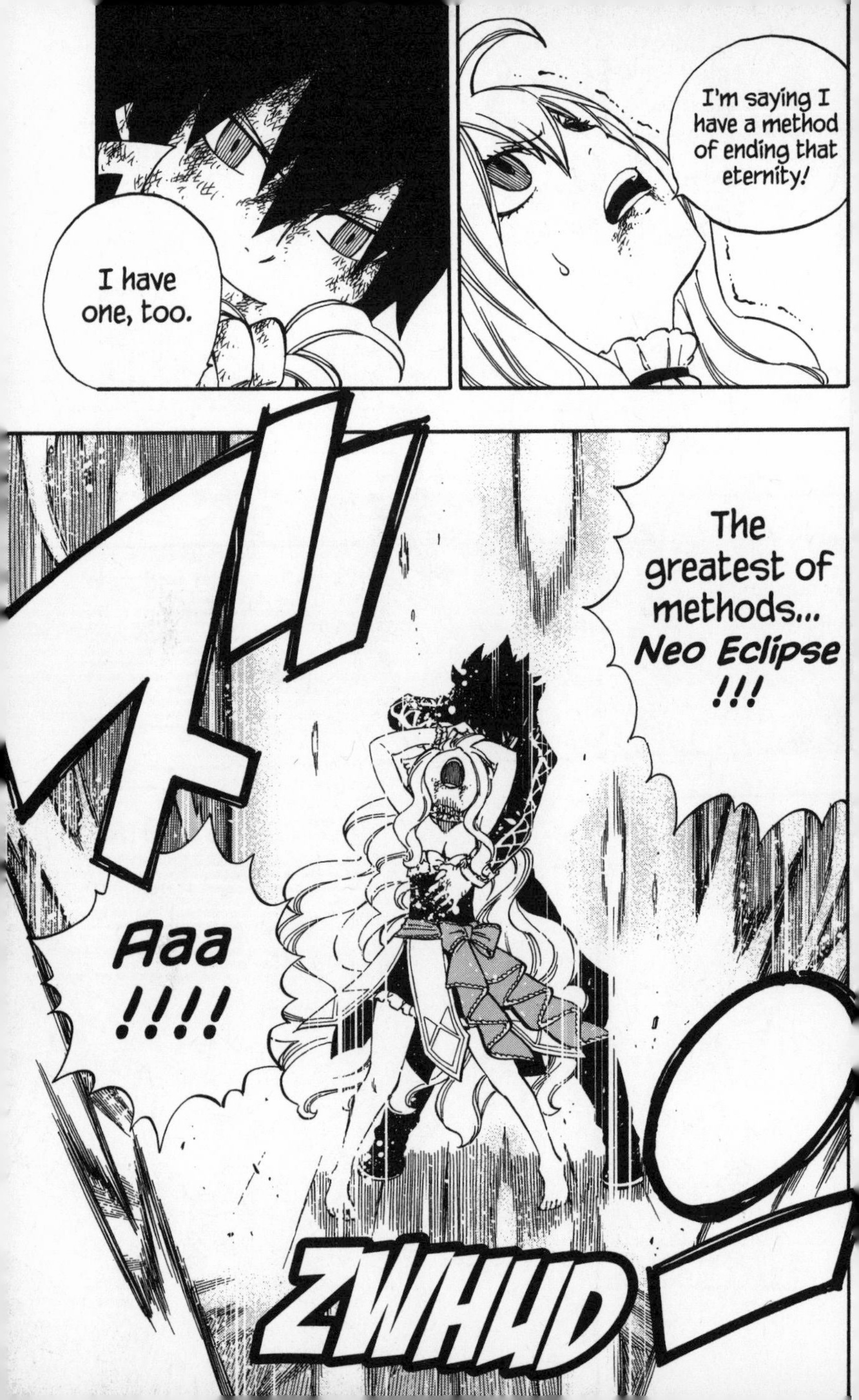
I'm saying I have a method of ending that eternity!
I have one, too.
The greatest of methods... *Neo Eclipse* !!!
Aaa !!!!
ZWHUD

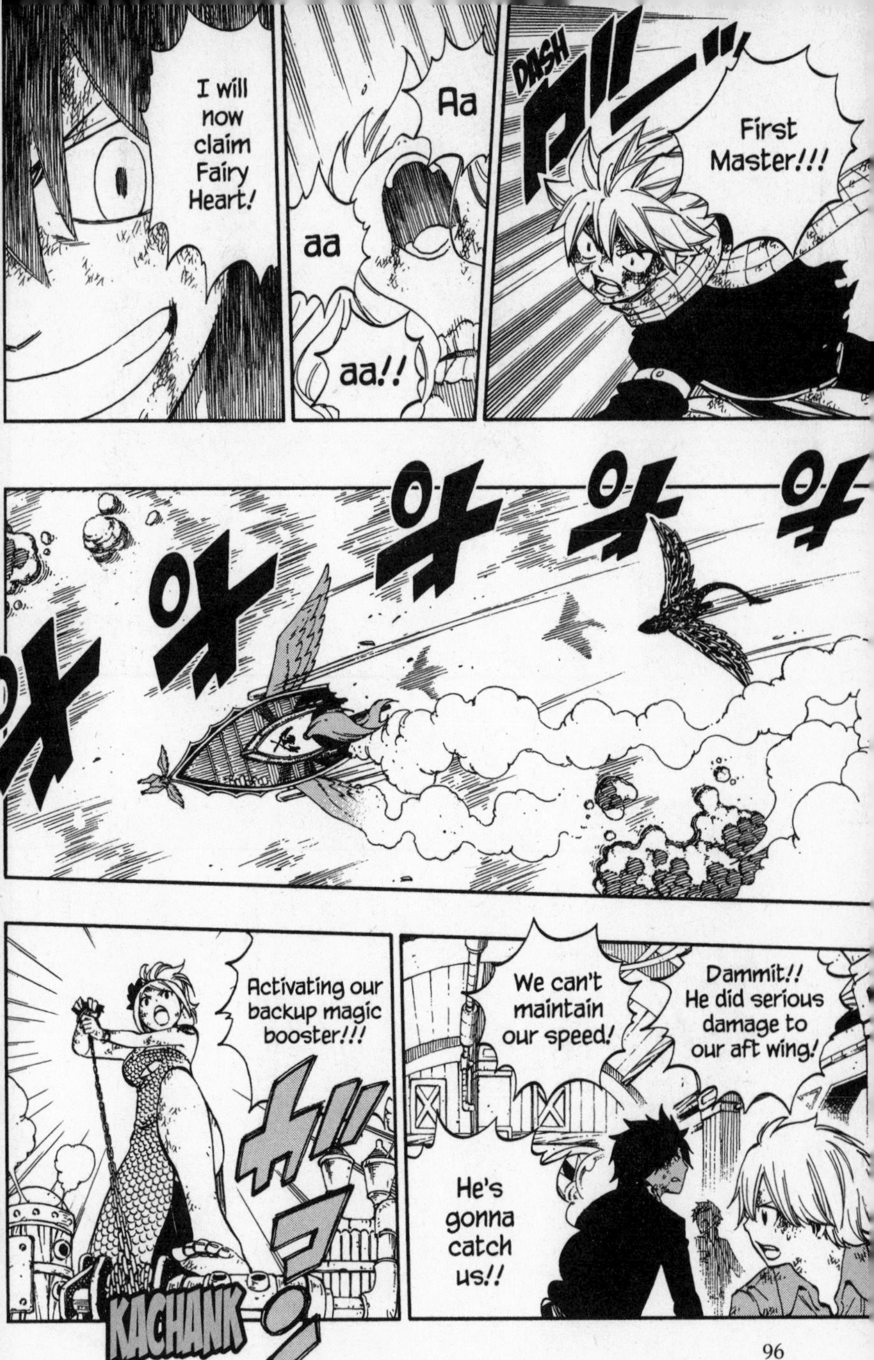
DASH
First Master!!!
Aa
aa
aa!!
I will now claim Fairy Heart!
Dammit!! He did serious damage to our aft wing!
We can't maintain our speed!
He's gonna catch us!!
Activating our backup magic booster!!!
KACHANK

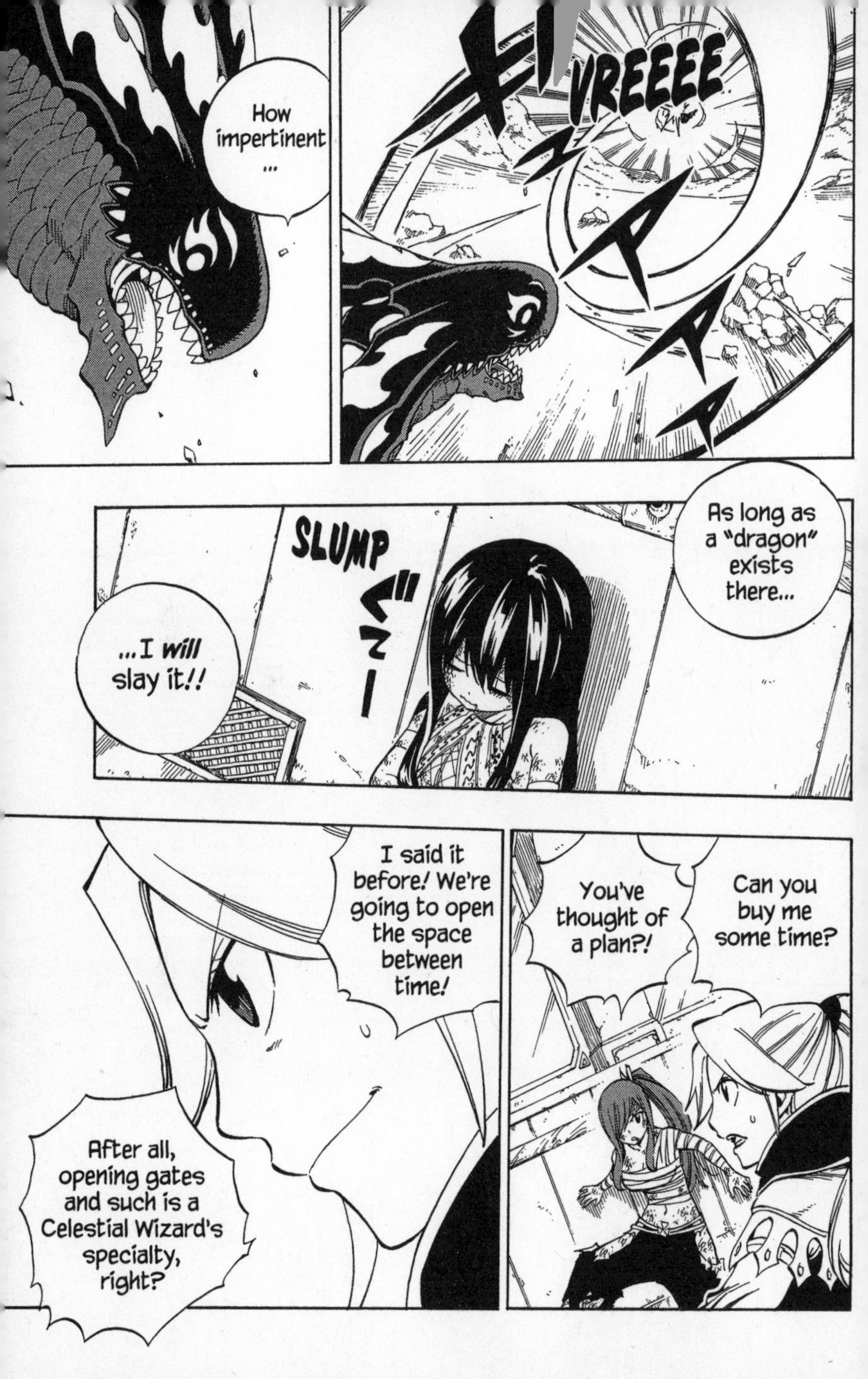
VREEEE
How impertinent ...
As long as a "dragon" exists there...
SLUMP
...I will slay it!!
Can you buy me some time?
You've thought of a plan?!
I said it before! We're going to open the space between time!
After all, opening gates and such is a Celestial Wizard's specialty, right?

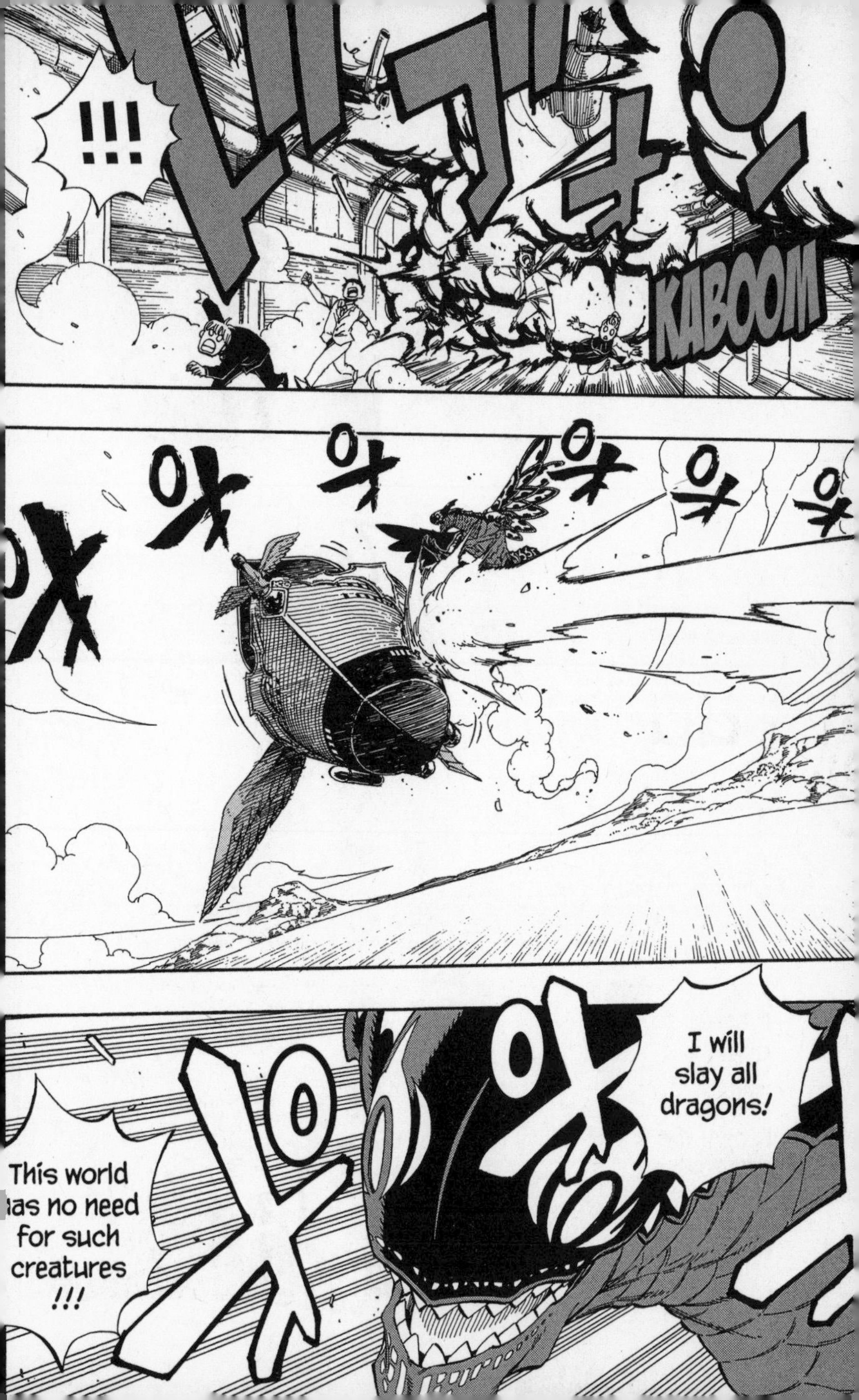
KABOOM
!!!
I will slay all dragons!
This world has no need for such creatures !!!

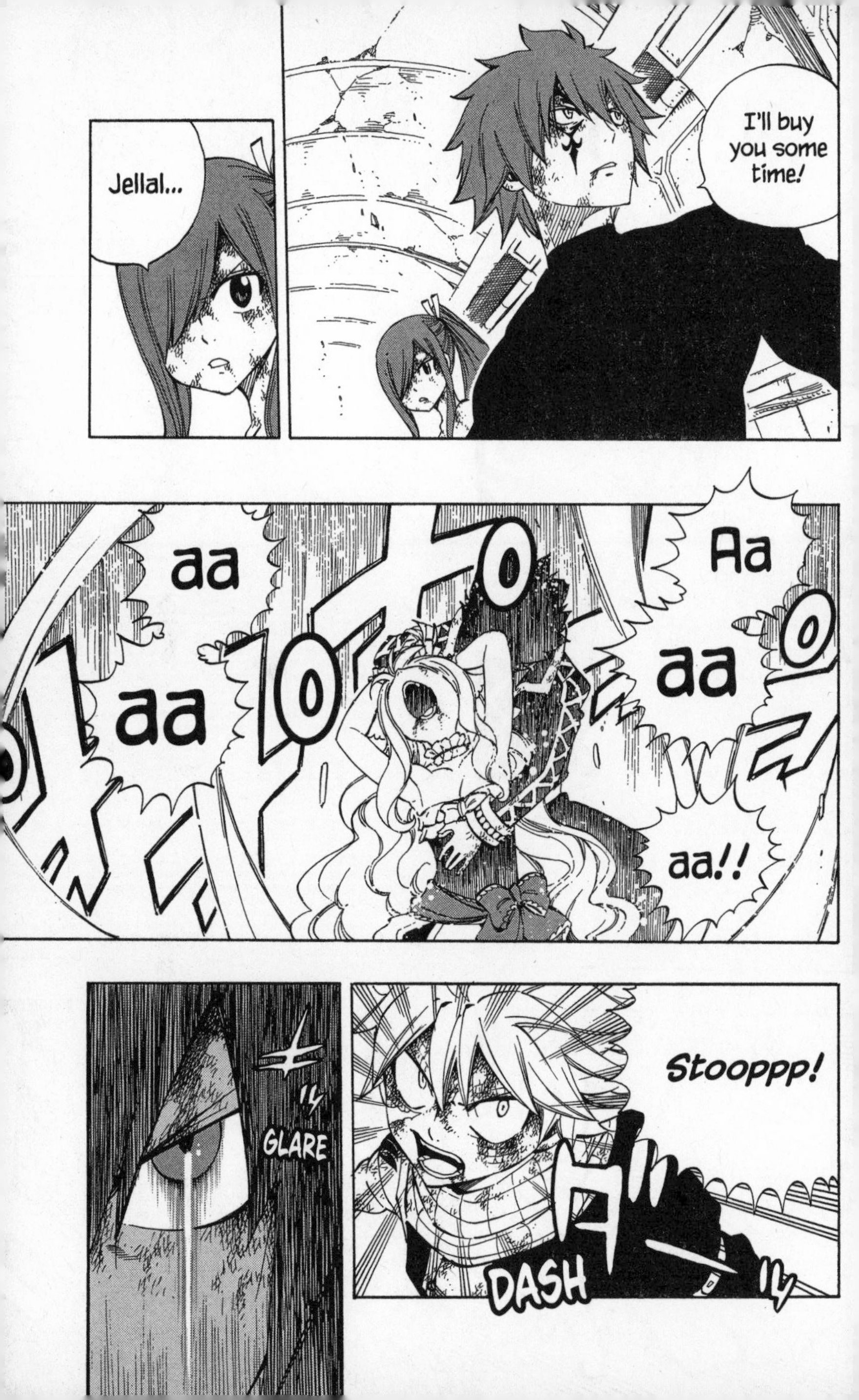

I'll buy you some time!
Jellal...
Aa
aa
aa!!
aa
aa
Stooppp!
DASH
GLARE

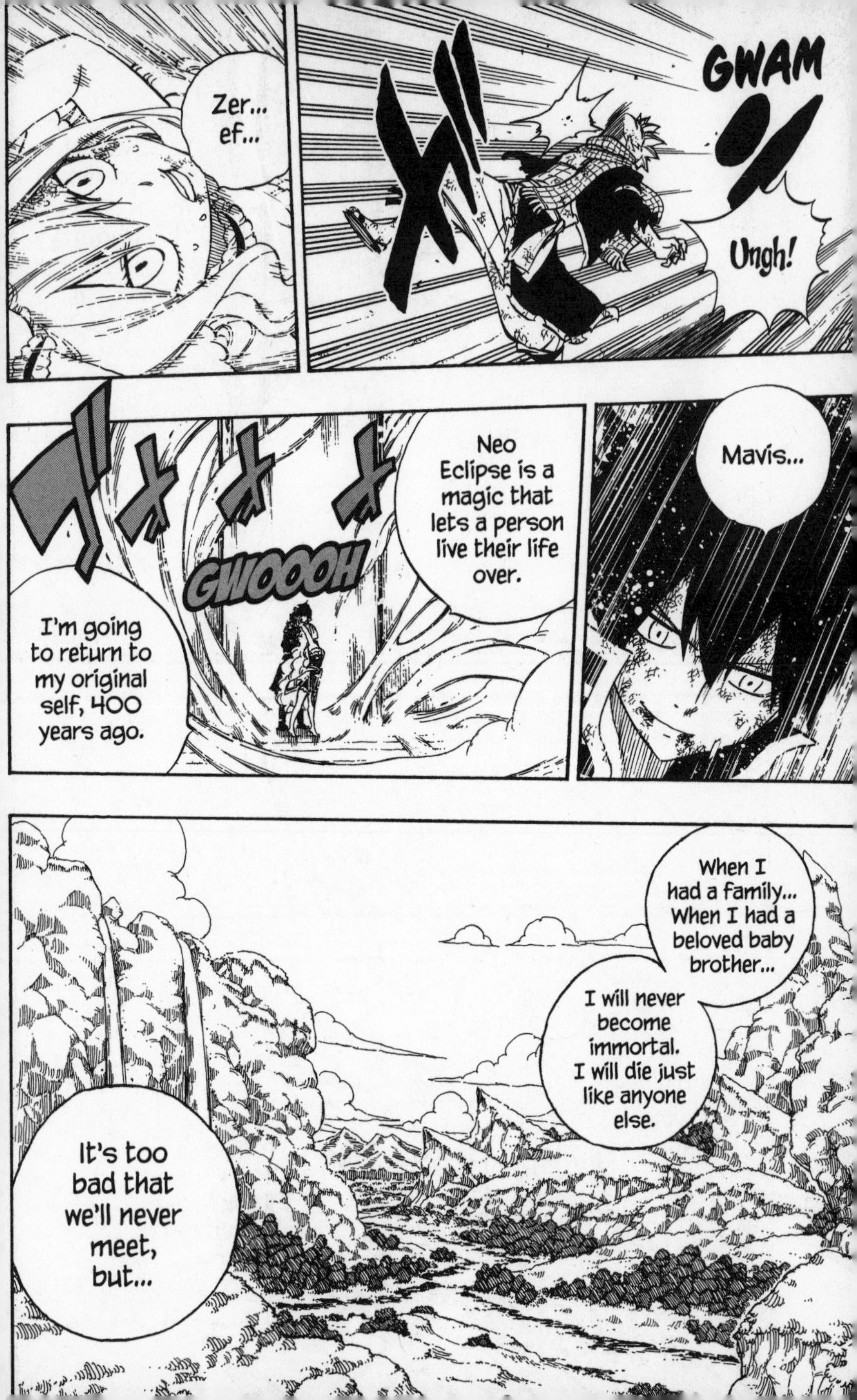
GWAM
Ungh!
Zer... ef...
Mavis...
Neo Eclipse is a magic that lets a person live their life over.
GWOOOH
I'm going to return to my original self, 400 years ago.
When I had a family... When I had a beloved baby brother...
I will never become immortal. I will die just like anyone else.
It's too bad that we'll never meet, but...

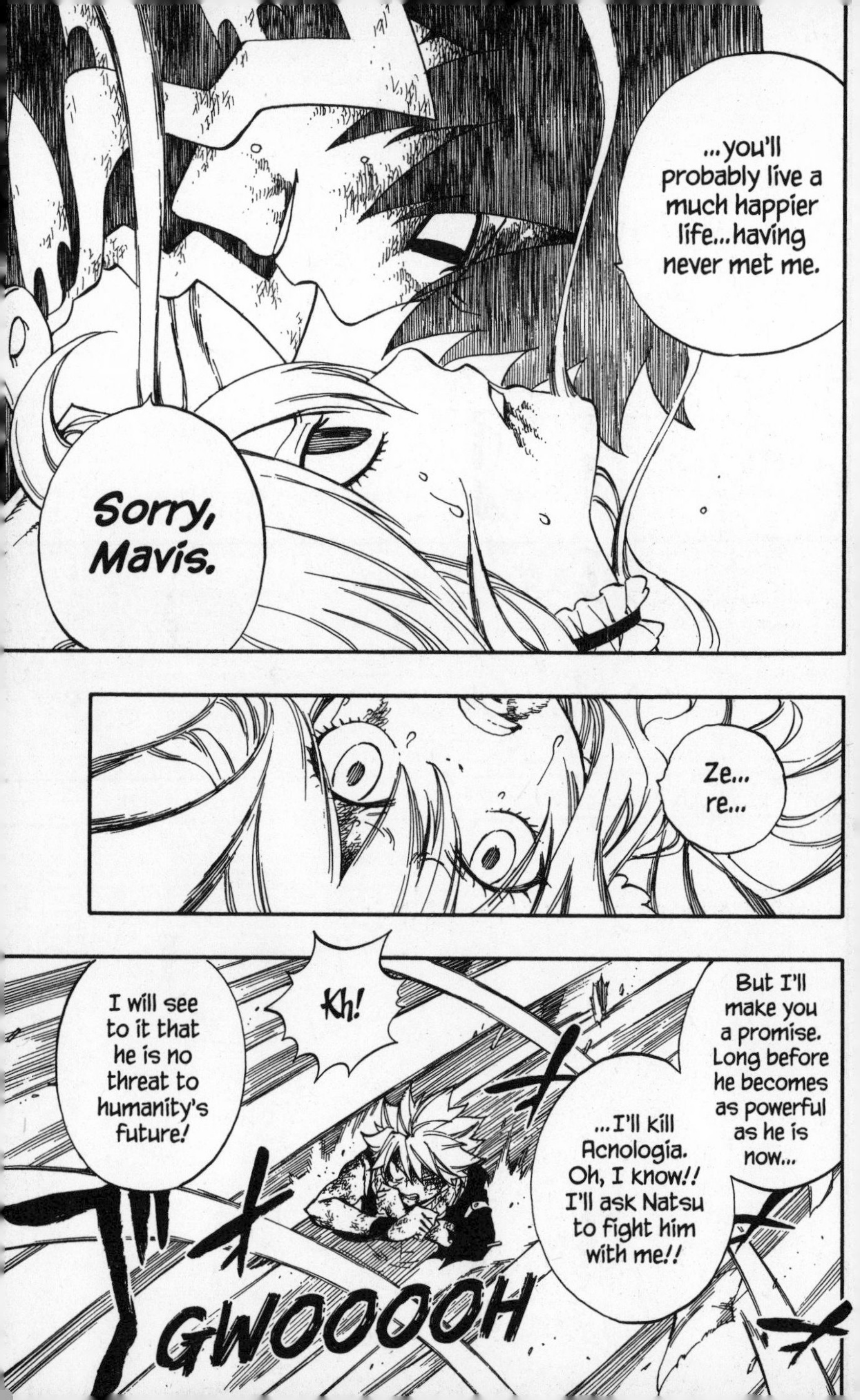

...you'll probably live a much happier life...having never met me.
Sorry, Mavis.
Ze... re...
But I'll make you a promise. Long before he becomes as powerful as he is now...
...I'll kill Acnologia. Oh, I know!! I'll ask Natsu to fight him with me!!
Kh!
I will see to it that he is no threat to humanity's future!
GWOOOOOH

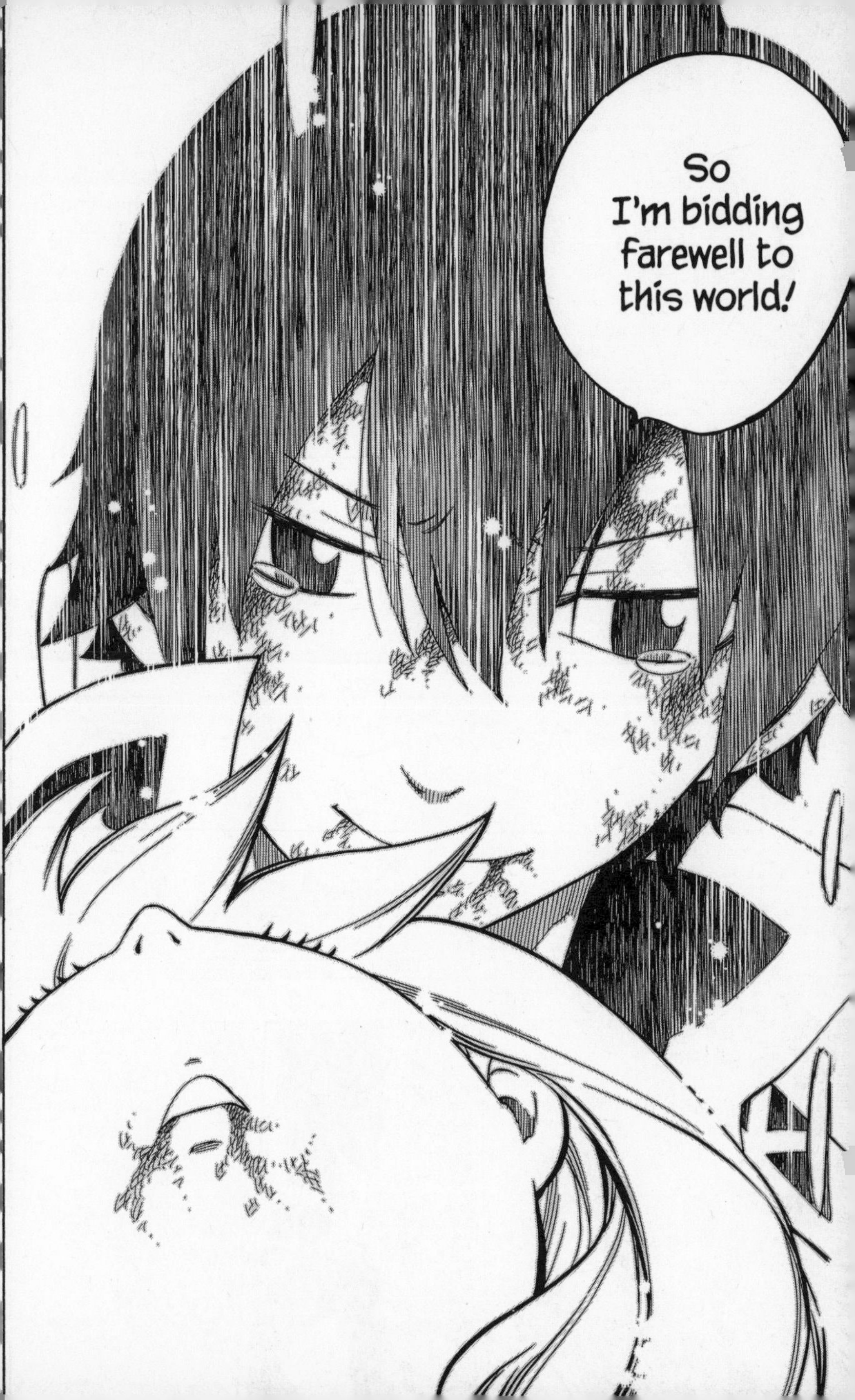
So I'm bidding farewell to this world!

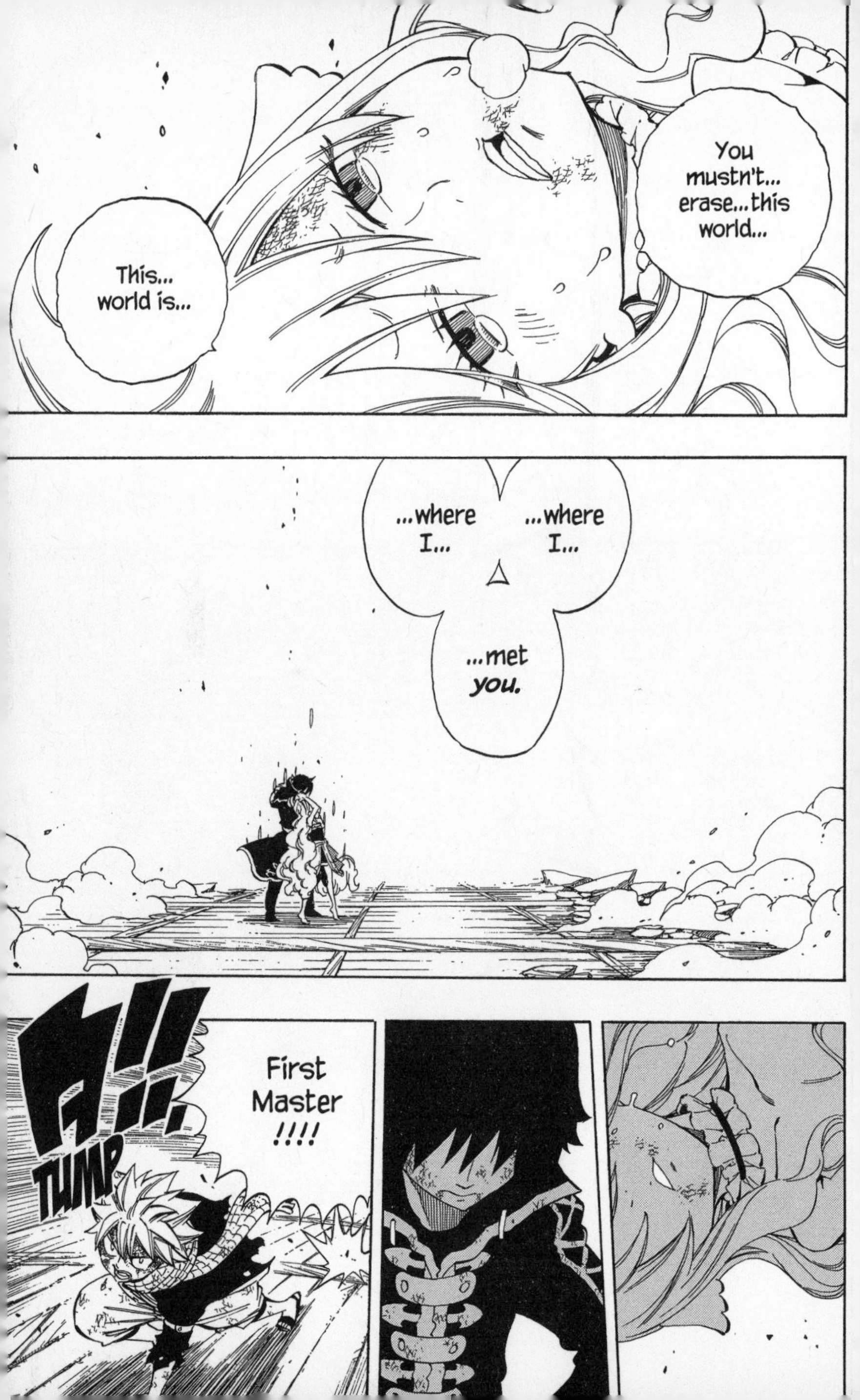
You mustn't... erase...this world...
This... world is...
...where I... ...where I... ...met *you.*
First Master !!!!
TUMP

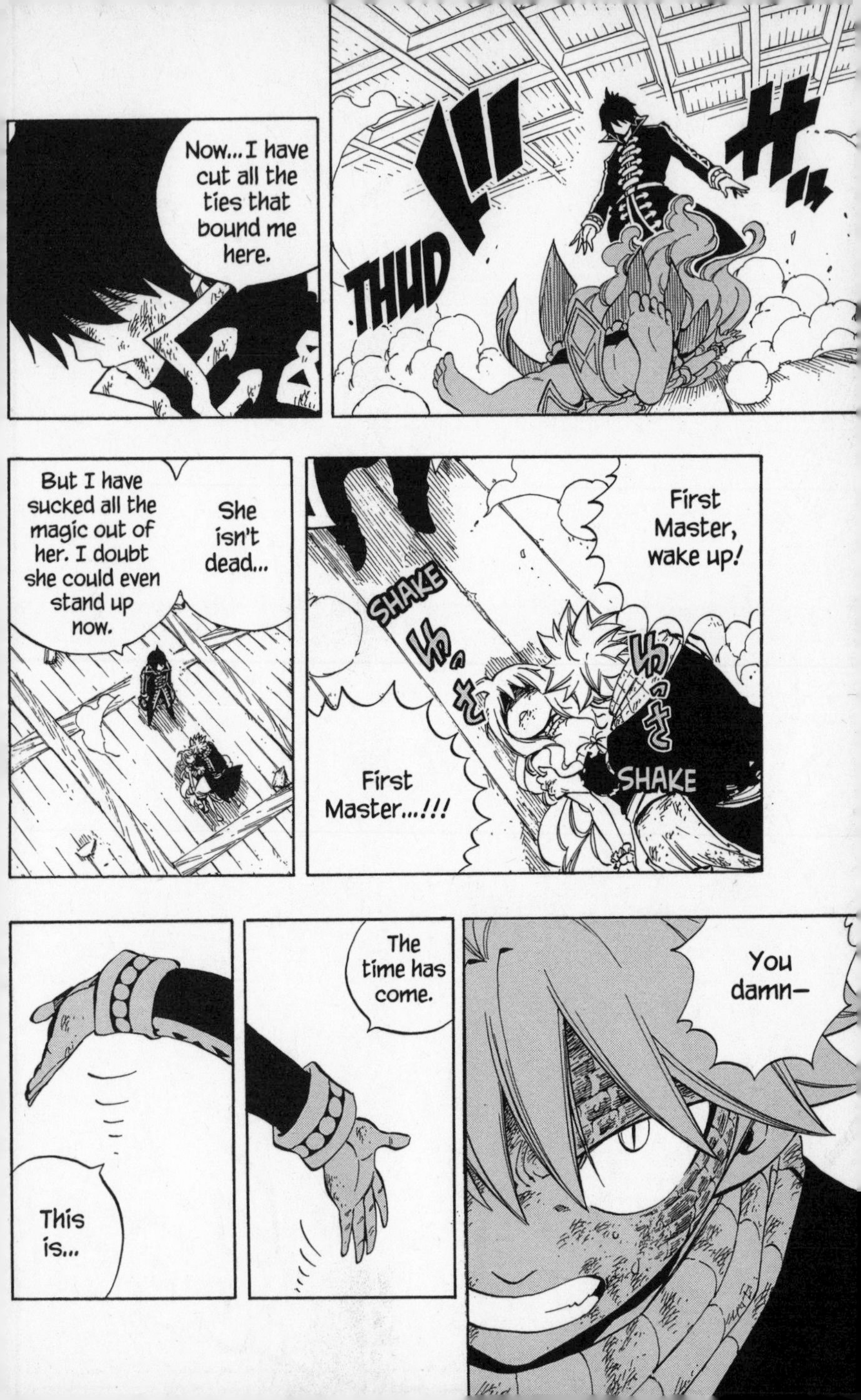
THUD
Now... I have cut all the ties that bound me here.
First Master, wake up!
SHAKE
SHAKE
First Master...!!!
She isn't dead...
But I have sucked all the magic out of her. I doubt she could even stand up now.
You damn—
The time has come.
This is...

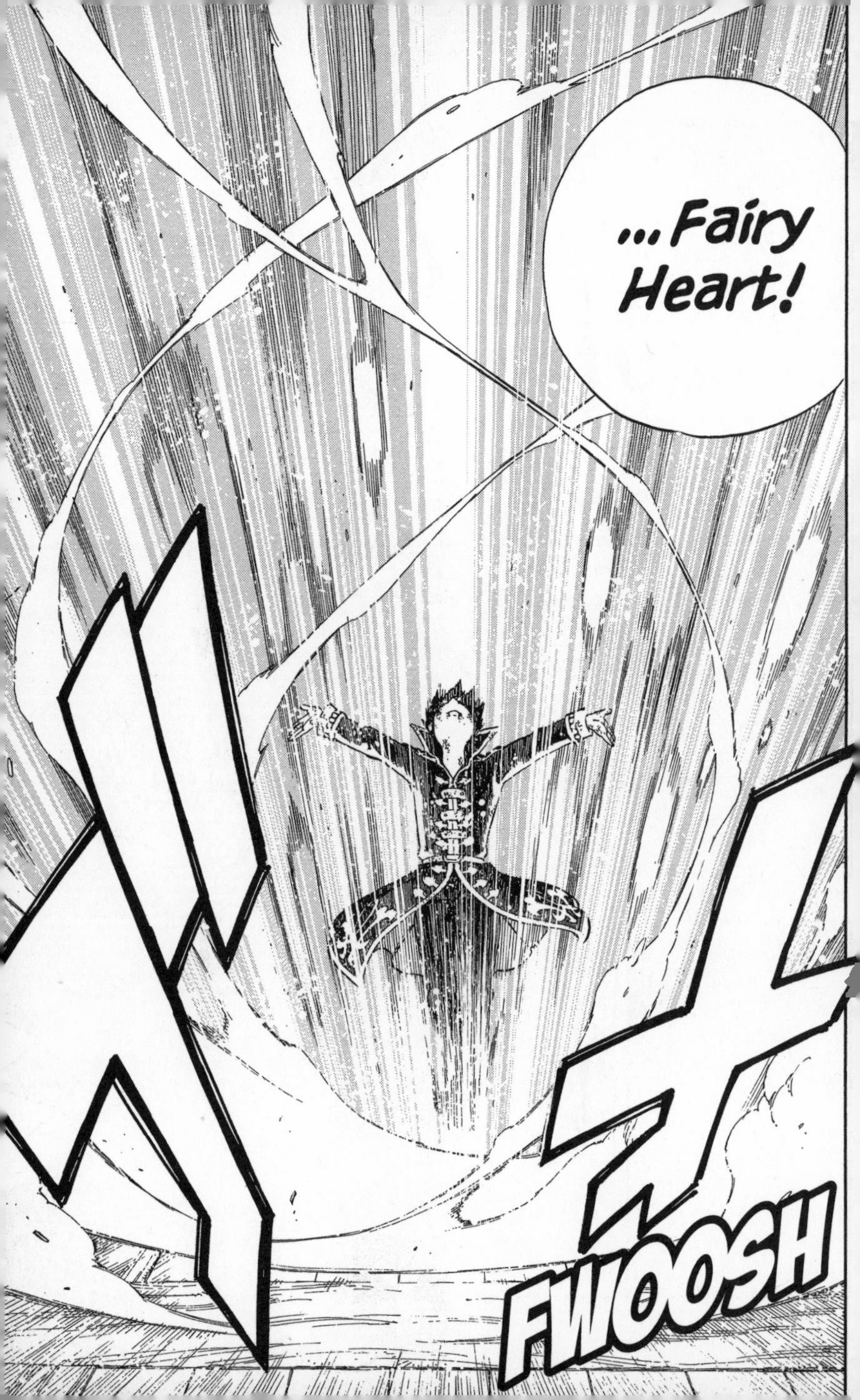
...Fairy Heart!
FWOOSH

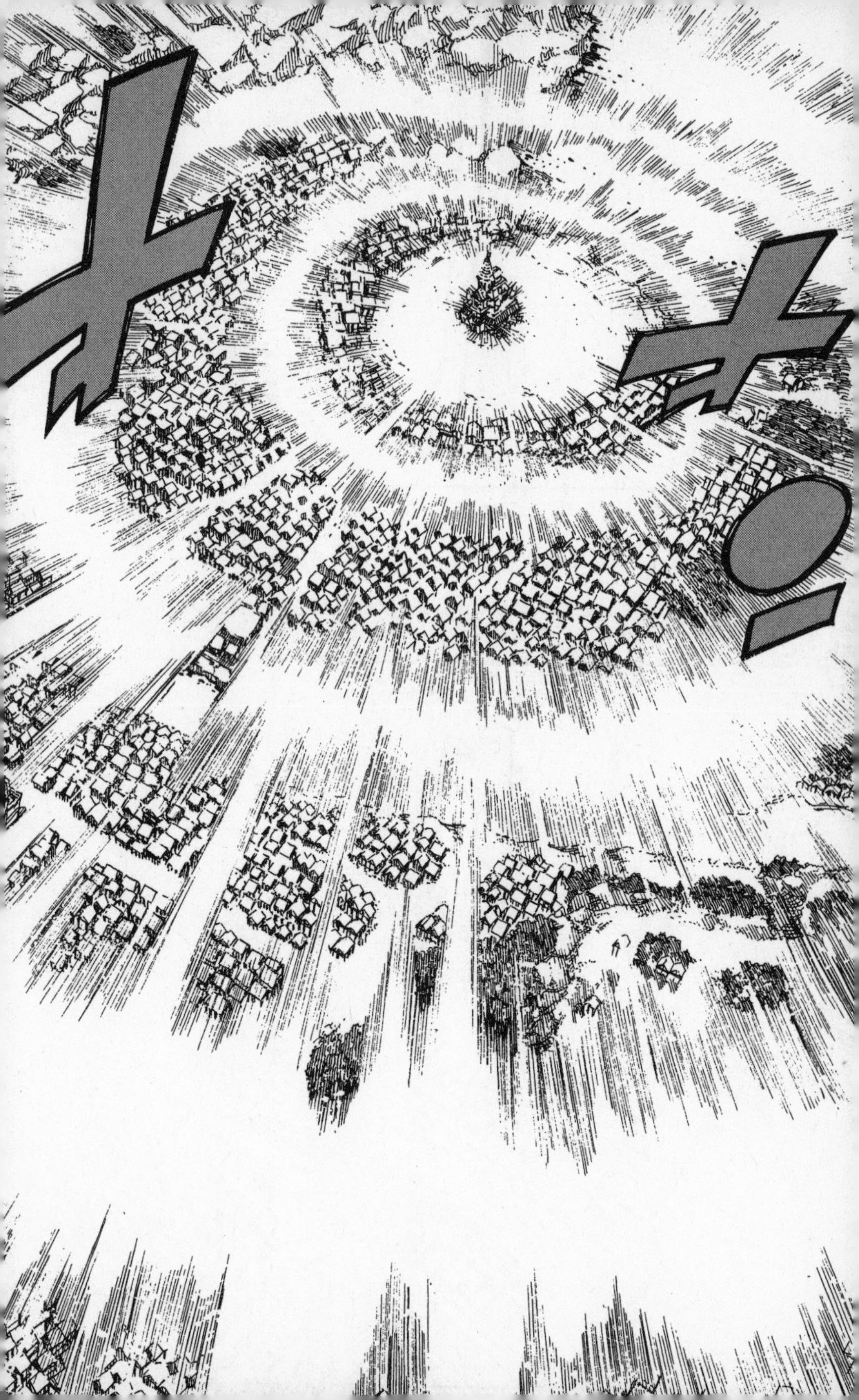

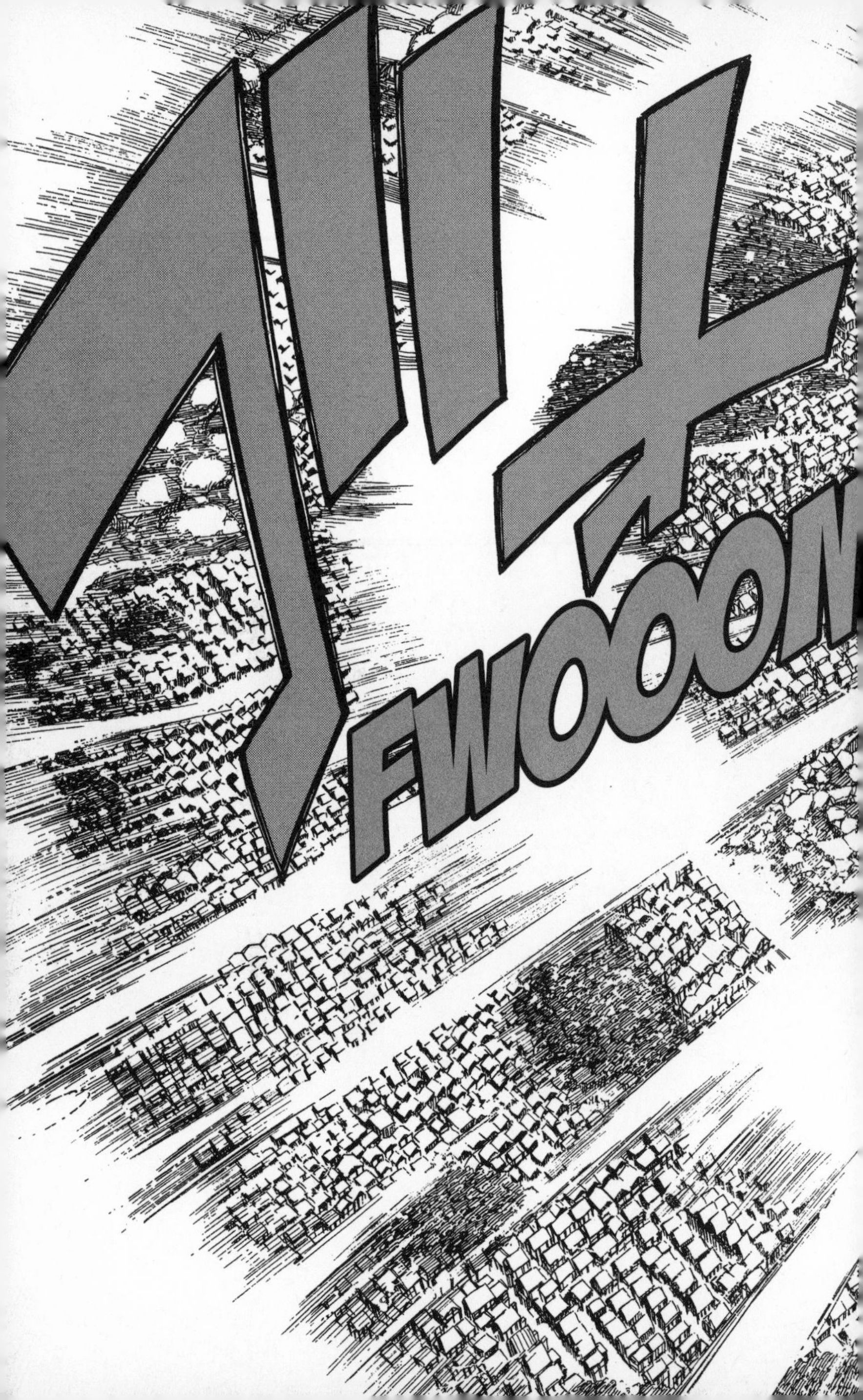
FWOOOM

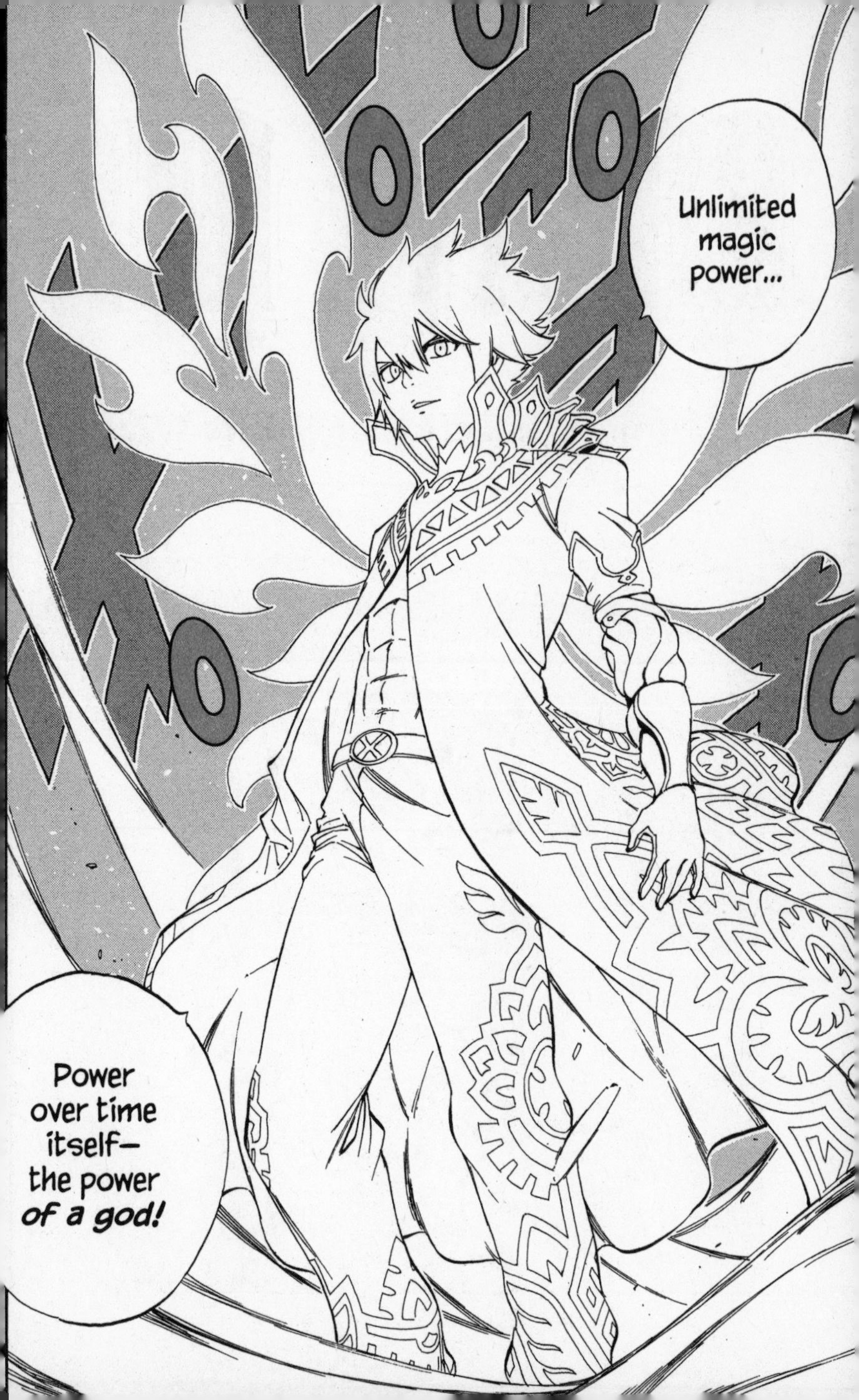
Unlimited magic power...
Power over time itself—the power of a god!

FAIRY TAIL

フェアリーテイル

Chapter 533: Zeref the White Wizard

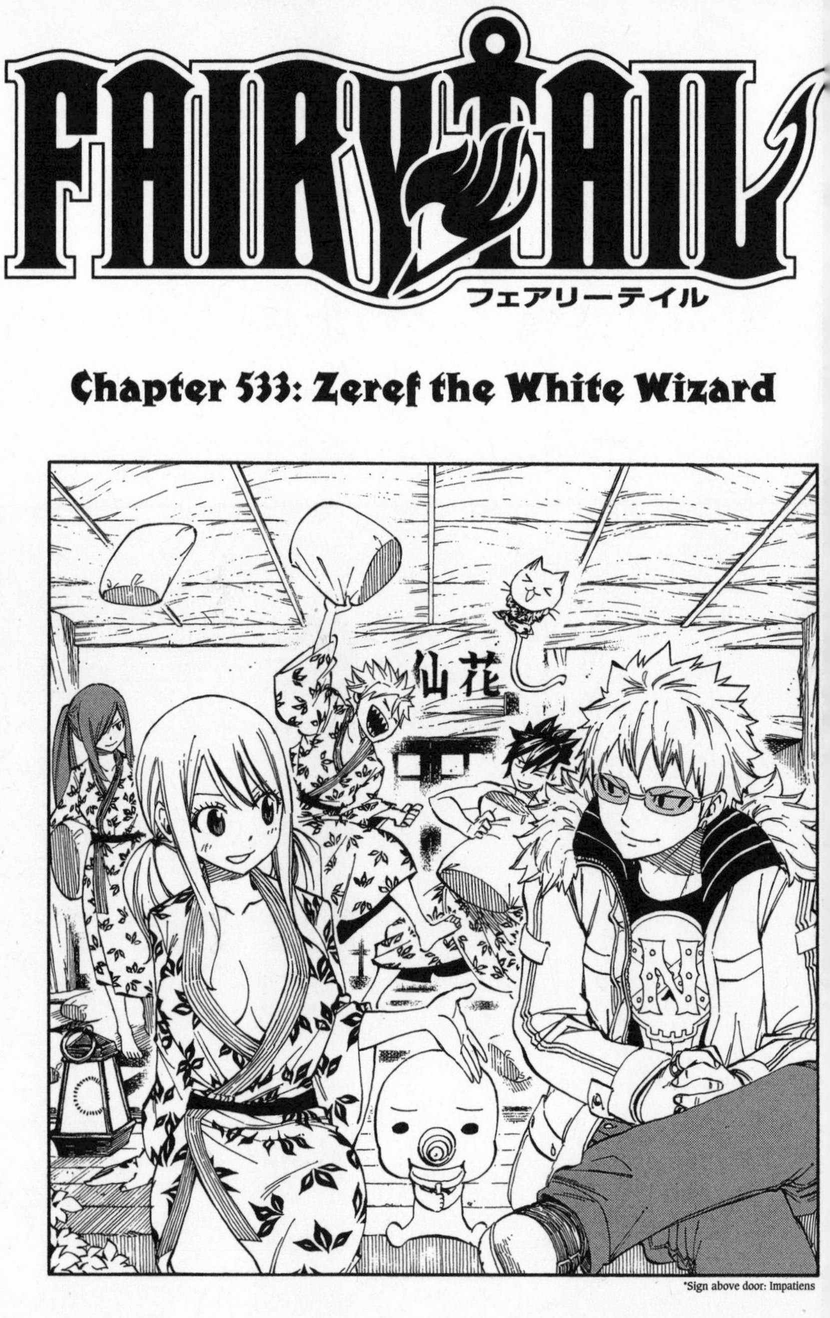
仙花

*Sign above door: Impatiens

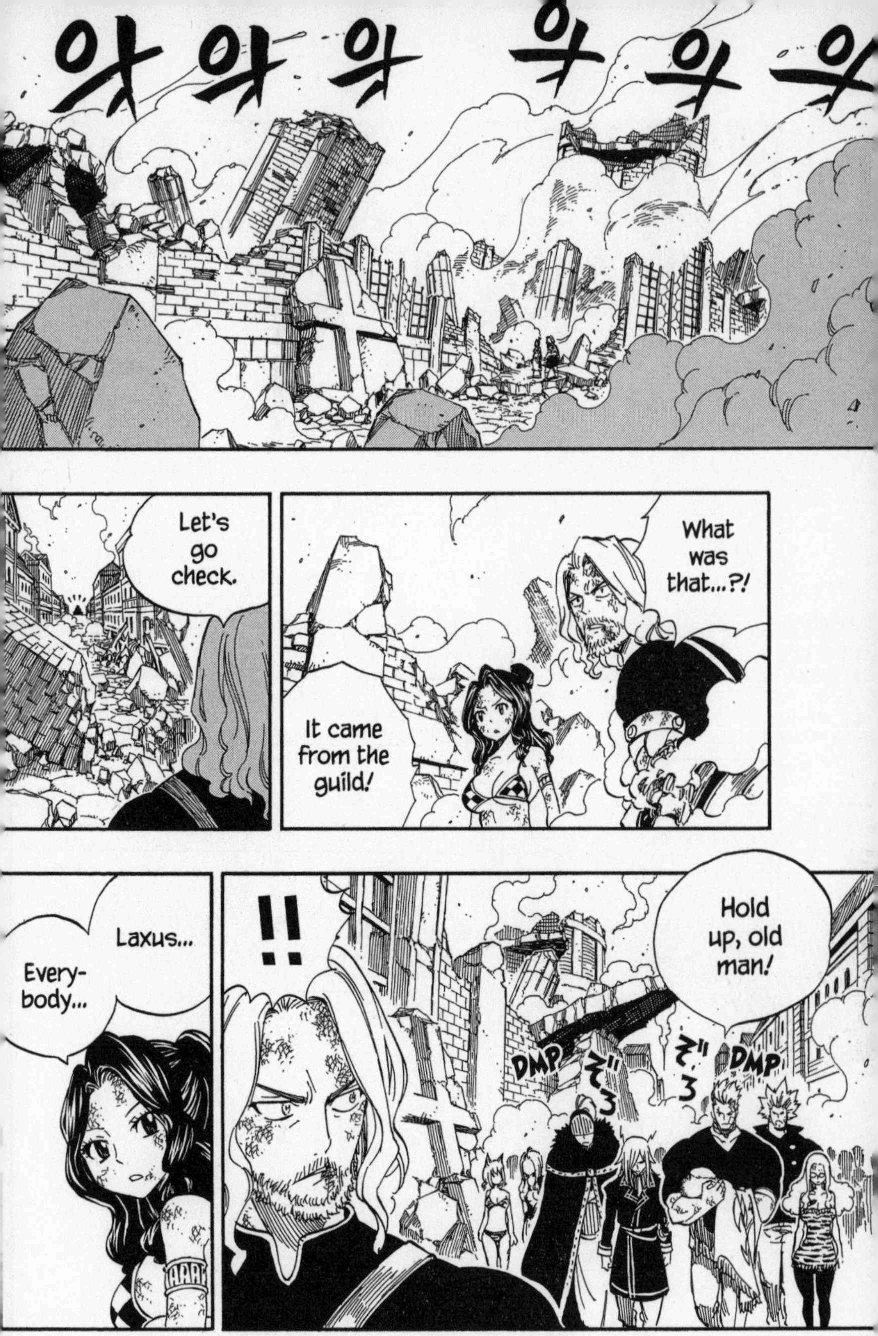
약약약 약약약
What was that...?!
It came from the guild!
Let's go check.
Hold up, old man!
DMP
DMP
!!
Laxus...
Every-body...

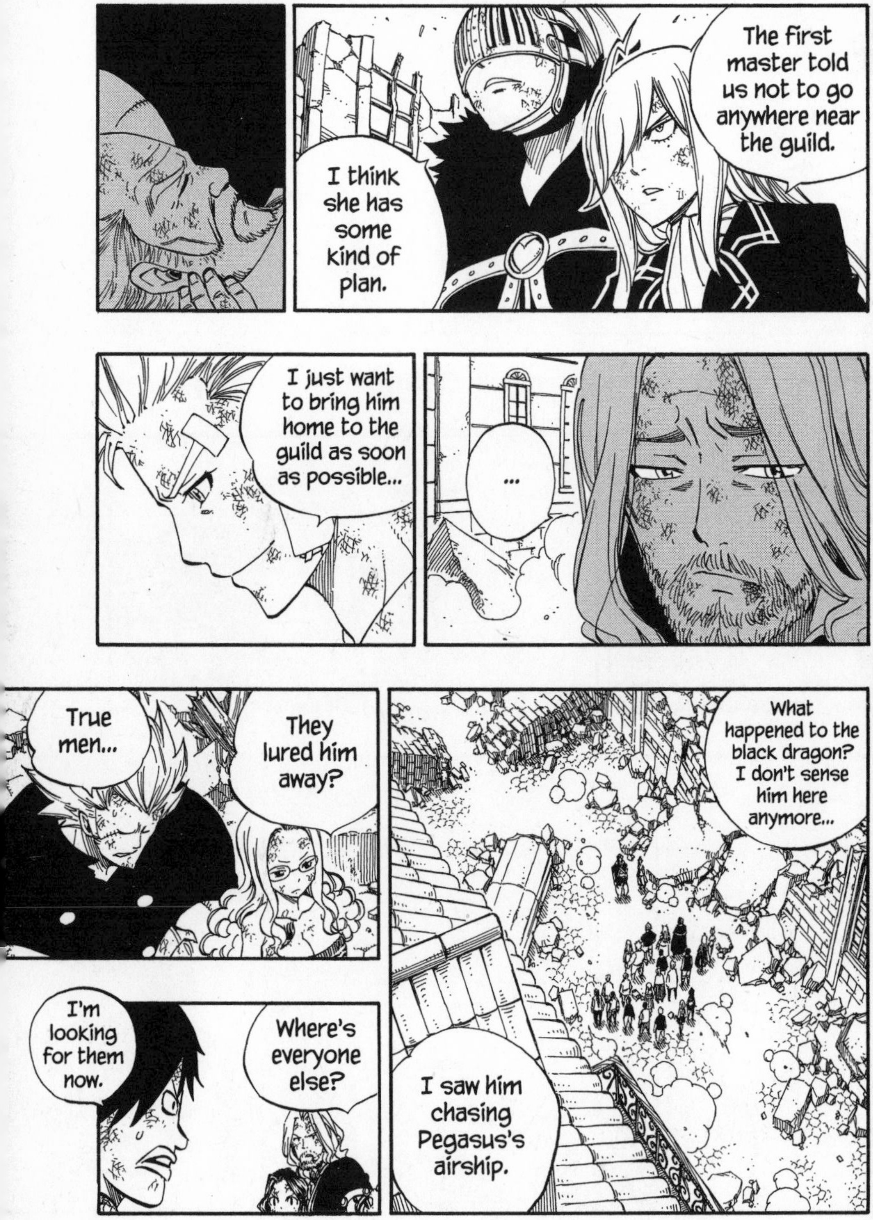

The first master told us not to go anywhere near the guild.
I think she has some kind of plan.
...
I just want to bring him home to the guild as soon as possible...
What happened to the black dragon? I don't sense him here anymore...
I saw him chasing Pegasus's airship.
They lured him away?
True men...
Where's everyone else?
I'm looking for them now.

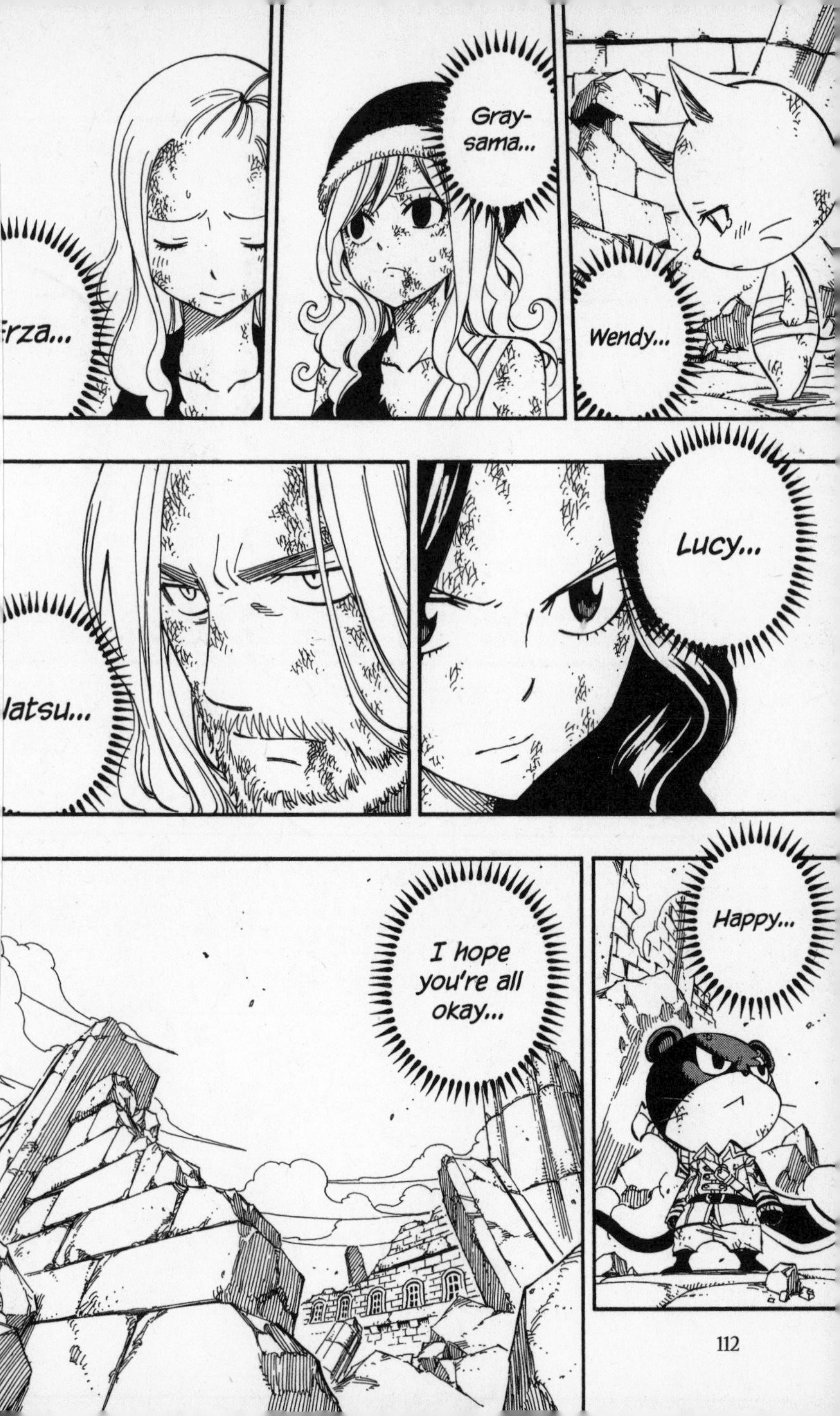
Wendy...
Gray-sama...
rza...
Lucy...
latsu...
Happy...
I hope you're all okay...

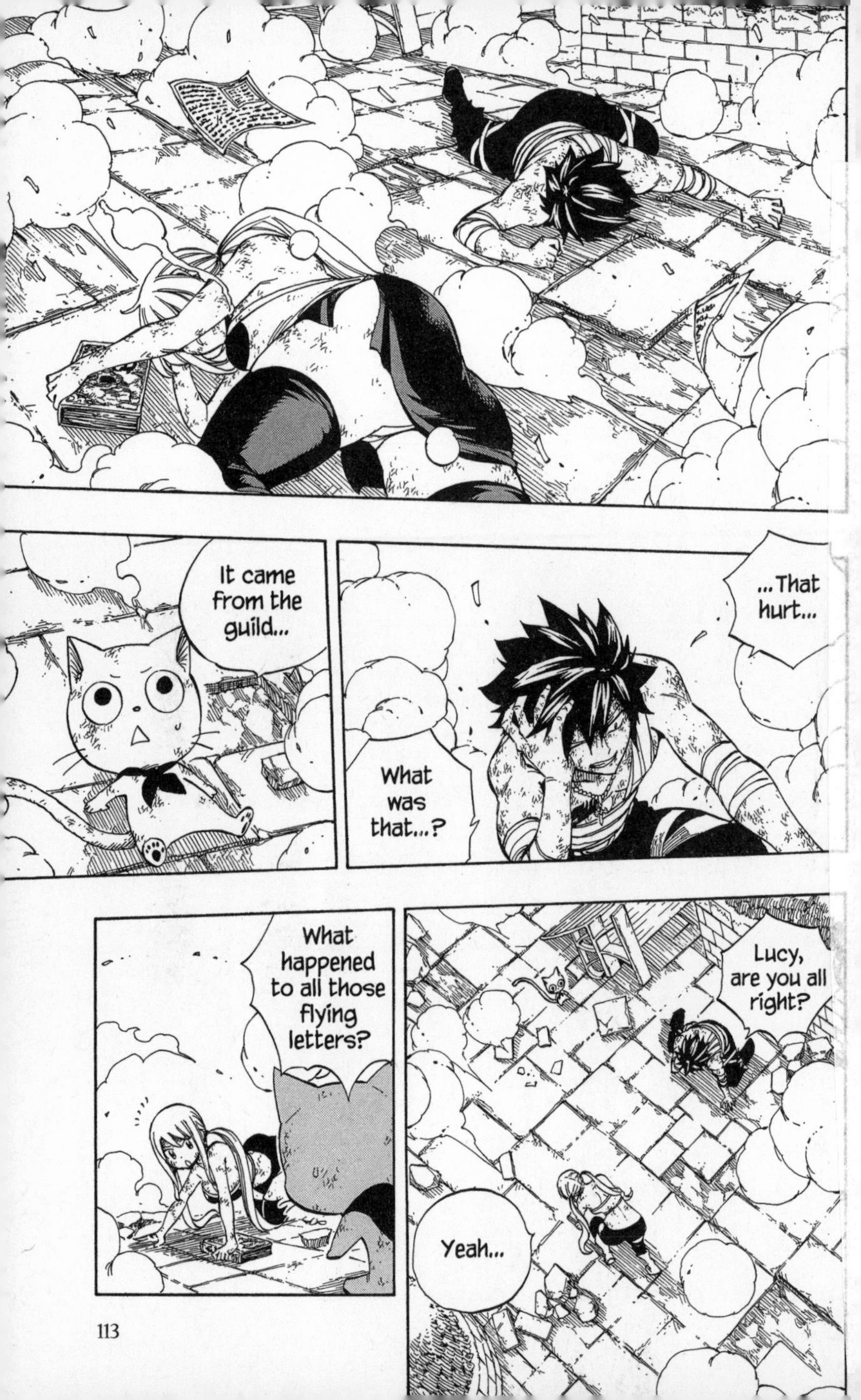
...That hurt...
What was that...?
It came from the guild...
Lucy, are you all right?
Yeah...
What happened to all those flying letters?

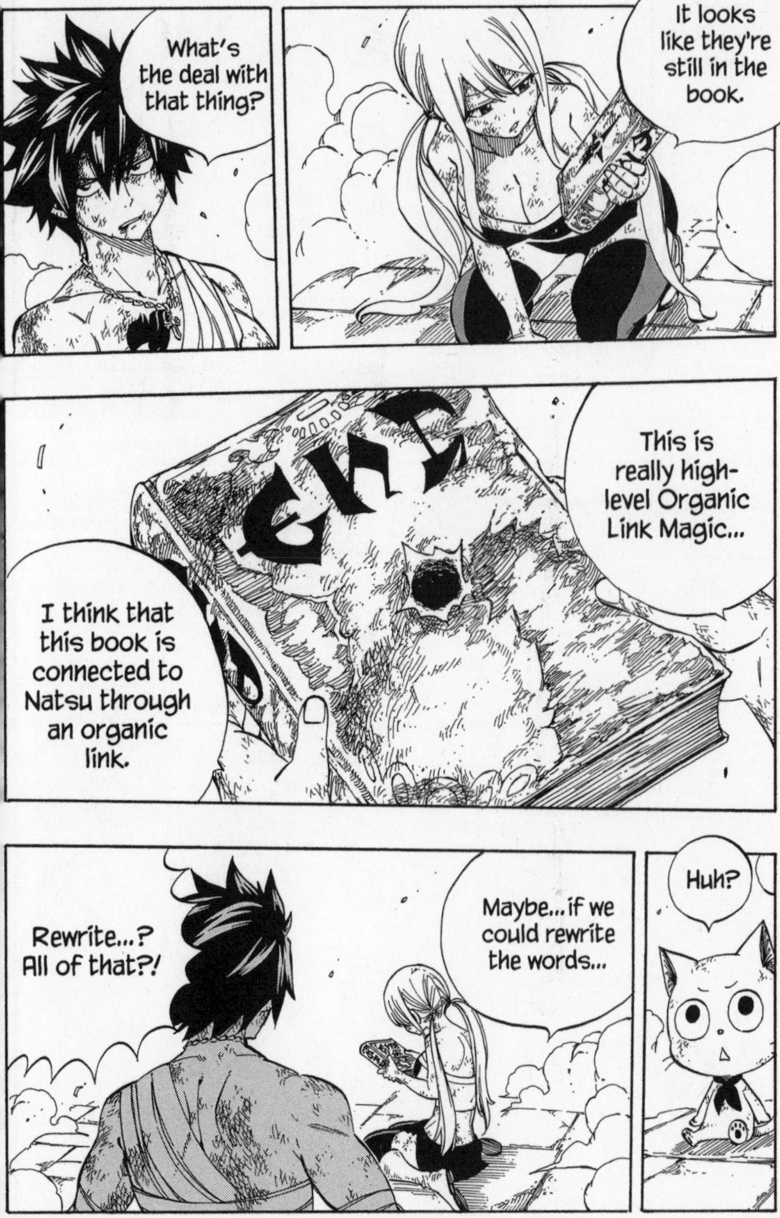
It looks like they're still in the book.
What's the deal with that thing?
This is really high-level Organic Link Magic...
I think that this book is connected to Natsu through an organic link.
Huh?
Maybe...if we could rewrite the words...
Rewrite...? All of that?!

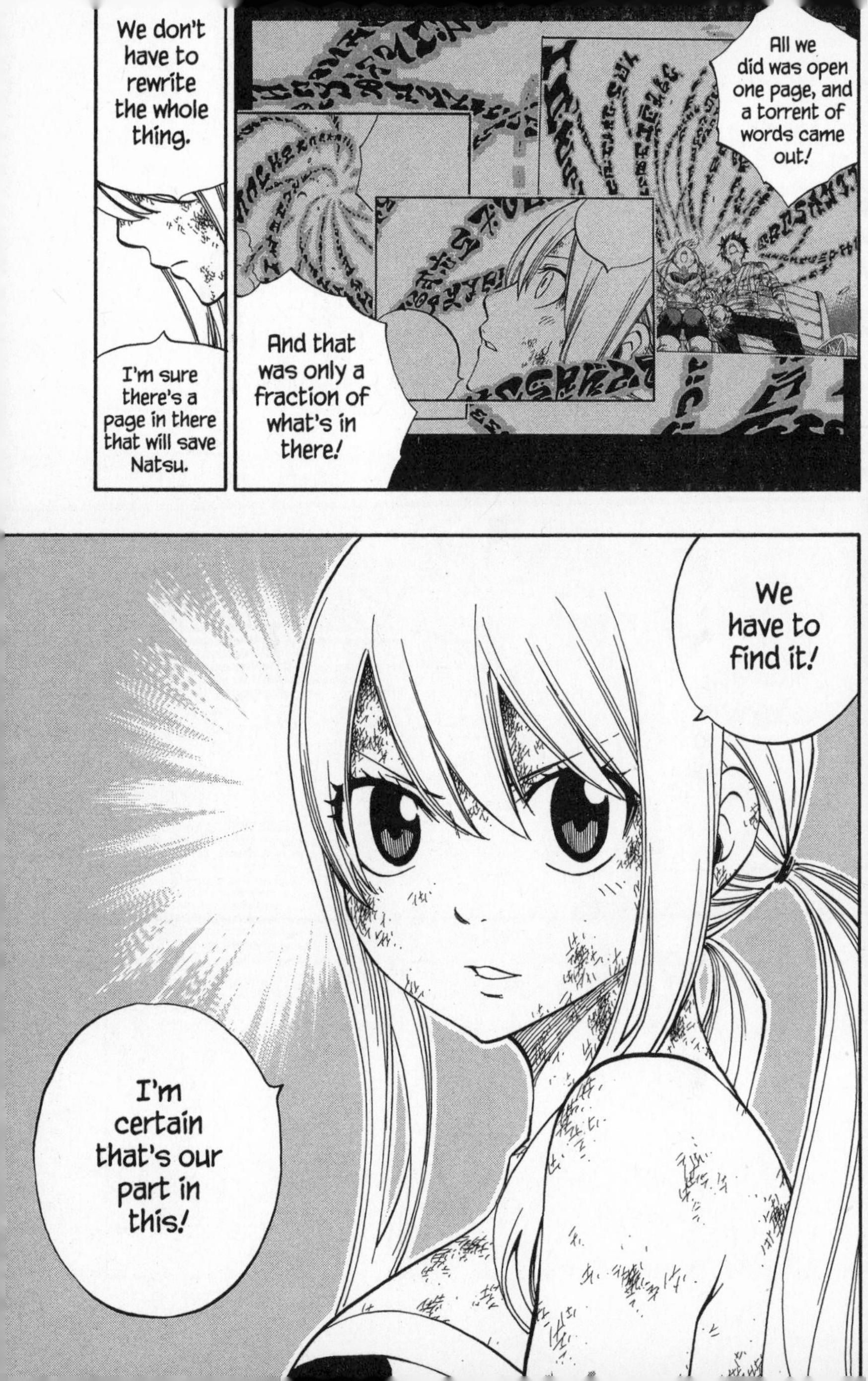
All we did was open one page, and a torrent of words came out!
And that was only a fraction of what's in there!
We don't have to rewrite the whole thing.
I'm sure there's a page in there that will save Natsu.
We have to find it!
I'm certain that's our part in this!

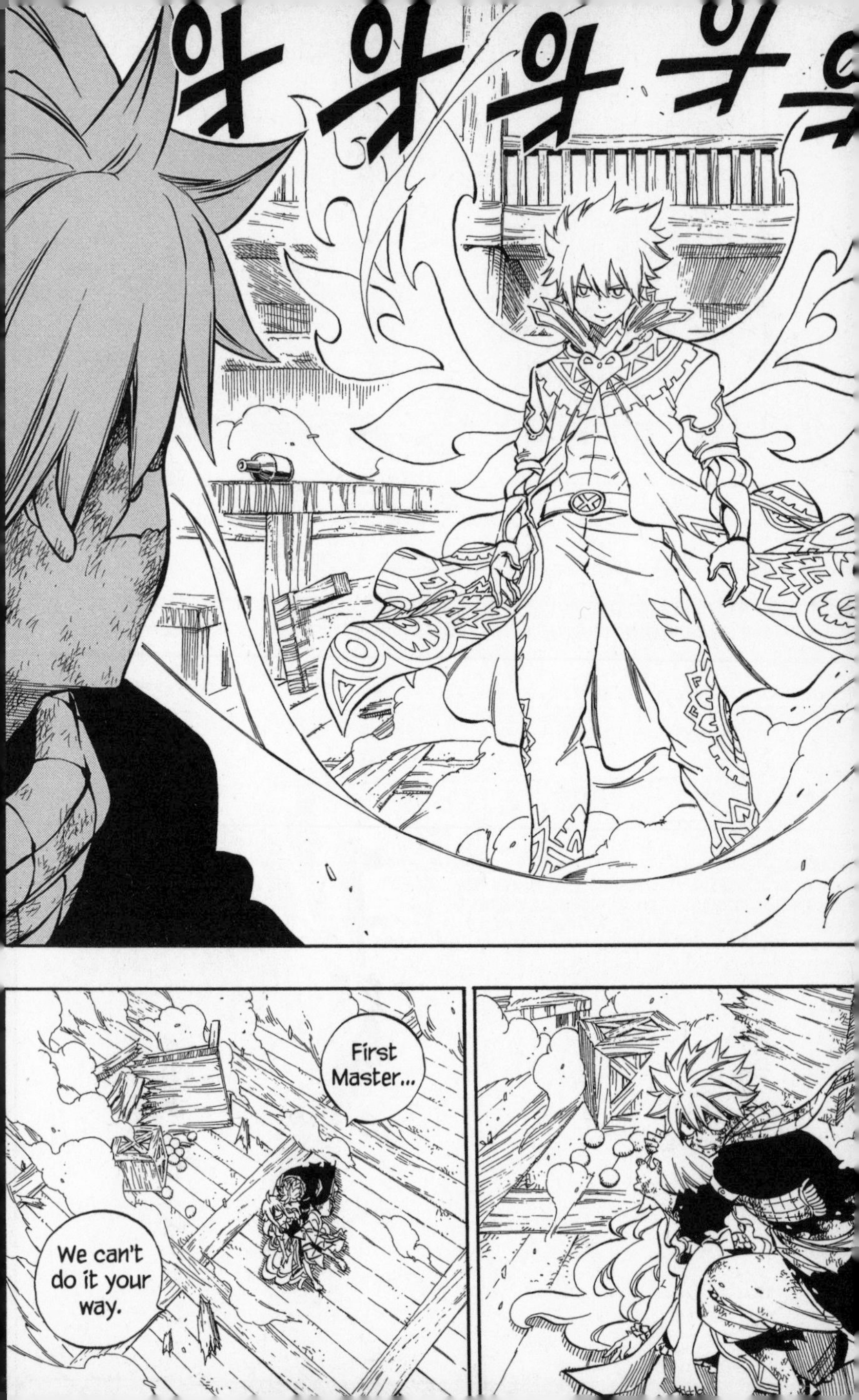
First Master...
We can't do it your way.

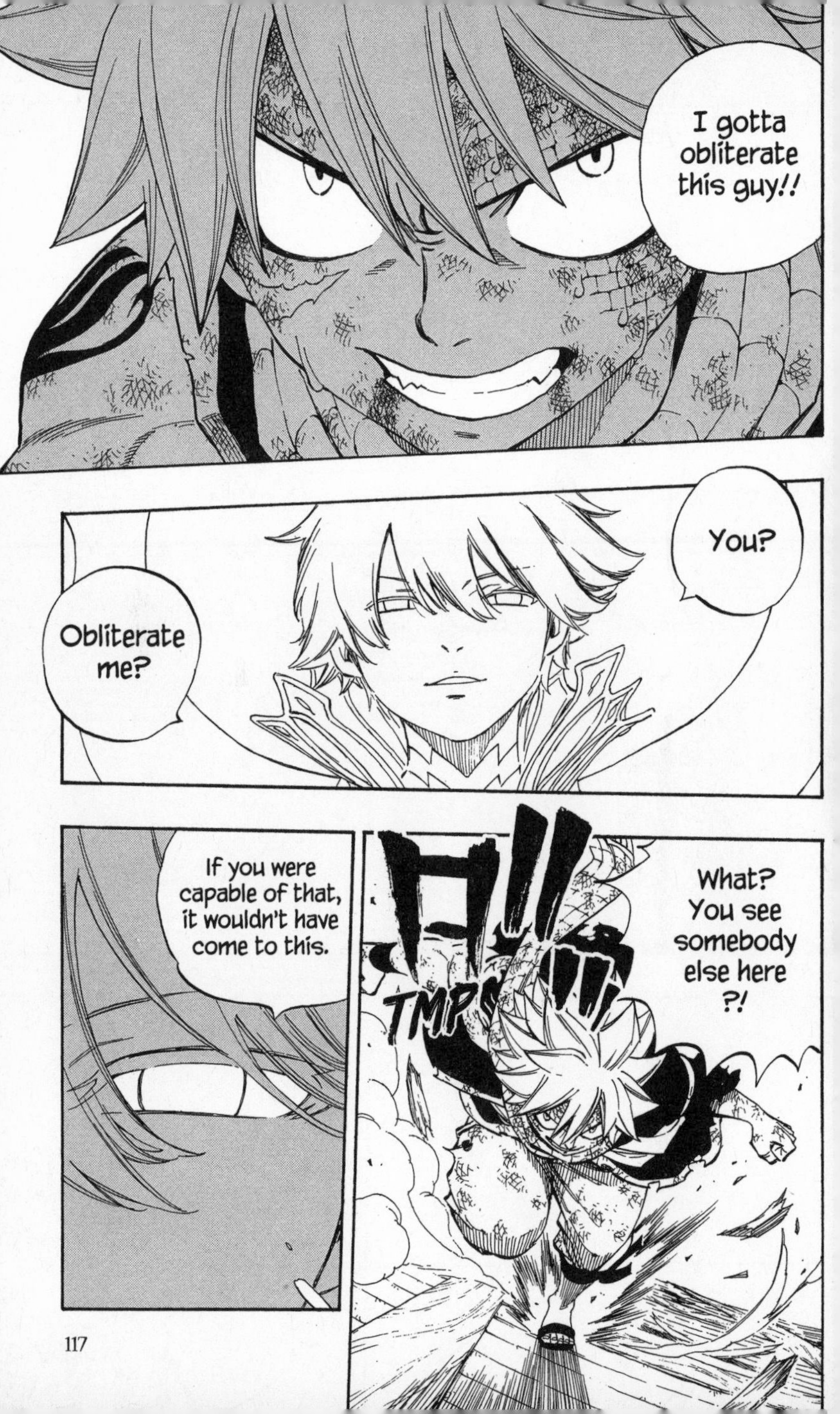

I gotta obliterate this guy!!
You?
Obliterate me?
TMP
What? You see somebody else here ?!
If you were capable of that, it wouldn't have come to this.

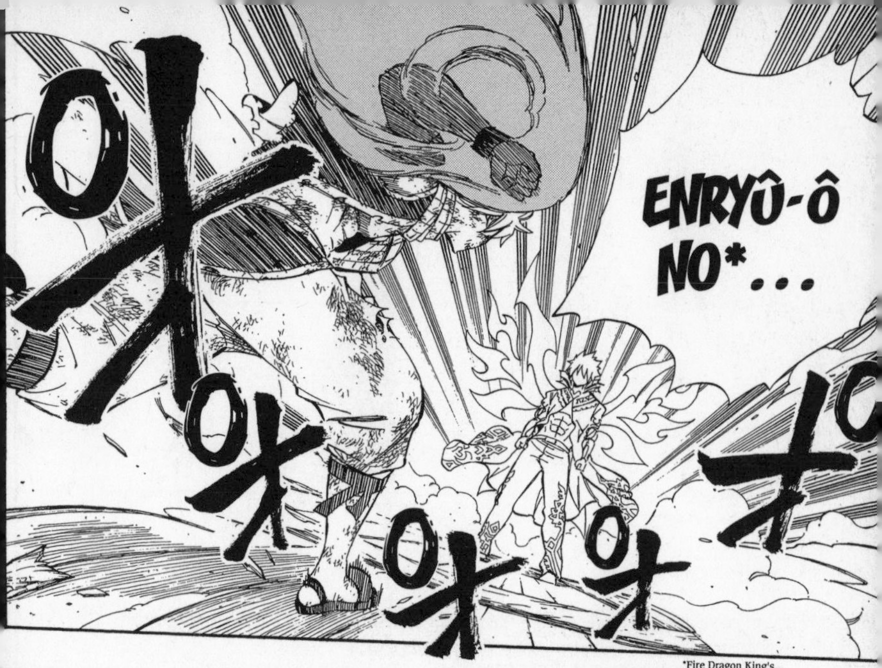
ENRYÛ-Ô NO*...
オオオオオオ

*Fire Dragon King's...

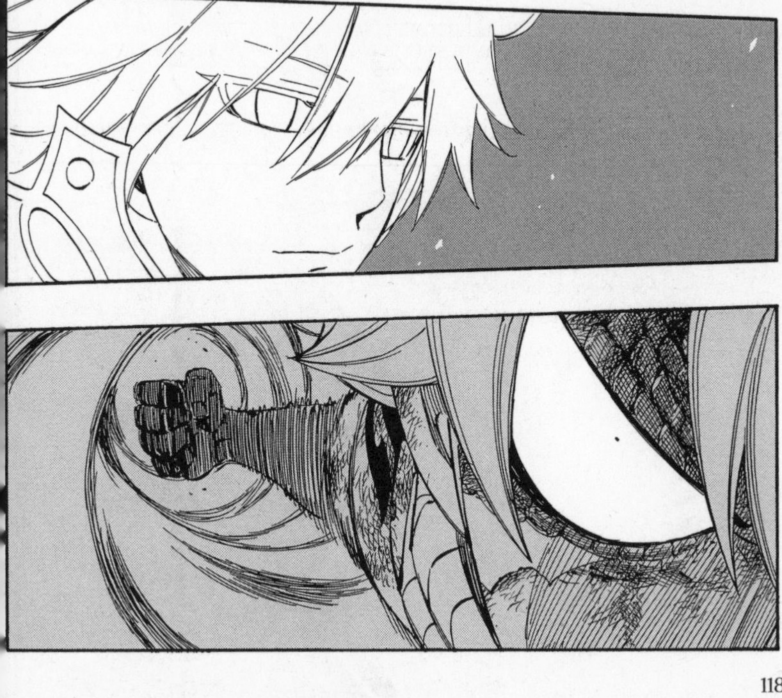

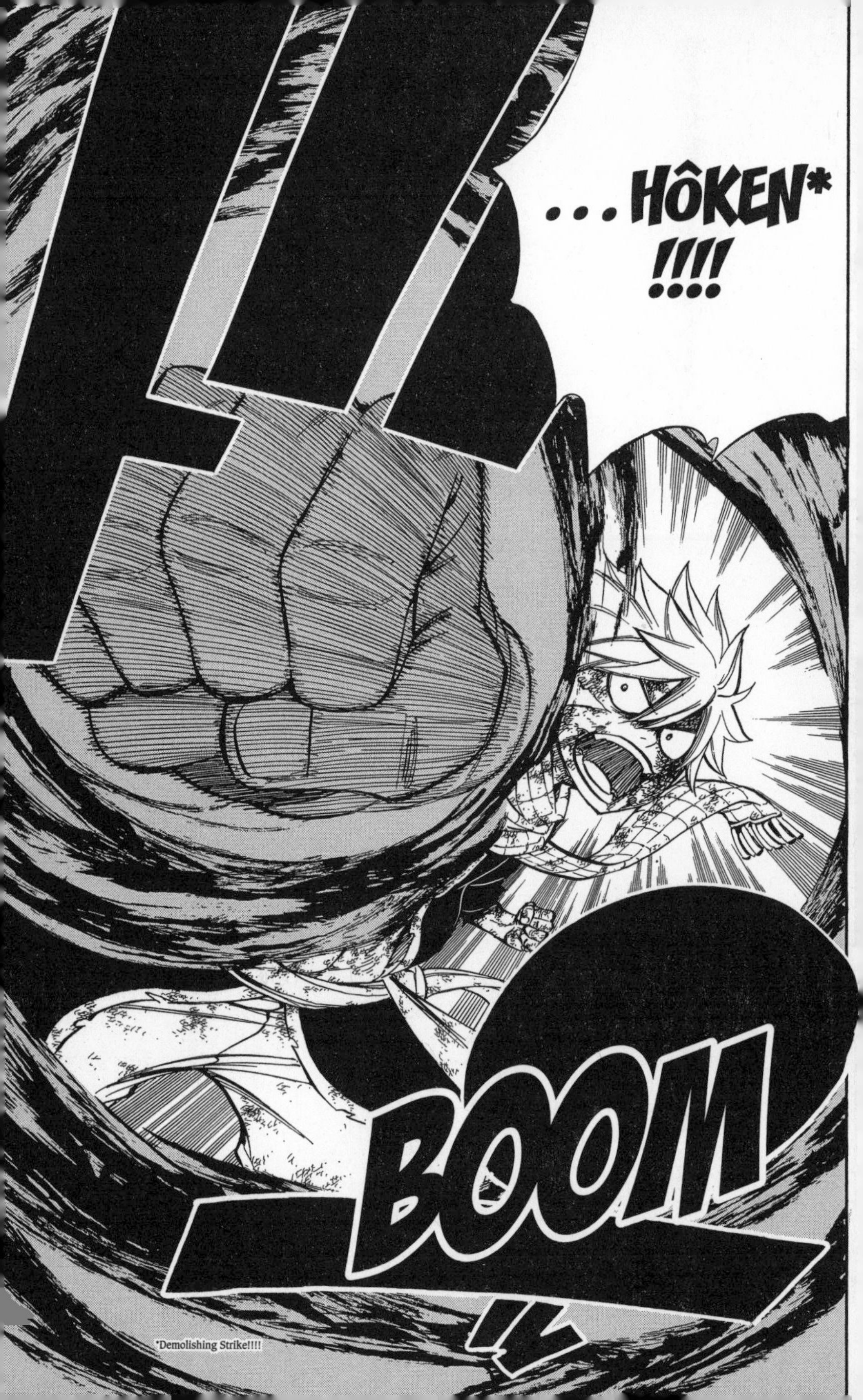
...HÔKEN*
!!!!
BOOM
*Demolishing Strike!!!!

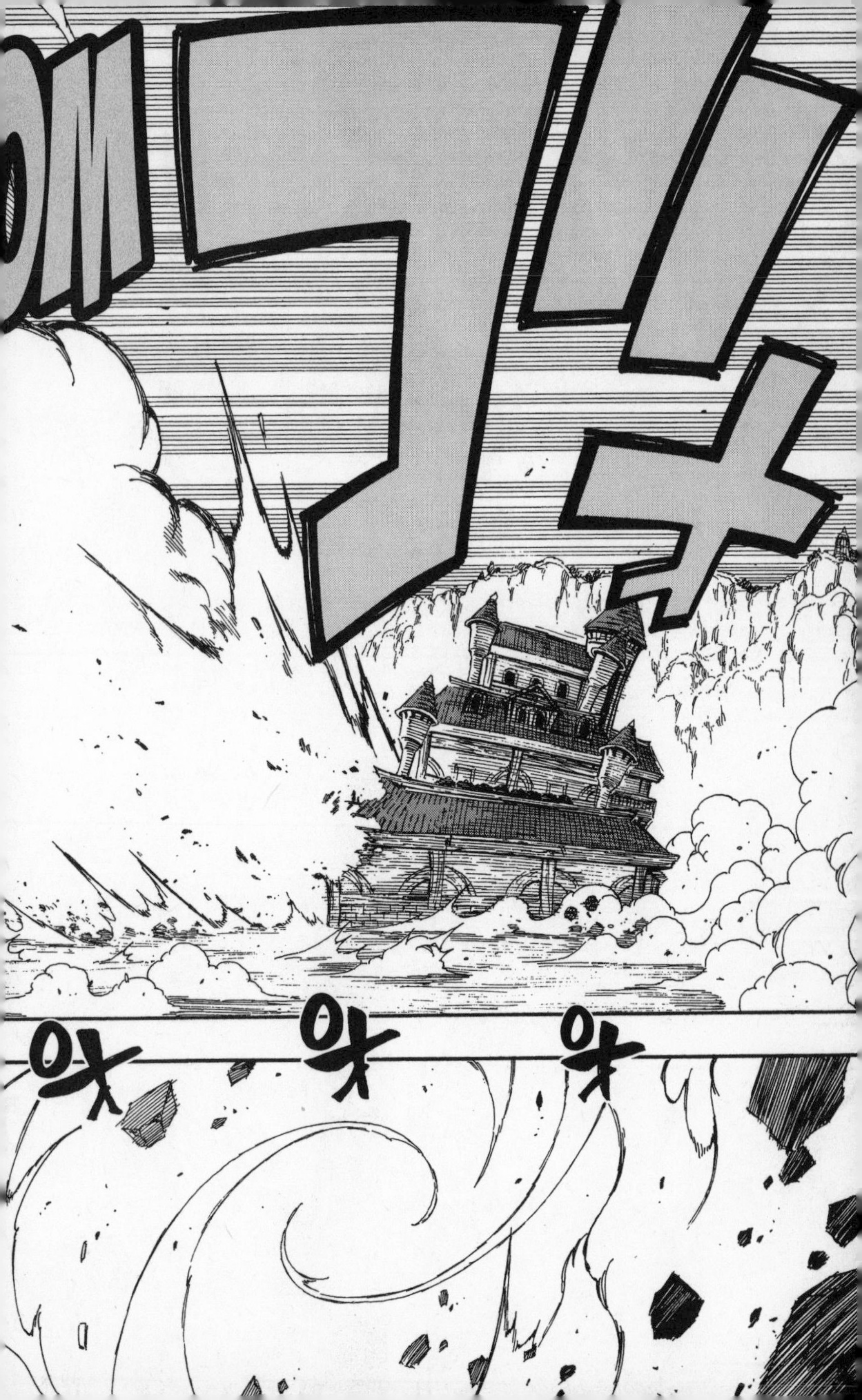
OM

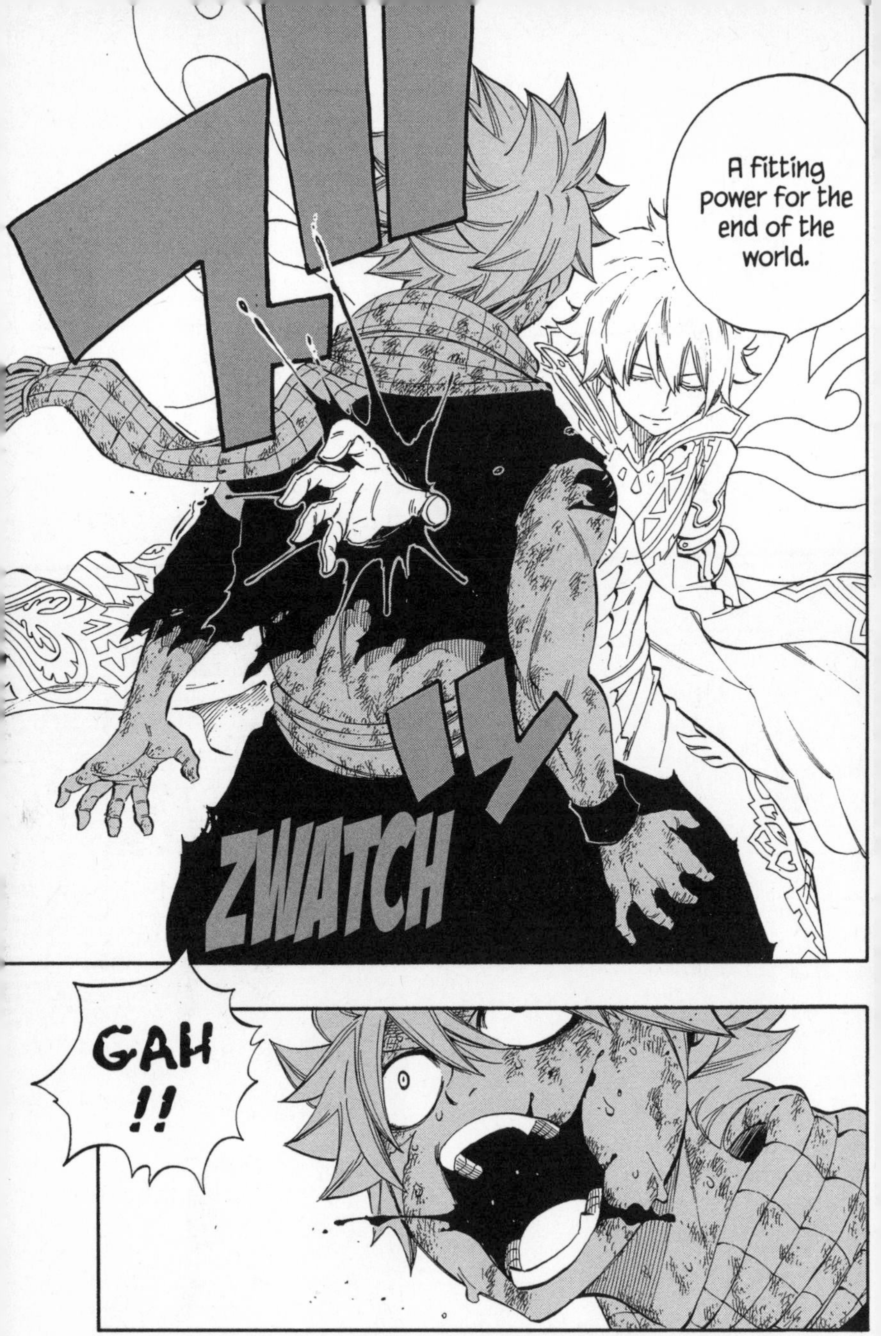
A fitting power for the end of the world.
ZWATCH
GAH !!

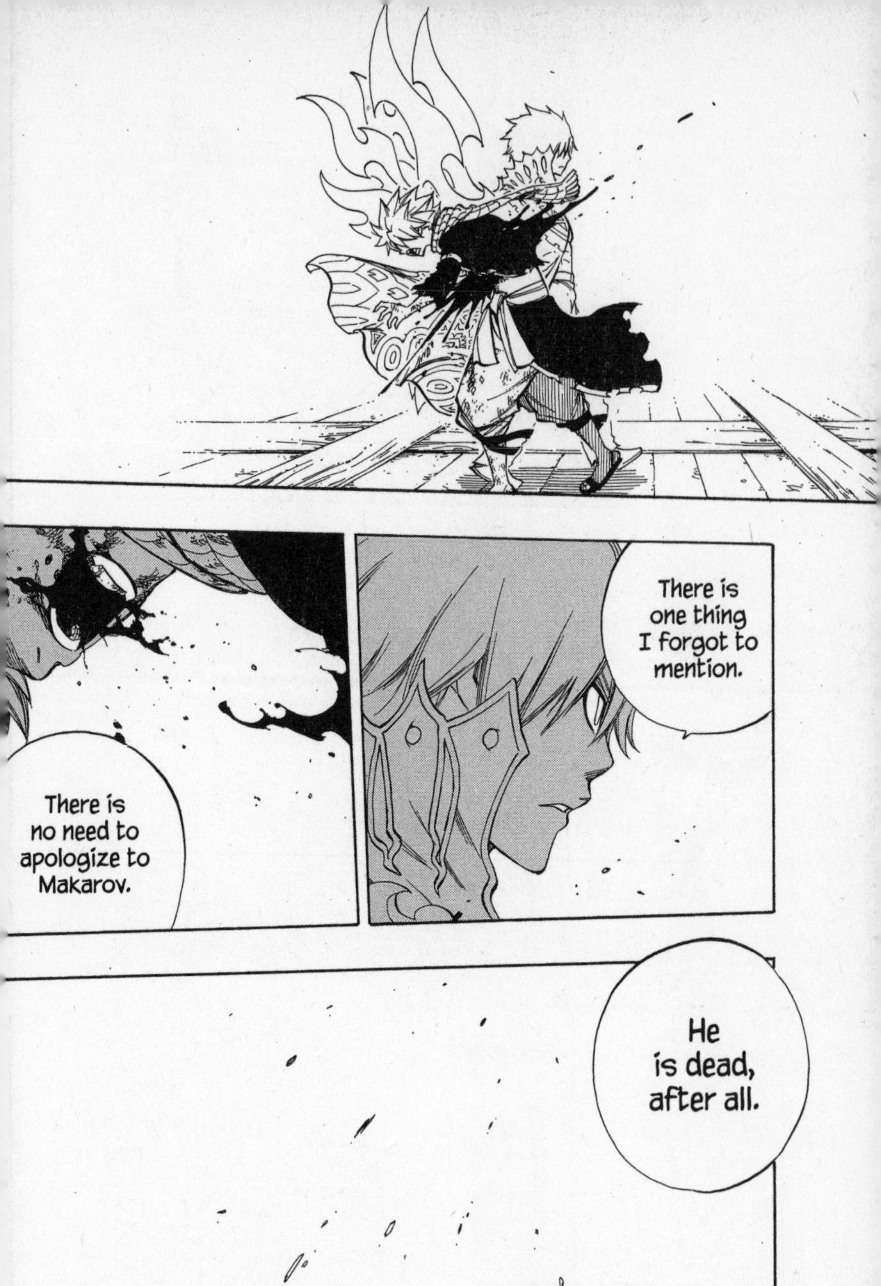
There is one thing I forgot to mention.
There is no need to apologize to Makarov.
He is dead, after all.

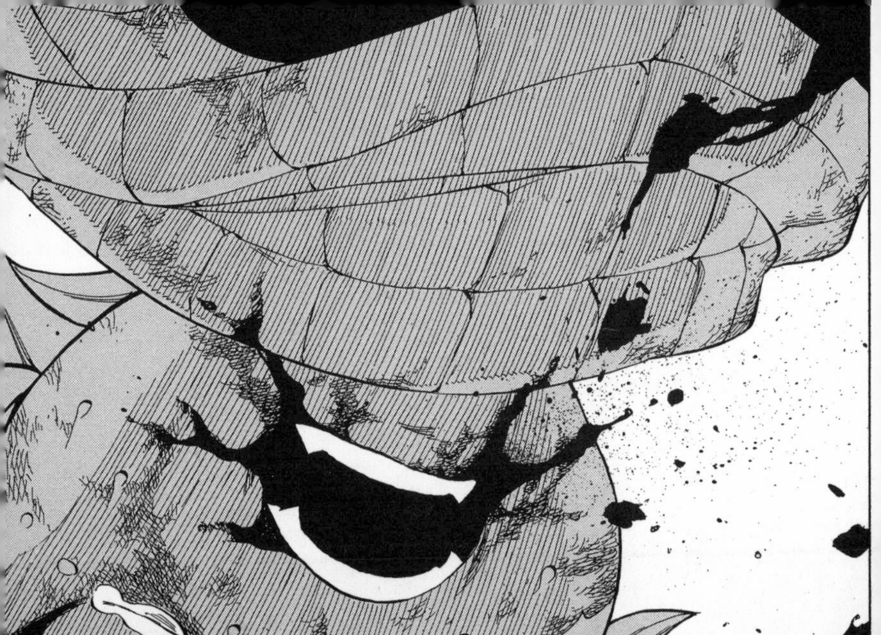

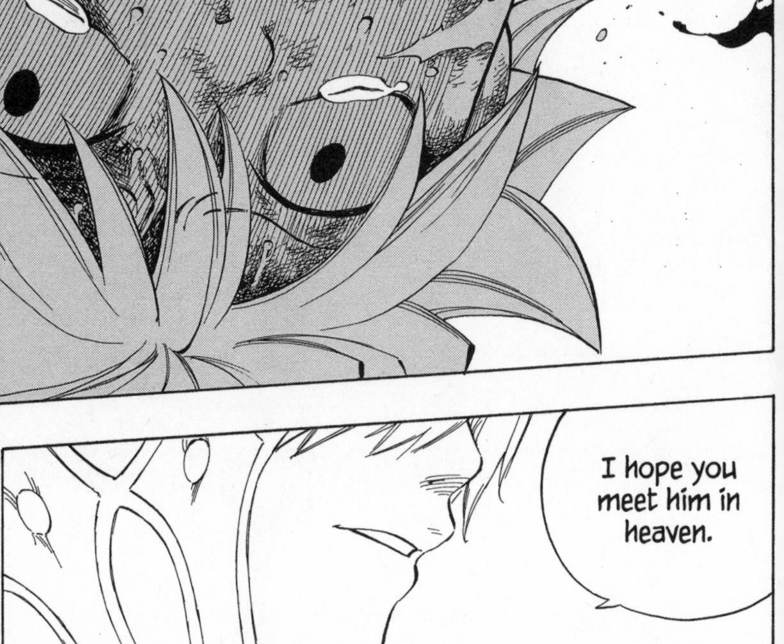
I hope you meet him in heaven.

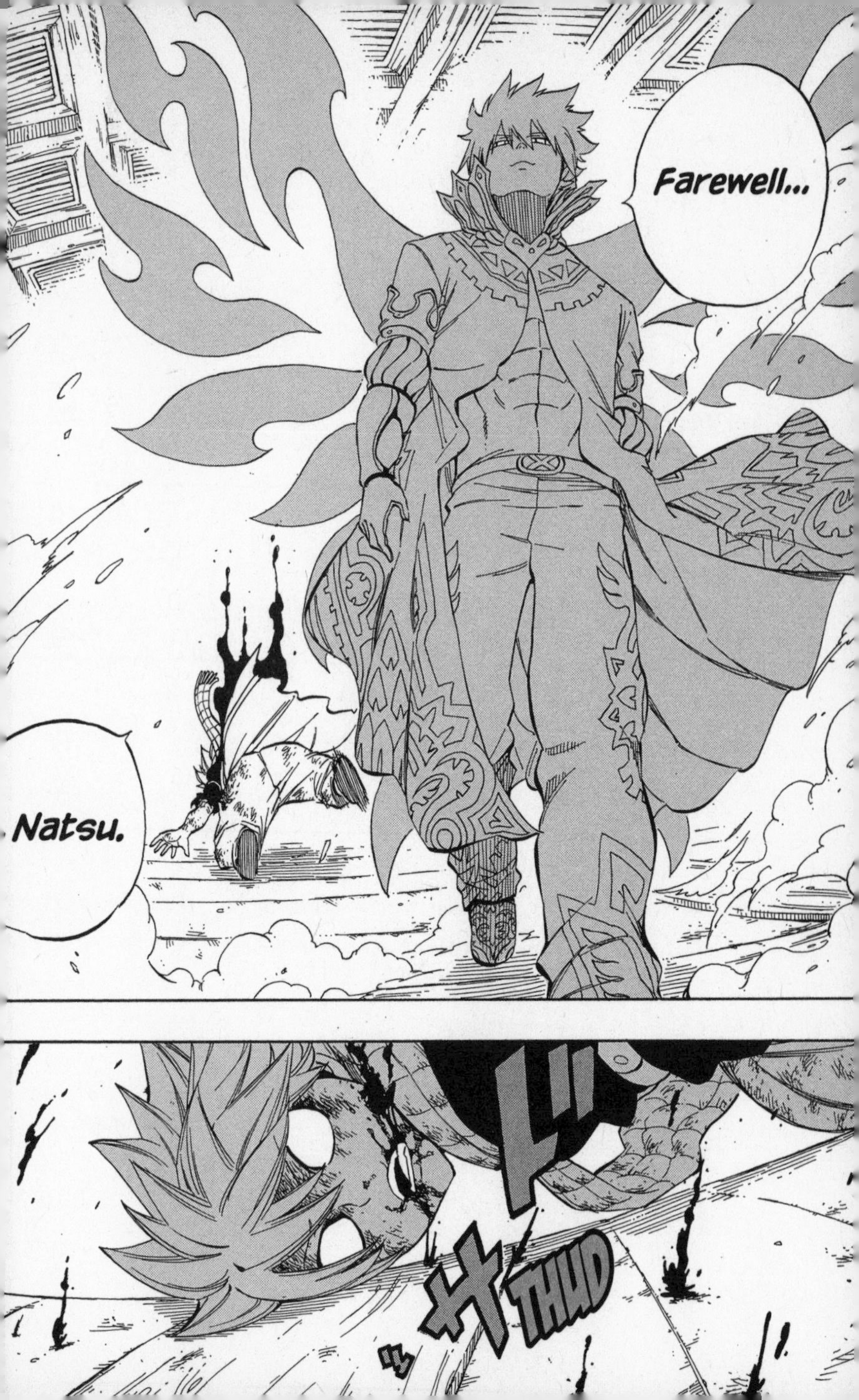
Farewell...
Natsu.
THUD

FAIRY TAIL

フェアリーテイル

Chapter 534: The Vow of the Doors

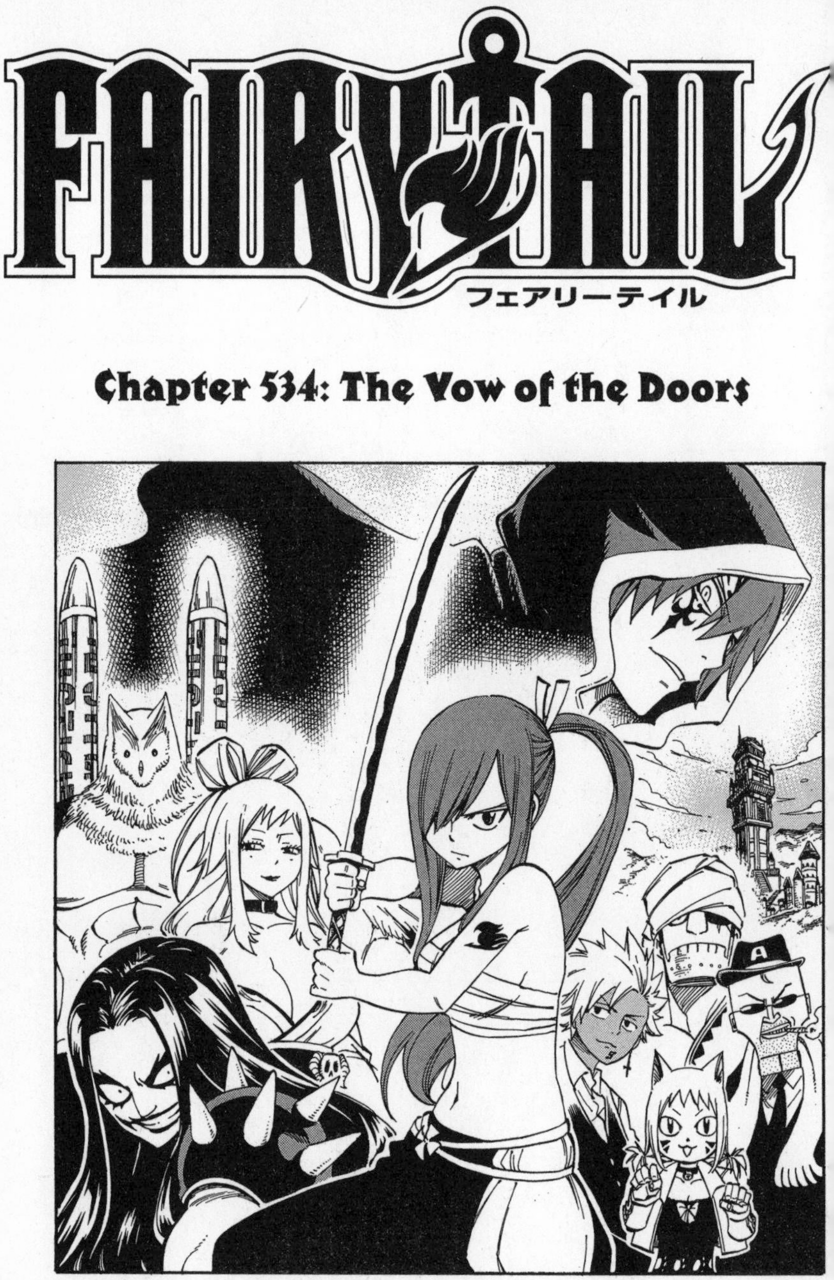

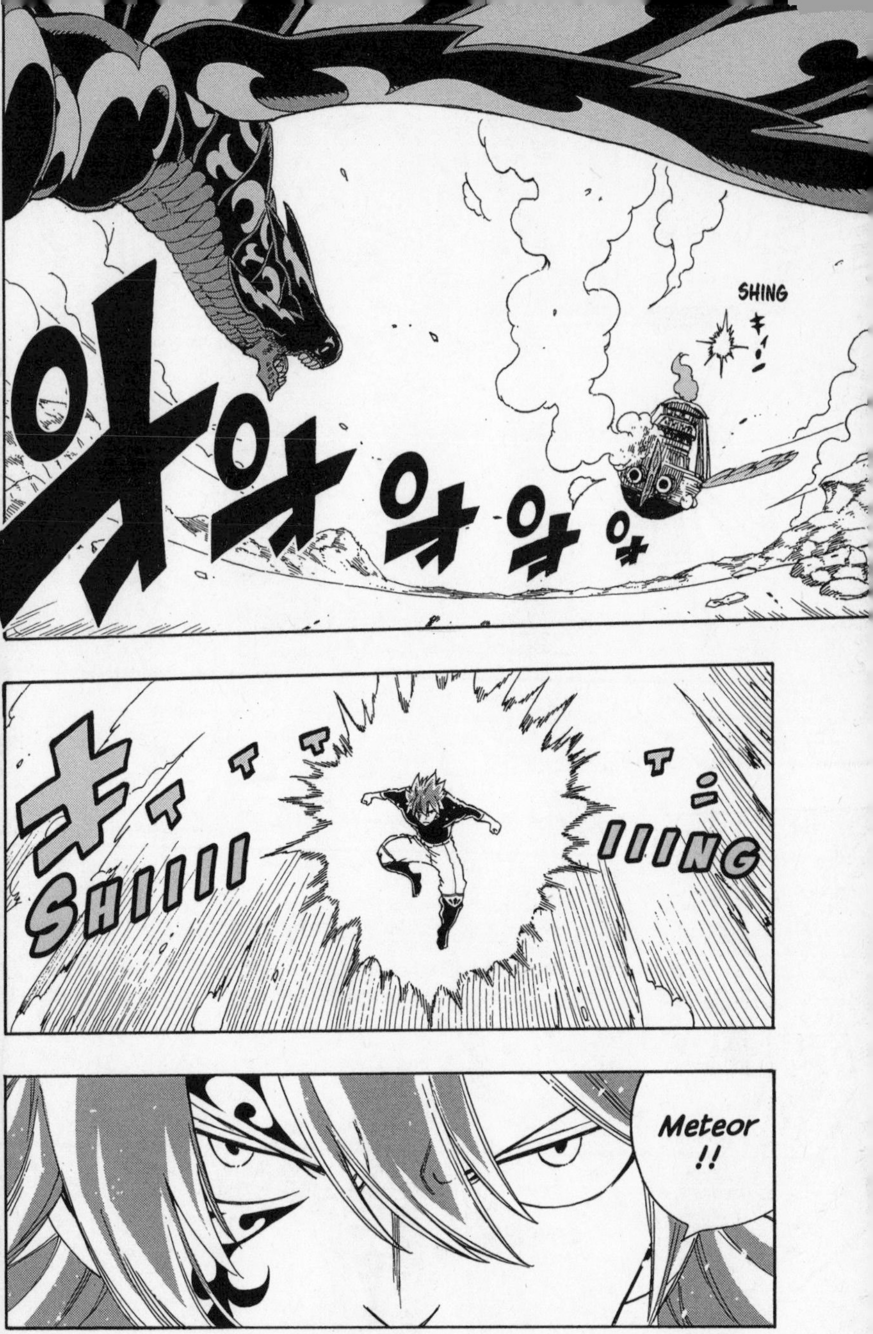
SHING
SHIIIII
IIING
Meteor !!

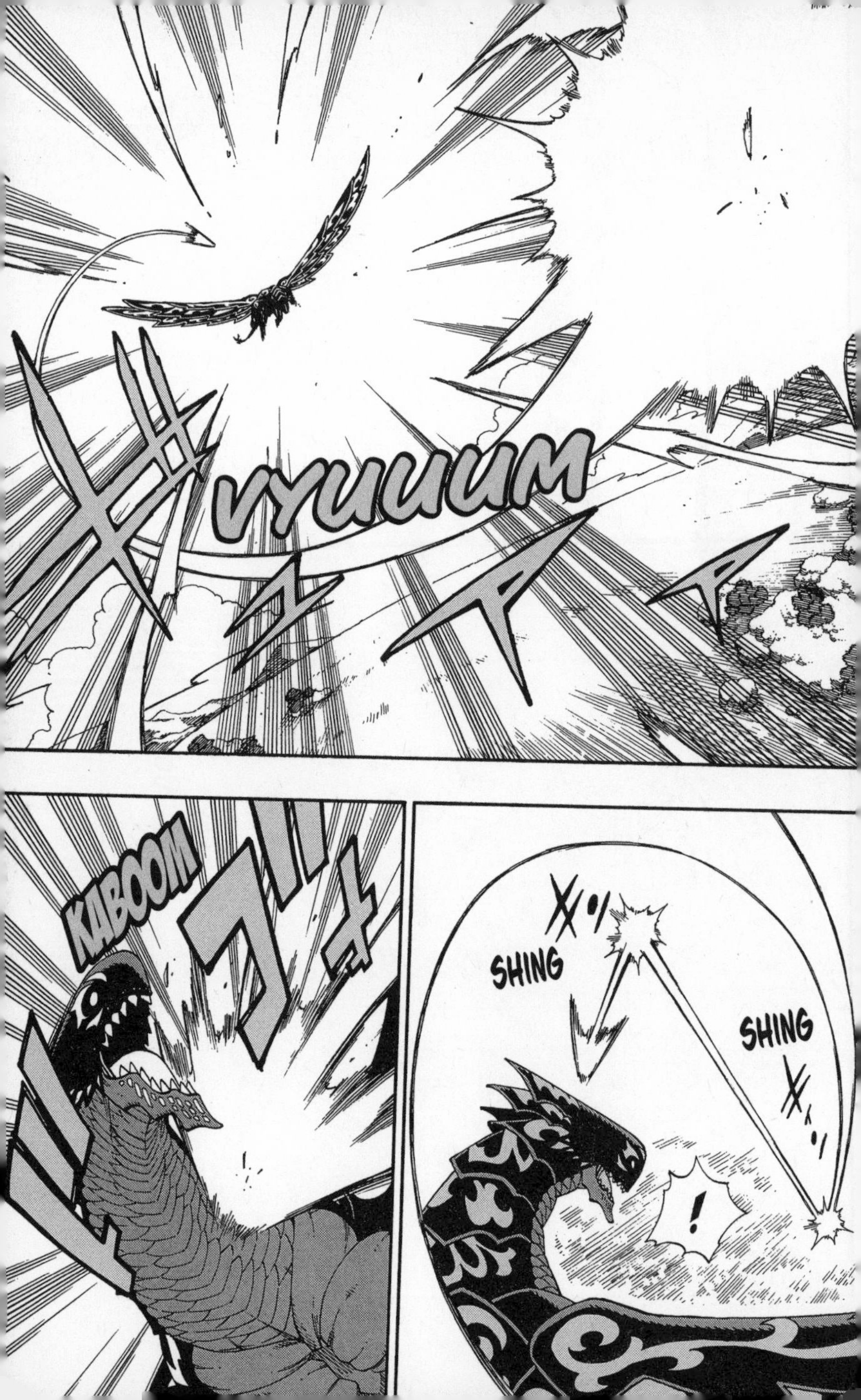
VYUUUM
SHING
SHING
!
KABOOM

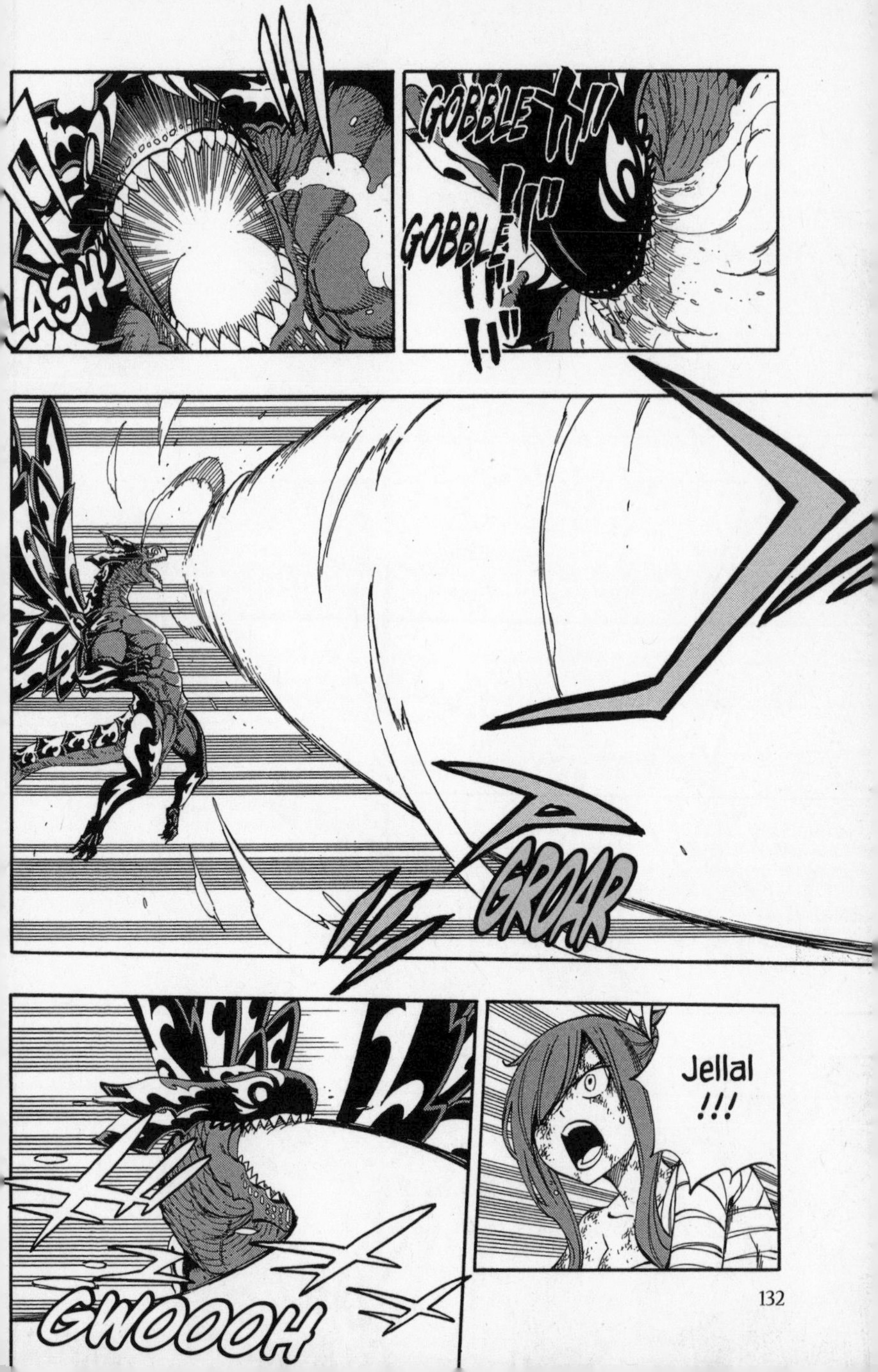
GOBBLE
GOBBLE
LASH
GROAR
Jellal !!!
GWOOOH

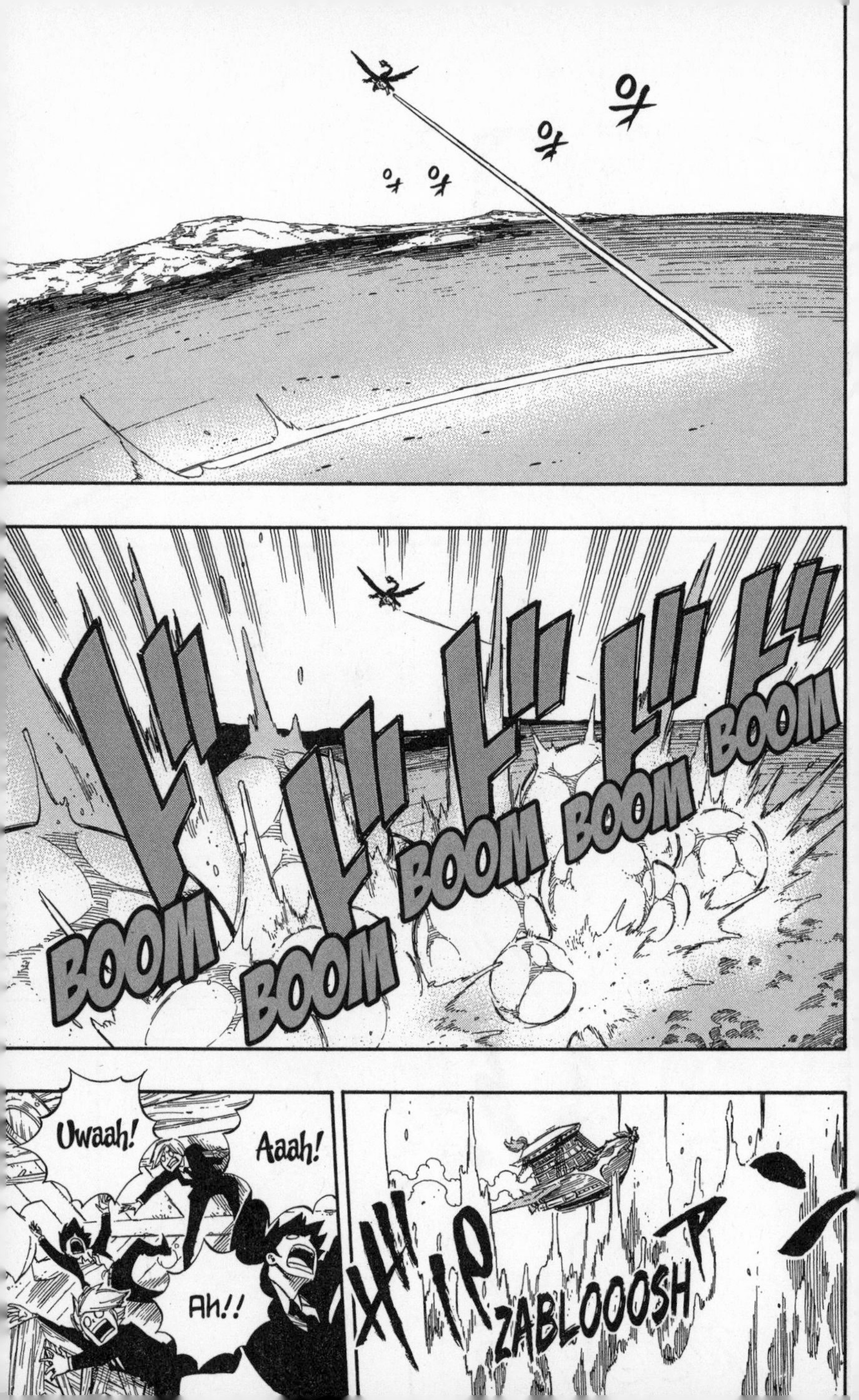
ドドドドド
BOOM
BOOM
BOOM
BOOM
BOOM
ZABLOOOSH
Uwaah!
Aaah!
Ah!!

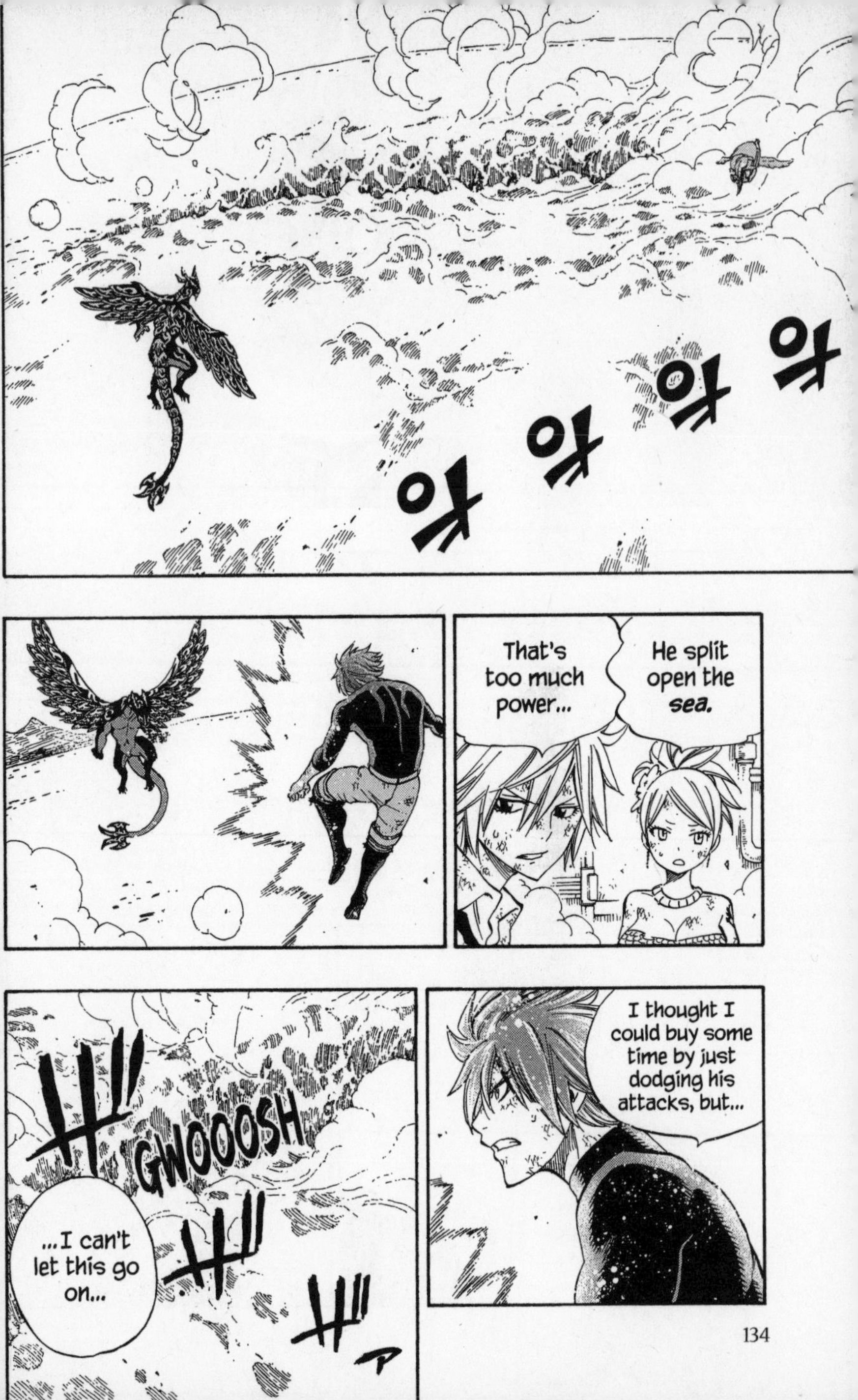
He split open the *sea.*
That's too much power...
I thought I could buy some time by just dodging his attacks, but...
GWOOOSH
...I can't let this go on...

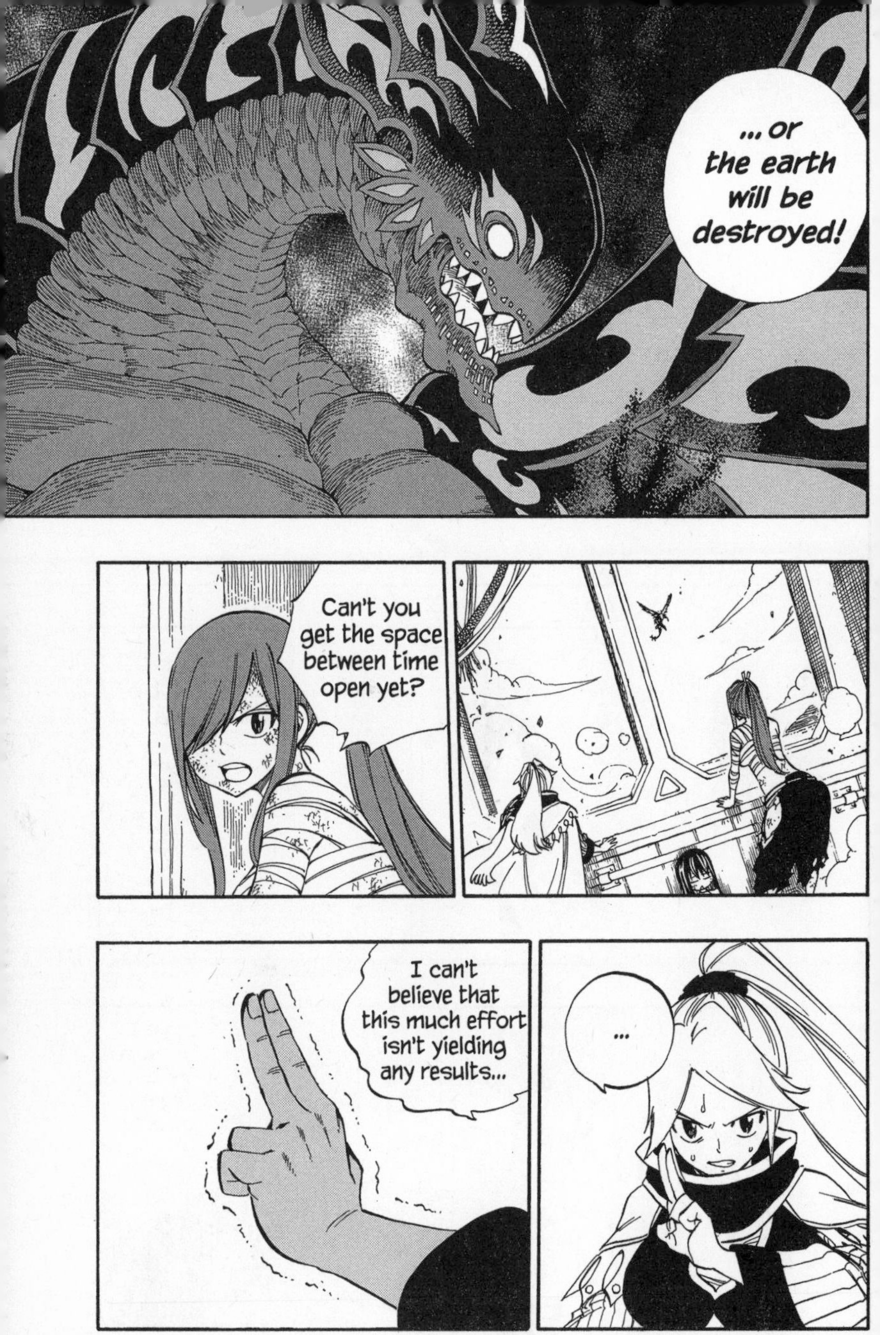
...or the earth will be destroyed!
Can't you get the space between time open yet?
...
I can't believe that this much effort isn't yielding any results...

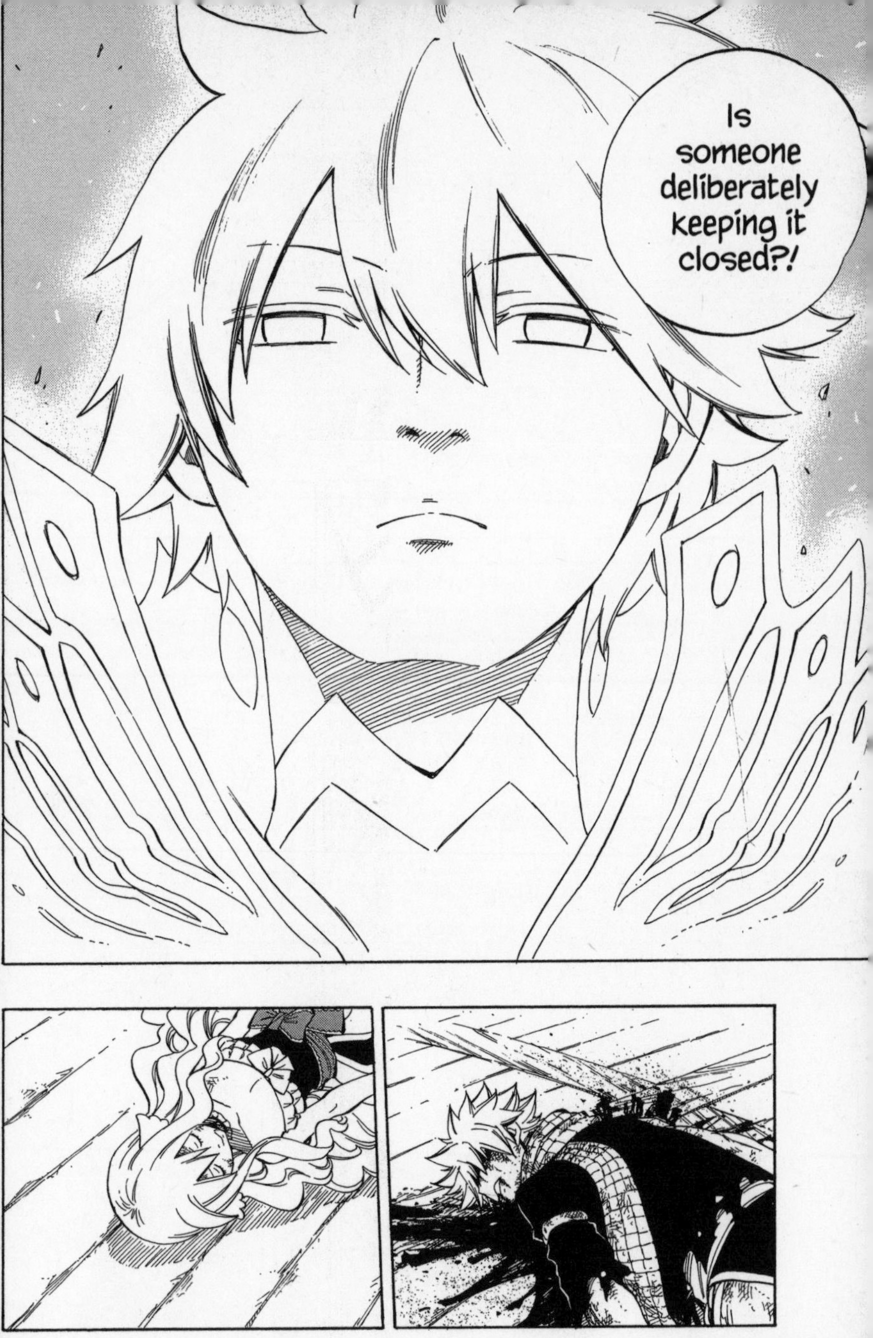
Is someone deliberately keeping it closed?!

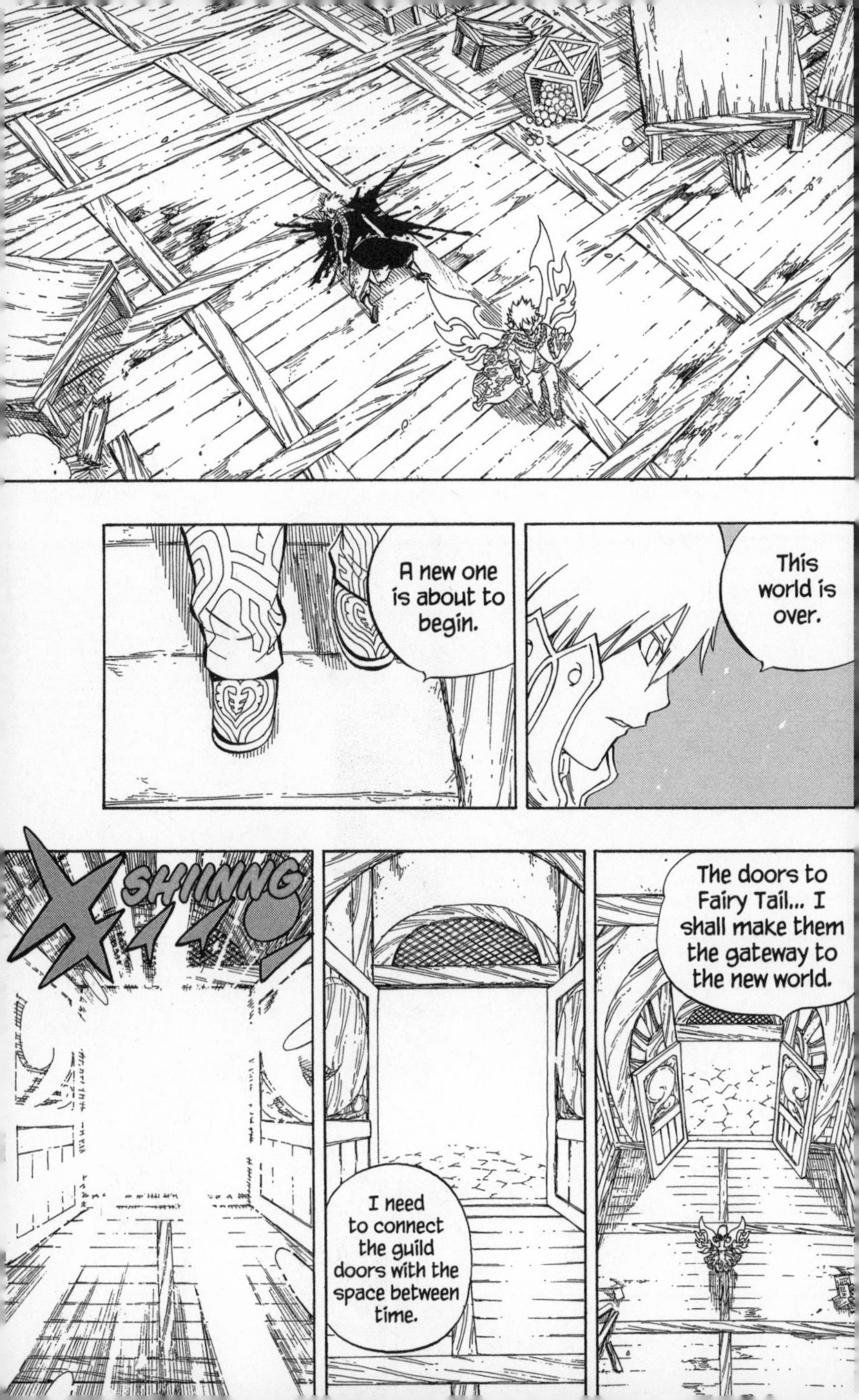
This world is over.
A new one is about to begin.
The doors to Fairy Tail... I shall make them the gateway to the new world.
I need to connect the guild doors with the space between time.
SHIINNG

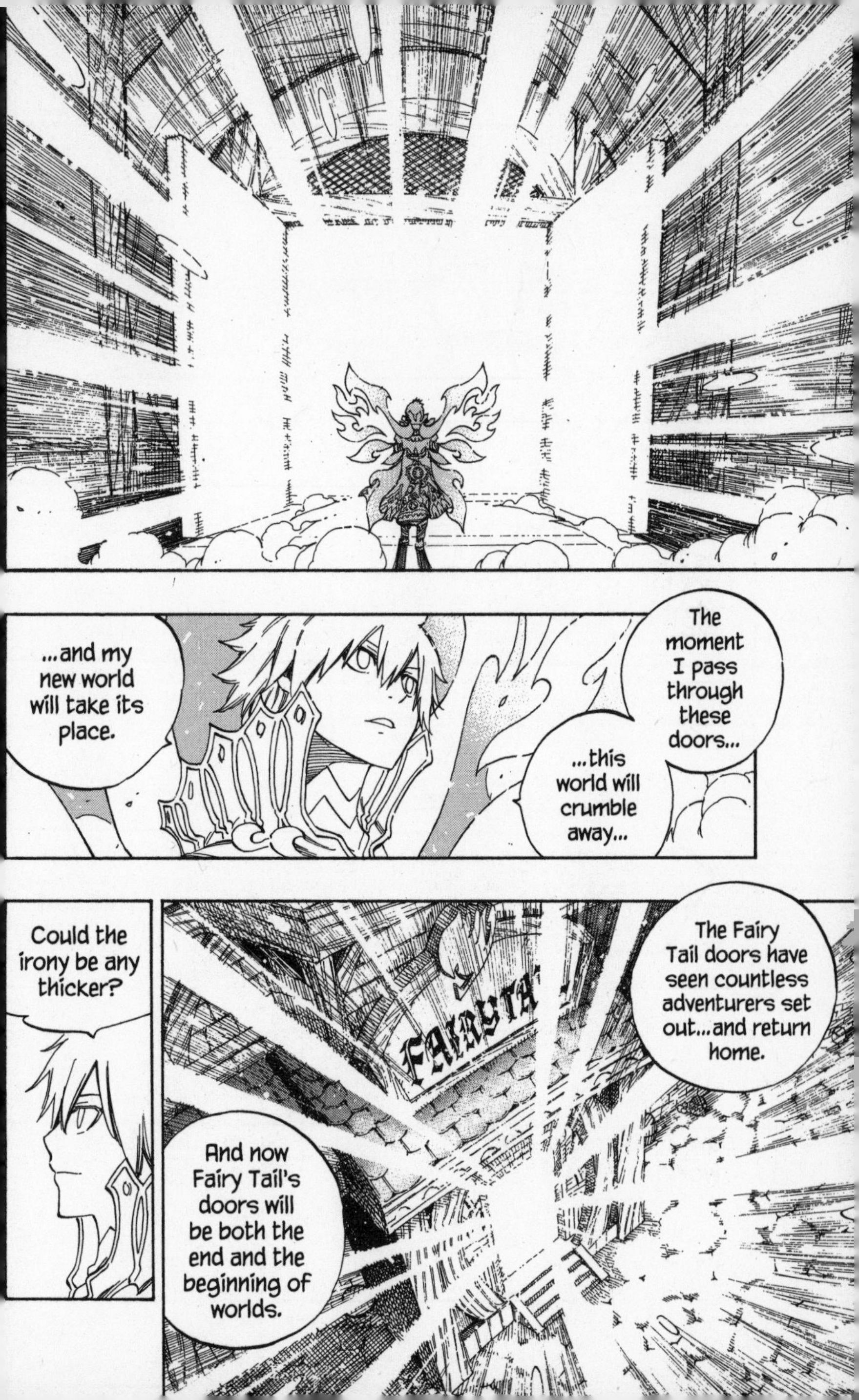
The moment I pass through these doors...
...this world will crumble away...
...and my new world will take its place.
The Fairy Tail doors have seen countless adventurers set out...and return home.
And now Fairy Tail's doors will be both the end and the beginning of worlds.
Could the irony be any thicker?

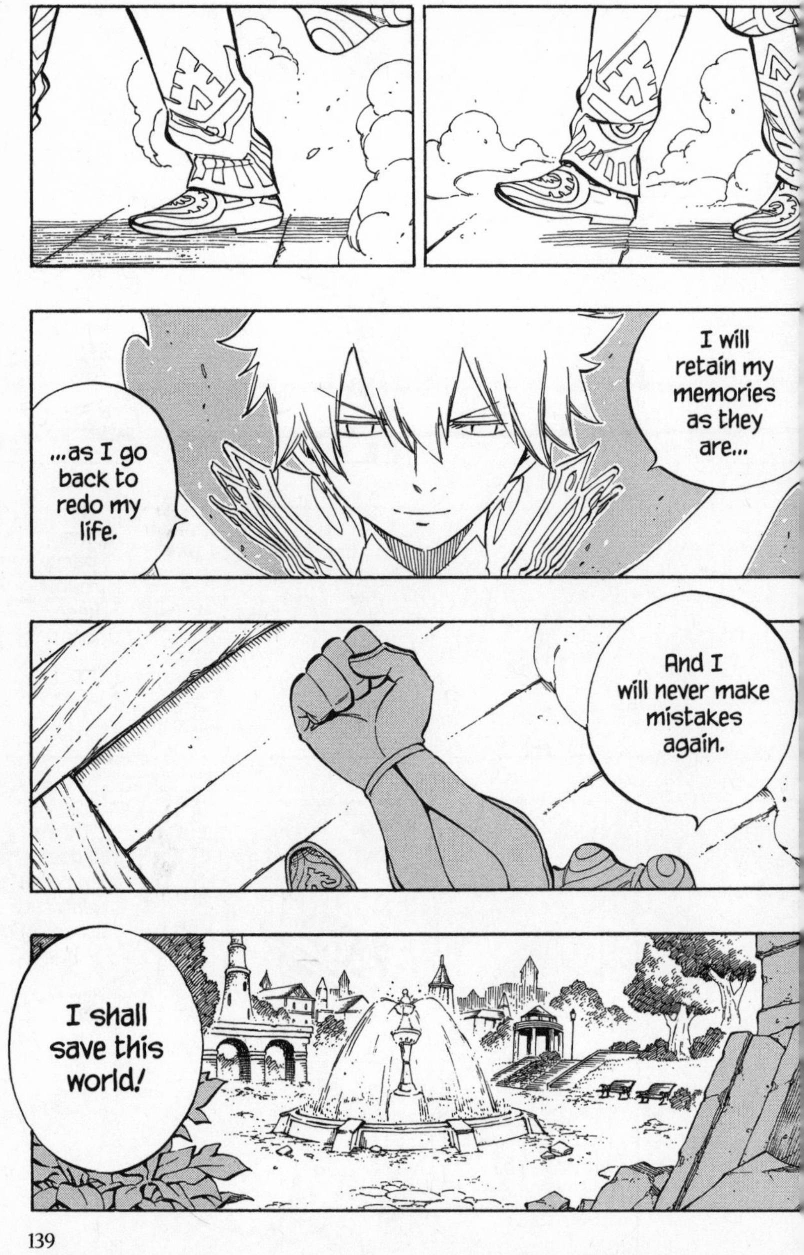
I will retain my memories as they are...
...as I go back to redo my life.
And I will never make mistakes again.
I shall save this world!

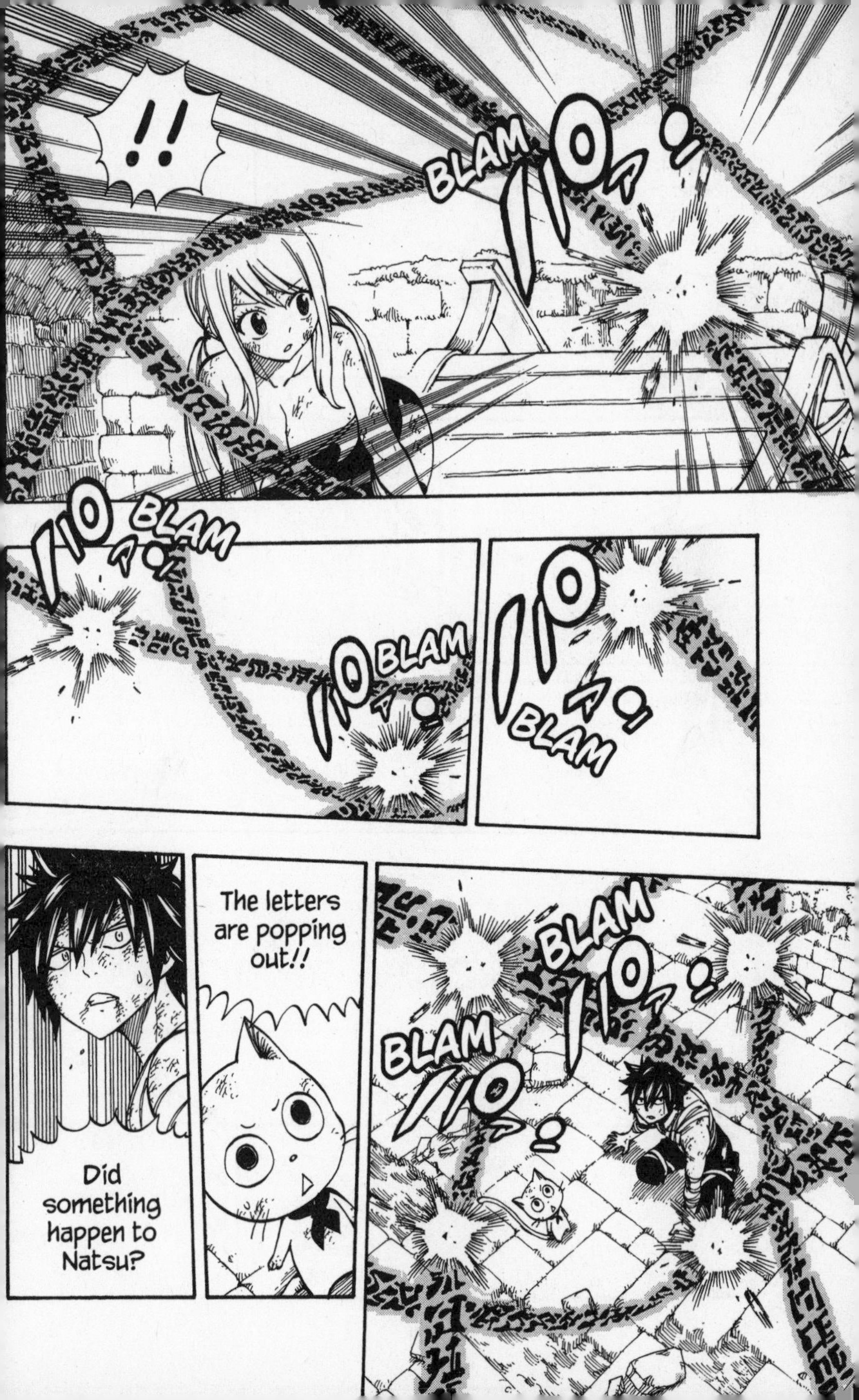
BLAM
!!
BLAM
BLAM
BLAM
BLAM
BLAM
The letters are popping out!!
Did something happen to Natsu?

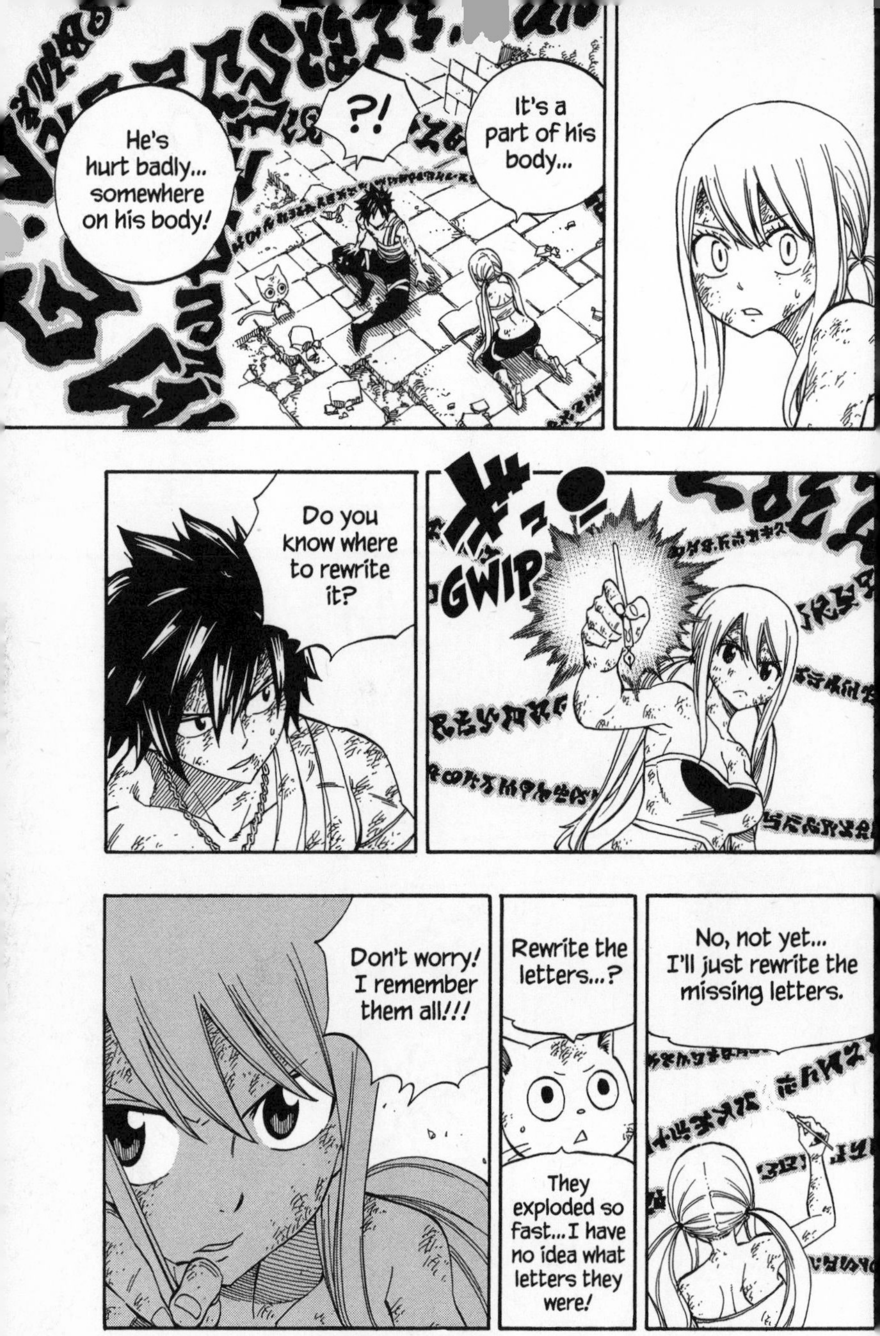
It's a part of his body...
?!
He's hurt badly... somewhere on his body!
GWIP
Do you know where to rewrite it?
No, not yet... I'll just rewrite the missing letters.
Rewrite the letters...?
They exploded so fast...I have no idea what letters they were!
Don't worry! I remember them all!!!

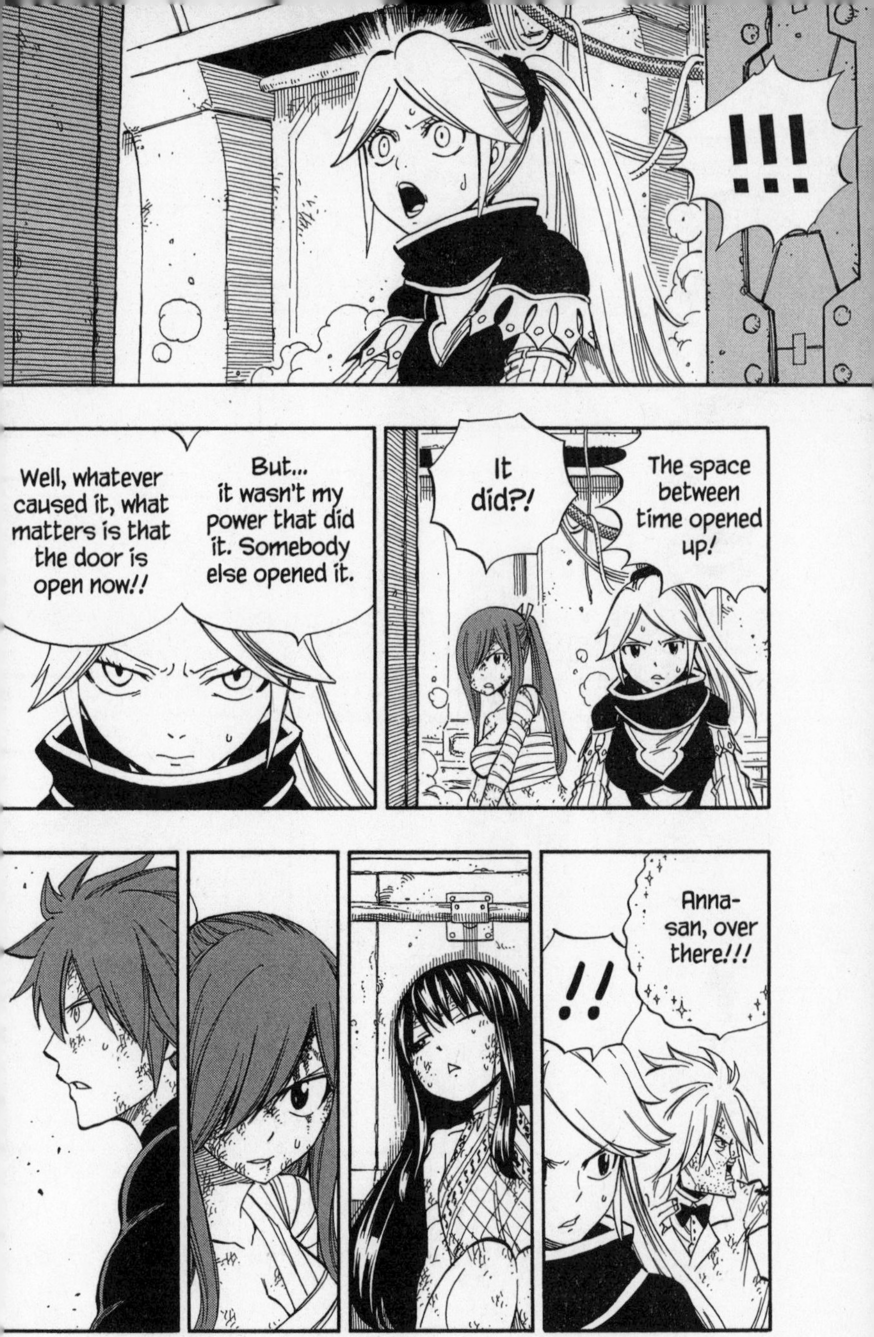
!!!
The space between time opened up!
It did?!
But... it wasn't my power that did it. Somebody else opened it.
Well, whatever caused it, what matters is that the door is open now!!
Anna-san, over there!!!
!!

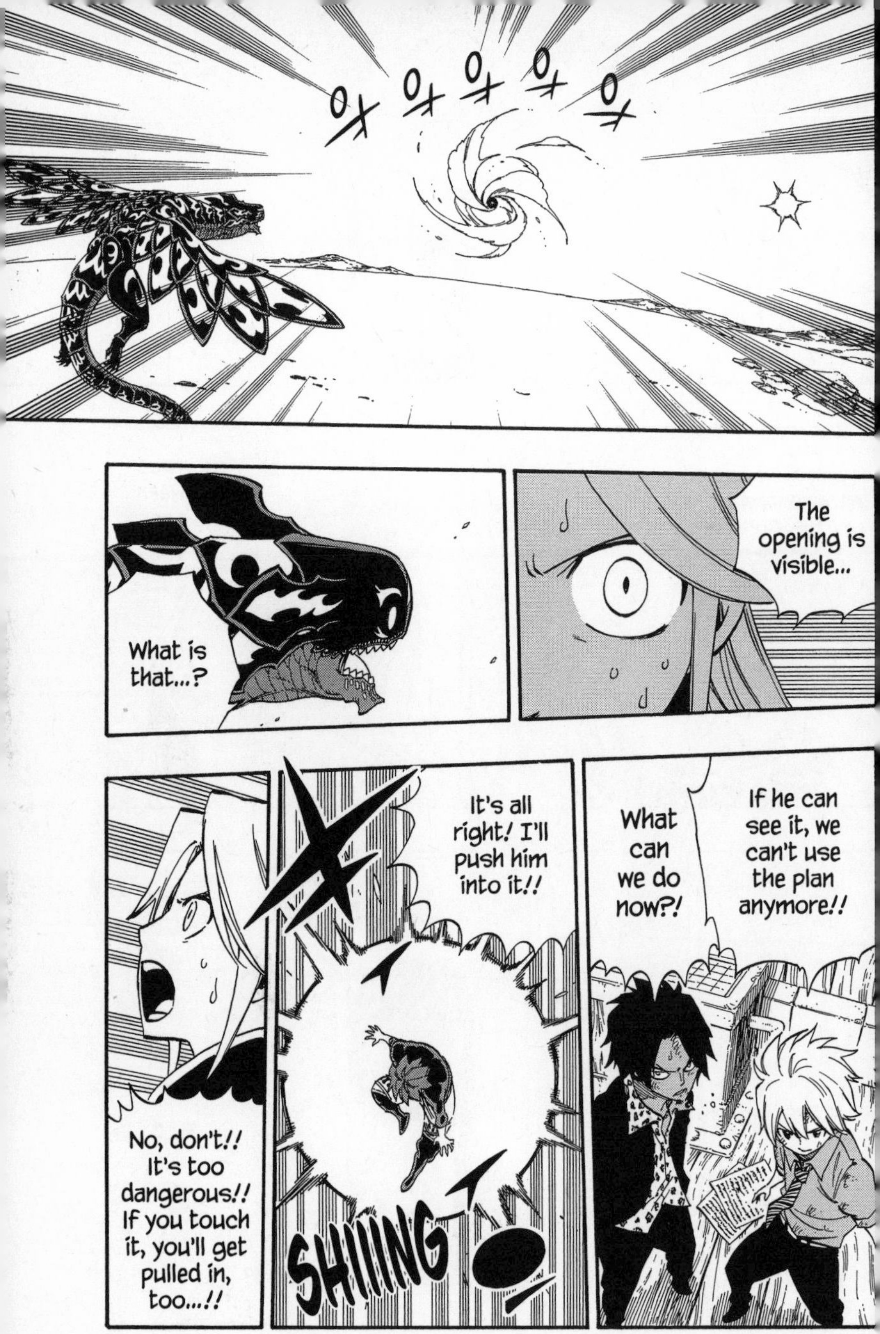

The opening is visible...
What is that...?
If he can see it, we can't use the plan anymore!!
What can we do now?!
It's all right! I'll push him into it!!
SHIIING
No, don't!! It's too dangerous!! If you touch it, you'll get pulled in, too...!!

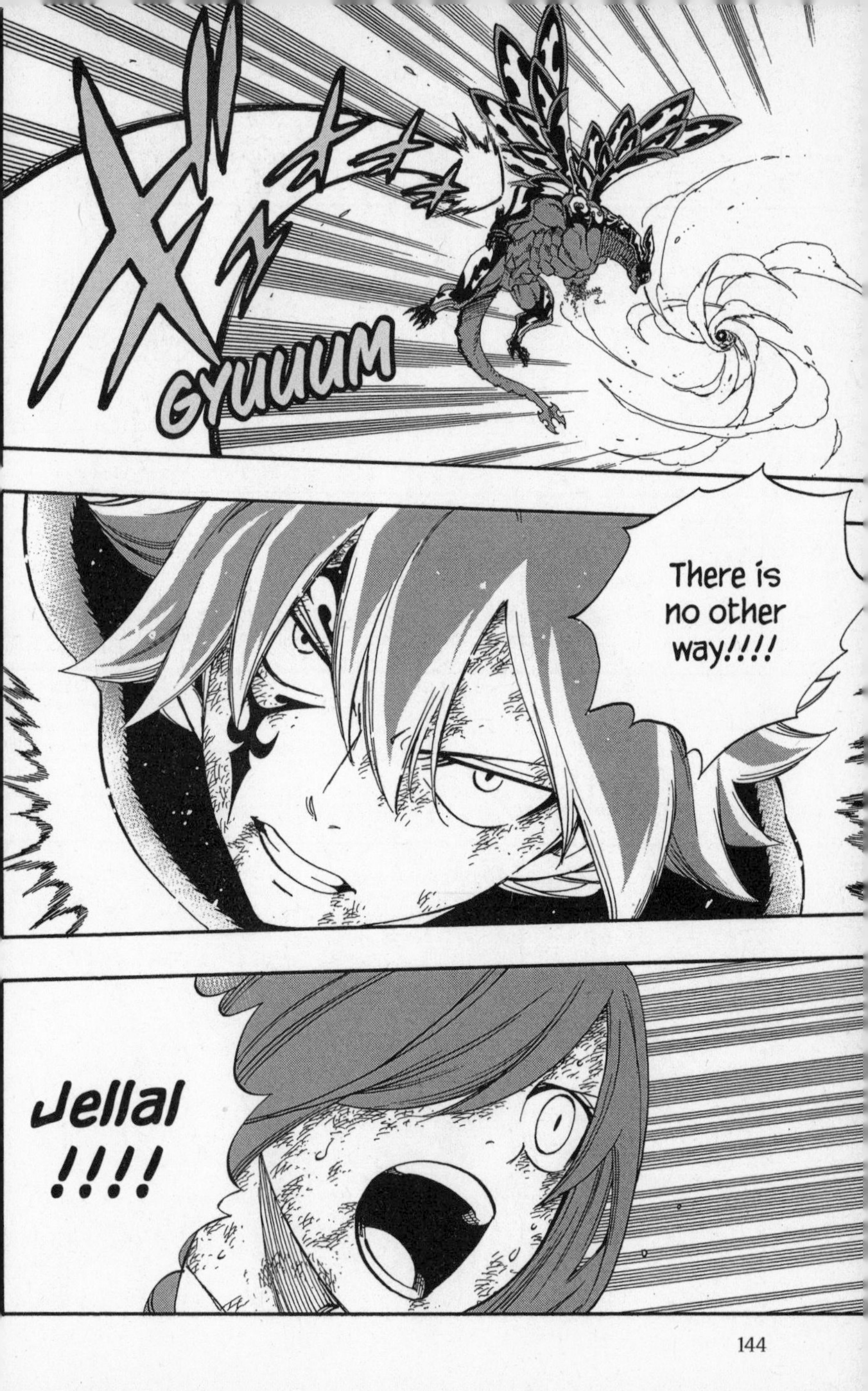
GYUUUM
There is no other way!!!!
Jellal !!!!

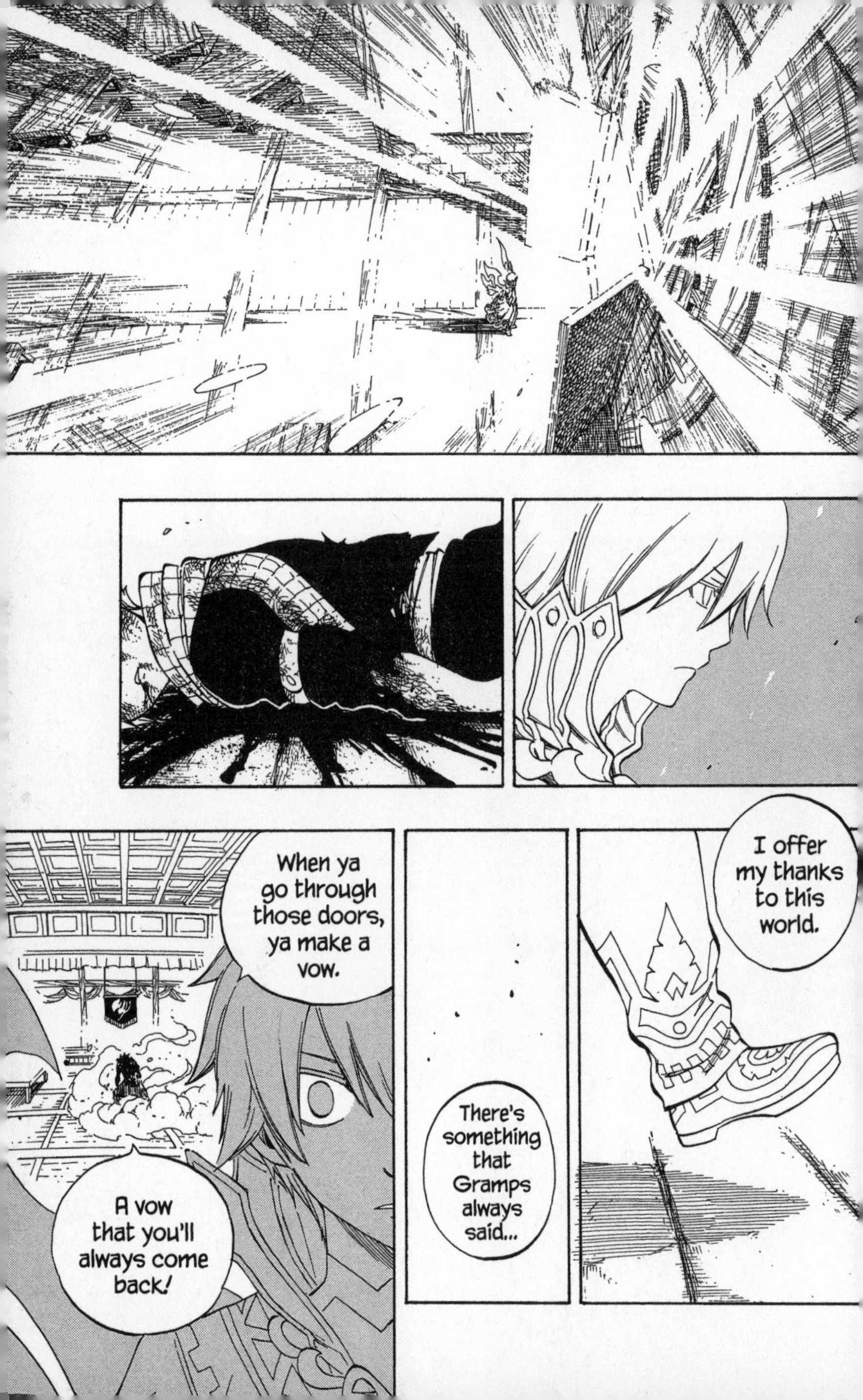
I offer my thanks to this world.
There's something that Gramps always said...
When ya go through those doors, ya make a vow.
A vow that you'll always come back!

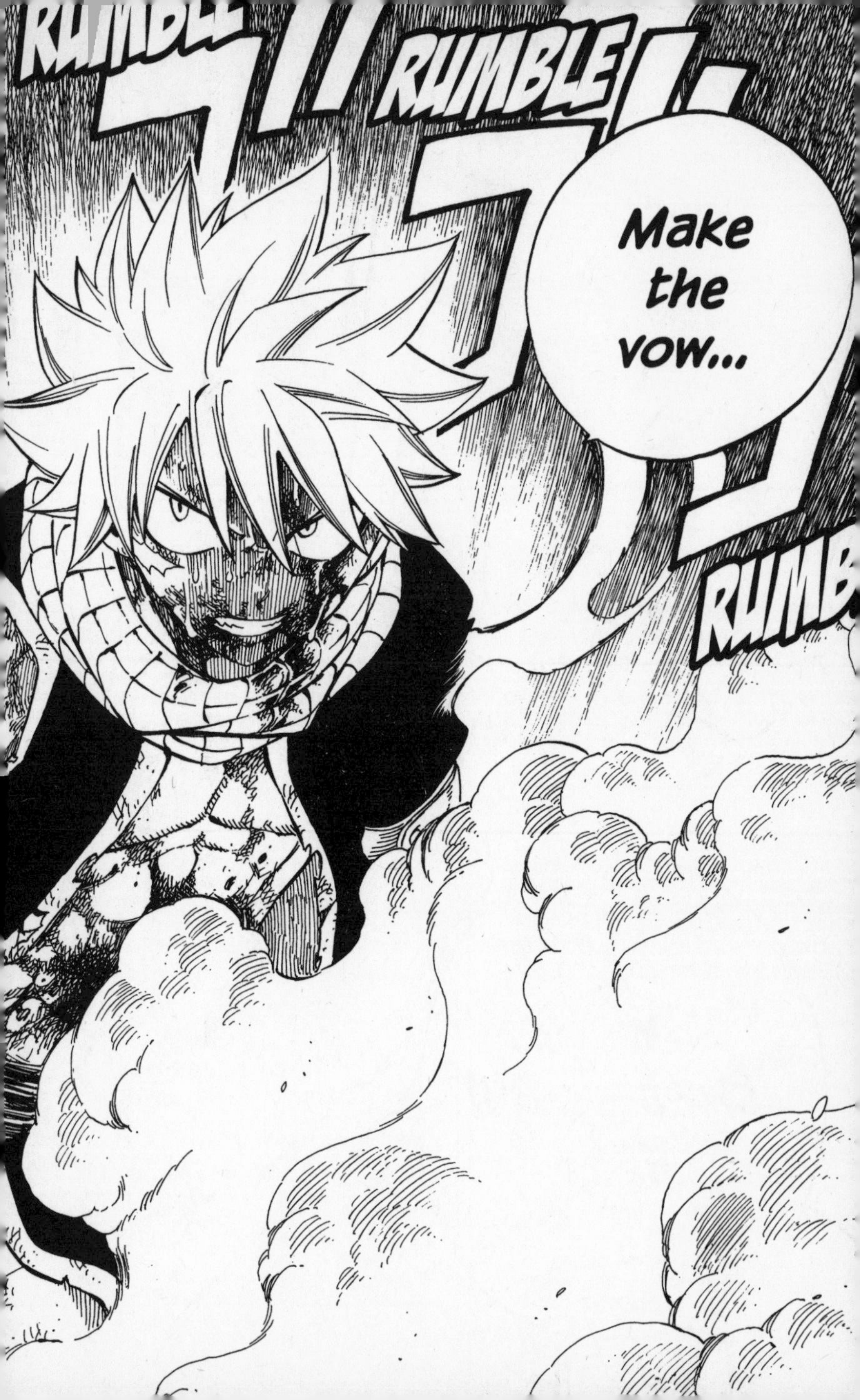
RUMBLE
RUMBLE
Make the vow...
RUMB

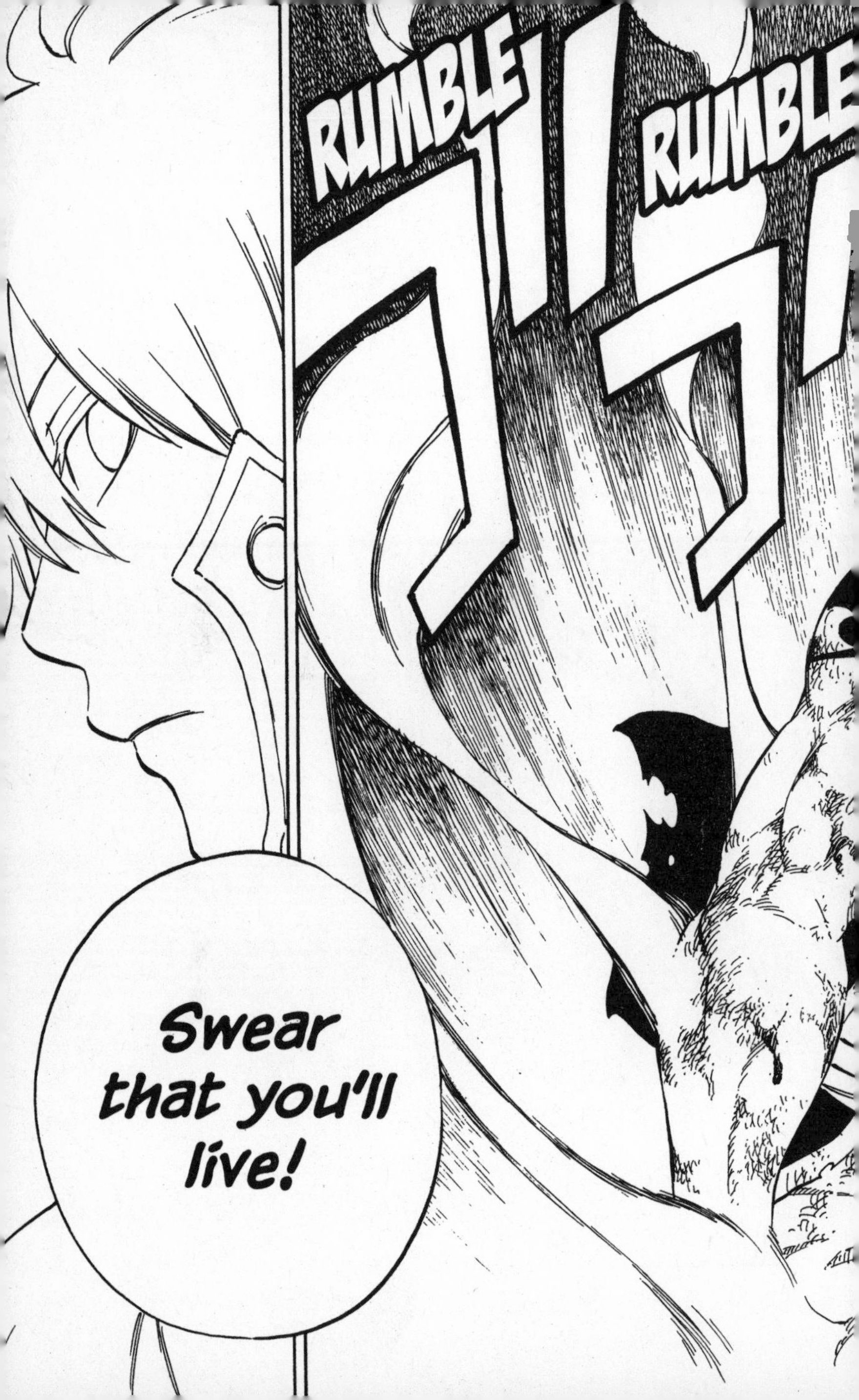
RUMBLE
RUMBLE
Swear that you'll live!

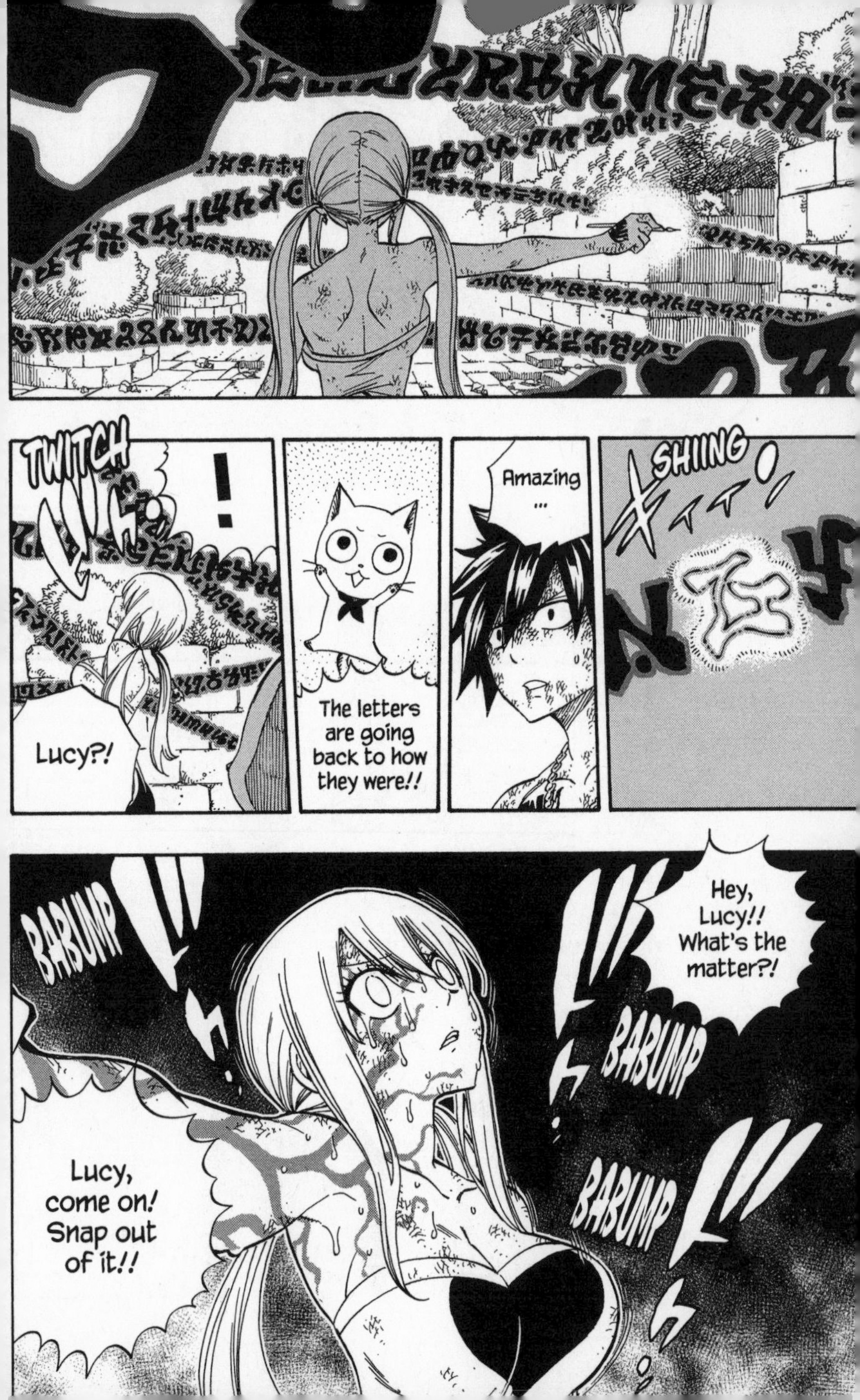
SHIING
Amazing ...
The letters are going back to how they were!!
TWITCH
!
Lucy?!
Hey, Lucy!! What's the matter?!
BABUMP
BABUMP
BABUMP
Lucy, come on! Snap out of it!!

FAIRY TAIL

フェアリーテイル

Chapter 535: The Greatest Power

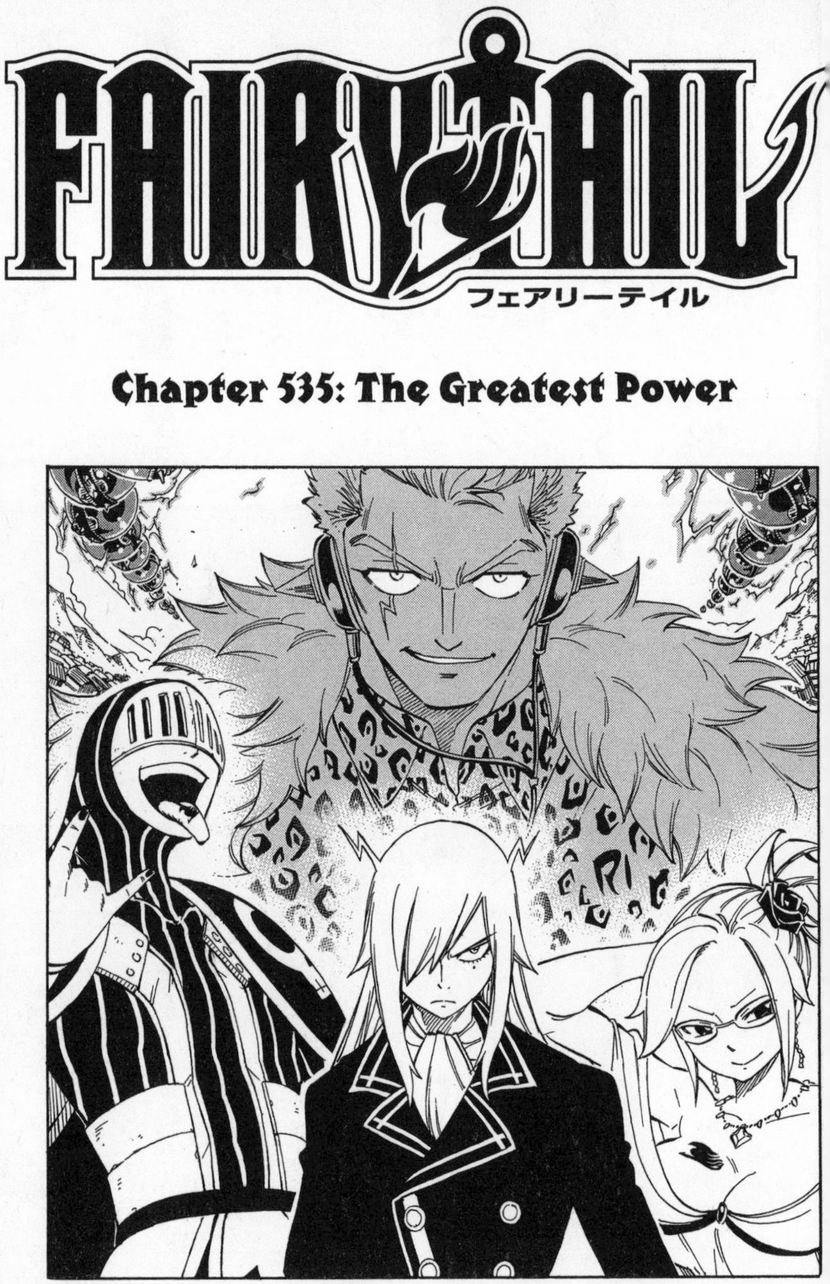

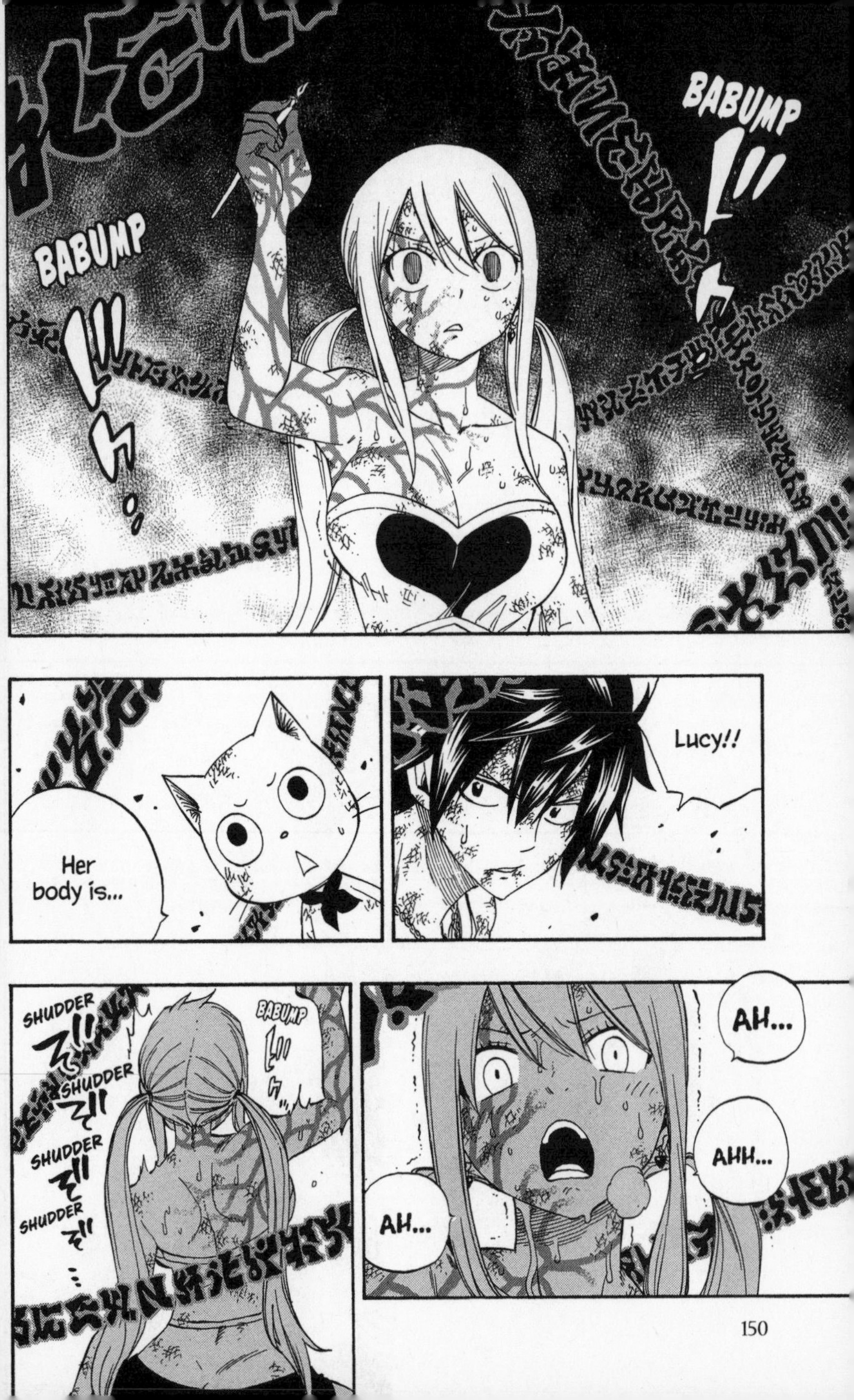

BABUMP
BABUMP
Lucy!!
Her body is...
AH...
AHH...
AH...
BABUMP
SHUDDER
SHUDDER
SHUDDER
SHUDDER

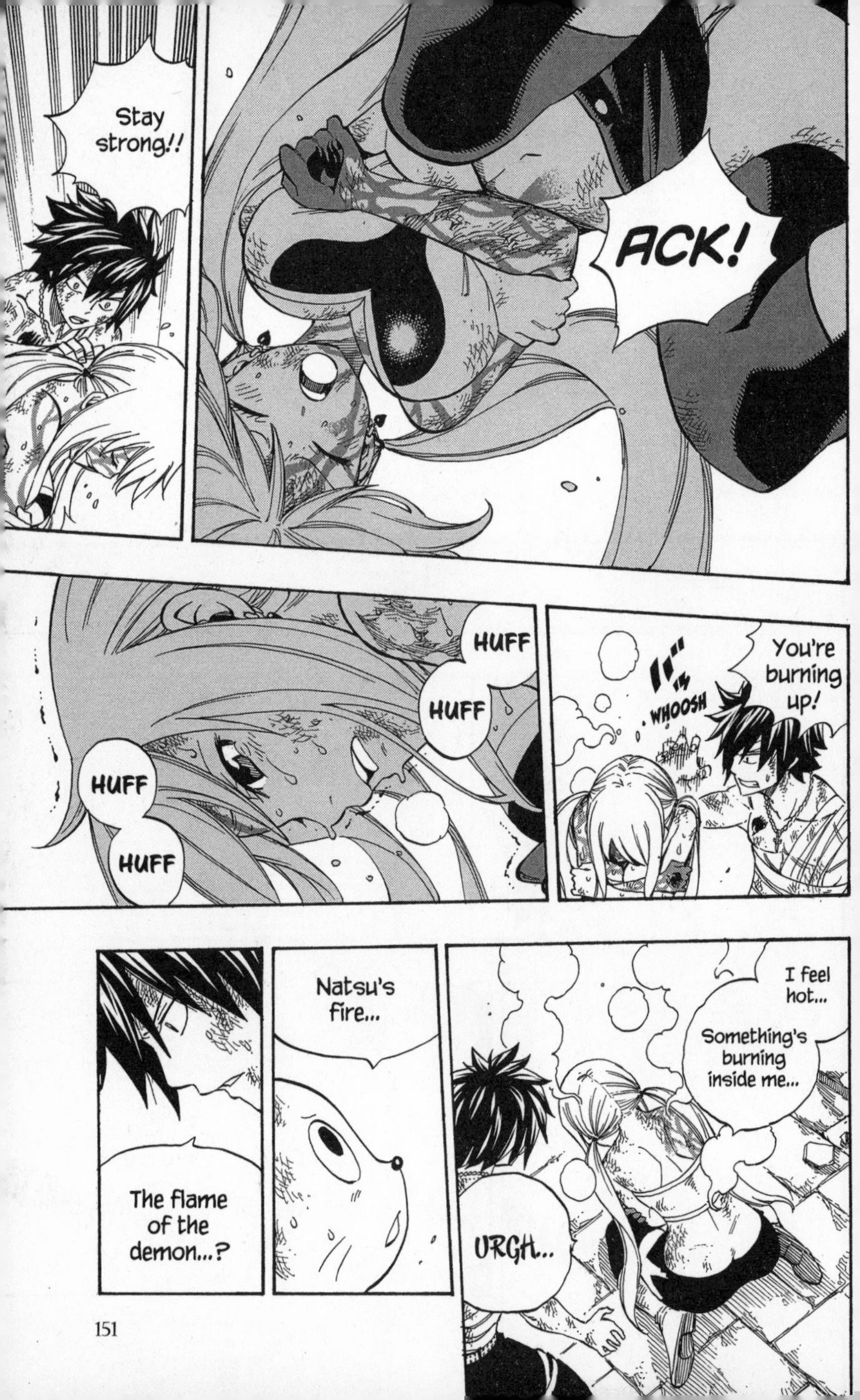
ACK!
Stay strong!!
You're burning up!
WHOOSH
HUFF
HUFF
HUFF
HUFF
I feel hot...
Something's burning inside me...
URGH...
Natsu's fire...
The flame of the demon...?

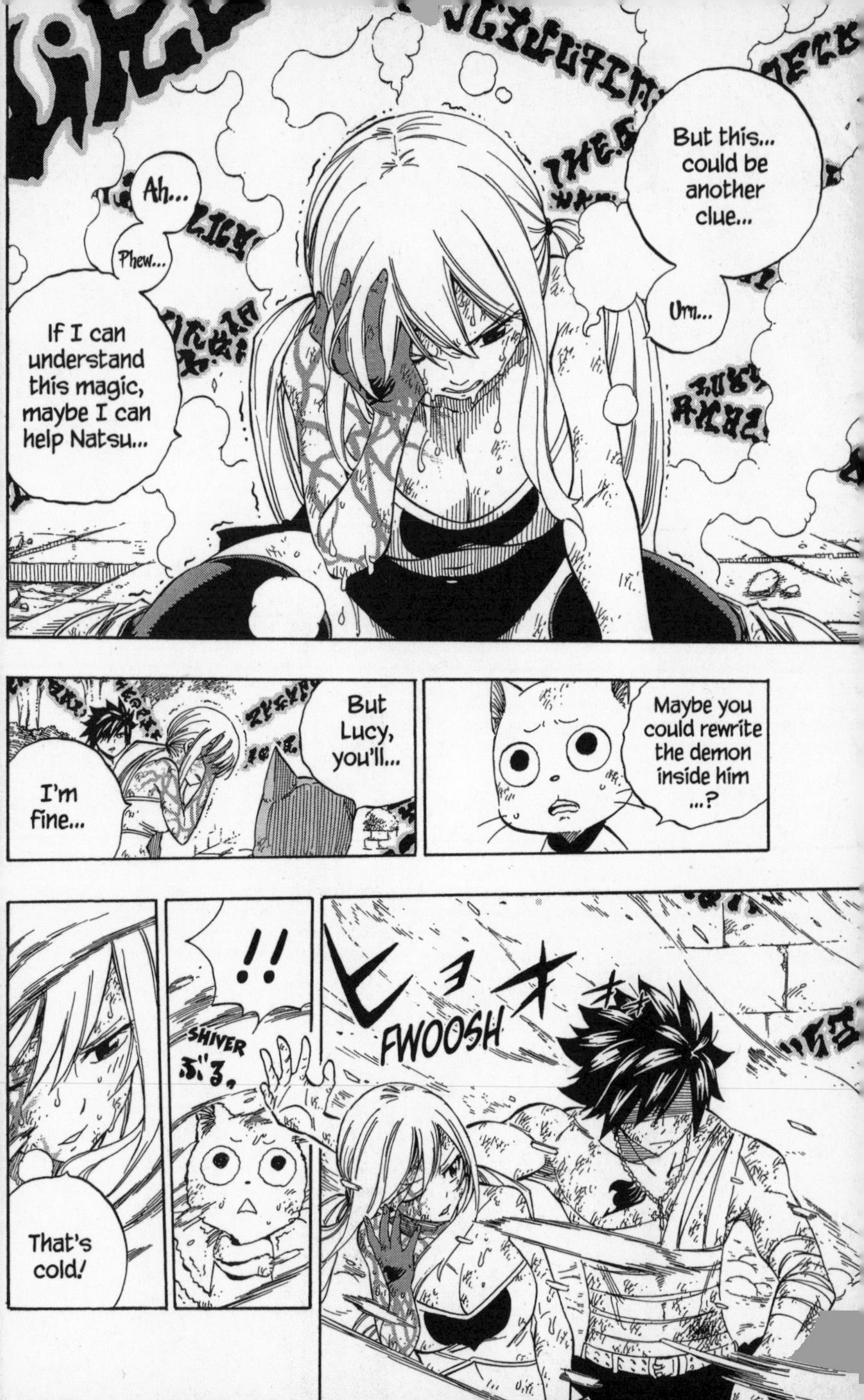
But this... could be another clue...
Um...
Ah...
Phew...
If I can understand this magic, maybe I can help Natsu...
Maybe you could rewrite the demon inside him ...?
But Lucy, you'll...
I'm fine...
ヒョオ
FWOOSH
!!
SHIVER
ぶる
That's cold!

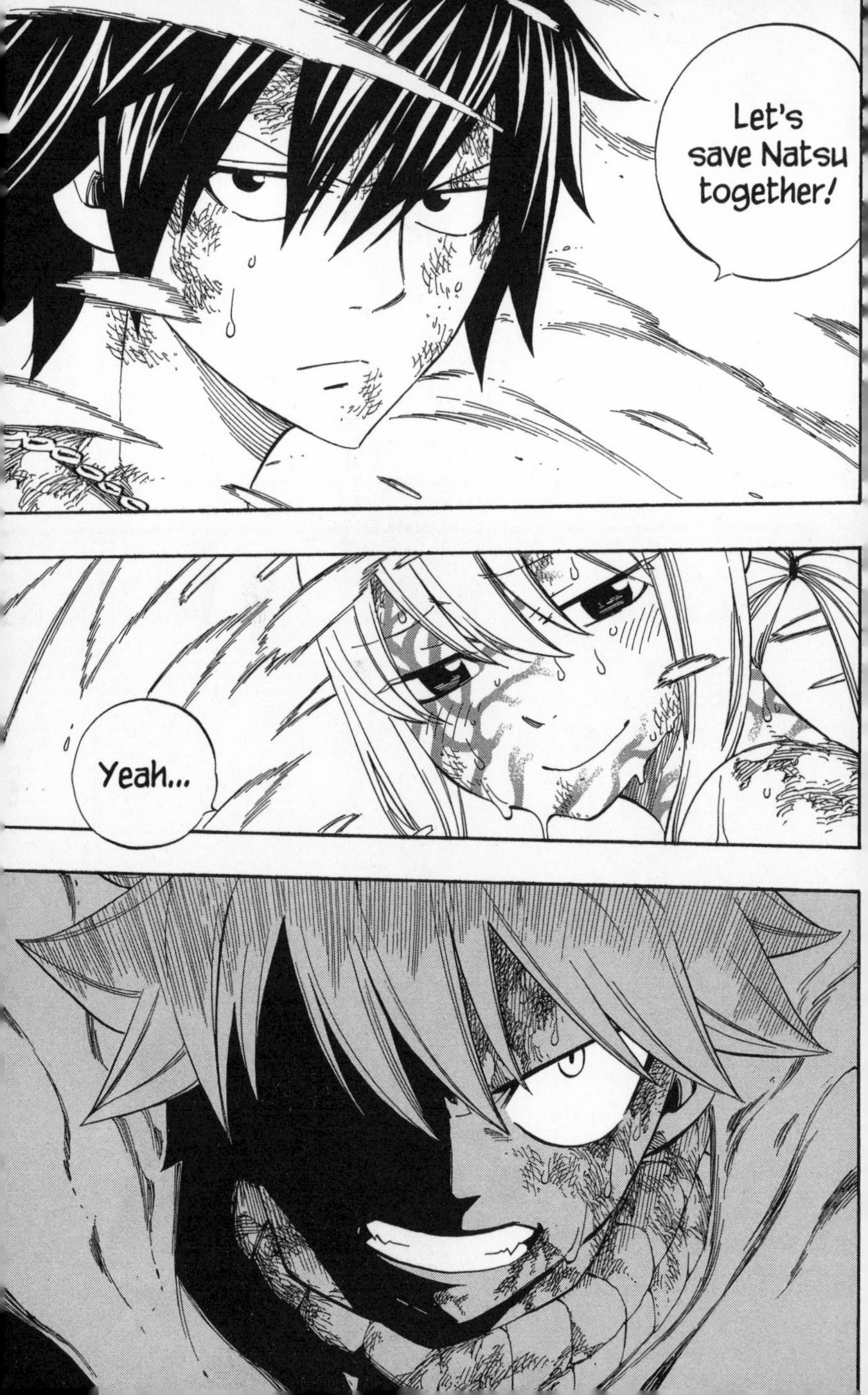
Let's save Natsu together!
Yeah...

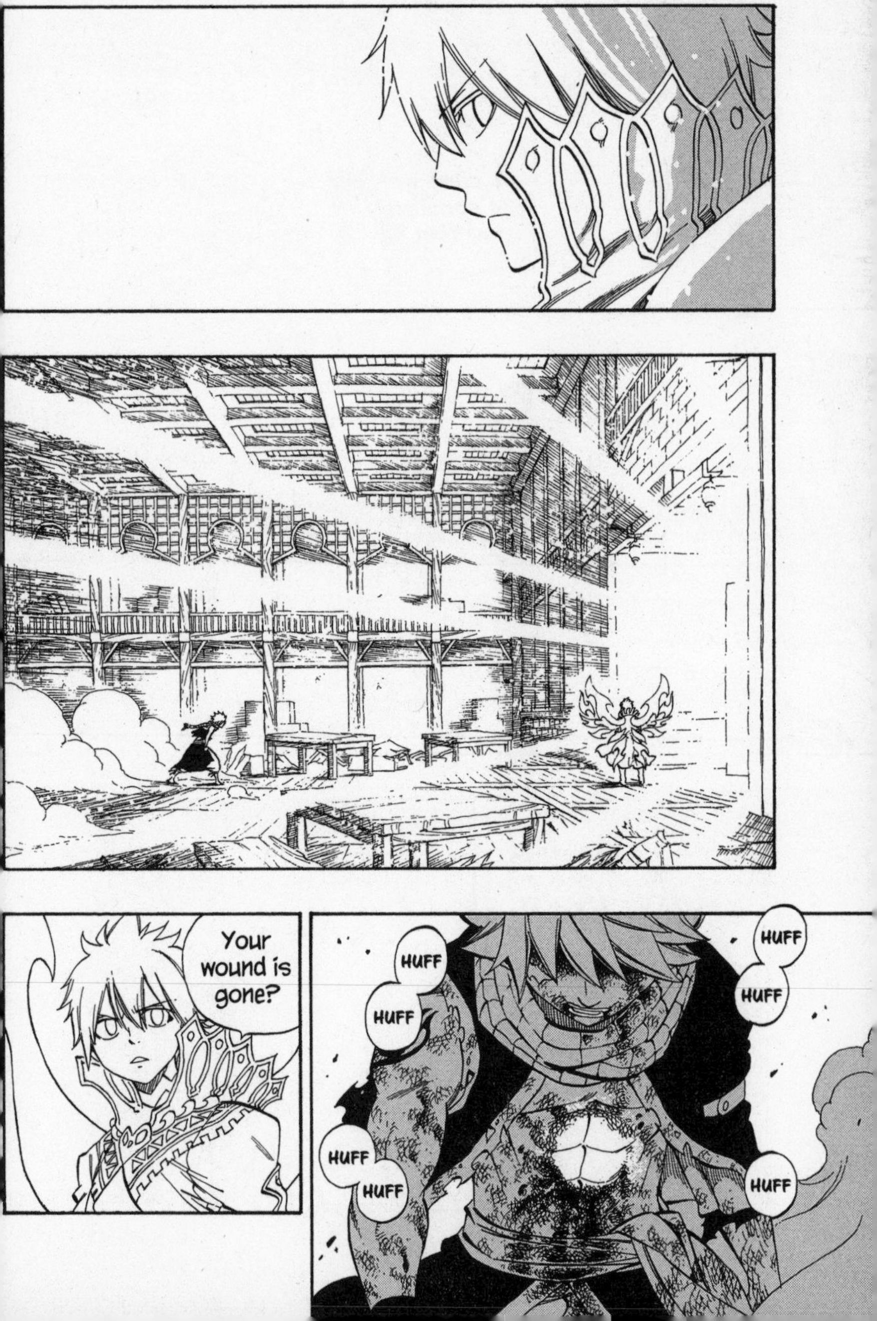
HUFF
HUFF
HUFF
HUFF
HUFF
HUFF
HUFF
Your wound is gone?

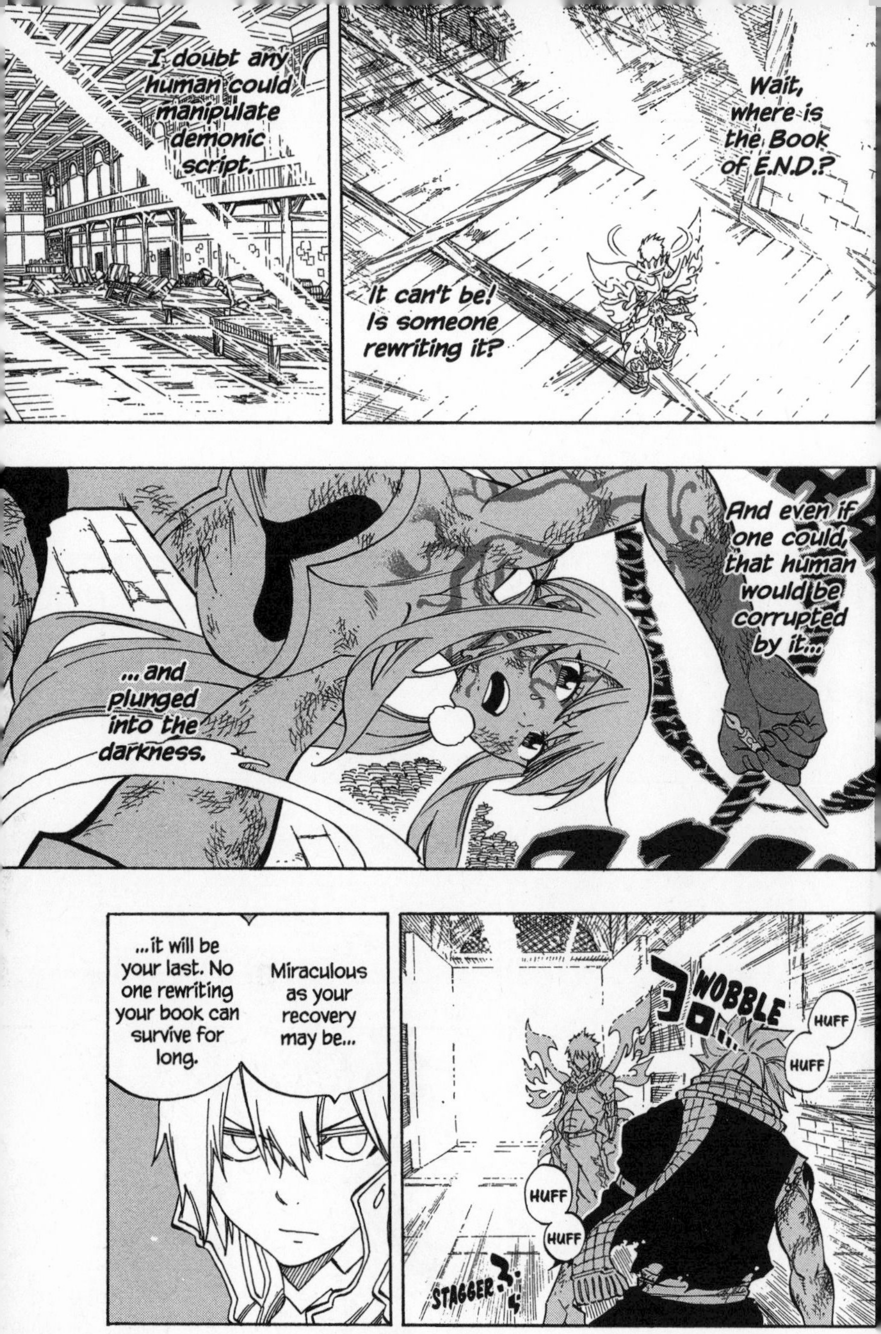
Wait, where is the Book of E.N.D.?
It can't be! Is someone rewriting it?
I doubt any human could manipulate demonic script.
And even if one could, that human would be corrupted by it...
...and plunged into the darkness.
WOBBLE
HUFF
HUFF
HUFF
HUFF
STAGGER
Miraculous as your recovery may be...
...it will be your last. No one rewriting your book can survive for long.

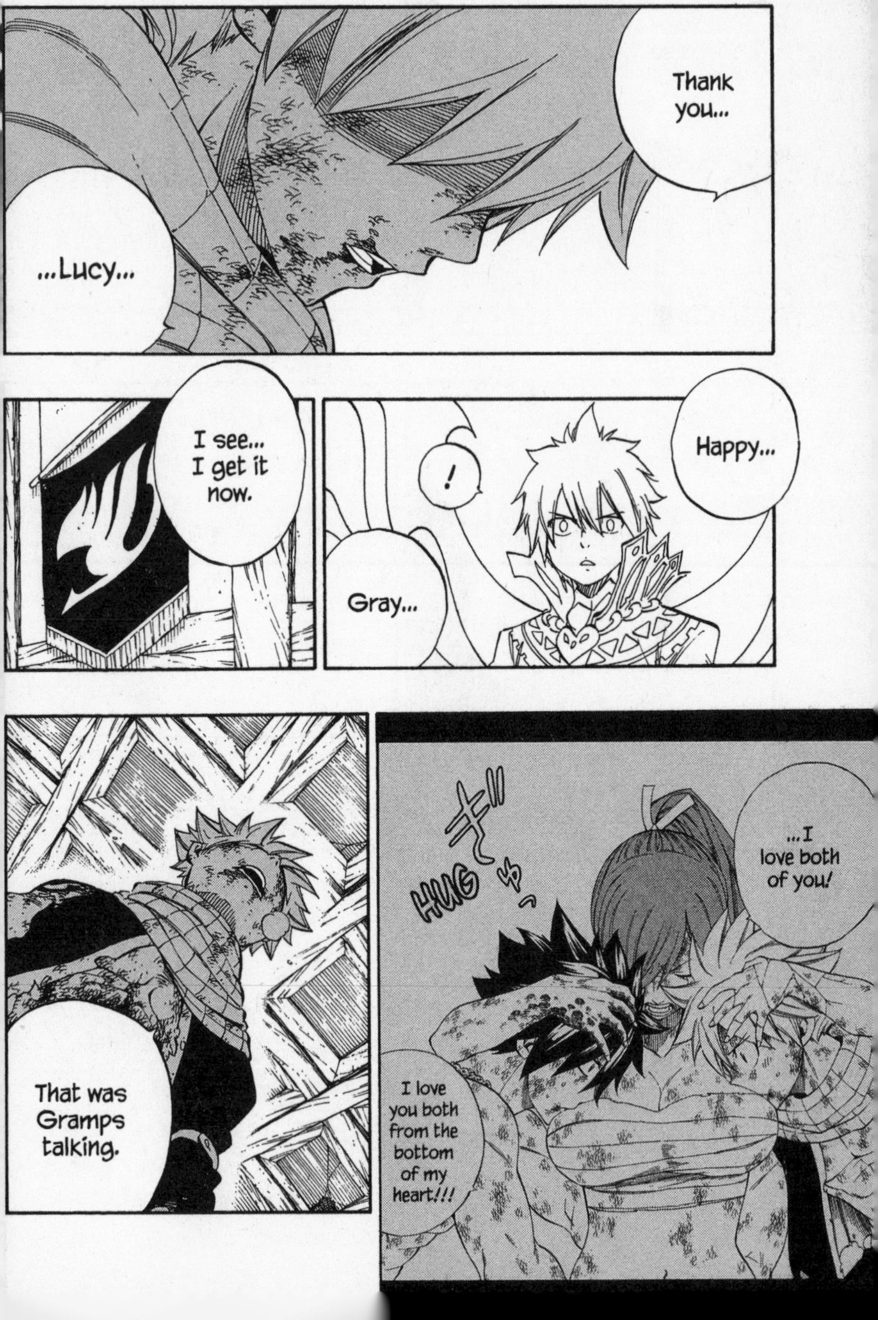
Thank you...
...Lucy...
Happy...
!
Gray...
I see... I get it now.
HUG
...I love both of you!
I love you both from the bottom of my heart!!!
That was Gramps talking.

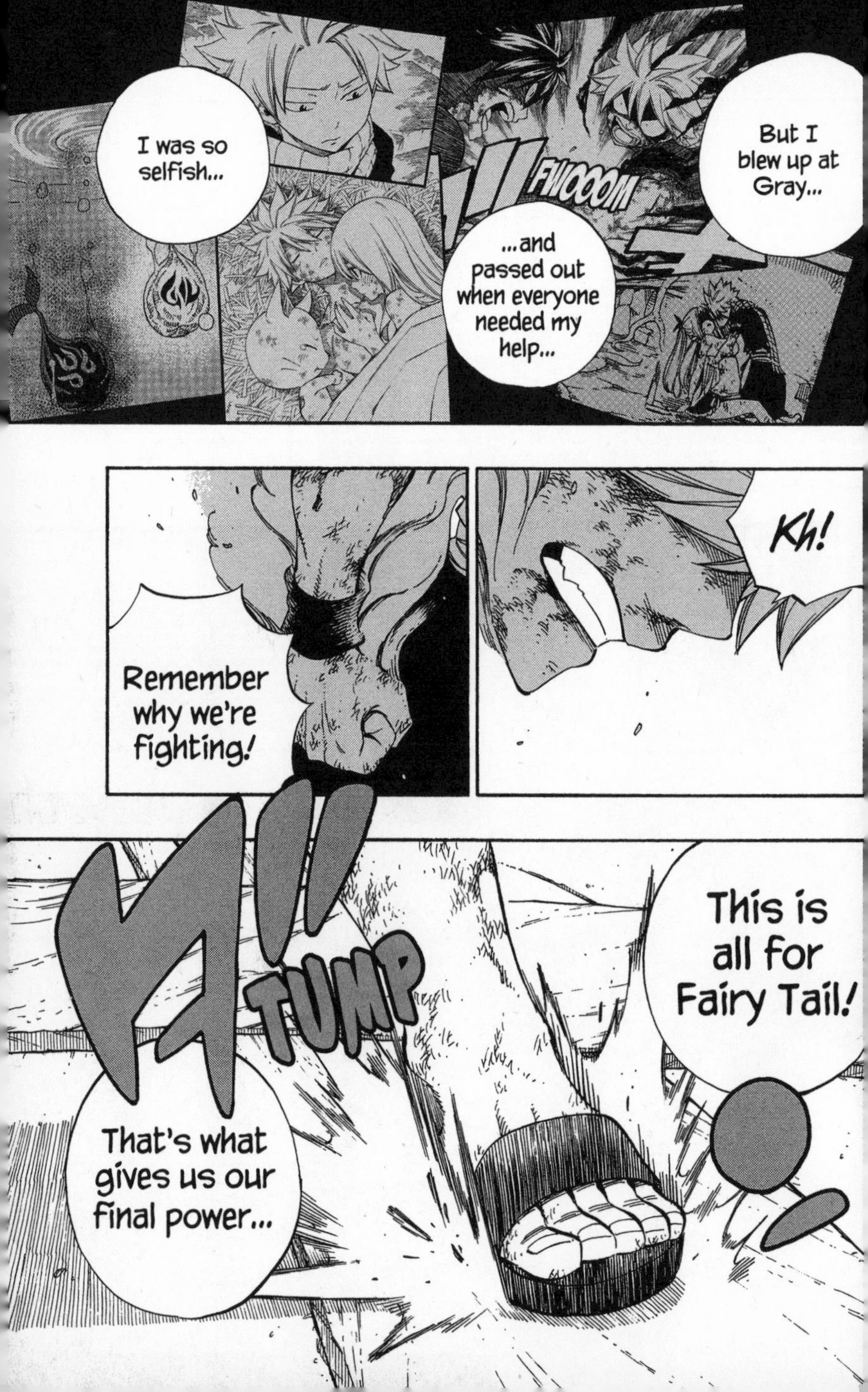
But I blew up at Gray...
FWOOOM
...and passed out when everyone needed my help...
I was so selfish...
Kh!
Remember why we're fighting!
This is all for Fairy Tail!
TUMP
That's what gives us our final power...

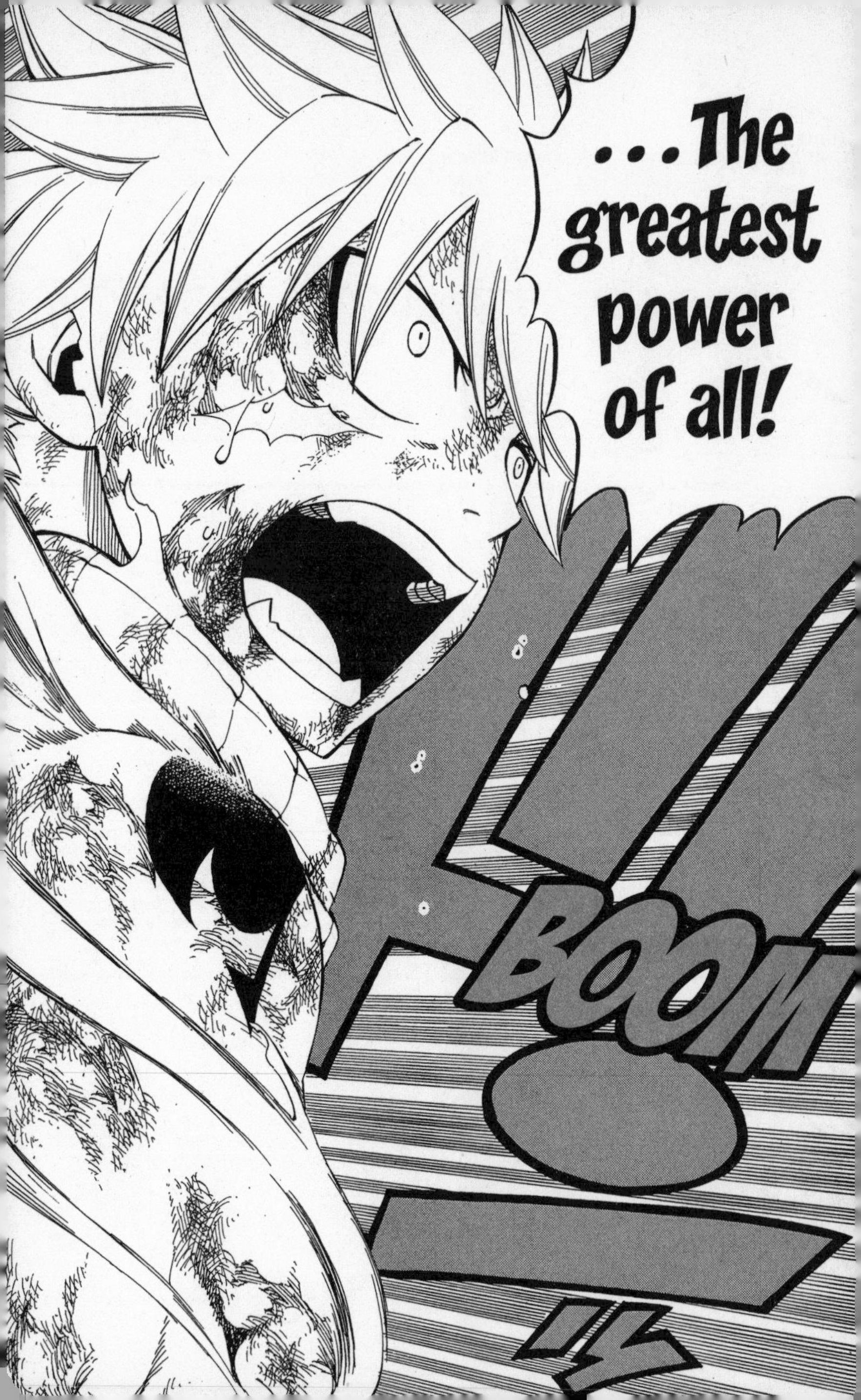
...The greatest power of all!
BOOM

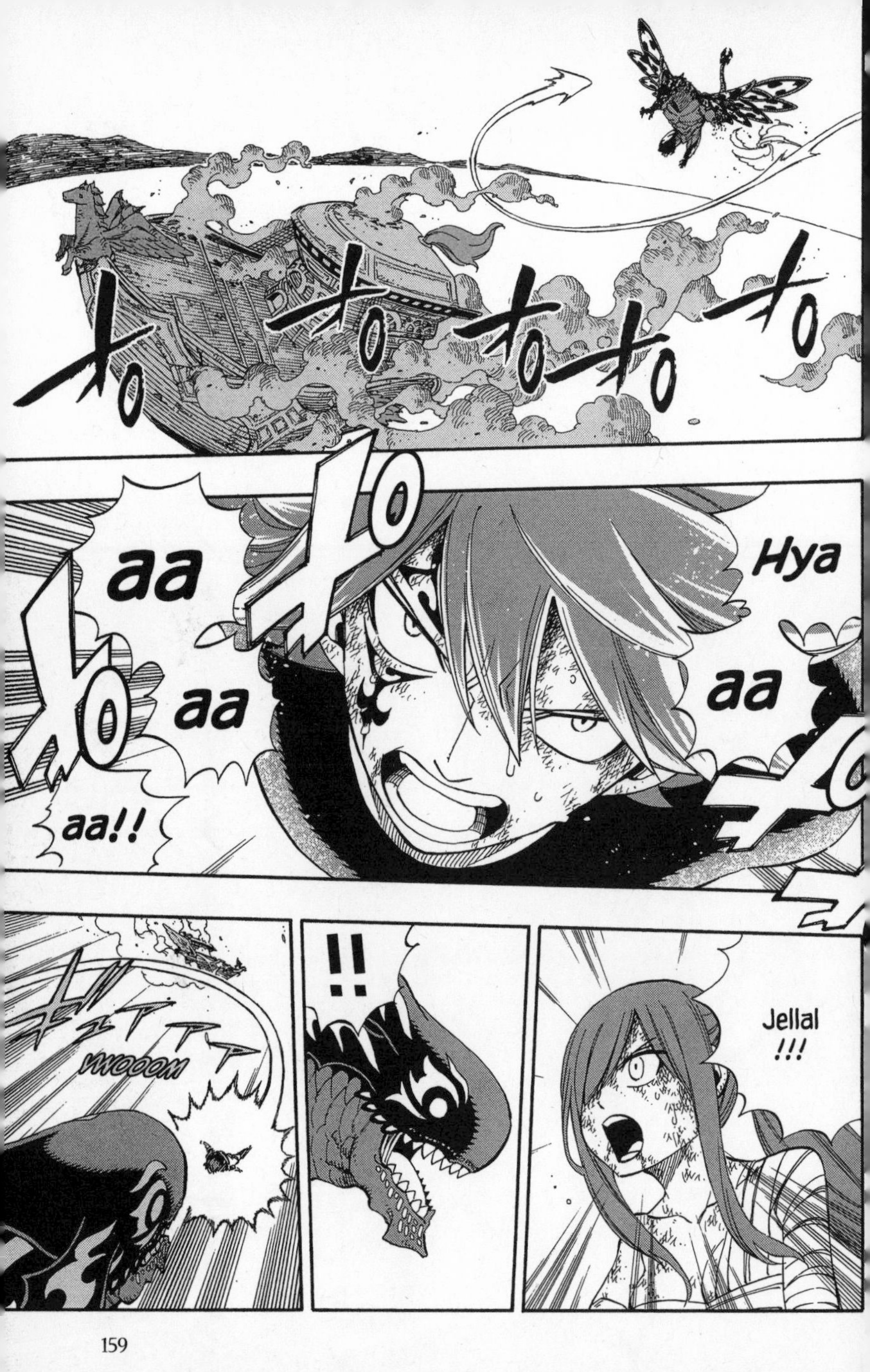
Hya
aa
aa
aa
aa!!
Jellal
!!!
!!
VWOOOM

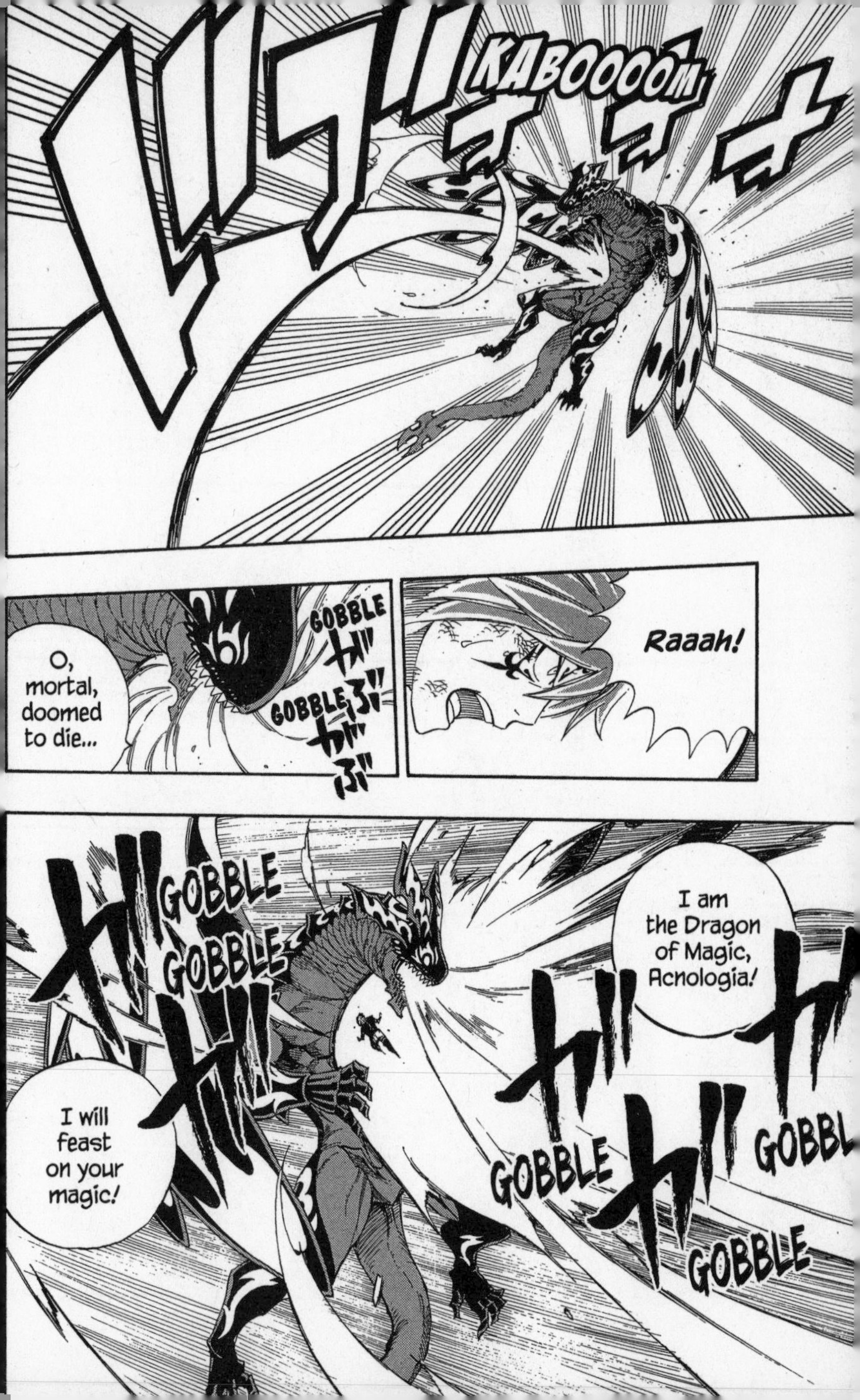
KABOOOOM
Raaah!
O, mortal, doomed to die...
GOBBLE
GOBBLE
I am the Dragon of Magic, Acnologia!
GOBBL
GOBBLE
GOBBLE
GOBBLE
GOBBLE
I will feast on your magic!

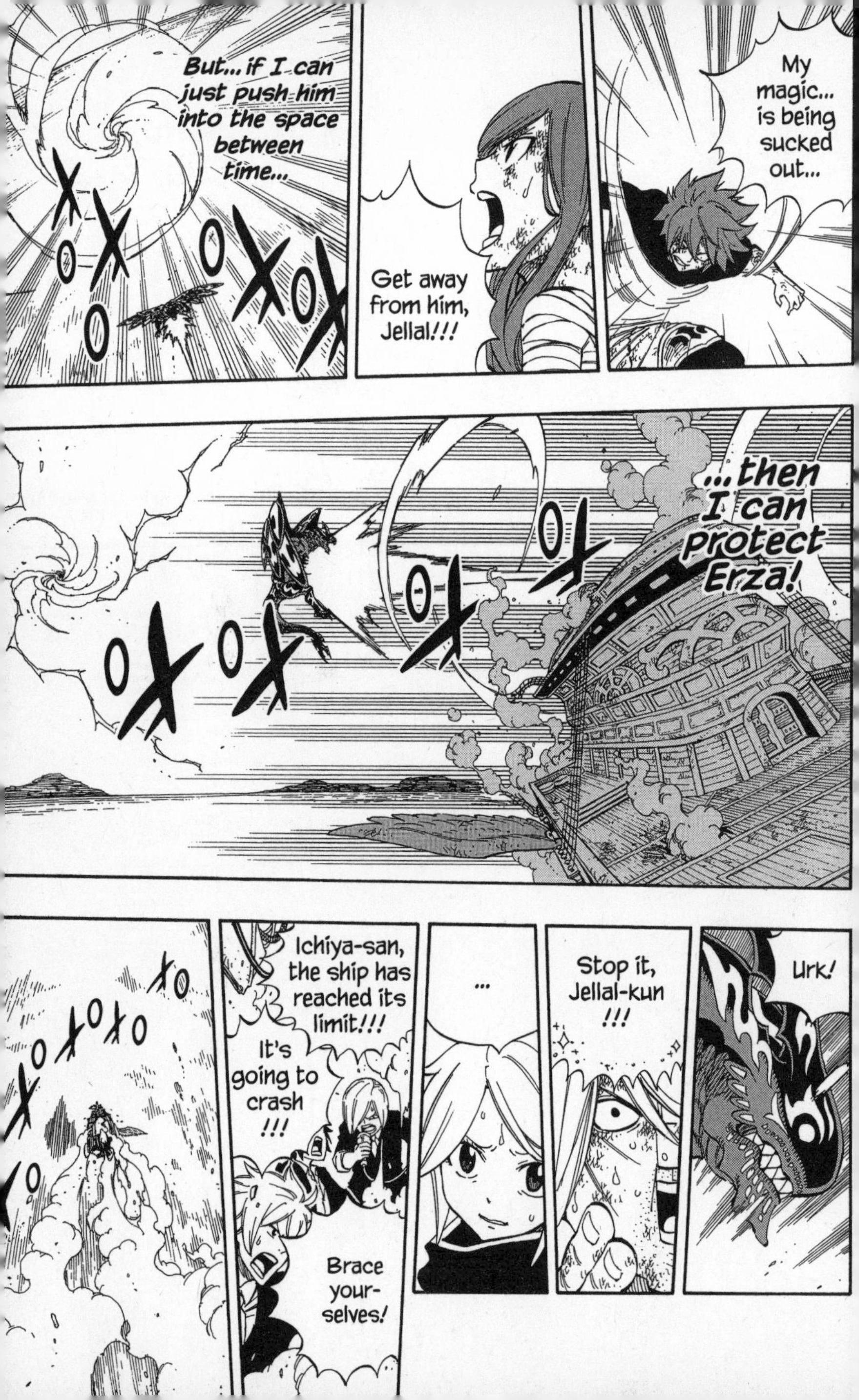
My magic... is being sucked out...
Get away from him, Jellal!!!
But... if I can just push him into the space between time...
...then I can protect Erza!
Urk!
Stop it, Jellal-kun !!!
...
Ichiya-san, the ship has reached its limit!!!
It's going to crash !!!
Brace your-selves!

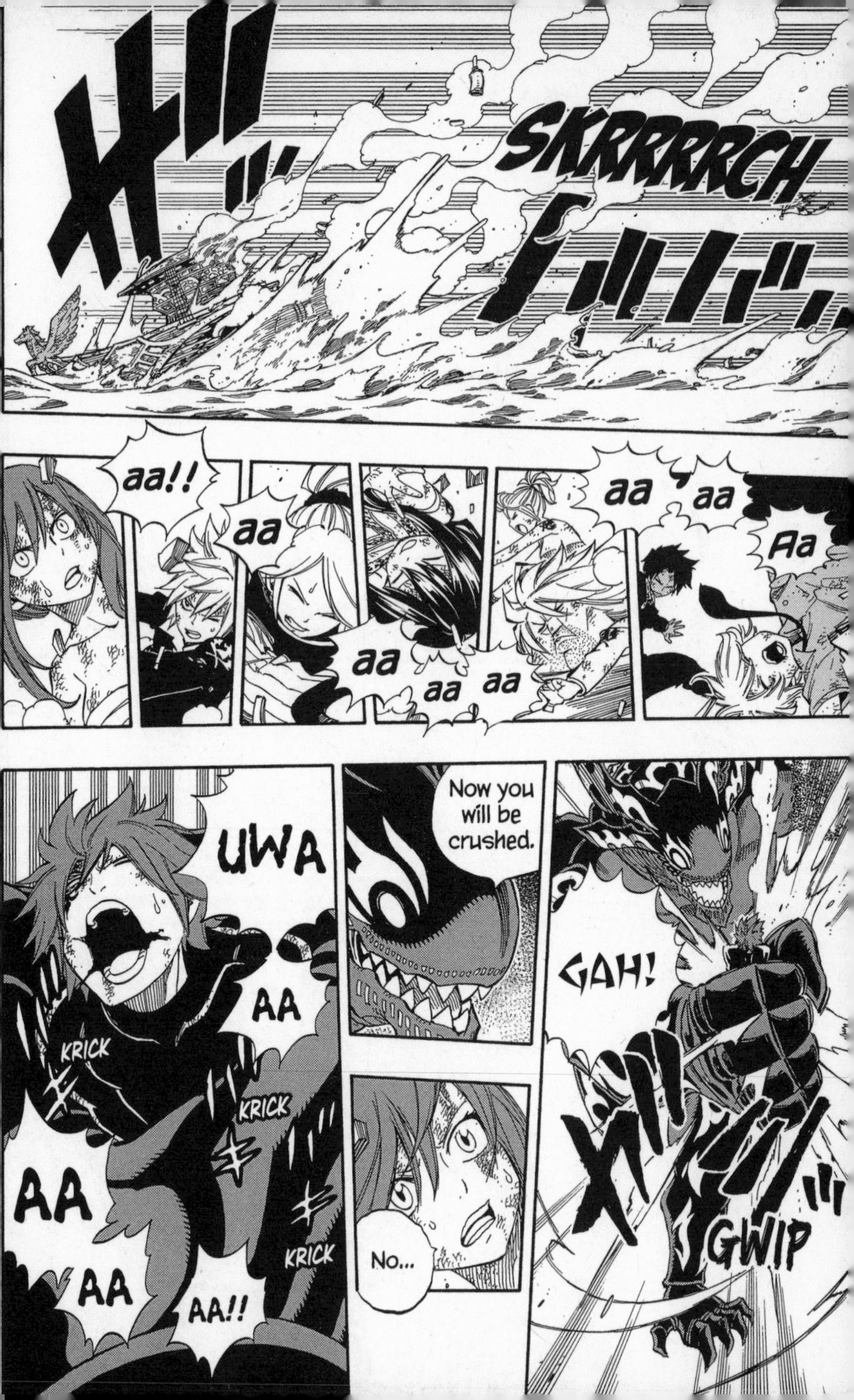
SKRRRRCH
aa aa Aa
aa aa aa
aa
aa!!
Now you will be crushed.
GAH!
GWIP
No...
UWA
AA
KRICK
KRICK
KRICK
AA
AA
AA!!

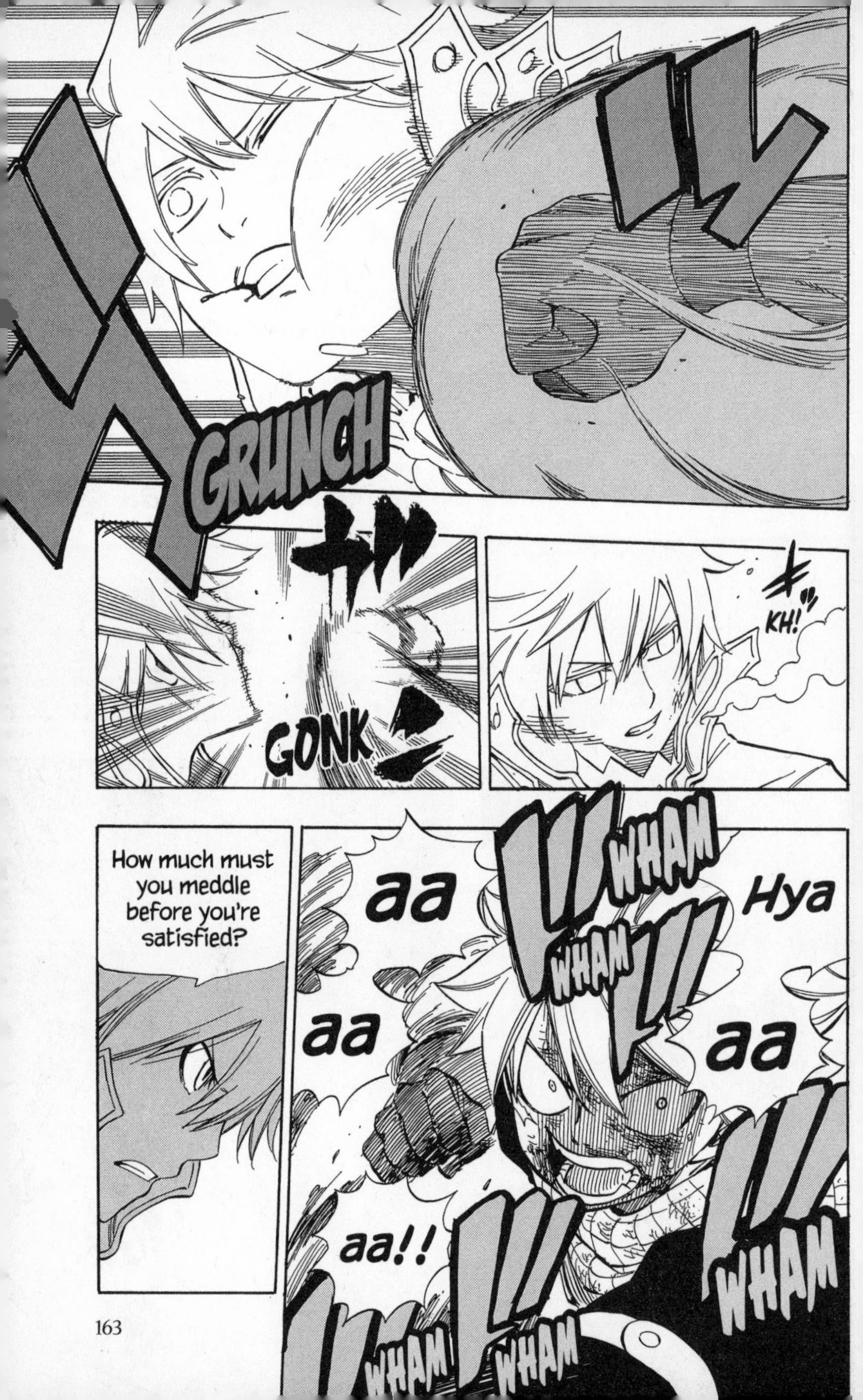

GRUNCH
KH!
GONK
WHAM
Hya
aa
WHAM
aa
aa
aa!!
WHAM
WHAM
WHAM
How much must you meddle before you're satisfied?

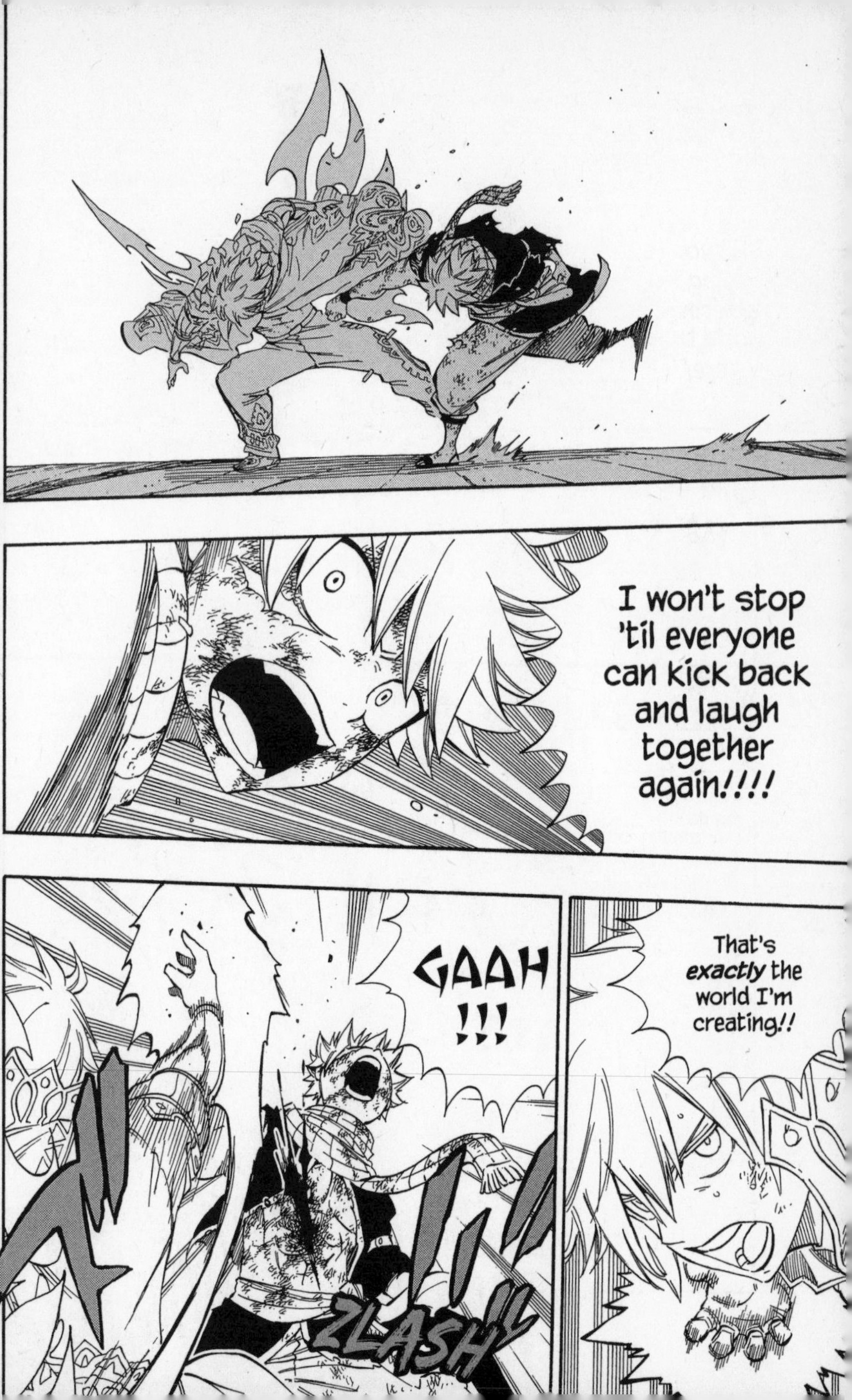
I won't stop 'til everyone can kick back and laugh together again!!!!
That's *exactly* the world I'm creating!!
GAAH !!!
ZLASH

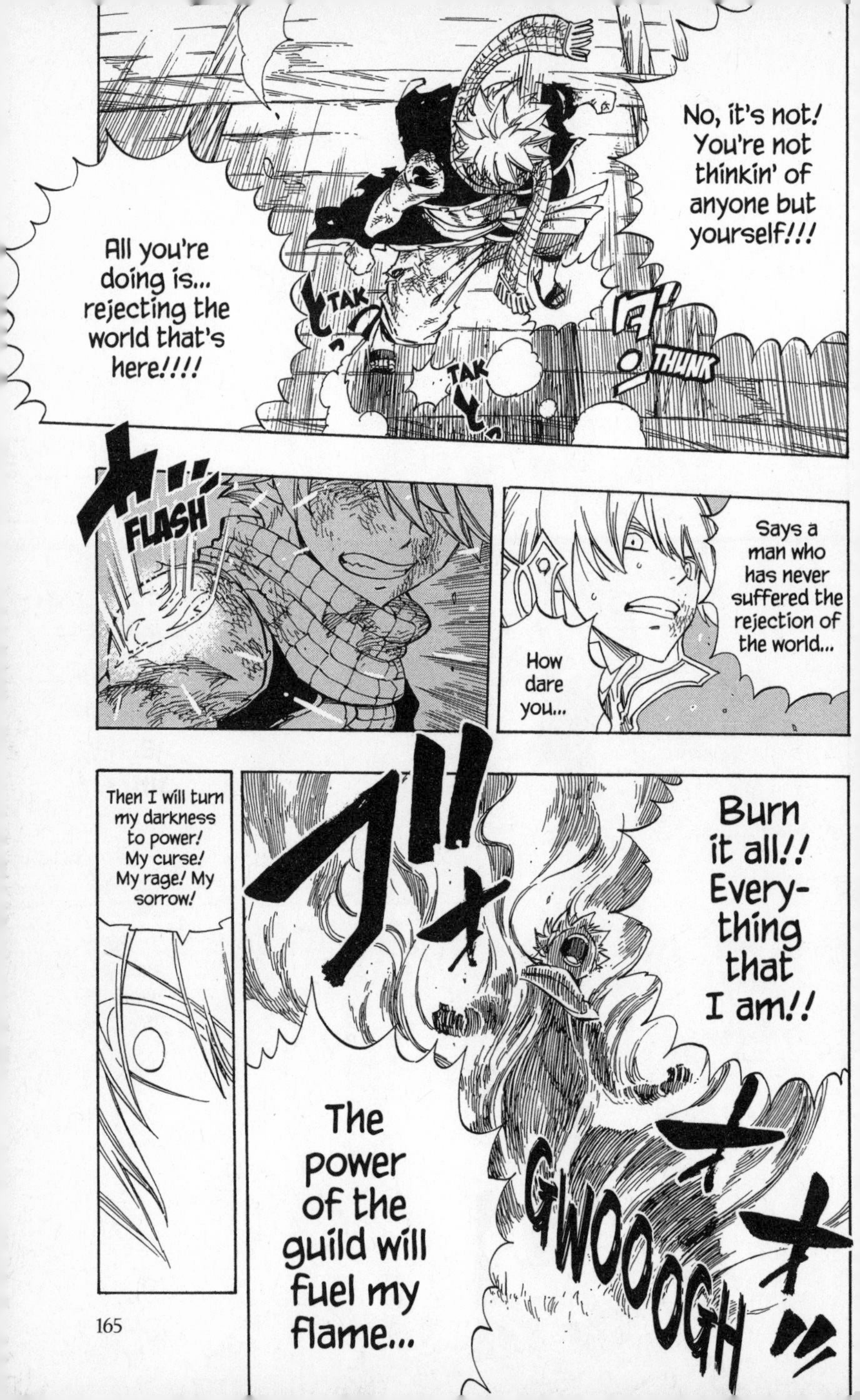
No, it's not! You're not thinkin' of anyone but yourself!!!
All you're doing is... rejecting the world that's here!!!!
THUNK
TAK
TAK
Says a man who has never suffered the rejection of the world...
How dare you...
FLASH
Burn it all!! Everything that I am!!
The power of the guild will fuel my flame...
GWOOOGH!!
Then I will turn my darkness to power! My curse! My rage! My sorrow!

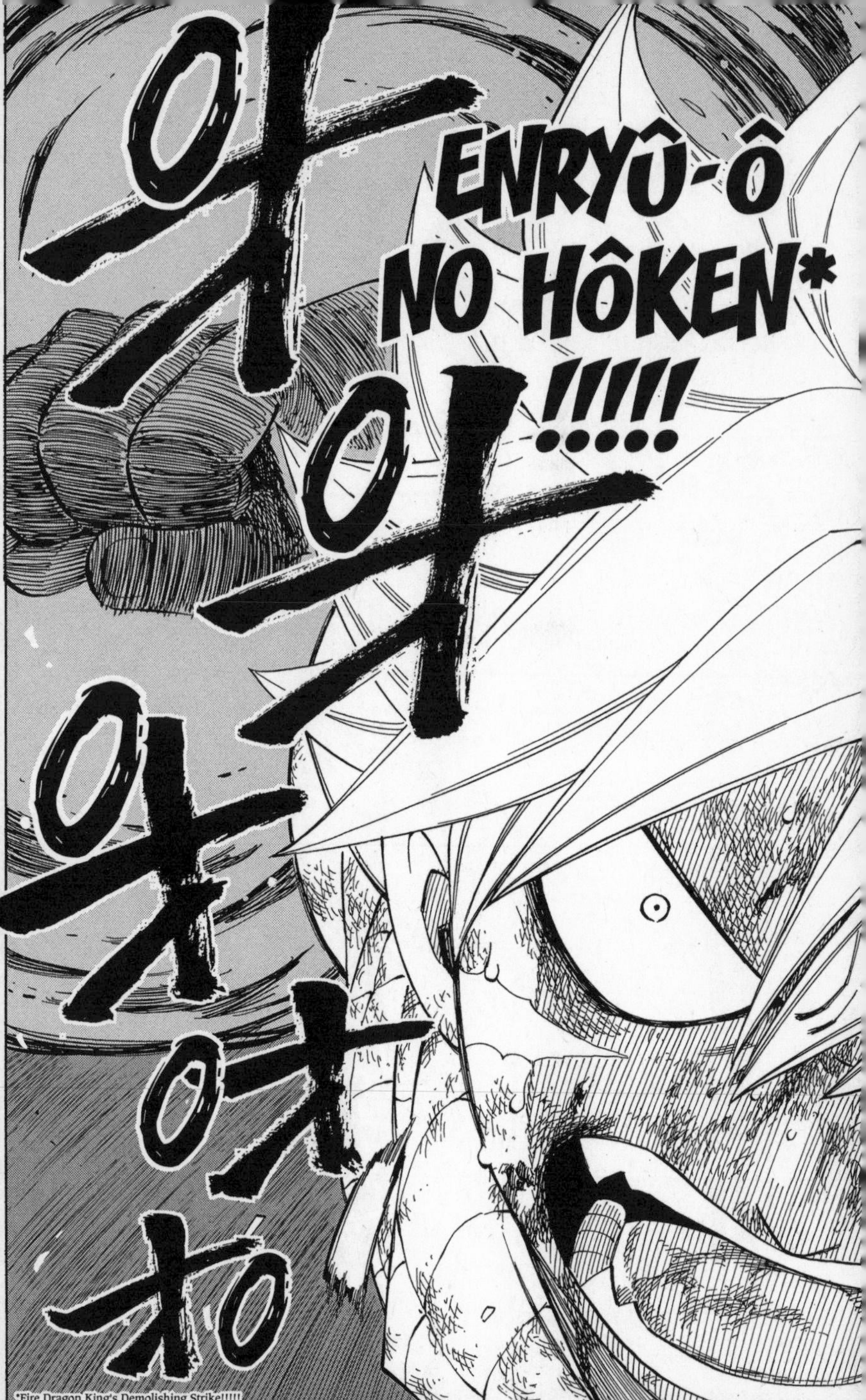
ENRYÛ-Ô NO HÔKEN* !!!!!

*Fire Dragon King's Demolishing Strike!!!!!

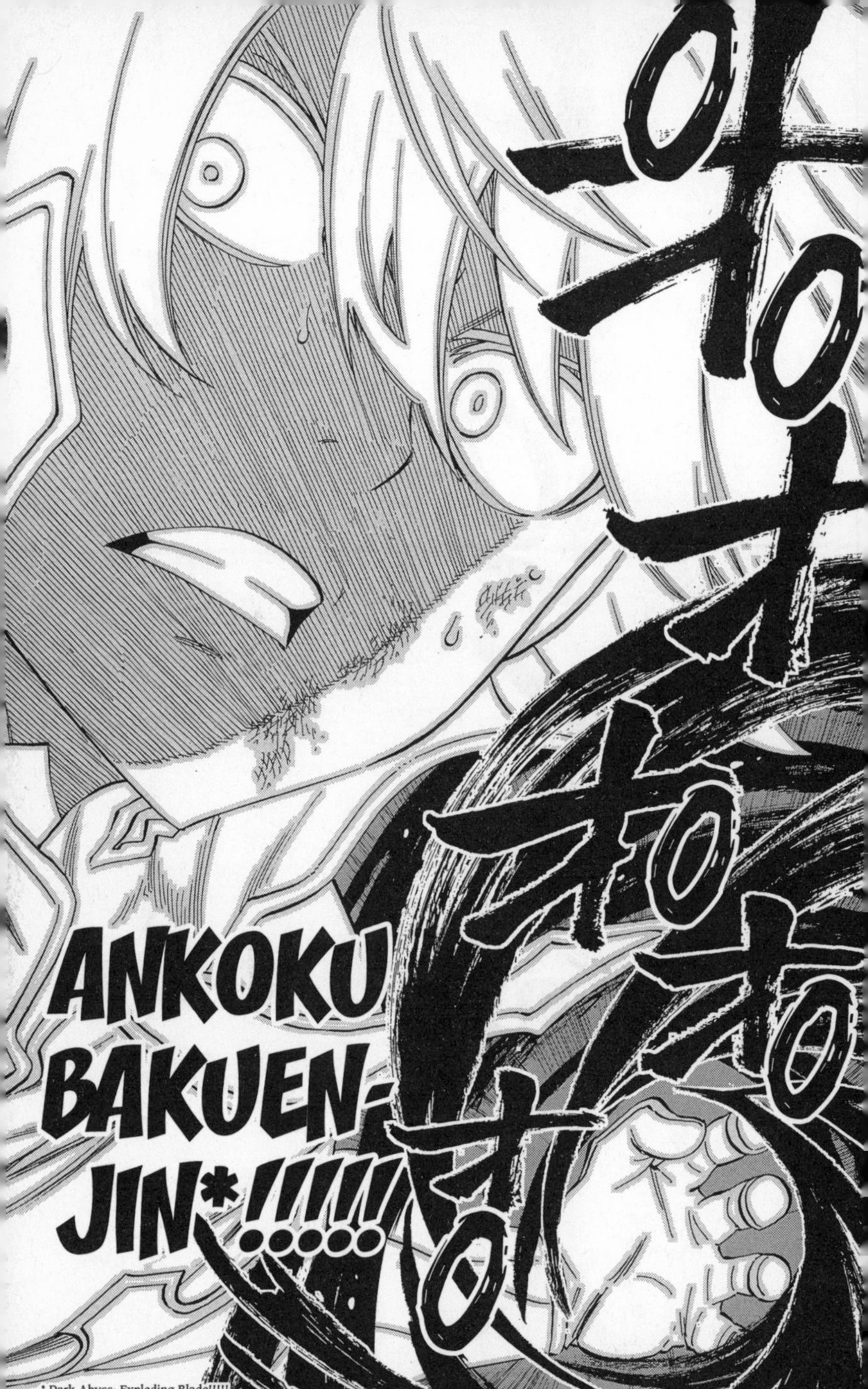
ANKOKU BAKUEN-JIN*!!!!!

* Dark Abyss: Exploding Blade!!!!!

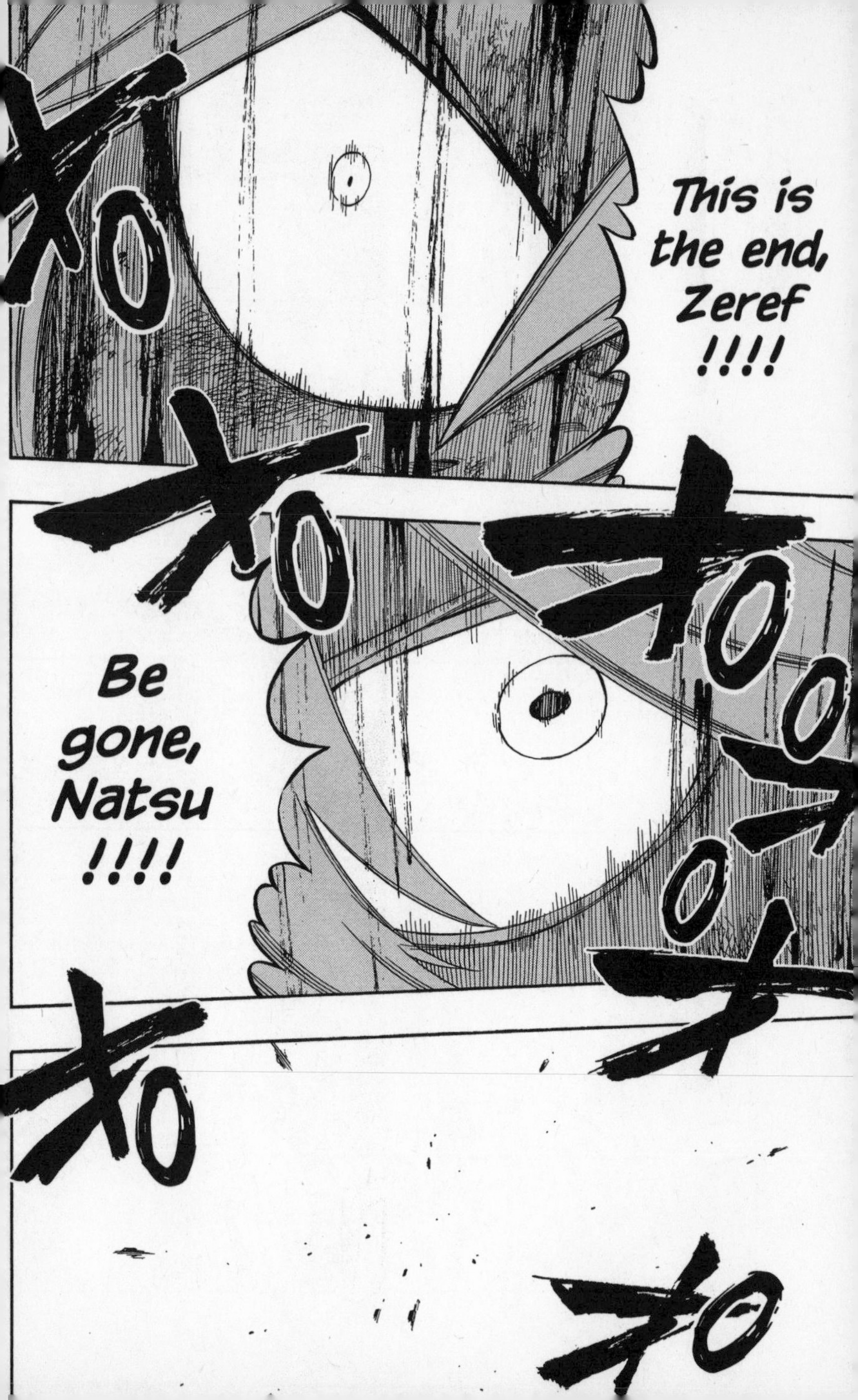
This is the end, Zeref !!!!
Be gone, Natsu !!!!

FAIRY TAIL

フェアリーテイル

Chapter 536: Savage Dragon Fire

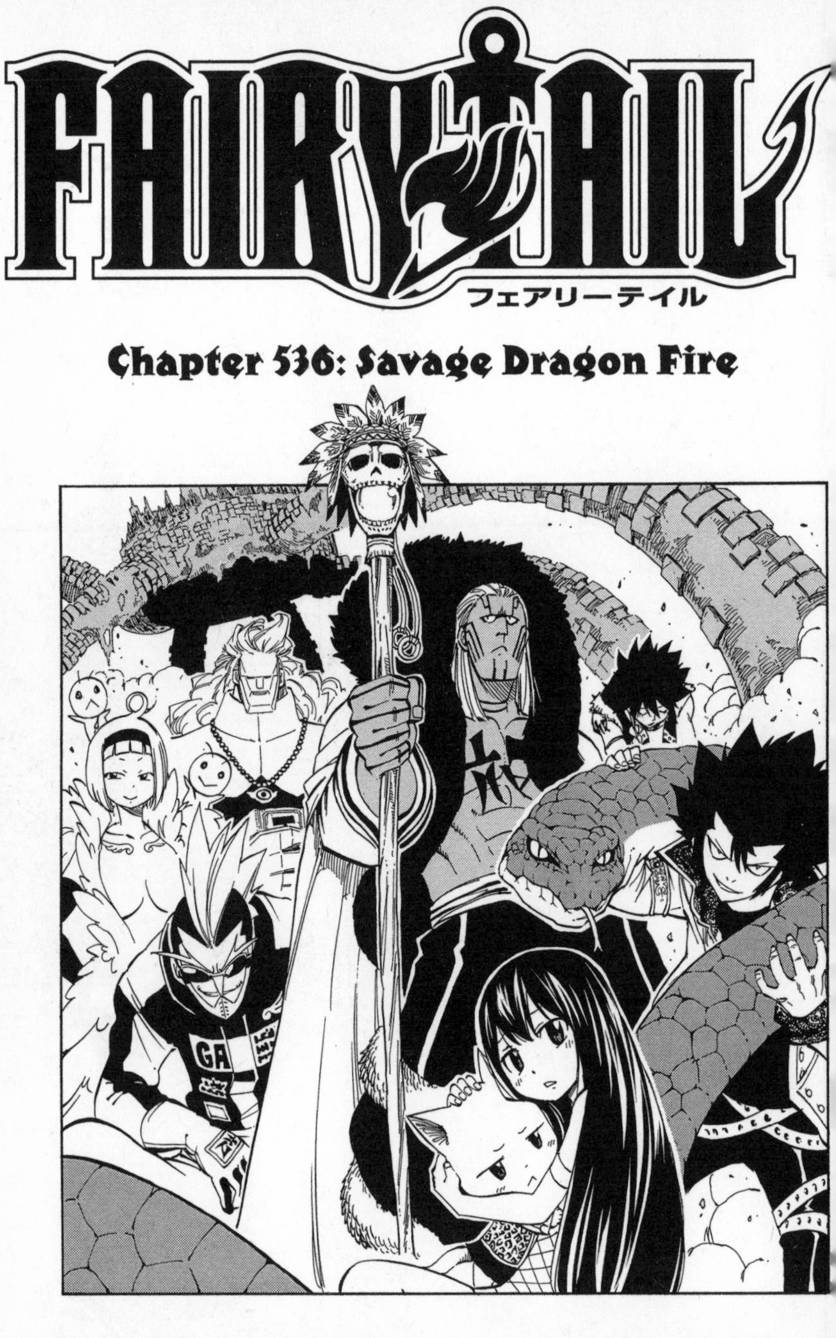

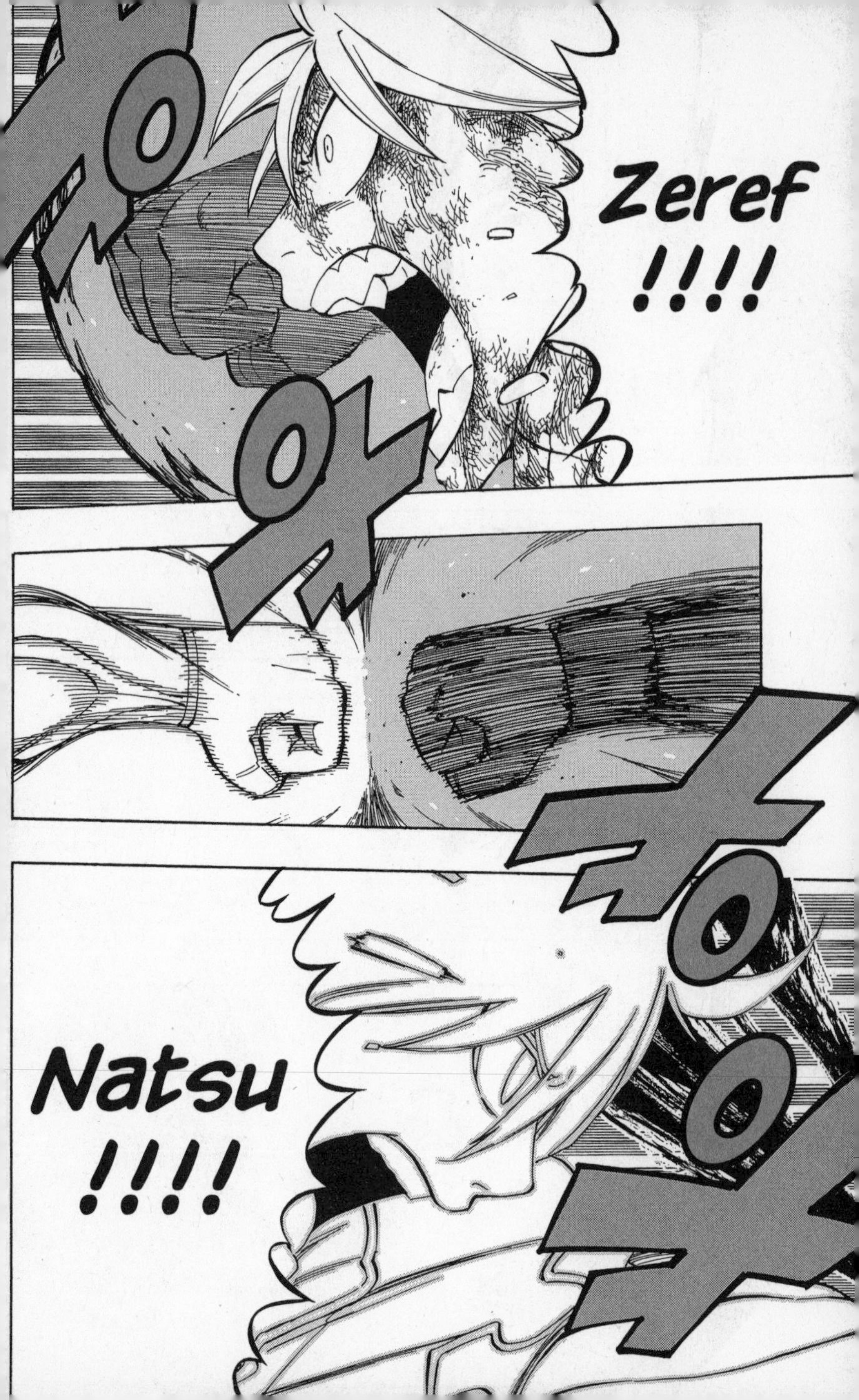
Zeref !!!!
Natsu !!!!

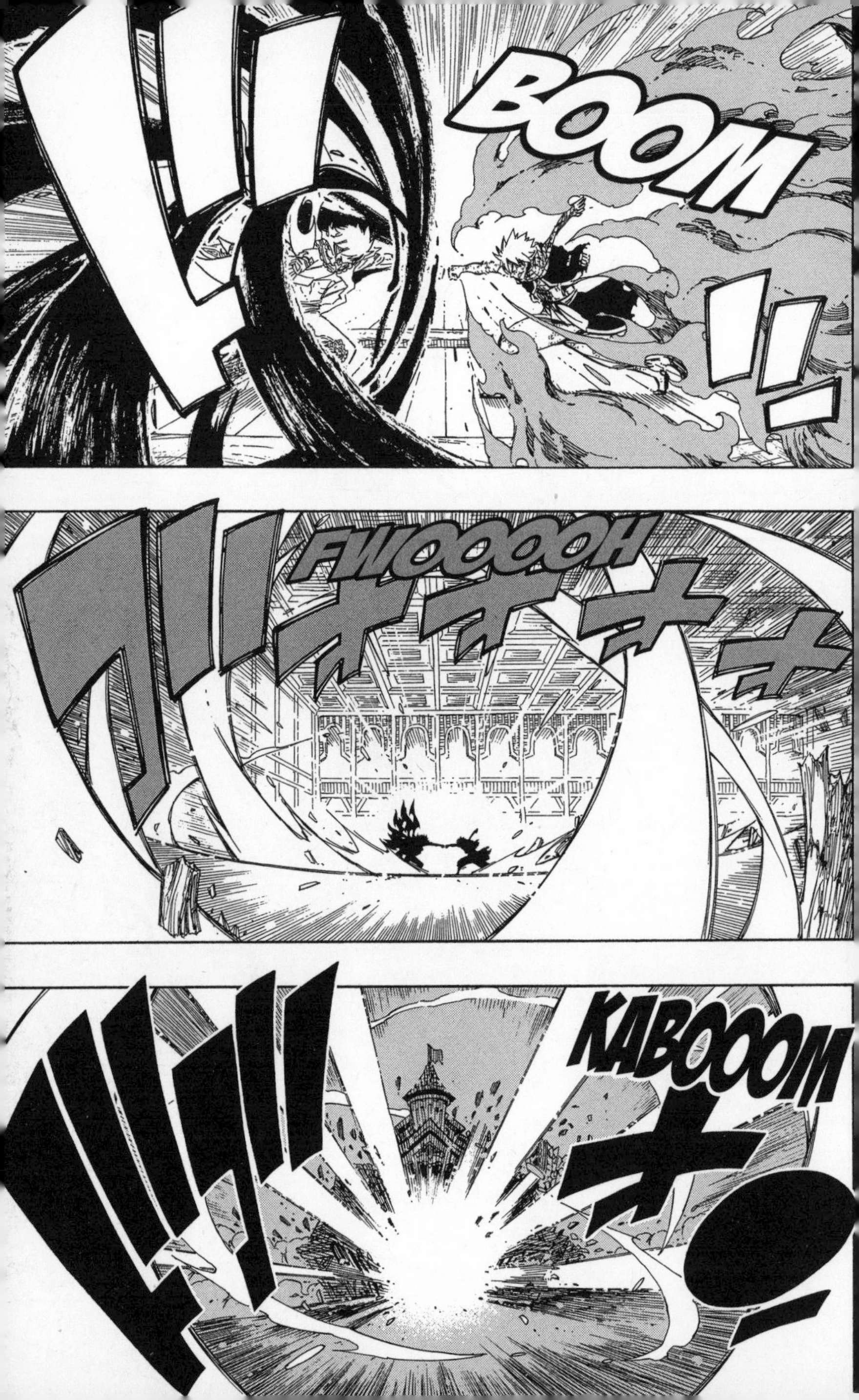
BOOM
FWOOOOH
KABOOOM

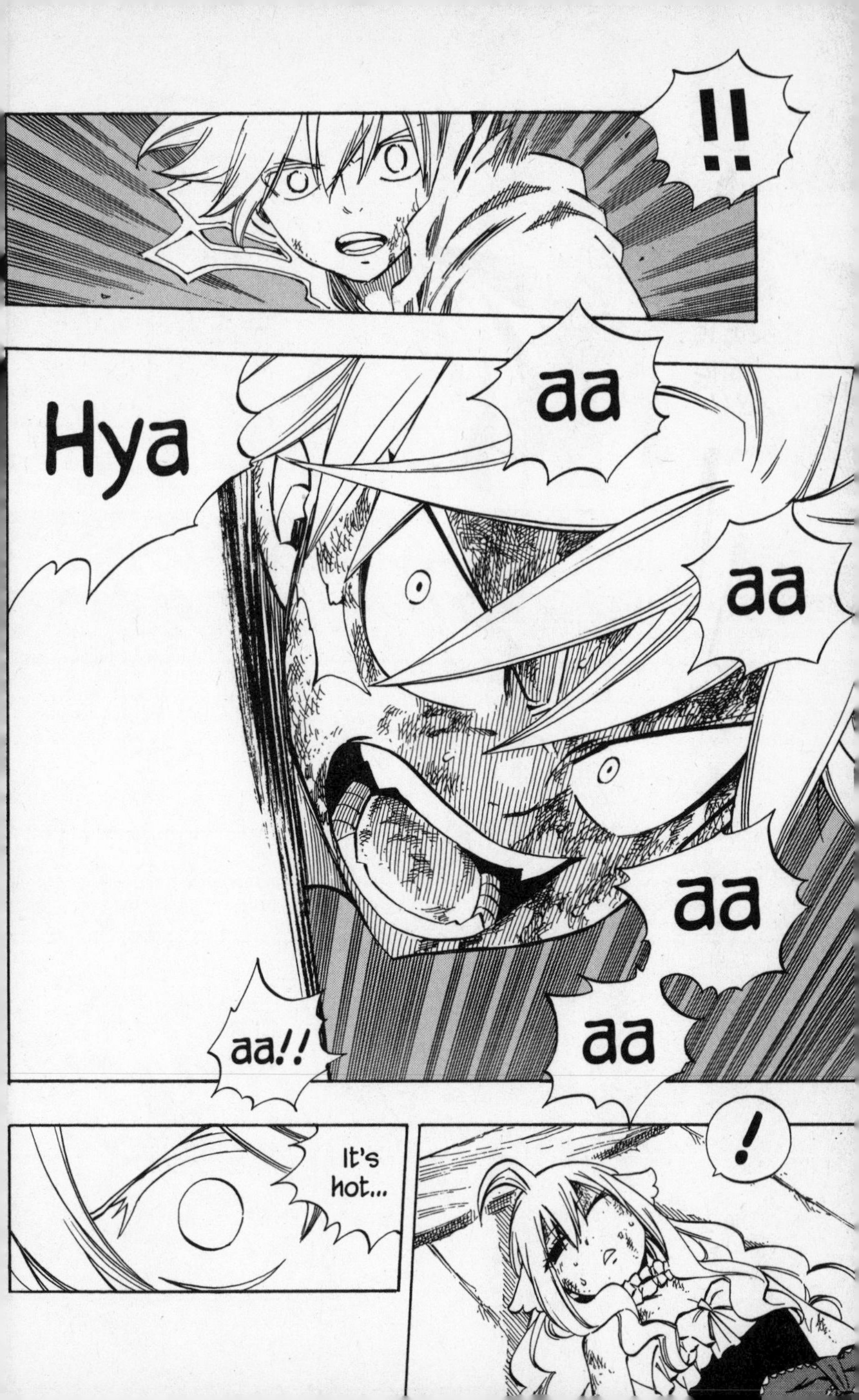
!!
Hya
aa
aa
aa
aa
aa!!
!
It's hot...

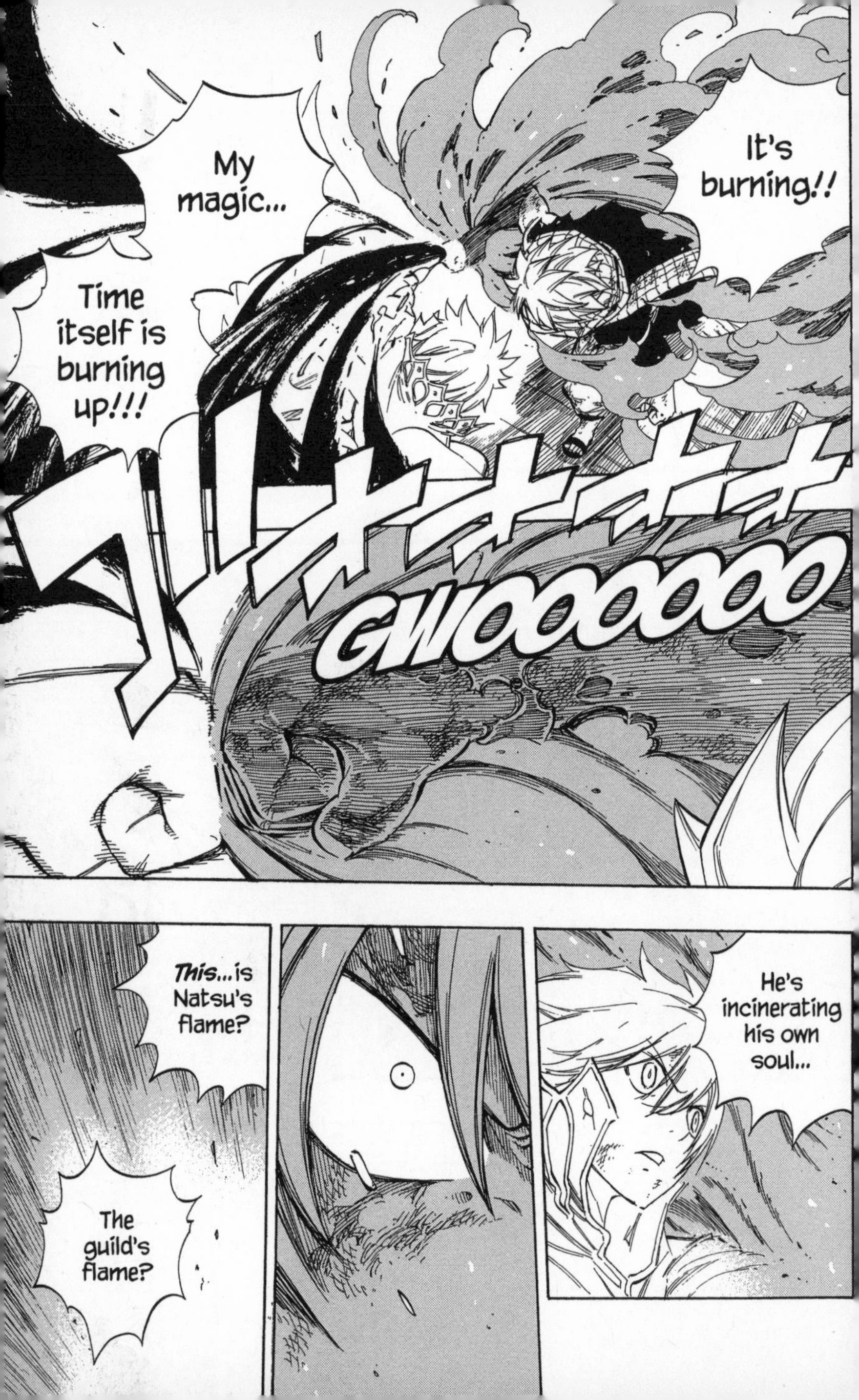
It's burning!!
My magic...
Time itself is burning up!!!
GWOOOOOO
He's incinerating his own soul...
This...is Natsu's flame?
The guild's flame?

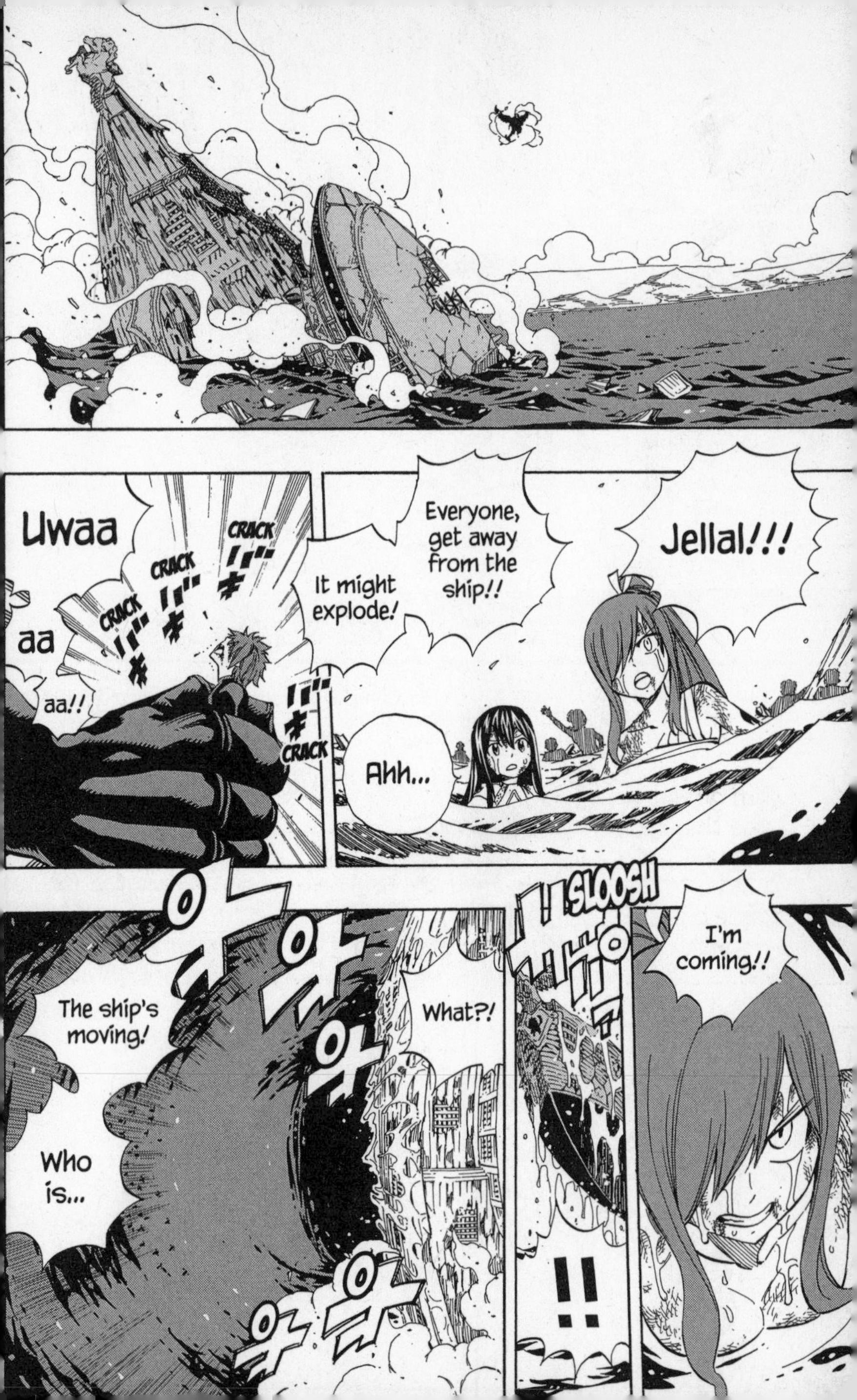
Jellal!!!
Everyone, get away from the ship!!
It might explode!
Ahh...
Uwaa
aa
aa!!
CRACK
CRACK
CRACK
CRACK
I'm coming!!
SLOOSH
!!
What?!
The ship's moving!
Who is...

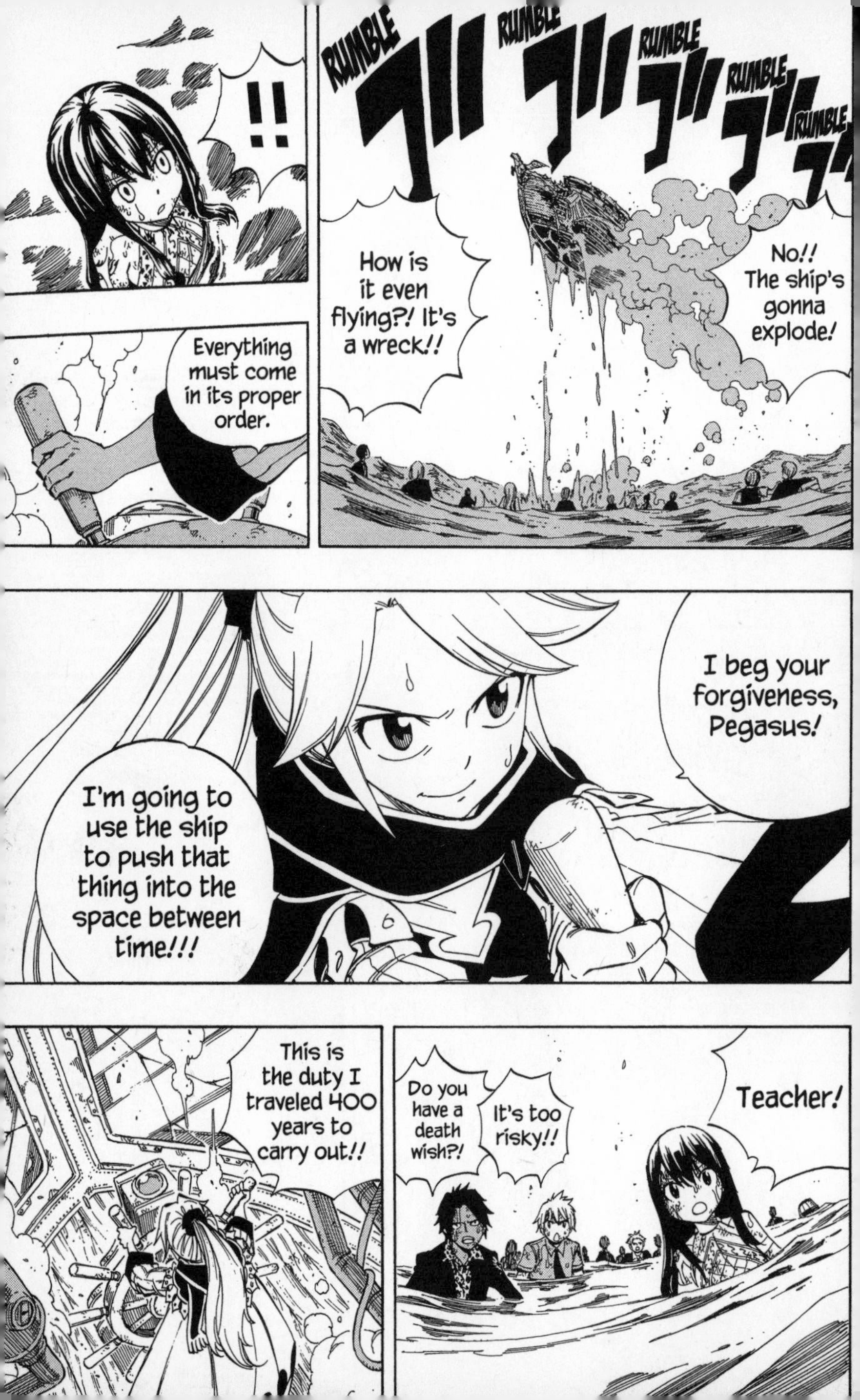
RUMBLE
RUMBLE
RUMBLE
RUMBLE
RUMBLE
No!! The ship's gonna explode!
How is it even flying?! It's a wreck!!
!!
Everything must come in its proper order.
I beg your forgiveness, Pegasus!
I'm going to use the ship to push that thing into the space between time!!!
Teacher!
It's too risky!!
Do you have a death wish?!
This is the duty I traveled 400 years to carry out!!

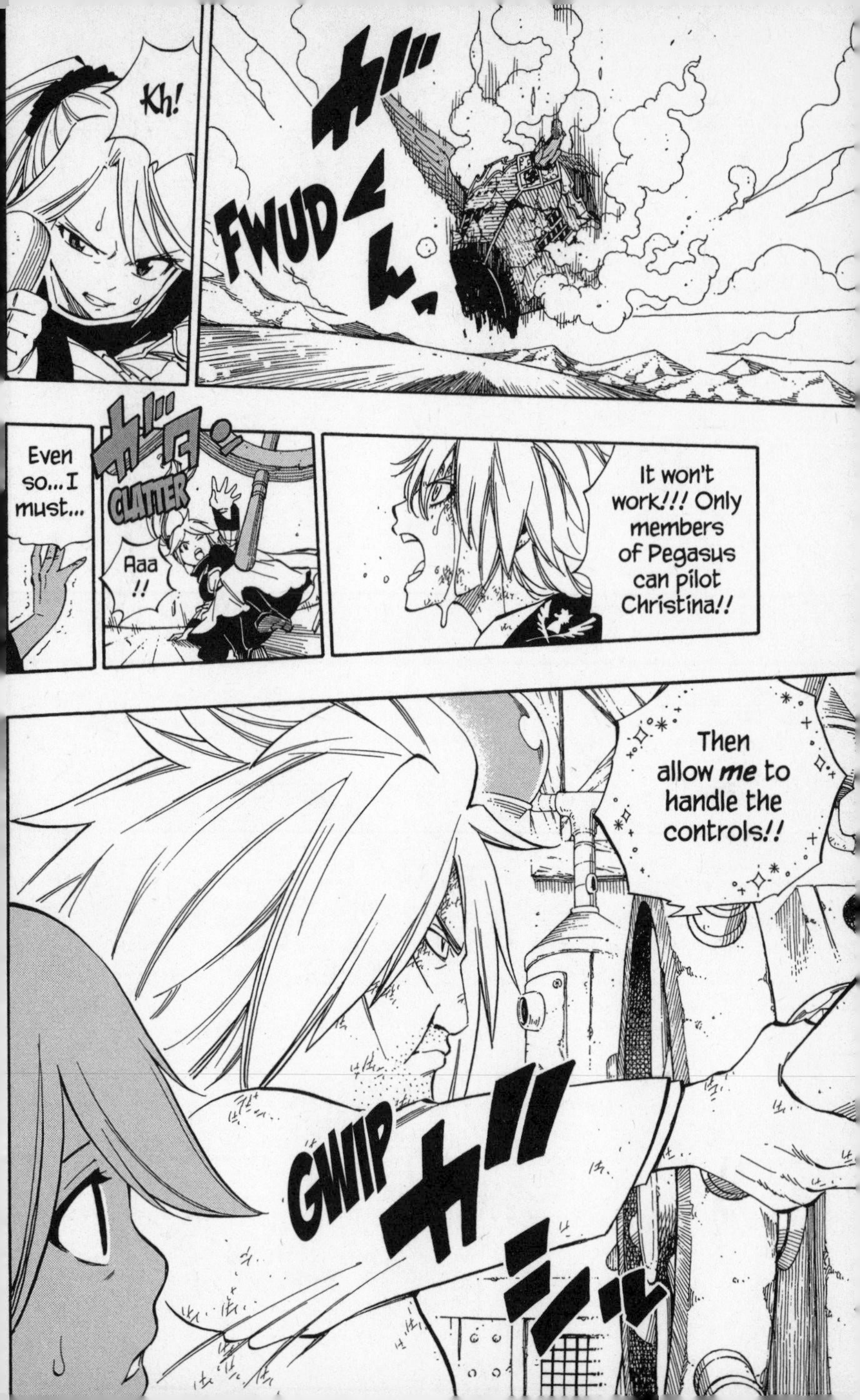
FWUD
Kh!
It won't work!!! Only members of Pegasus can pilot Christina!!
CLATTER
Aaa!!
Even so...I must...
Then allow *me* to handle the controls!!
GWIP

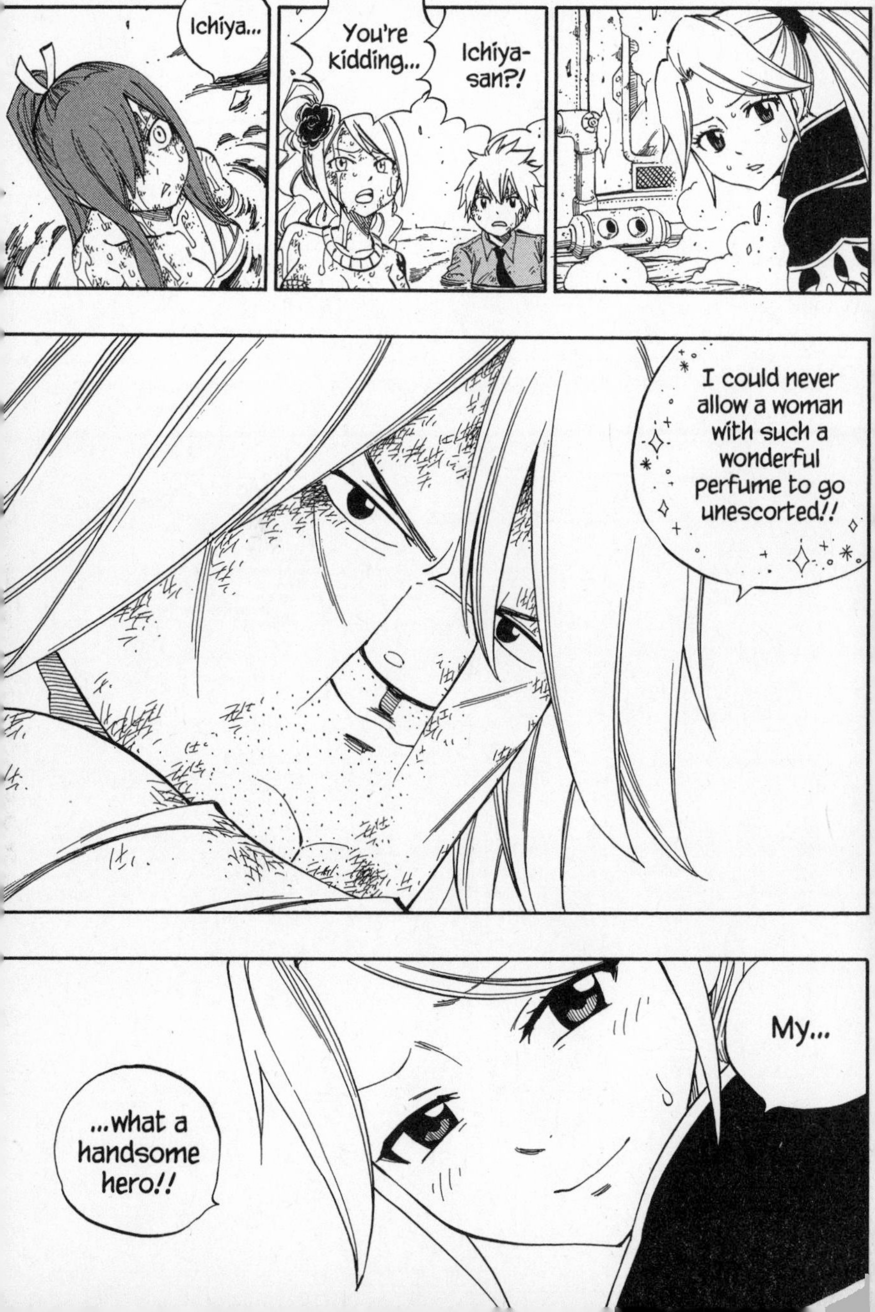
Ichiya-san?!
You're kidding...
Ichiya...
I could never allow a woman with such a wonderful perfume to go unescorted!!
My...
...what a handsome hero!!

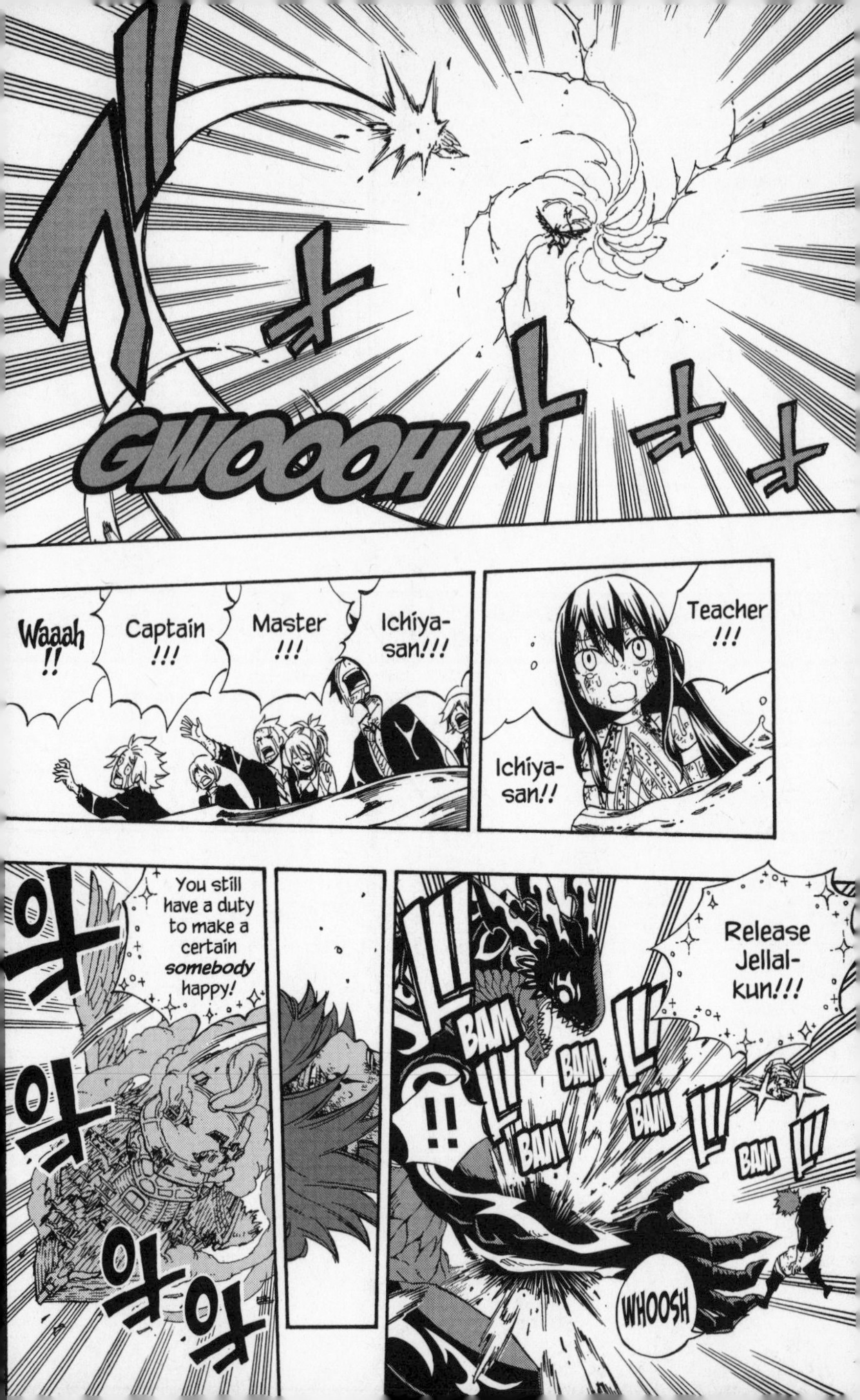
GWOOOH
Teacher!!!
Ichiya-san!!
Ichiya-san!!!
Master!!!
Captain!!!
Waaah!!
Release Jellal-kun!!!
BAM
BAM
BAM
BAM
BAM
!!
WHOOSH
You still have a duty to make a certain *somebody* happy!

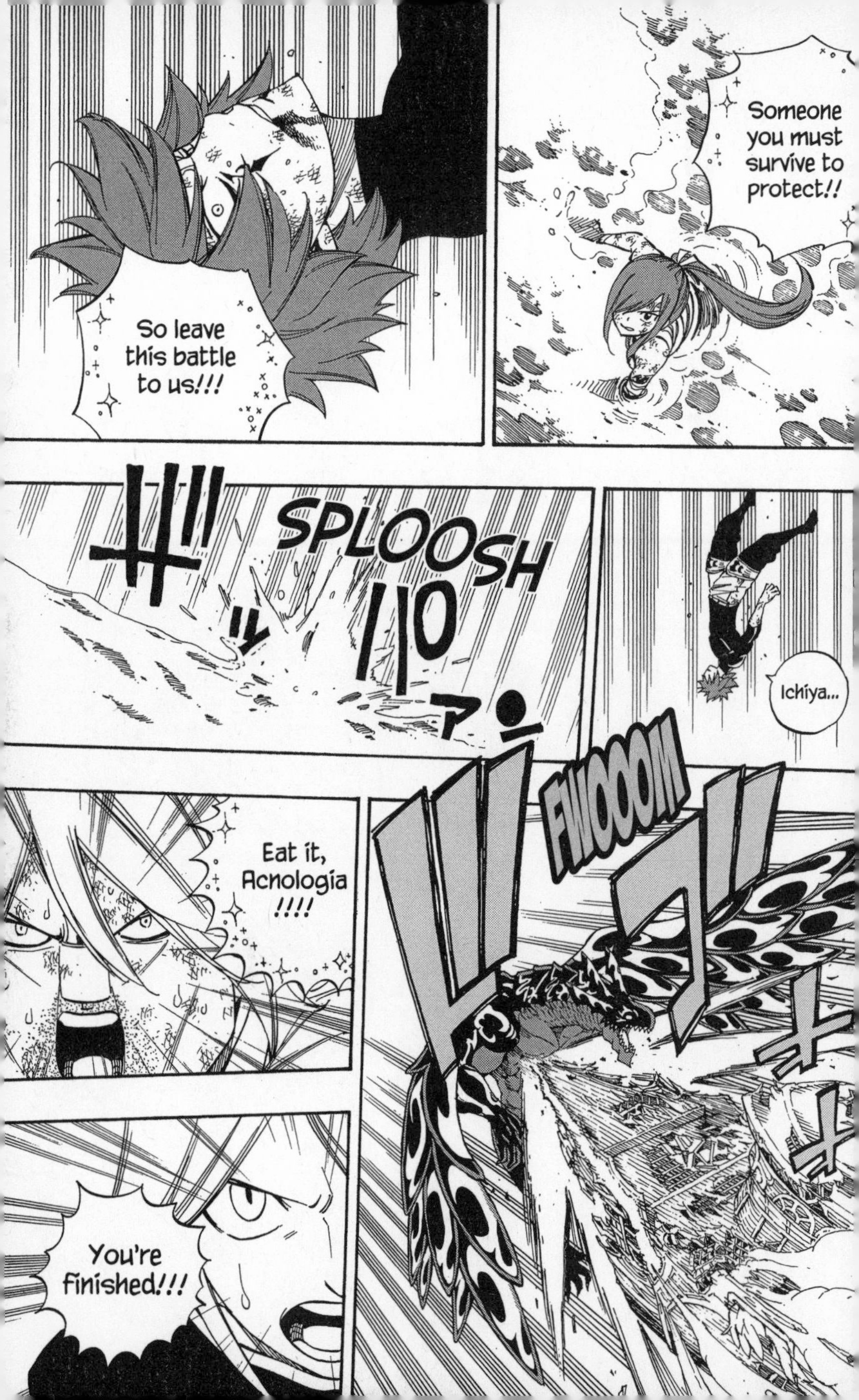

Someone you must survive to protect!!
So leave this battle to us!!!
Ichiya...
SPLOOSH
FWOOOM
Eat it, Acnologia!!!!
You're finished!!!

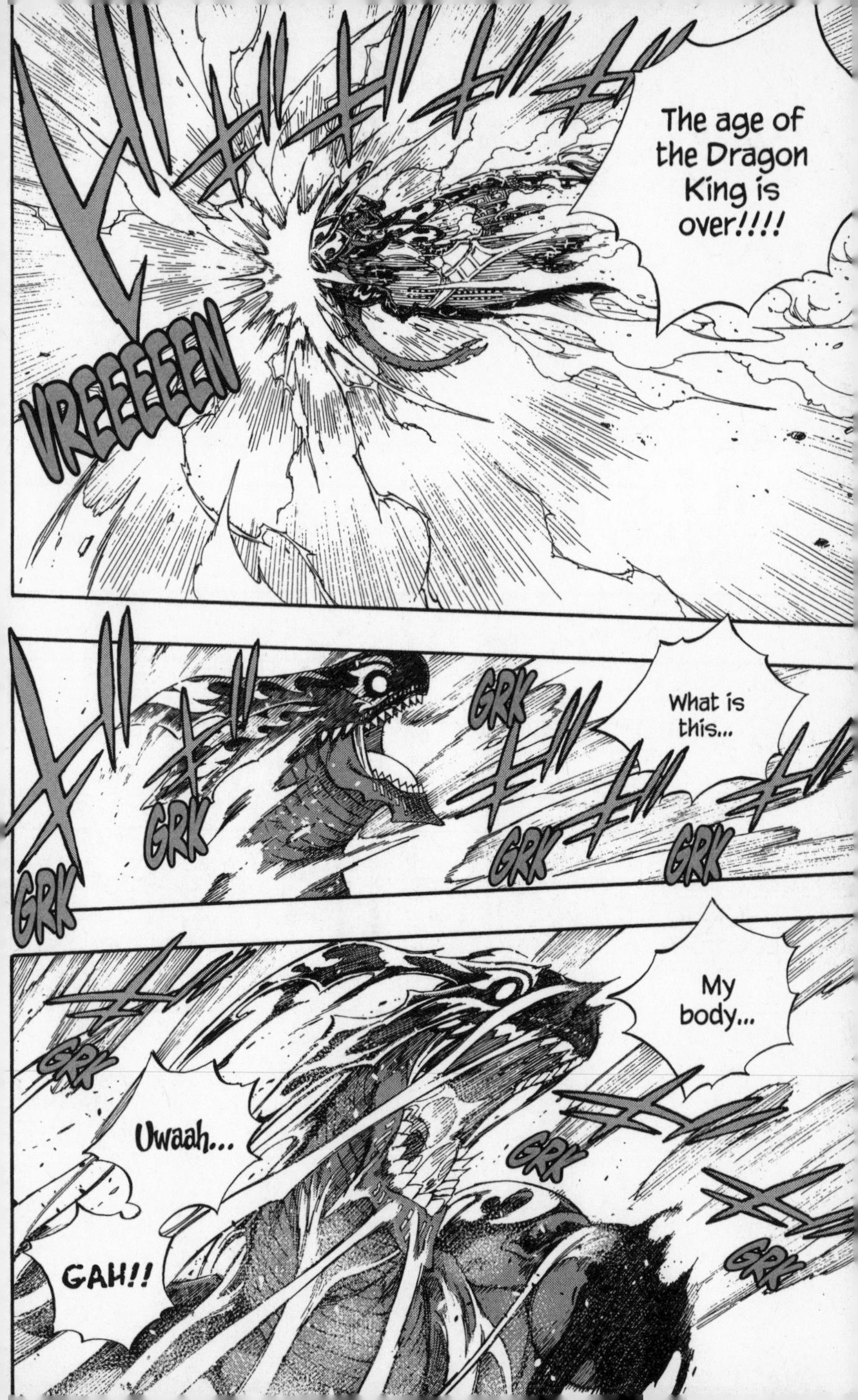
The age of the Dragon King is over!!!!
VREEEEEEN
What is this...
GRK
GRK
GRK
GRK
GRK
My body...
GRK
GRK
Uwaah...
GRK
GAH!!

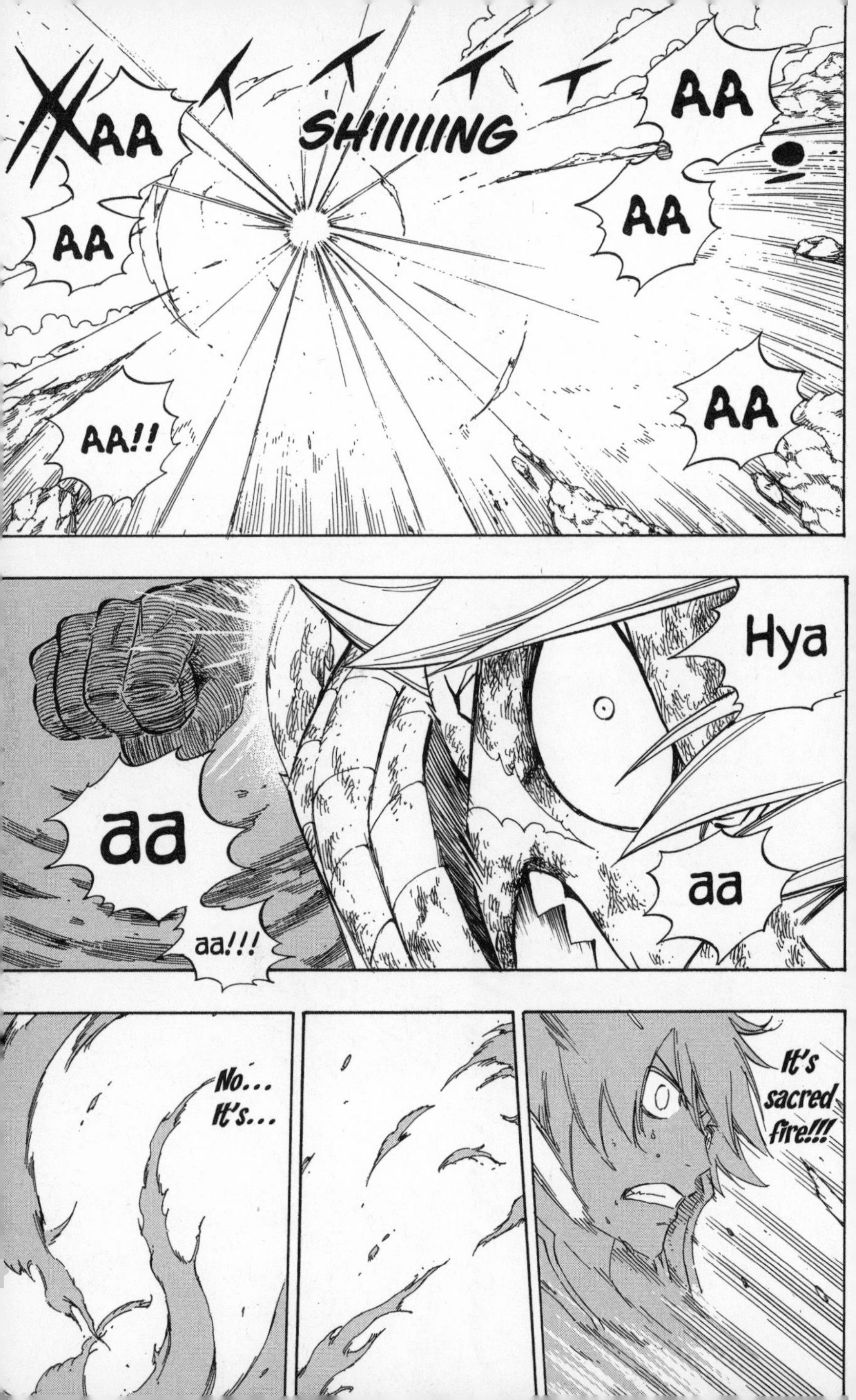
AA
AA
SHIIIIING
XAA
AA
AA
AA!!
Hya
aa
aa
aa!!!
It's sacred fire!!!
No... It's...

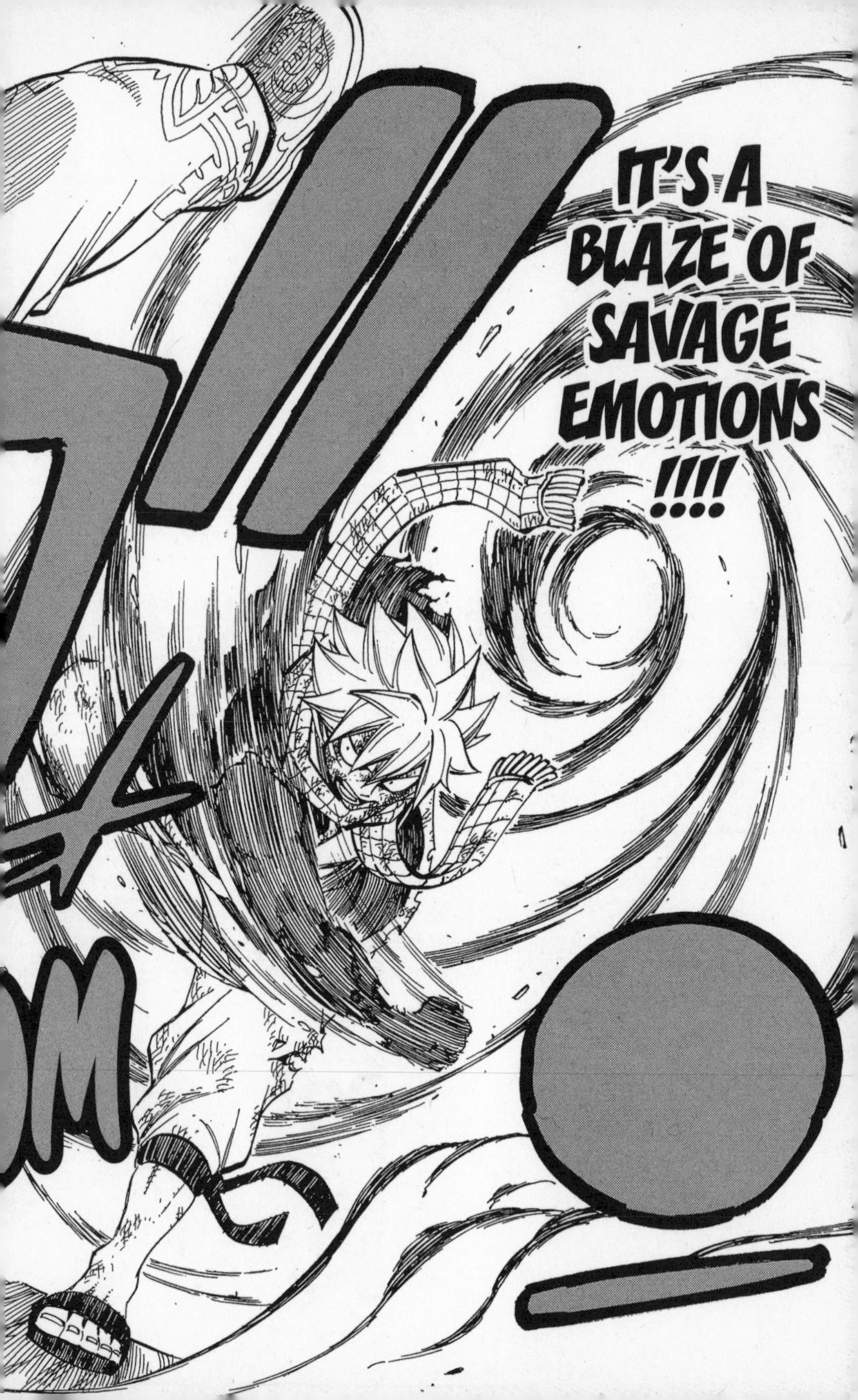
IT'S A BLAZE OF SAVAGE EMOTIONS !!!!

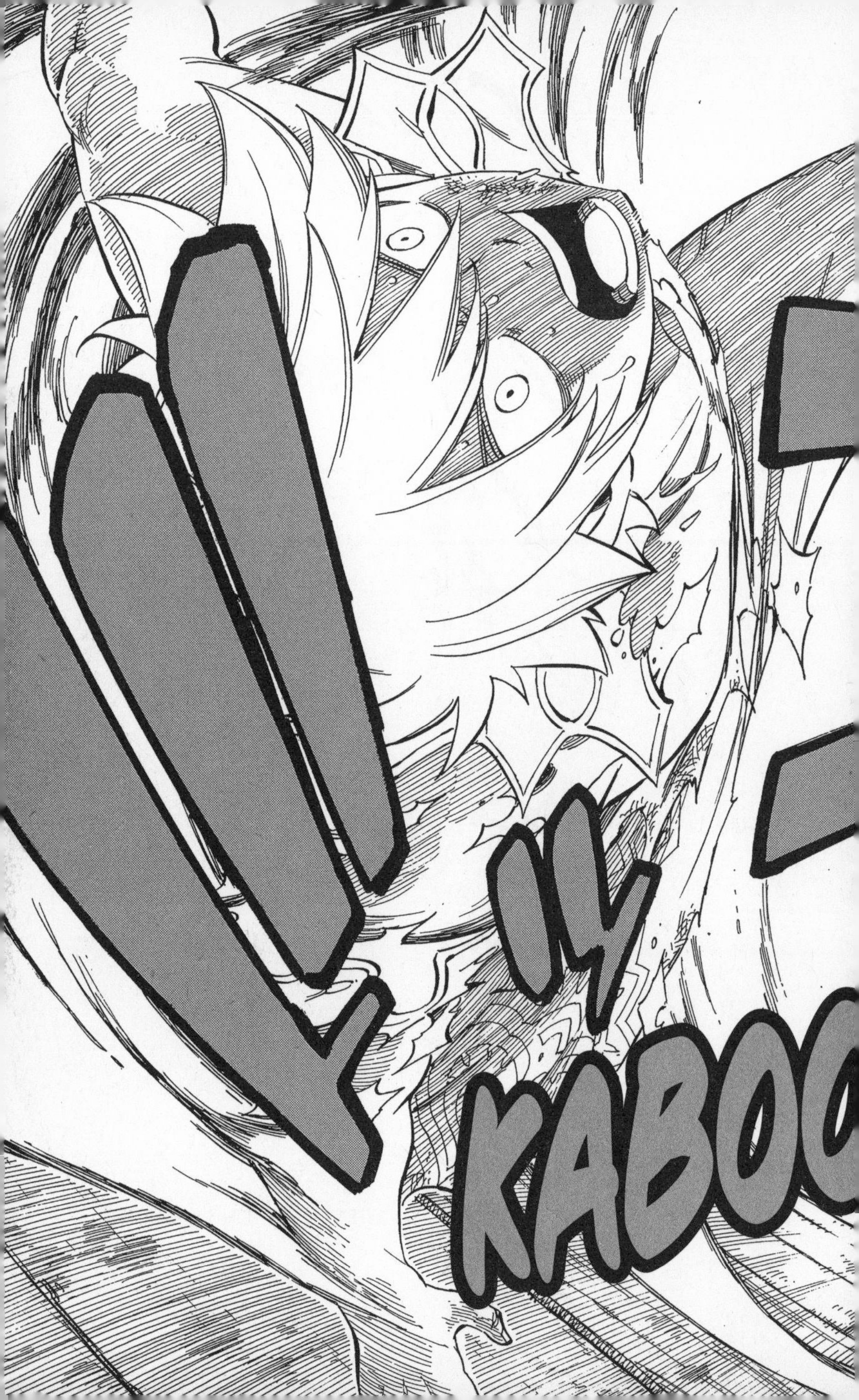
KABOO

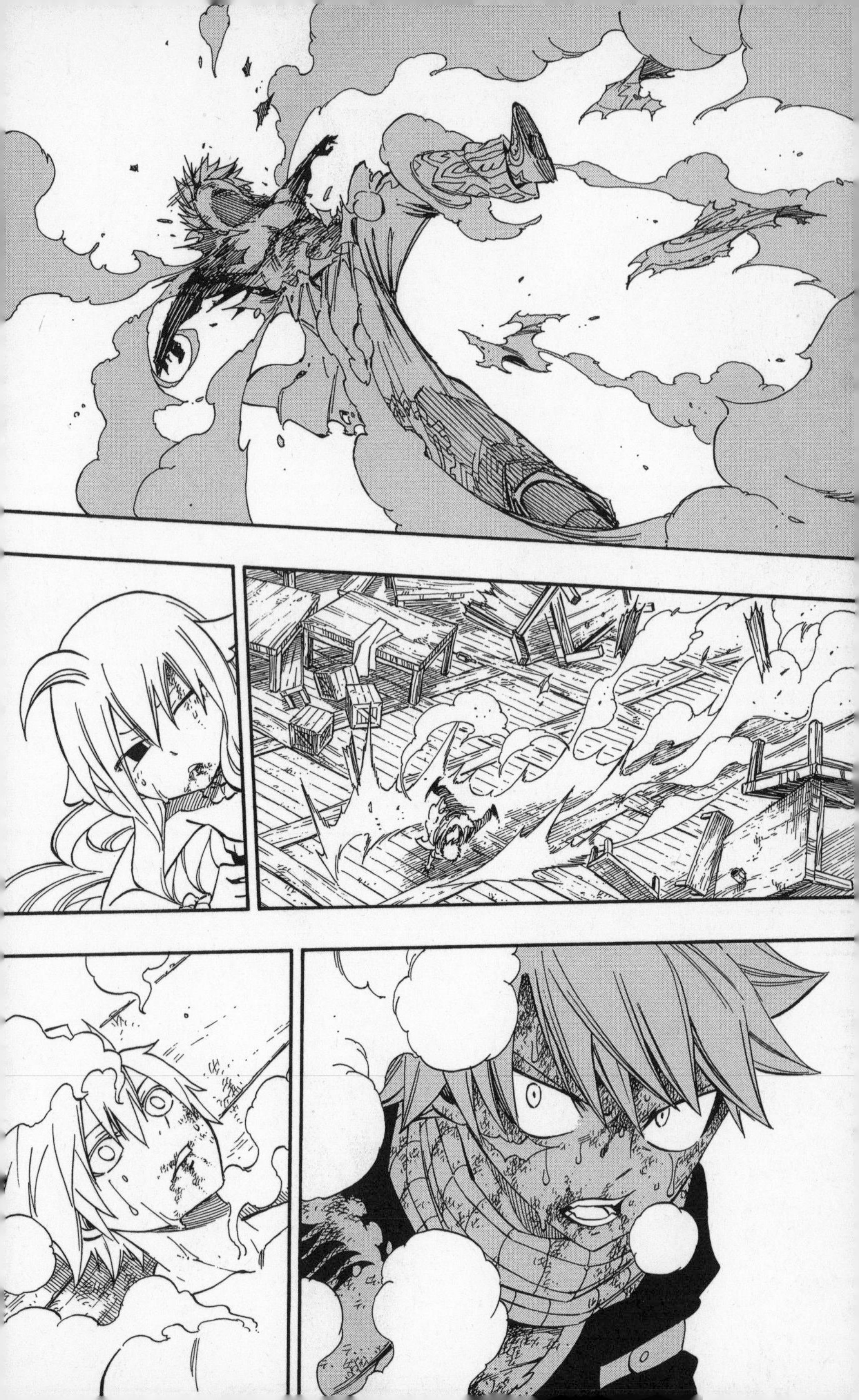

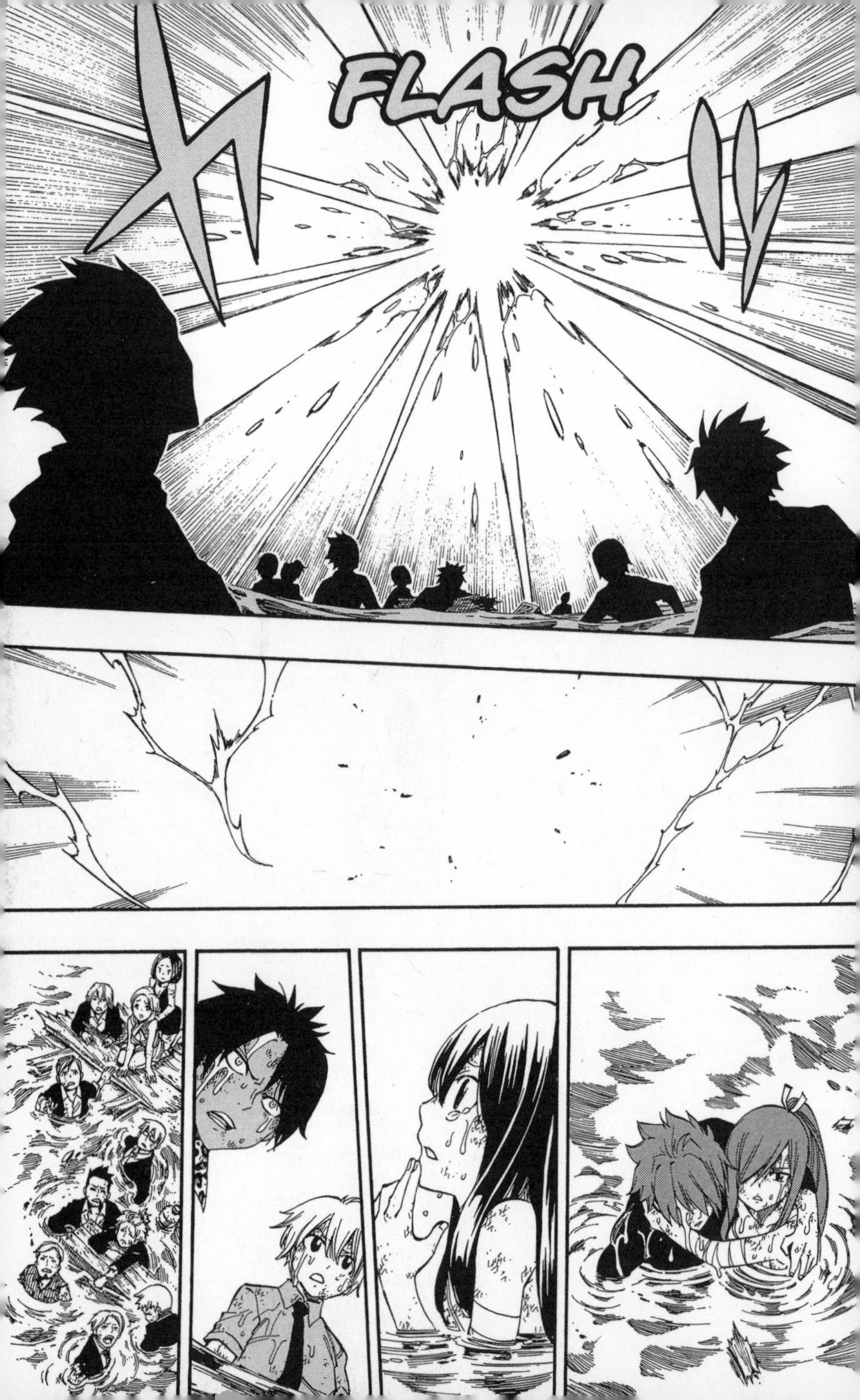
FLASH

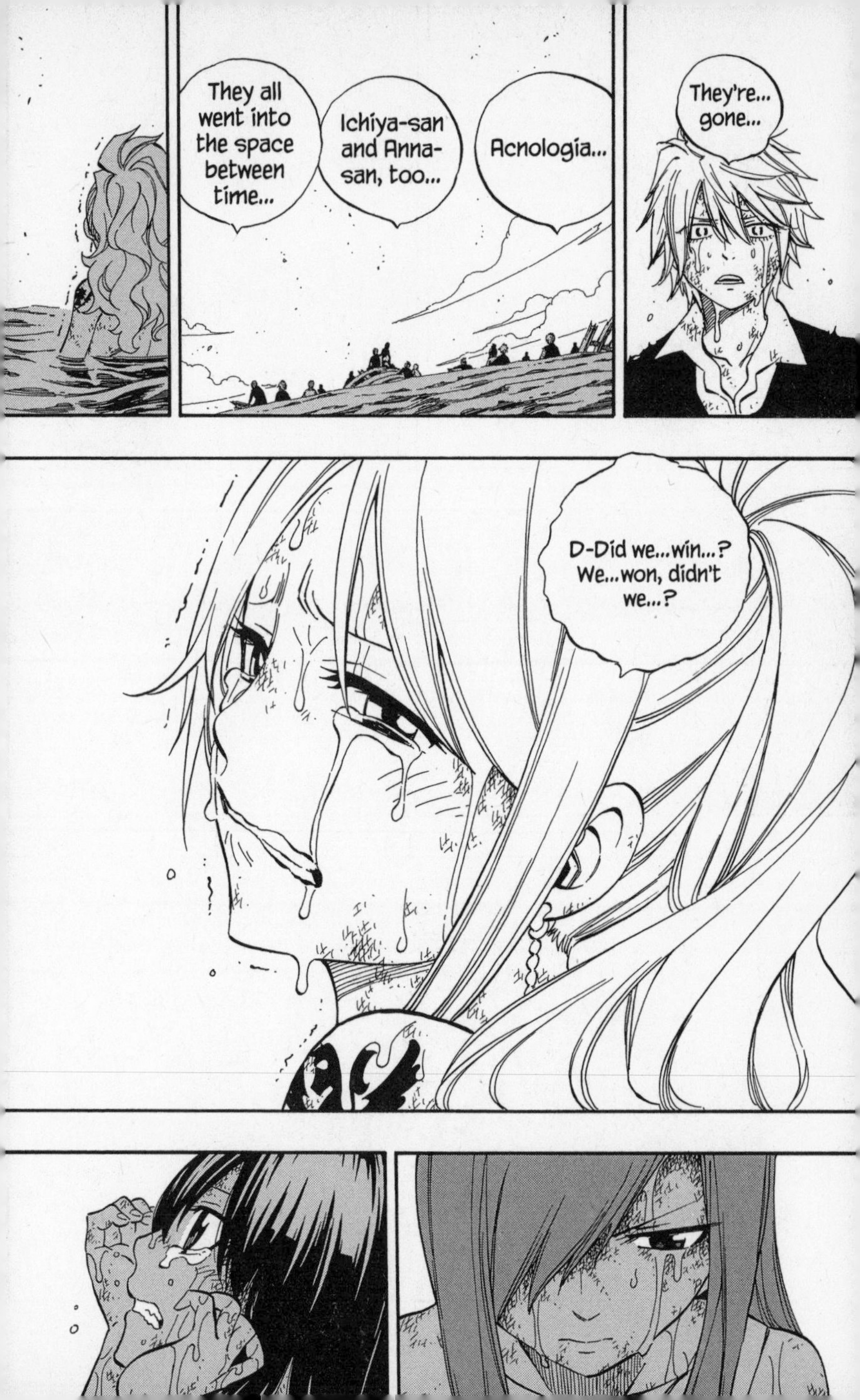
They're... gone...
Acnologia...
Ichiya-san and Anna-san, too...
They all went into the space between time...
D-Did we...win...? We...won, didn't we...?

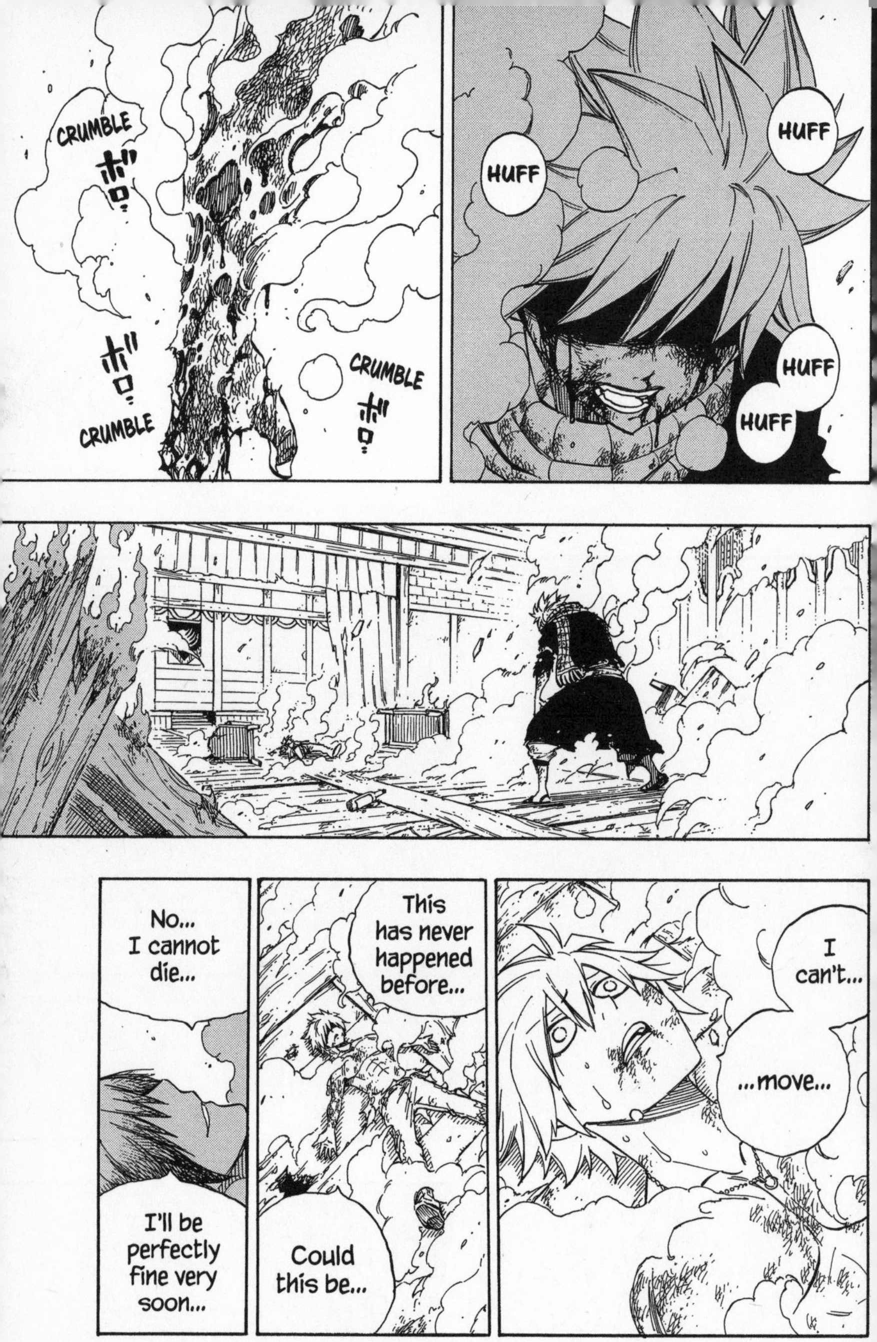
HUFF
HUFF
HUFF
HUFF
CRUMBLE
ボロ
CRUMBLE
ボロ
CRUMBLE
ボロ
I can't...
...move...
This has never happened before...
Could this be...
No... I cannot die...
I'll be perfectly fine very soon...

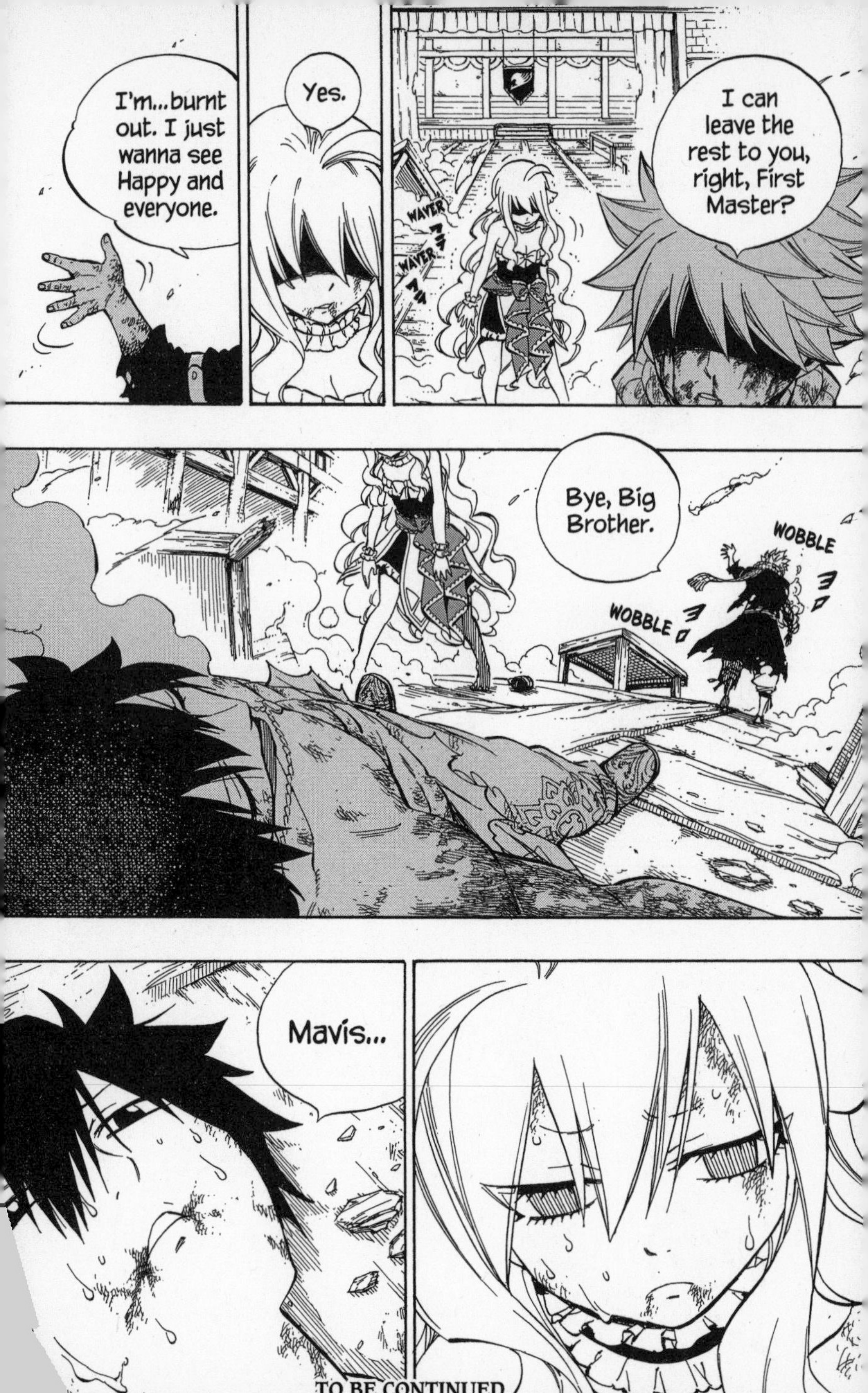
I can leave the rest to you, right, First Master?
WAVER
WAVER
Yes.
I'm...burnt out. I just wanna see Happy and everyone.
Bye, Big Brother.
WOBBLE
WOBBLE
Mavis...

TO BE CONTINUED

FAIRY TAIL
フェアリーテイル

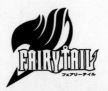

FROM HIRO MASHIMA

All right, so the next volume of *Fairy Tail* is the last one…but as I write this note, I realize it's actually been a week since I finished the final chapter. The work never ends (haha)! Wait, what? I was planning on taking it easy after this serialization ended, but the work just doesn't let up! I wonder why… This is a photo of a commemorative piece that my awesome staff gave me!

Original Jacket Design: Hisao Ogawa

A Kodansha Comics Trade Paperback Original.

Published in the United States by Kodansha Comics, an imprint of Kodansha USA Publishing, LLC, New York.

Publication rights for this English edition arranged through Kodansha Ltd., Tokyo.

First published in Japan in 2017 by Kodansha Ltd., Tokyo
ISBN 978-1-63236-475-3

Printed in the United States of America.

www.kodanshacomics.com

9 8 7 6 5 4 3 2 1

Translation: William Flanagan
Lettering: AndWorld Design
Editing: Haruko Hashimoto
Kodansha Comics edition cover design by Phil Balsman

TOMARE!

止まれ

[STOP!]

You're going the wrong way!

Manga is a completely different type of reading experience.

To start at the beginning, go to the end!

That's right! Authentic manga is read the traditional Japanese way—from right to left, exactly the opposite of how American books are read. It's easy to follow: Just go to the other end of the book and read each page—and each panel—from right side to left side, starting at the top right. Now you're experiencing manga as it was meant to be!